*Disorder in the Court*

# DISORDER IN THE COURT

*Report of the Association of the Bar of the City of New York, Special Committee on Courtroom Conduct*

*by NORMAN DORSEN, Executive Director
and LEON FRIEDMAN, Associate Director*

*Roberta Ribner, Administrative Assistant*

PANTHEON BOOKS / A DIVISION OF RANDOM HOUSE / NEW YORK

*Library of Congress Cataloging in Publication Data*

Association of the Bar of the City of New York.
  Special Committee on Courtroom Conduct.
Disorder in the Court.

Bibliography: pp. 384–86
  1. Conduct of court proceedings—United States. 2. Criminal justice, Administration of—United States. I. Dorsen, Norman. II. Friedman, Leon. III. Title.
KF9655.A97    347′.73′5    73-7019
ISBN 0-394-48222-0

Manufactured in the United States of America

FIRST EDITION

## ACKNOWLEDGMENTS

Grateful acknowledgment is made to the following for permission to reprint previously published material:

American Bar Association: Excerpts from the American Bar Association Standards Relating to the Prosecution and Defense Functions and Relating to the Judge's Role in Dealing with Trial Disruptions (A.B.A., 1155 E. 60 St., Chicago, Ill. 60637). · *American Bar Association Journal:* Excerpts from "The Responsibilities of the Legal Profession" (Brennan), 54 *American Bar Association Journal* 121 (1968). · American Judicature Society: Excerpts from "The Federal Prosecutor" by Robert Jackson, reprinted from *Judicature* 24. · Association of the Trial Lawyers of America: Excerpts from "Is the Problem Simple" (Newman) and "Its Argument" (Kodas and Joost), reprinted from the Jan./Feb. 1971 issue of *Trial* Magazine. · Atheneum Publishers, Inc.: Excerpt from "William Kunstler and the New Bar," from *Obiter Dicta* by Joseph W. Bishop, Jr. Copyright © 1971 by Joseph W. Bishop, Jr., First published in *Esquire* Magazine. · Doubleday & Company, Inc.: Excerpts from *In Brief Authority* by Francis Biddle. Copyright © 1962 by Francis Biddle. Copyright © 1962 by American Heritage Publishing Company, Inc. · The Legal Aid Society: Excerpts from "Our Lower Courts are Disgraceful" by Robert P. Patterson, Jr., from 67 *Legal Aid Review* 5, pp. 8–9 (1970). · The Harvard Law Review Association: Excerpts from Note, "The Supreme Court, 1970 Term," 85 *Harvard Law Review* 3 (1971). Copyright © 1971 by The Harvard Law Review Association. · *Newsweek:* Excerpt from "How Justice Worked—The People v. Donald Payne" by Peter Goldman and Don Holt, reprinted from *Newsweek*, 3/8/71. Copyright © Newsweek, Inc. 1971. · *The New York Times:* Excerpts from "Can a Black Man Get a Fair Trial in this Country" by Haywood Burns, of 7/12/70 *Magazine.* Copyright © 1970 by the New York Times Company. · Praeger Publishers, Inc., and *The Washington Monthly:* Excerpt from "Crime in the Courts" by Lenoard Downie, Jr. Reprinted from *Justice Denied: The Case for Reform of the Courts* by Leonard Downie, Jr. Copyright © 1971 by Praeger Publishers, Inc., N.Y. · Fred B. Rothman & Co.: Excerpts from "Courtroom Misconduct by Prosecutors and Trial Judges" by Albert Alschuler, 50 *Texas Law Review* 629 (1971). · University of Pennsylvania and Fred B. Rothman: Excerpts from "Lawyers and Civilization" by Anthony Lewis, from *University of Pennsylvania Law Review* 860 (1972). · Warren, Gorham & Lamont, Inc.: Excerpts from "Judges as Tyrants" by Herman Schwartz, from *Criminal Law Bulletin*, 1971. · Judge Jack Weinstein: Excerpts from a letter to Senator Harry F. Byrd. By permission of the author. · Wisconsin Law Review: Excerpts from Note, "Criminal Law—Contempt—Conduct of Attorney during Course of Trial," 1971 *Wisconsin Law Review* 329.

# THE COMMITTEE

*On this and the succeeding page are listed the members of the Committee and its staff, together with public and professional positions held by them.*

BURKE MARSHALL, *Chairman* • *Deputy Dean and Professor of Law, Yale Law School; former Assistant Attorney General for the Civil Rights Division, Department of Justice; Chairman, National Advisory Commission on Selective Service; Chairman, Vera Institute of Justice; Member, New York State Special Commission on Attica.*

STANLEY S. ARKIN • *Partner: Arkin & Horan, P.C., New York City; former Chairman, Committee on Criminal Courts Law and Procedure of the Association of the Bar of the City of New York; criminal defense attorney; former Special Prosecutor, New York City, against Department of Correction Personnel.*

BRUCE BROMLEY • *Partner: Cravath, Swaine & Moore, New York City; former Judge, New York Court of Appeals; former Chairman, New York City Board of Ethics.*

ROBERT L. CARTER • *United States District Judge, Southern District of New York; former General Counsel, NAACP; former President, National Committee Against Discrimination in Housing; former Co-Chairman, National Conference of Black Lawyers; member, New York State Special Commission on Attica; former member, Temporary Commission on the State Court System; former member, New York Mayor's Committee on the Judiciary.*

ROBERT M. KAUFMAN • *Partner: Proskauer, Rose, Goetz, & Mendelsohn, New York City; former legislative assistant to Senator Jacob K. Javits; former Chairman, Committee on Civil Rights, Association of the Bar of the City of New York; former Chairman, Committee on Civil Rights, New York County Lawyers Assocation; Chairman, Special Committee on Campaign Expenditures, Association of the Bar of the City of New York.*

GEORGE N. LINDSAY • *Partner: Debevoise, Plimpton, Lyons & Gates; former Co-Chairman, Lawyers' Committee for Civil Rights Under Law.*

ROBERT B. MCKAY • *Dean and Professor of Law, New York University School of Law; Chairman, New York State Special Commission on Attica.*

FREDERICK A. O. SCHWARZ, JR. • *Partner: Cravath, Swaine & Moore; former Assistant Commissioner for Law Revision, government of Northern Nigeria (1961– 62); Director/Trustee, New York City Lawyers' Committee for Civil Rights Under Law.*

BETHUEL M. WEBSTER • *Partner: Webster, Sheffield, Fleischmann, Hitchcock & Brookfield; former President, Association of the Bar of the City of New York; former member, Permanent Court of Arbitrition under the Hague Conventions; Chairman, Drug Abuse Council.*

## THE STAFF

### Executive Director

NORMAN DORSEN • *Professor of Law, New York University School of Law; former law clerk, Supreme Court Justice John M. Harlan; General Counsel, American Civil Liberties Union; author, Frontiers of Civil Liberties; coauthor, Political and Civil Rights in the United States; editor, The Rights of Americans.*

### Associate Director

LEON FRIEDMAN • *Executive Director, Committee for Public Justice; author, The Wise Minority; editor, The Justices of the United States Supreme Court; Southern Justice; The Law of War.*

### Administrative Assistant

ROBERTA RIBNER

# CONTENTS

# PREFACE

In early 1970, Francis Plimpton, who was then president of the Association of the Bar of the City of New York, appointed a Special Committee on Courtroom Conduct to study and report on the causes and implications for the profession of incidents of courtroom disorder that were of such wide concern at the time. The Committee received a generous grant from the Ford Foundation, which made extensive research and a full analysis possible.

This book is the report of the Committee. In preparing it the Committee worked from position papers from the consultants listed in the Appendix, and from drafts prepared by Professor Dorsen and Leon Friedman. But the individual members of the Committee worked page by page on that material, and the imprint of each of them appears throughout the report. The substantive conclusions and recommendations are the result of many hours of discussion and many meetings over the past two years. As is always the case, not all of the members agree with every conclusion, recommendation, or emphasis. The report nevertheless is unanimous.

If there is an unexpressed underlying message in the report, I think it is that at the time Mr. Plimpton appointed our committee, the bar as a whole misconstrued, both publicly and in its private councils, the dimensions and causes of courtroom disorders. In speeches, reports, panels, judicial conferences, and other forums, the law professors acted at that time as if the courts of this country had suddenly been taken over by an organized group of radical lawyers interested only in destroying the system that was protecting their clients. This panic did great and lasting damage to the public perception of the processes of the laws, for it exaggerated far out of proportion the problems that had occurred in a few courtrooms, particularly Judge Hoffman's in Chicago. Further, it confused zeal in the defense of clients with revolution, and thus moved in the direction, with threats of disbarment, of intimidating defense counsel.

It is my hope that this report will restore perspective by making available to everyone a more careful, systematic, and thorough look at the matter of courtroom disorder. The flaws in our system of justice are unquestionably many, and they are growing as the resources allocated to the courts fall increasingly behind the growing volume of work that they must do. But the system works in the great cases, and it has worked, by and large, in all of the cases that were of such concern to the bar two years ago. It is more in danger from interference with counsel fighting for justice for their clients than from whatever disruption—and it is not on the whole very great—is caused by their efforts.

—BURKE MARSHALL

*May 1, 1973*

*Disorder in the Court*

# CHAPTER ONE

# Introduction: The Dimensions of the Current Problem

There have always been disorderly trials. Throughout history, defendants, lawyers, and spectators—in the United States and in other countries—have at times been unruly and disrespectful to judicial authority. The administration of justice has always endured a degree of disorder.

Why, then, this study and report? The answer can be traced directly to the concern of the bar and the public over the disorder that took place in 1969 and 1970 in the Chicago conspiracy case and the New York Black Panther case. The extraordinary publicity that these trials received and the fears they generated for the system of criminal justice in the United States provoked a widespread response.

In particular, the judiciary, the organized bar, and some state legislatures reacted very strongly. One judge remarked that a "gale may have been raging in the courts at the time."[1] The American College of Trial Lawyers appointed a blue ribbon committee headed by Whitney North Seymour, former president of the American Bar Association, and including noted criminal lawyer Edward Bennett Williams, former federal judge Simon Rifkind, and Lewis F. Powell, Jr. (then president of the Trial Lawyers group and now a Supreme Court Justice), to look into the problem. The report they issued in July 1970 included the following comments in its preamble:

> The members of the American College of Trial Lawyers are deeply concerned by the tactics of trial disruption which on occasion have converted trials into spectacles of disorder and even violence.
>
> These tactics, involving contemptuous and obscene language and other techniques deliberately designed to break the judge and frustrate the judicial process, have been employed by defendants and tolerated and encouraged by some of their counsel. Indeed, some counsel appear to have been active participants in the disruption.

Prosecutors also from time to time have been guilty of courtroom misconduct.

In some instances judges have overreacted to these tactics.

At the American Bar Association meeting in St. Louis in August 1970, there were four panels devoted to the problem of trial disruption. Many speakers commented on the phenomenon, including Chief Justice Burger, who attacked the "spectacles that are undermining public confidence in the whole system" and proposed methods "for eliminating those unseemly, outrageous episodes we read about that have happened in our courtrooms."

The Chief Justice made more extensive comments about the problem before the American Law Institute in May 1971. He said, in an address entitled "The Necessity for Civility":

It is surely important for a gathering of lawyers, judges and law professors to focus our thoughts, for the few minutes I will detain you, on the conduct of members of our profession. Lawyers are granted a monopoly to perform essential services for hire, and it has long been almost an article of faith to us that monopolies are subject to strict regulation and public accountability for adherence to standards. Today more and more new and vexing problems reach the courts and they call for the highest order of thoughtful exploration and careful study. Yet all too often, overzealous advocates seem to think the zeal and effectiveness of a lawyer depends on how thoroughly he can disrupt the proceedings or how loud he can shout or how close he can come to insulting all those he encounters—including the judges. . . .

At the drop of a hat—or less—we find adrenalin-fueled lawyers cry out that theirs is a "political trial." This seems to mean in today's context —at least to some—that rules of evidence, canons of ethics and codes of professional conduct—the necessity for civility—all become irrelevant.[2]

The Chief Justice repeated the essence of his comments to a meeting of the A.B.A. in London in July 1971. In the meantime the A.B.A. adopted a special report of its Project on Standards for Criminal Justice relating to "The Judge's Role in Dealing with Trial Disruptions." Many other judges and numerous legal organizations spoke about or issued reports condemning courtroom disruption.[3]

In addition, many state legislatures passed new laws dealing with different aspects of disruptive behavior in court. California passed a law in 1970 making it a crime to picket or parade "in or near a building which houses a court of this state with the intent to interfere with, obstruct, or impede the administration of justice. . . ."[4] New York State amended its criminal procedure law to permit the trial of a defendant who was removed from the court for disorderly or disruptive conduct.[5] Nevada and Minnesota passed similar laws.[6] Massachusetts passed an act making it a criminal offense to disrupt court proceedings.[7]

New rules of court were also adopted in some jurisdictions,[8] including the Appellate Divisions of the First and Second Department in New York[9] (which has disciplinary control over lawyers in the New York City area). The Federal District Court for the Southern District of New York promulgated a new rule on April 23, 1971, providing for discipline of lawyers guilty of "conduct prejudicial to the administration of justice; conduct violative of the Code of Professional Responsibility . . . or the Code of Ethics."[10] Oklahoma also adopted new disciplinary rules which appended a set of rules on courtroom conduct.[11]

In addition, on June 10, 1971, Senator James Buckley introduced a bill relating to the disbarment of attorneys,[12] which, he announced, was designed to meet the situation "which urgently calls for reform."[13] He had previously made clear in a series of letters to the Association of the Bar of the City of New York that he was unhappy with the delay in bringing disciplinary proceedings against William Kunstler.[14]

Many of the new state laws and rules were based on *Illinois* v. *Allen,* the leading case on courtroom disruption, decided by the United States Supreme Court on March 30, 1970. The Court held that it was "essential to the proper administration of criminal justice that dignity, order and decorum be the hallmark of all court proceedings in our country."[15] Accordingly they gave the trial judge wide discretion in dealing with unruly defendants, permitting him to use a variety of sanctions, including civil or criminal contempt, exclusion from the courtroom, or as a last resort, binding and gagging.*

The reaction of the general public to the problem showed itself in newspaper editorials and news stories throughout the country. The adverse comments about disorder in the courts seemed to indicate a further deterioration of the public's confidence in the judicial system. There was a strong sense that something must be terribly wrong in the courts and the legal system generally if such outrages could take place.

It was in this atmosphere that the Special Committee on Courtroom Conduct of the Association of the Bar of the City of New York began a comprehensive analysis of the entire problem in its historical context. No other organization was making such a study, and the Committee concluded that a close and sustained look at the complex issues from the broadest possible perspective would be desirable.

One problem that we faced immediately was the lack of accurate facts on the extent and nature of courtroom misconduct. To overcome this obstacle, the Committee sent a detailed questionnaire to every trial judge of general jurisdiction in the country and to lower criminal court judges in New York City and California. Of 4,687 questionnaires sent, we received 1,602 responses—an unusually high return. The responses contained detailed information on the extent of disruption, those responsible for it, and the forms it takes.[16]

---

* For a fuller discussion of the *Allen* case see chapter 6.

By far the most startling revelation of the questionnaire returns was that there is no serious quantitative problem of disruption in American courts. The Chicago and Black Panther cases were not the tip of an iceberg, as feared by so many, but the larger part.

Of the 1,602 judges who responded, 107 reported that they had experienced a total of 112 cases of trial disruption in their entire lives on the bench. In the federal system, 112 of the 448 federal district judges responded to the questionnaire. They reported only five cases of disruption. Of the 1,490 state court judges who responded, 101 reported that they had experienced a total of 106 disruptive trials[17] (five state court judges described two trials each).

For the most part, disruption did not occur in politically oriented cases such as the Chicago trial or the Black Panther case. The greatest incidence of disruption occurred in ordinary felony cases. There were seventeen cases of disruption in murder trials, twelve in armed robbery cases, seven each in rape, burglary, and assault cases, five drug law violations, and four in larceny trials. There were also eight instances of disruption in divorce actions.

The defendant in a criminal case was held responsible for the disruption in seventy-four of the cases, and the spectators in seventeen cases. A lawyer was involved in only eight instances. In thirteen cases the defendant was acting without a lawyer (pro se).

The breakdown of the figures indicates that courtroom disruption is primarily a problem of highly emotional defendants, disturbed about serious criminal charges facing them, often unhappy with their lawyers and concerned that the proceedings are somehow stacked against them. Many factors may contribute to disruption in such cases: the long prison term facing the defendant, the tactics of the prosecution, the presence of friends or relatives, and the attitude of the judge. In many cases, the judges reported that they were able to handle the disruptions simply by impressing on the defendants that they would receive a fair trial and acting to protect the defendants' rights.

In twenty-one of the cases, the judges reported that there were some political overtones to the disruption. For the most part this involved spectators creating a disturbance in the court to show their support of the defendant and his political philosophy. The disorders were generally handled by ordering the court cleared. In other cases, the defendant in an ordinary criminal trial uttered certain radical slogans to attack the proceedings or to justify his actions although there was no political component to the crimes he was charged with. In only four cases were the defendants political activists charged with crimes with some political coloration (selective service violations, student demonstrations, etc.).

In another survey we conducted we received similar responses. A questionnaire was sent to the ninety-three United States attorneys and to the district attorneys of the sixty-nine largest jurisdictions. Fifty-three federal attorneys responded, reporting ten cases of disruption (some of which had already been reported by the judges). Five involved ordinary crimes such as murder or armed robbery and five had political overtones. All the disruption was caused by defendants or spectators, none by lawyers.

Twenty-five district attorneys responded and reported on fifteen cases of disruption, some of which overlapped with the judges' responses. Seven had some political overtones and the eight others were ordinary criminal cases. Defendants or spectators were primarily blamed for the disruption, but two of the district attorneys said that lawyers had contributed to the disorder in the cases they described.

Of the seventy-eight United States attorneys and district attorneys reporting to us, ten said there had been an increase in disorderly trials, fifty-five reported no increase, and thirteen did not answer the question.

Questionnaires on disruption were also sent to each of the fifty attorneys general of the states and to the presidents of the eighty-nine largest bar associations in the nation. In answer to specific questions about whether disruption had increased in their jurisdictions we obtained the following responses:

Thirty-nine attorneys general reported that there was no increase in disruptive trials in their jurisdictions, and three reported that there was. Only two described cases not referred to in other questionnaires. One response was generally about cases "involving members of black militant groups."

Twenty-six of the bar association presidents reported no increase in their jurisdictions, while three reported that disruption had increased.

The officially reported cases of courtroom misconduct (i.e., published decisions of trial or appellate courts) are also sparse. From 1960 to the end of 1972 we found only twelve published cases of defendant misconduct that led to a contempt conviction that was upheld on appeal.[18] The reported cases of lawyer misconduct are also small. We found only seventeen cases from 1960 to 1972 in which lawyer misbehavior in court led to a successful contempt conviction,[19] and only one case in which it led to disciplinary proceedings against the lawyer by the bar.[20]

Certain published data confirm our results. In 1971 the *New York Times* conducted a survey and independent interviews with legal authorities around the country and reported that courtroom disorder was "not a serious or growing problem."[21] The Administrative Office of the United States Courts also reported comparatively low figures on convictions for criminal contempt in the federal system over the past five years.[22]

Based on these figures the total incidence of courtroom disorder leading to a contempt conviction in the federal system is less than one-fifth of 1 percent of the criminal trials, and an even lower percentage of the total trials.

It is more difficult to arrive at the ratio of disorderly trials in the state court systems. Our estimate of the total number of criminal trials in the United States each year is about 630,000. This includes approximately 130,000 jury trials and 500,000 non-jury trials.[23] If the results of our survey and the reported cases are any indication of the total amount of disruption in the state courts—one-third of the nation's judges of general jurisdiction reported only 112 cases in their entire experience—the problem cannot be considered statistically important.

It is true that our survey did not reach the lower court judges who dispose of the less serious cases—those generally involving penalties of six months or less. But the type of disorder in those courts (which we shall discuss in chapter 2) is not what recently prompted the profession to take steps against disruptive trials. It is the more serious disruptions before juries that led to this concern, and the incidence of those disruptions is very, very small.

The *Georgetown Law Journal* in 1971 conducted a survey and reported that 25 percent of the judges it contacted "had been forced to take disciplinary action against a disruptive defendant."[24] The Georgetown results seem to be inconsistent with our survey, but we believe that our conclusions on the low incidence of disruption are correct. The Georgetown survey was deliberately sent to a very small sampling of judges—only 133 nationwide. Moreover, it was sent primarily to judges in jurisdictions where disruption was likely to be at a maximum —New York, Baltimore, Washington. In addition, a higher percentage of lower criminal court judges, who generally experience more disorder, were asked to respond. In contrast, our survey was comprehensive, reaching all trial judges throughout the country. Most important, the Georgetown survey considered even a warning to a defendant or lawyer to be "disciplinary action." The judges responding to our inquiry evidently did not consider this a satisfactory index of disruption.

The evidence that disruption occurs infrequently did not dampen the Committee's enthusiasm for the project. On the contrary, it concluded that an in-depth study would be valuable for five reasons: 1) to reassure the public and the profession that the incidence of courtroom misbehavior is low and relatively insignificant; 2) to define the proper roles of all the participants in judicial proceedings—lawyers, defendants, and prosecutors, as well as judges, bailiffs, and court officers—and thereby to promote a system of orderly judicial procedures that earns public respect; 3) to re-examine the often outmoded legal rules governing the behavior of these parties, including the law of contempt; 4) to appraise the legal proposals offered by other groups, such as the A.B.A.; and 5) to consider the possible relationship to courtroom disorder of stresses in society and in the legal system that produce injustice.

In choosing to proceed with a full study we made one concession to the questionnaire results. It was evident that almost all cases of disorder occurred in criminal trials. To be sure, there were a few civil cases, mainly involving divorce and custody proceedings, where the tension of the parties erupted in the courtroom and a disturbance ensued. But these were relatively rare, and pale in significance compared to the cases of disorder in criminal proceedings. Accordingly, we have principally stressed the criminal case, although our conclusions apply to all courtroom proceedings.

The Committee's conclusions, which are interspersed throughout this book, are summarized on pages 255–266. At the most general level we have concluded that courtroom disorder—whether caused by defendants, lawyers, prosecutors, spectators, or others—is not surprising and has been overemphasized, but is nevertheless severely prejudicial to a system of orderly justice.

Disorder should not be surprising in a proceeding where the state is acting to deprive an individual of his freedom and reputation; where there are stresses in the system, such as racism and the pressures on due process; where there are occasional political prosecutions and overbearing judges; and where the proceeding is essentially polemic and competitive, with emotion and temper never far from the surface.

Disorder has been overemphasized because, as we have already indicated, its incidence in American trials is low; and because both public and bar tend to focus on dramatic and publicized confrontations without bearing in mind that these are highly exceptional.

Disorder is dangerous, nevertheless, because any interference with an orderly system of justice is threatening; because some causes of disruption, if not eliminated, could lead to more extensive interruption of trial proceedings and a more serious deterioration in the legal process; and because the disruptions that have occurred, and the conditions in the courts that partly explain them, threaten to erode the public's confidence in the fairness and health of our judicial system.

# CHAPTER TWO

---

## *The Need for Orderly Justice*

We begin with a case involving a brief episode of courtroom disruption of the type that has worried the legal profession and the public—the shouting of obscenities in court by a representative of a militant political group. Although the incident received little public attention, it illustrates three themes that appear throughout this report. First, we are concerned with orderly justice, not merely the absence of disorder but the affirmative order of a properly organized and functioning system of criminal justice which acts to protect the rights of the people. Secondly, we are concerned with the immediate consequences and dangers of disrupted trials. Finally, we are interested in the complex relationship between courtroom disorder and injustice in the criminal courts.

## The Roldan Incident

On October 13, 1970, two young teenagers who belonged to the Young Lords, a militant Puerto Rican group in New York City, were arrested by three plainclothes policemen in front of a slum building on 110th Street in New York's Spanish Harlem. The police accused them of setting garbage on fire inside the hall of a tenement during a protest against Sanitation Department neglect of their neighborhood. Both men disputed the policemen's story, insisting they were trying to put the fires out and that they would never try to burn down the houses of their own people.

The police took the young men, Julio Roldan and Robert Lemus, to the nearest precinct, booked them, called attorneys on their behalf, but would not let them speak to the defendants without an officer present. The two were placed in a single cell overnight with no blankets although the weather was quite cold. They were taken to the criminal court building for arraignment at 7:30 the next morning, but the police again refused to allow their attorneys access to them on the ground that there were no proper facilities for consultation. When their case was finally called at 2:30 P.M., the following events occurred, as described by the court reporter:

> *The Court [Judge Hyman Solniker of the New York Criminal Court]:* What's the story, gentlemen?
>
> *Mr. [Dan] Pochoda [attorney for Roldan]:* Your Honor, we would like a couple of minutes to speak to these defendants. We have not had a chance.
>
> *The Court:* You are not going to have any opportunity to talk to them. I'll give you a short adjournment, and you will make arrangements. It is prohibited security-wise and otherwise. We haven't got the facilities; as you can see right now. We are working under adverse conditions.
>
> *Mr. Pochoda:* I understand, Your Honor. We have been waiting all day.
>
> *The Court:* I can't create the Utopia here.
>
> *Mr. Pochoda:* I understand that.
>
> *The Court:* All right. Second call.
>
> *The Defendant:* I want my rights in this fucking Court, man. . . .
>
> (WHEREUPON, AT THIS POINT IN THE PROCEEDINGS, THERE WAS A DISTURBANCE AT THE BAR, CREATED BY ONE OF THE DEFENDANTS APPEARING BEFORE THE JUDGE; AT WHICH TIME, THE COURT REPORTER REMOVED HERSELF FROM THE IMMEDIATE AREA. SAID DEFENDANT WAS CARRIED INTO THE PEN BY POLICE OFFICERS AND COURT OFFICERS. DURING THIS INTERIM, AN INDIVIDUAL WHO WAS STANDING NEAR THE ENTRANCE TO THE PEN, BEGAN PROTESTING TO THE COURT ABOUT THE ALLEGED BEATING OF SAID PRISONER AS HE WAS BEING PLACED BACK INSIDE THE PEN. THE COURT REPORTER ASSUMED HER POSITION AT THE MACHINE WHEN ORDER WAS RE-STORED IN THE COURTROOM.)[1]

During the uproar, one of the defendants shouted:

> There is no justice in this court. There is no one here to represent us. Our lawyers have not had a chance to speak with us. This is only happening because I'm Puerto Rican.

The judge ordered the defendants to the back of the courtroom. At 4:00 P.M. the case was recalled:

> *The Court Officer:* This is a recall on Docket Number A-20005 and A-20006, Julio Roldan and Robert Lemus, charged with attempted arson. This is being recalled.
>
> *Mr. [Alan] Fraser [assistant district attorney]:* The People recommend twenty-five hundred dollars as to each defendant.
>
> *The Court:* What sort of a building was this?

*Mr. Fraser:*   This was an occupied dwelling; a multiple dwelling. And this fire was set inside the hallway of the building.

*The Defendant:*   There was no fire set anywhere.

*Mr. Pochoda:*   Your Honor, this charge that I am—both defendants are admitted members of the Young Lords Party. To say that members . . .

*The Defendant:*   I want my own lawyer. . . .

*Miss [Barbara] Handschu [attorney for defendant Lemus]:*   Your Honor, there has been tremendous strain. I'm sorry.

*Mr. Pochoda:*   They were standing on the corner when the fires—when some fires were burning. . . .

*The Defendant:*   I want my own lawyer.

*The Court:*   You will get your own lawyer on the adjourned date. You get any lawyer you want. You retain your own lawyer on the adjourned date. Now, you be quiet right now. Otherwise, I will hold you in contempt of Court and I will delay the proceedings for thirty days, and put you in for thirty days; then you come back and start from scratch. If you want to do that, it's all right with me. What do you want to say?

*Mr. Pochoda:*   Your Honor, they are both admitted and very active members of the Young Lords Party. To think these persons in this capacity attempted to set fire in the building . . .

*The Defendant:*   I want . . .

*Mr. Pochoda:*   (continuing) . . . attempted to set fire in the building that was occupied by Puerto Rican families, is totally absurd. They don't have a prior record. One defendant had a prior record. Lived in the Bronx all their lives.

*The Court:*   What date?

*Mr. Fraser:*   October 20.

*Mr. Pochoda:*   We would like an early date, Your Honor. They could not meet this bail.

*Mr. Pochoda:*   It's clearly an absurd charge.

*The Court:*   Possibly they won't be reached until the middle of November. I'm giving them a preference by putting it over to the 20th. Bail, fifteen hundred dollars, each defendant.[2]

Neither defendant could raise bail and they were both remanded to the Tombs—the Manhattan House of Detention. Two days later, early in the morning of October 16, 1970, Julio Roldan committed suicide in his cell by hanging himself with his belt.

An investigation of the suicide was made by the New York City Board of Corrections. It observed about the courtroom conditions at Roldan's arraignment:

> The courtroom is crowded and noisy. The judges who preside are themselves offended by the lack of decorum and the practical necessities of moving the calendar of cases. It is little wonder that a defendant, and the Judge as well, are not left to feel that justice is being done.[3]

The chairman of the Board of Corrections, William vanden Heuvel, concluded:

Julio Roldan died by his own hand on October 16, 1970, but the intricate system of criminal justice which we have designed to protect the community and the individual succeeded only in deranging him and ultimately, instead of protecting him, it permitted his destruction.[4]

# A Functioning System of Criminal Justice . . . Not Mob Rule

We expect our courts to provide the basis for a free and open society. They protect the freedom and property of all citizens by punishing those who violate social peace and order. They perform this function while preserving the civil liberties of all persons, particularly those of minorities (such as Roldan) who may lack the economic and political power of other groups. The alternative to a legal system that operates fairly and effectively is either mob rule or tyranny. As Justice Brennan has written:

> Constitutional power to bring an accused to trial is fundamental to a scheme of "ordered liberty" and prerequisite to social justice and peace. History has known the breakdown of lawful penal authority—the feud, the vendetta, and the terror of penalties meted out by mobs or roving bands of vigilantes. It has known, too, the perversion of that authority. In some societies the penal arm of the state has reached individual men through secret denunciation followed by summary punishment. In others the solemn power of condemnation has been confided to the caprice of tyrants. Down the corridors of history have echoed the cries of innocent men convicted by other irrational or arbitrary procedures.[5]

This country has experienced some of the worst and most persistent breakdowns of orderly justice through the pressure of lynch mobs and mass terror. Such outrages were almost always directed against minority groups. One of the prime aims of the Ku Klux Klan after the Civil War was to terrorize the courts so that whites committing crimes against the black population would be promptly acquitted and blacks accused of crimes against the white population would be given the maximum penalties possible. A federal judge wrote in 1875:

> In no country but our own is the discreditable fact true that where murder, and cruel and shocking outrages, are perpetrated by a dominant party in a narrow region of the country, there is no power of punishment, save through the impracticable instrumentality of those who have either committed or sympathized with the crime. When conspiracies and combinations against the property, well-being, and life of classes of persons in the small divisions of our country include large portions of the constabulary, the magistracy, and the jurors, grand and traverse, the inevitable consequence must be that the offenses they commit, or with which they sympathize, will be perpetrated with impunity. . . . It

has been our painful duty in repeated instances to charge juries that the
federal court had no cognizance of offenses where crimes so cruel and
shocking have been proved that court, jury, and audience could scarcely
refrain from tears of sympathy, and where the elegantly dressed, so-
cially well-connected and shameless murderers had, in the communities
where they had shed innocent blood, not only confessed but boasted of
their crimes and who had either not been indicted at all, or, when tried,
had been acquitted by juries, their coadjutors in crime, amid the ac-
clamations of their co-conspirators.[6]

Fifty years later, the same kind of justice was still being dispensed
in many Southern courts. In one case in Arkansas involving five black
men who had been accused of killing a white man while defending a
Negro church against an armed attack, a mob marched to the jail for
the purpose of lynching them, but were prevented by the presence
of United States troops. A committee of leading citizens of the town
promised the mob that if they went home, the defendants would be
executed by the state after a trial. On October 27, 1919, a grand jury
of white men was organized consisting of many members of the lynch
mob, and on October 29, it returned an indictment. On November 3
the five black defendants were brought into court, informed that a
certain lawyer was appointed their counsel, and placed on trial before
a white jury (blacks being systematically excluded from both grand
and petit juries). The court and neighborhood were surrounded by
an adverse crowd that threatened the most dangerous consequences
to anyone interfering with the desired result. The defendants' counsel
did not ask for a change of venue or challenge a single juryman. He
called no witnesses for the defense and did not put the defendants on
the stand. The trial lasted about three-quarters of an hour and in less
than five minutes the jury brought in a verdict of guilty of murder
in the first degree. Oliver Wendell Holmes wrote about the case:

> [N]o juryman could have voted for an acquittal and continued to live
> in Phillips County and if any prisoner by a chance had been acquitted
> by a jury he could not have escaped the mob.[7]

While blacks were the chief target of such pressure in the South,
other members of minority groups were also subjected to terror-filled
trials which brought about legalized lynchings. In 1913, Leo Frank,
a Jewish factory superintendent in Atlanta, was accused of killing a
fourteen-year-old girl who worked for him. The evidence implicating
him was dubious but he was found guilty nevertheless. The trial was
carried on in a court packed with spectators and surrounded by a
crowd outside, all strongly hostile to the defendant. On the morning
that the case was given to the jury the solicitor general was greeted
with applause, stamping of feet, and clapping of hands when he entered the court, and the judge, before beginning his charge, had a

private conversation with Frank's lawyer in which he expressed the opinion that there would be "probable danger of violence" if there should be an acquittal or a disagreement.

> When the verdict [of guilty] was given and before more than one of the jurymen had been polled, there was such a roar of applause that the polling could not go on until order was restored. The noise outside was such that it was difficult for the judge to hear the answers of the jurors, although he was only ten feet from them.[8]

While mob violence is no longer the problem it once was in this country, it is all too plain that a functioning judiciary is one of the most important protections of all citizens in our society, particularly unpopular minorities. Anthony Lewis of the *New York Times* has written of the Supreme Court:

> There are closed minds in the Supreme Court on this issue or that. But on the whole it is a more open forum, more subject to persuasion, less moved by money or influence than any other institution of government. Anyone who sits in that courtroom and watches even briefly must be impressed by the simplicity of access, the directness of the process, the very real consideration given to interests that have little power in the material world. The Court listened to blacks when Congress did not, and to Communists and to pornographers. Would prisoners under death sentence be more likely to get a sympathetic hearing today from a state governor or legislature or from the courts? It would be very hard to convince me that the despised and rejected in our society would be better off if we gave up our vision of law in Freud's sense, one marked by detachment, and went over to what could be called revolutionary justice, committed to particular interests.[9]

It is therefore essential that the courts function as efficiently as possible and that they are protected in their role of preserving constitutional rights.


# The Dangers of Disruption

Although the criminal justice system has serious flaws and, as we show throughout this report, many of those caught up in the process have suffered genuine injustice, courtroom disruption is not a desirable or appropriate response to these problems. Disruption of courtroom proceedings even of the minor type involved in the Roldan incident can be extremely dangerous and threatening to the cause of orderly justice. Chief Justice Warren E. Burger stated in a widely publicized address to the American Law Institute in May, 1971, that

> "order in the court" articulates something very basic to the mechanisms of justice. Someone must teach that good manners, disciplined behavior

and civility—by whatever name—are the lubricants that prevent law-
suits from turning into combat. More than that it is really the very glue
that keeps an organized society from flying apart.[10]

It is apparent that a defendant who disrupts a trial undermines
the strong public investment in a fair judicial process. He also makes
the possibility of a fair trial for himself that much more difficult. But,
as we shall see later in this report, disruption can be instigated by
judges or prosecutors as well as by defendants or their lawyers. If
what we have said about the stresses in the legal process has any
validity, individual defendants have a difficult enough time in the
courts without the additional handicap of an emotion-filled courtroom brought about by abusive or disorderly conduct, from whatever source.

Courtroom disruption is dangerous to society for other reasons. A
public trial plays an extremely important role in the continuing sociali-
zation of members of any community. It serves as a vast morality play,
in which deeply felt notions of justice, of rewards for good deeds and
punishment for immoral acts, are reinforced through identification
with one or more of the participants. This may be the reason for the
overwhelming public interest in sensational criminal trials which occur
from time to time. Thurman W. Arnold has explained the process as
follows:

> [T]he public judicial trial . . . symbolizes for them [the mass of people]
> the heaven of justice which lies behind the insecurity, cruelty, and ir-
> rationality of an everyday world. In the public trial we find the govern-
> ment speaking ex cathedra. Other actions of the government may be
> subject to political attack or may be called corrupt or foolish. The ac-
> tion of a court in a trial cannot be so considered without seeming to
> endanger the very fabric of the State.
> The judicial trial thus becomes a series of object lessons and exam-
> ples. It is the way in which society is trained in right ways of thought
> and action, not by compulsion, but by parables which it interprets and
> follows voluntarily.[11]

Many psychiatrists have also pointed out how important is the entire
system of criminal justice for the collective psyche of society.[12]

A disrupter who interferes with the "grandeur of court procedure,"
as Hannah Arendt describes the process,[13] touches an extremely sensitive nerve in the body politic. He undermines the public's view of the
courts as the great teacher and protector of ethics and morality. With
public confidence in the courts already at a low level—Chief Justice
Burger cited a survey showing that only a small percentage of the
public approved of the way they are operating[14]—those who introduce
more disorder in the courts threaten the system in a vital way.

More important, they may make it impossible for significant reform
to take place. Individual acts of disruption may distract attention from

the structural disorders of the system itself. Rather than wake people up to the evils that the disrupters are complaining of, such actions tend to convince the public that the disrupters are the enemies of social justice. A federal appellate judge has written:

> . . . it may be argued that there are some things in the judicial process more important than decorum in a courtroom. . . . Dissent is a healthy manifestation of the freedoms we as a nation profess and cherish. And a criminal trial might serve as the seed around which a point of view may crystallize. But a courtroom is not an arena in which dissension, particularly of a disruptive nature, may supplant, or even take precedence over, the task of administering justice.[15]

Thus, in a very fundamental way courtroom disruption threatens the system of orderly justice. It makes it more difficult for a defendant to obtain a fair trial. It hampers the ability of the courts to protect those members of society who most need protection. It undermines the public's confidence in and respect for the legal process. It may interfere with the possibility of significant reform in the judicial system. In almost every way it is inconsistent with the rule of law in an open democratic society.

# Disorder and Injustice

In this study we also must take account of an often overlooked type of courtroom disruption: the disorder of a criminal justice system that is not performing as it should, that often produces not justice but delays, chaos, and confusion. The Roldan incident illustrates some of these inadequacies—crowded calendars and courtrooms, overworked legal aid lawyers, lack of facilities for consultation, short tempered judges, and the imposition of high bail. Two principal shortcomings that require special note are 1) the structural defects in the criminal justice system and 2) racism among the participants in the legal process. Apart from their intrinsic qualities, each of these has a bearing, as we shall see, on the disrupted trial proceedings that have caused such widespread concern.

## Structural Inadequacies in the Judicial System

Within the last few years two presidential commissions have expressed shock at the inadequacy and unfairness of the lower criminal courts, particularly in urban centers. The President's Commission on Law Enforcement and the Administration of Justice wrote, in 1967:

The Commission has been shocked by what it has seen in some lower courts. It has seen cramped and noisy courtrooms, undignified and perfunctory procedures, and badly trained personnel. It has seen dedicated people who are frustrated by huge caseloads, by the lack of opportunity to examine cases carefully, and by the impossibility of devising constructive solutions to the problems of offenders. It has seen assembly line justice.[16]

A year later, the National Riot Commission reported:

Some of our courts, moreover, have lost the confidence of the poor. This judgment is underwritten by the members and staff of this Commission, who have gone into the courthouses and ghettoes of the cities torn by the riots of 1967. The belief is pervasive among ghetto residents that lower courts in our urban communities dispense "assembly-line" justice; that from arrest to sentencing, the poor and uneducated are denied equal justice with the affluent, that procedures such as bail and fines have been perverted to perpetuate class inequities. We have found that the apparatus of justice in some areas has itself become a focus for distrust and hostility. Too often the courts have operated to aggravate rather than relieve the tensions that ignite and fire disorders.[17]

There has been far from sufficient improvement since these words were written. A special report on the Detroit Recorder's Court issued in 1970 indicated that confusion and disorder occurred in a majority of the cases heard there and that any attempt to reach a fair or just verdict was seriously jeopardized by the noisy courtroom atmosphere.[18] Similarly a study of the New York City criminal justice system in 1971 concluded that the residents "now have a system for the administration of justice that is neither efficient enough to create a credible fear of punishment nor fair enough to command sincere respect for its values."[19]

Directly related to this chaos are a host of other problems plaguing the system of criminal justice. Some police officers in our major cities have a quota system of arrests, make dragnet arrests of suspected drug addicts or prostitutes, harass members of minority groups, and too often ignore the constitutional rights of suspects.[20]

Once arrested, tens of thousands of persons must stay in jail because they cannot make bail. A census of city and county jails conducted by the federal government in 1970 indicated that of the 160,000 persons incarcerated at that time, 83,000 or 52 percent had not been convicted of a crime but were being held for failure to post bond. The large majority of them could not raise bail of less than $1,000.[21]

The long delays before a case can be tried have now reached the dimensions of a national scandal, and many courts and the Congress are insisting upon speedy trials. However, the pressure to move matters along in court has led to a crisis in plea bargaining. On the one hand, defendants accused of serious crimes are given the opportunity to plead to lesser offenses and receive minimal sentences. On the other hand, accused persons loudly protesting their innocence are compelled to plead guilty to lesser charges by the implied threat of heavier sentences if they go to trial and by their own attorney's desire to dispose of a case as quickly as possible.[22]

The quality of representation of poor defendants in the criminal courts is often woefully inadequate, not so much because the lawyers are incompetent but because they are overwhelmed by the number of cases they must handle.[23] Some judges in the lower courts are abusive, intimidating, and prejudiced against minority groups and young people that appear before them. In the Boston area, some judges openly acknowledged that they would increase the sentences for all defendants who asserted the right of appeal to a lower court verdict.[24] In Washington, D.C., some judges have been frequently reprimanded for mocking criminal defendants and belittling the attorneys who appear before them.[25] In New York, dossiers have been prepared by community law offices on some of the civil court judges who have been particularly biased against minority group litigants.[26]

The problems revealed by this brief outline of the inadequacies in the criminal justice system provide the backdrop against which specific incidents of courtroom disruption initiated by defendants, lawyers, and others must be examined. We of course do not suggest that every episode of disruption is the immediate result of the sense of outrage that defendants or others feel when confronted with the shortcomings of the legal system. Nor does every instance of injustice produce a courtroom outburst. As we have seen, the incidence of disruption by defendants and lawyers is far less than popular accounts indicate, despite the injustice that many of them meet every day in the courts.

## Racism

One of the most serious complaints that has been raised against the judicial system is that racism pervades its administration at all levels. That racism is one of the most significant problems in American law has been amply documented by a series of presidential reports and independent studies over the past decades.[27]

Many of the witnesses appearing before the Committee have pointed out the dangers that this situation creates. Haywood Burns, executive director of the National Conference of Black Lawyers, told us:

> Blacks feel and see that the law is used against black people. There is a situation where they are society's victims, and the law has been society's weapon. This places an undue burden on the legal system. The defendants are there due to problems related to society, not the legal system. Blacks don't believe it is impossible to win in court, but they are skeptical. The law has been the vehicle and handmaiden of racism. The

law has been used to continue and preserve a racist society. We have
had the experience of Jim Crowism and of slavery, both of which have
been legally protected institutions. But this is not just an historical
legacy, it is today's experience also. . . .

. . . I would give you a few illustrations. First, we see the attitudes of
the court personnel, both the ancillary judicial personnel and judges.
You should go sit in Arraignment Part and listen to the insults, racial
and other, that are directed to defendants and especially to members
of minority groups. These things go beyond mere staffing problems.
They reflect an entire attitude.

Professor Derrick Bell of the Harvard Law School wrote a careful
report for the Committee about the potential of disruption because of
these and other shortcomings in the judicial system.[28] He cited three
studies of lower criminal courts in three separate areas of the nation—
Detroit, Boston, and Florida—to show the handicaps that the black
population suffers in the courts. One was a 1969 study in the Detroit
Recorder's Court, based on examination of 787 misdemeanor cases.[29]
The study found that cases were generally heard in noisy courtrooms
where decorum was continually disrupted by police, court personnel,
attorneys, witnesses, and spectators, and that inadequate physical facilities contributed to confusion. Bell analyzed this report from the
perspective of black defendants.

While the judge spent little time on any of the cases (four of five being
concluded in less than ten minutes and two of five receiving less than
three minutes), cases involving black defendants were generally heard
in less time than those involving whites. Black defendants with counsel
were almost twice as likely to plead guilty as a white defendant with
counsel, even though defendants without counsel tended to plead guilty
at approximately the same rate, regardless of race.

The result is that

in terms of a jail sentence without other alternatives permitted we find
that half again as many blacks as whites receive such a sentence. . . .
in regard to the penalty incurring the least lasting stigma and not involving a loss of one's liberty—a fine—we observe that whites are twice
as likely as blacks to receive such a disposition of their case.

Wherever discretion exists in the legal system, it is likely to be exercised against blacks. For example, the state of Florida has a procedure
under which a judge may withhold an adjudication of guilty from
defendants who are placed on probation. Thus the defendant avoids
the stigma of being a convicted felon. A study made by the Florida
Probation and Parole Commission showed that black defendants were
not treated in the same way as whites.

A 1969 study of 2,419 consecutive felony cases received by the Florida
Probation and Parole Commission during an eight month period, revealed that blacks (41.1%) are adjudicated guilty more often than

whites (28.3%), and are placed on probation with a felony charge in less than one-third of the 2,402 probation cases for whom race was recorded. "Thus," states the report, "it appears that blacks accused of a felony are much less likely than whites to be placed on probation, and when placed on probation, they are less likely to avoid being labeled 'convicted felon.'"

Professor Bell cited an independent study of sentencing patterns[30] which showed a peculiar pattern of indulgence and nonindulgence with respect to black defendants. If they commit offenses against other blacks their sentences are generally lower than what white defendants would receive. But if the black crime crosses racial lines, is committed against whites, the sentences are much higher than for any other group. This pattern indicates that race is almost always a factor in sentencing and that the "indulgence" granted in intraracial crime may itself be prejudicial: it does not show sympathy for the black defendant but contempt for the black victim.[31]

Our questionnaire results show that a substantial number of disrupted trials involved black defendants. The trial judges reported that more than one-third of all defendant disorder had "racial overtones." Nevertheless, the problem of racism has not erupted in widespread courtroom disorder. Professor Bell explains:

> Blacks, lawyers and clients, despite the provocation of racism and injustice, have been so beaten by the system that, as Frederick Douglass could have predicted, they contributed but little to whatever cause exists for this concern [courtroom disruption]. The danger for the future is less that blacks will disrupt the courts than that they will ignore them.

Despite Professor Bell's prediction, the potential exists for a more vigorous reaction in the courts by black defendants and lawyers. The patience of blacks has been put under great stress. If other means of improving conditions fail, blacks and other minority groups may choose to engage in more active protest within the courtroom.


## The Problem of Justification

Throughout this report we describe instances of courtroom disruption which, like the Roldan incident, are understandable. Many of the cases described in the next chapter deal with people or causes later vindicated by history. It is therefore important at the outset to consider whether anyone is ever "justified" in deliberately disrupting court proceedings.

As already noted, many of those arrested and tried in the courts feel that they are not being treated fairly. One lawyer who appeared before our committee, Professor Sheila Rush Okpaku, said:

> If we took, in viewing our own courts, the perspective of an American watching the South African court system operate, we would not censure attempts by defendants to bring world and media attention to the injustice being done to them. It is the fact that it is our own court system, our own homeground, that is being protested that limits our perspective.

This point was underscored to the Committee by Melvin L. Wulf, legal director of the American Civil Liberties Union. Those who feel strongly about what they see as injustice in the courts or in society are not likely to be impressed by the dangers of disruption. From their perspective, the system does not deserve their respect.

On a more theoretical level, it is possible to advance an argument in support of courtroom disruption based on considerations similar to those said to justify civil disobedience. At our request, one of the consultants to our committee, Professor Graham Hughes of the New York University Law School, offered a hypothetical justification for such conduct. In his paper he posits a case where law enforcement authorities ignore various forms of gambling engaged in by white middle-class citizens, such as poker playing and public gambling activities conducted by religious groups. But they vigorously enforce the gambling laws against dice games, which are usually played by blacks or Spanish-speaking Americans. Feeling aggrieved by the policy, these minorities work in an orderly democratic fashion to change it, to no avail. The police continue to enforce the gambling laws selectively against them. At this point, says Professor Hughes, disruption may be justifiable from the defendants' point of view.

> . . . there are plausible grounds for contending that, with respect to gambling laws, an unjust and unequal enforcement policy has been countenanced by the law and the courts so that on this issue at least the usual moral arguments in favor of cooperating with judicial processes have been overborne by countervailing arguments derived from principles of justice and fairness. Here again we begin to find a case for starting civil disobedience in the courtroom, but again this is not at all the same as a general case for revolution or a general argument for behaving criminally or even a general argument for always violating the tranquility of the courts. It asserts only that in one small and very particular context the administration of justice has generally deteriorated into arbitrary caprice and deserves no respect. It would be a perfectly proper position to be maintained by a generally law-abiding and orderly group.

Professor Hughes argues that many defendants brought within the judicial system feel that the courts do operate in many areas with "arbitrary caprice." Thus the disrupter may feel he is performing a necessary political act. His argument, according to Professor Hughes, would be:

Where people are brought before courts as a result of the operation of laws which impinge on them in an unjust and racist manner because of their socioeconomic background and race, then, even though a general revolutionary posture may not be justified and even though the courts themselves behave in a fair and equitable manner, nevertheless noncooperation with the judicial process is justified as a form of civil disobedience designed to evangelize the community as to the injustice protested against.

But even if we take the extreme example offered by Professor Hughes, disruption of court proceedings cannot be tested in the same way as other acts of civil disobedience. The justification for civil disobedience is that some laws are so immoral that men of conscience cannot obey them. Violations of law lead to punishment which they accept as witness to their acts of conscience. Implicit in this model is recognition of the importance of court procedures to punish those who disobey the law and allow them to show the world how deeply they feel about the laws in question.

On the other hand, a courtroom disrupter is attacking the heart of the system accepted by the civil disobedient. His acts are not a witness to a law's immorality but a direct threat to the judicial process. While we recognize that court disorder can draw attention to shortcomings in the courts, this extra dimension makes us question the model that Professor Hughes presented. Furthermore, as lawyers we cannot endorse any form of courtroom disruption because we believe orderly justice is vitally important for an open and free society.

Nevertheless, we recognize the force of the contrary arguments. We have seen reforms in prison conditions being considered only after a series of riots have taken the lives of many inmates and guards. We hope that the reforms necessary to make the courts more responsive to the needs of all members of society will not need the same kind of spur.

# CHAPTER THREE

# *The Historical Background*

Disorderly trials are not unique to contemporary America. From 1970 to the end of 1972 disruption of court proceedings took place in Spain, England, Canada, Egypt, and France. In Spain in December 1970 a group of Basque separatists were tried by a military court-martial for planning the killing of a secret police inspector. The defendants admitted being members of a guerrilla group but denied any part in the murder. During their trial restrictions were placed on the political testimony they could offer. Finally, the defendants began struggling with the policemen guarding them, one prisoner advanced threateningly on the tribunal, and spectators began shouting and singing.[1]

In England, twenty Welsh protestors marched into a London courtroom in February 1970 to complain about the jailing of a Welsh singer. The group began singing "We Shall Overcome" in Welsh and passed out leaflets objecting to discrimination against the Welsh language. Fourteen of them were held in contempt of court and summarily given three-month sentences by the presiding judge.[2]

In another English case in October and November 1971, nine black West Indians (called the Mangrove Nine) were arrested and tried for "making an affray" after a fight between some black demonstrators and police in the Notting Hill section of London. Tensions between the police and the West Indian community were high because of police raids on a West Indian restaurant—the Mangrove—which was the headquarters for militants in the area. A magistrate had dismissed most of the serious charges against the nine but the English Director of Public Prosecutions reintroduced some of them, creating more tension. The defendants demanded an all-black jury, interrupted witnesses, and complained about their treatment by court officers. At one point a fight broke out in court between four defendants and the marshals. All the defendants were acquitted on the most serious charges and five were found guilty of minor offenses.[3]

Members of a radical separatist group in Canada, the Front for the

Liberation of Quebec, were tried in Montreal in February 1971 in two cases which were often disrupted by outbursts. Paul Rose had been indicted for strangling Pierre LaPorte, the Quebec labor minister who had been kidnapped by the Front. Rose frequently accused the presiding justice of collusion with the prosecutor and insisted on asking prospective jurors their political views about Quebec separatism despite the judge's ruling that "political questioning" was not in order. In another courtroom, Michel Chartrand, a labor leader, and other Quebec separatists were being tried for seditious conspiracy under the Canadian War Measures Act. The prosecutor demanded that only the defendants' lawyers be permitted to confer with them in the courtroom, and the defendants responded with a barrage of abusive language. The judge ordered proceedings halted.[4]

In August 1971, a group of former high government officials in Egypt were put on trial for treason in Cairo. The *New York Times* reported: "Angry shouts from defense attorneys challenging the legality of a three-man revolutionary tribunal disrupted the opening session this morning of the trial of the former Vice President, Aly Sabry, and other high officials arrested in May after a challenge to the leadership of President Anwar el-Sadat."[5]

Late in 1972 in Paris, eleven members of an underground organization seeking political autonomy for Brittany were tried for terrorism before the French National Security Court. One defendant spoke only in Breton, the native Celtic language of the province. There were melees between the defendants and court guards, and those on trial used their days in court to speak out on the political and economic problems of their region.[6]

Historically, both the civil law countries on the European continent and the common law jurisdictions in Great Britain and the United States have experienced recurrent patterns of disorderly court proceedings when one or a combination of the following conditions has occurred:

1. The courts are used to enforce or implement an unpopular policy of the government and thus become the battleground for the contending political forces of the time.

2. Individual opponents of the prevailing regime or members of dissident groups challenging basic government policies are brought before the courts for any reason.

3. The basic criminal procedures under which defendants are tried are thought to be unjust, discriminatory, or improperly invoked by the government.

## European Cases

Many of the famous trials of the past century on the European continent were "disorderly," primarily because of the first and second of the above causes. That is, the judicial systems were being buffeted by powerful political currents that periodically affected all European institutions.

The anarchists who were tried for assassinating monarchs and prime ministers in the 1890s generally used their trials as an opportunity to expound the philosophy of "the deed." Thus the trials of Vaillant (who dynamited the French Chamber of Deputies in 1894), Michel Angiollilo (who killed the Spanish premier in 1897), and Gaetano Bresci (who killed King Humbert of Italy in 1899) saw frequent sharp exchanges on politics between the defendants and the judges.[7]

Most of the court proceedings relating to the Dreyfus affair in France were not conducted according to the ordinary rules of court decorum. When Emile Zola was tried for criminal libel for accusing the army of covering up evidence of Dreyfus's innocence and exonerating the real culprit, Major Ferdinand Esterhazy, it was in a circus atmosphere. The public invaded "not only the places reserved for the audience, but took the seats around the judges and jurors, sat on window sills. Some climbed on the stoves. . . . Some young men sat on the floor . . . in front of the jury."[8] Frequent arguments occurred between Zola's lawyers and the judges whenever any attempt was made to offer evidence that Dreyfus was innocent. The audience openly cheered the army officers who testified against Zola. Witnesses shouted at each other and threatened to fight. When Dreyfus himself was retried at a court-martial in Rennes, he frequently interrupted the proceedings to ask questions or berate the generals who testified against him.[9]

A few years after the Dreyfus affair, Leon Trotsky was tried for leading an abortive insurrection against the Russian government in Petrograd in 1905. His trial was held before a special high court in June 1906. Most of the witnesses or defendants "took the stand to denounce the government and to call upon the proletariat to free the prisoners and try their prosecutors." Trotsky himself spoke for hours to explain the Social Democratic political platform and to indict "the regime which had put him on trial."[10]

During World War I, a young Austrian Socialist, Friedrich Adler, assassinated Count Stürgkh, the Austro-Hungarian prime minister, and used the trial to denounce the government's war policy. He claimed he was no more guilty than a soldier who killed in battle. At the trial, he said that he "had the duty of standing up for his beliefs" and revealing all the sins of the imperial government. Despite the judge's warnings not to introduce extraneous matters, he explained the political motives of his acts—his attempt to prompt a revolution of the Austrian people.[11]

During the Weimer Republic in Germany, there were a series of disorderly court proceedings arising from the political fragmentation and bitterness of the postwar years. The murderers of Karl Liebknecht and Rosa Luxemburg (leaders of the left-wing Sparticists) were exonerated of the most serious charges against them in 1920 in a courtroom filled with their cheering supporters from the *Freikorps*. Libel actions by or against leading members of the government were heard in raucous courtroom settings.[12]

Immediately after Hitler came to power in 1933, Georgi Dimitrov, a Bulgarian Communist, was tried in Berlin for conspiracy in the burning of the Reichstag—an event which the Nazis used as a basis for suppressing the Communist party. Dimitrov refused a lawyer and defended himself. He repeatedly asked each government witness "had not the Reichstag fire, in fact, been the signal for the destruction of the working class parties and a means of solving difficulties within the Hitler government." He often was dragged out of the courtroom when he insisted on asking inadmissible questions, and he engaged in a shouting match with Hermann Goering, who appeared as a witness. With representatives of the world press covering the trial, the German government did not directly interfere in the verdict and Dimitrov's brilliant defense led to his acquittal.[13]

About the same time, in France, a group of Croat nationalists led by a Fascist agent named Ustaschi were being tried for the assassination of King Alexander of Yugoslavia and Louis Barthou, the foreign minister of France, who had been riding together in Marseilles when the assassins struck. The murderers were tried in Aix-en-Provence in 1935 and their lawyers conducted such an uproarious defense that the court dismissed them from the case.[14]

After World War II, France saw a series of disorderly trials arising out of the terrorist activities of the F.L.N., the Algerian nationalist movement. The attempted murderers of Jacques Soustelle, the Algerian governor-general, were tried by a Paris military tribunal in 1959 and their lawyers were removed from the case for overstepping the lines of judicial propriety.[15] Within a year the same type of disorder took place —also resulting in removal of the attorneys—when a group of French intellectuals led by Professor Francis Jeanson were tried for giving aid to the Algerian rebels and encouraging young men called to military service to refuse service in Algeria.[16]

Similar politically oriented trials took place in Asia during the twentieth century. Indian nationalists, including Mahatma Gandhi, often used their trials for civil disobedience offenses as a platform to explain their opposition to continued British rule. In Japan the ultranationalist officers who assassinated older politicians in the 1930s openly proclaimed in court that they were trying to awaken the nation to Japan's great military destiny and were greeted with loud applause from the spectators.[17]

This small sampling of cases shows that the courts are seldom insulated from the turmoil of the political sphere in any nation. When political opponents of the prevailing regime are brought into the courts (whether for murder, conspiracy, or sedition) they are not inclined to sit quietly by without trying to justify their actions, rally their followers, and thwart their prosecutors.[18] These tactics generally involve a disregard of the normal rules of courtroom decorum.

This is not to say that every trial in periods of political turmoil and every trial of political dissidents will necessarily be disorderly. An opponent of the existing regime may conclude that fighting and winning according to the rules of the government may better serve his purposes. Or the political component of the case may be minimal. But particularly when the government singles out its political enemies for special treatment through the use of the criminal laws—charging them with sedition, conspiracy, or treason for their political actions—the defendants will not assume that they must stop their campaigns of opposition and agitation at the courthouse doors.

# English Cases

Because of the relative political stability that England has enjoyed in recent centuries, the disorderly trials that occurred there generally resulted from procedural complaints raised by the defendants, although there were often political overtones to the trials as well.

In a number of notorious trials in the seventeenth century, defendants noisily claimed that they were being illegally tried and that the basic protections of English law were not being afforded them. While the episodes of contention seem mild today, the trials were considered disorderly by the judges of the time and have been so regarded under the stiff standards of decorum of the English bar. These cases include the trials of Sir Walter Raleigh for high treason in 1603, John Lilburne and John Bastwick for sedition in 1637, and William Penn for unlawful assembly in 1670.*

Sir Walter Raleigh insisted at his trial for high treason in 1603 that

* An additional problem in these cases was the fact that, until the mid-eighteenth century, lawyers were not permitted to appear in an English court to defend those accused of a crime. Unskilled defendants had to rely on their own talents in court and frequently found themselves in contention with the prosecution and judge.

he should have the right to confront and cross-examine the witnesses who had signed confessions implicating him. Raleigh and the attorney general at the time, Sir Edward Coke, engaged in frequent exchanges about his guilt and the procedural rights he was entitled to.[19]

Thirty years later, in 1637, another disorderly trial occurred which had far-reaching effects on English and American law. John Lilburne, a twenty-three-year-old clothier's apprentice, was accused of "sending factious and scandalous Books out of Holland into England" without "any examination" and an appropriate license. In accordance with the usual procedures of the time, Lilburne was asked a series of questions by Sir John Banks, the king's attorney. These related to his activities in Holland and people he knew there. After answering some of them, Lilburne declared that he would answer only questions relating to the offense with which he was charged. He also asked to confront his accusers.

Eventually Lilburne was brought to the Star Chamber court where he was told to place his hand upon the Bible and to swear:

> To what?
> That you shall make true answer to all things that are asked of you.
> Must I so sir? but before I swear, I will know to what I must swear.
> As soon as you have sworn, you shall, but not before.[20]

The Star Chamber was trying to impose the oath ex officio on Lilburne. Under that procedure a defendant had to swear to answer truthfully any questions asked of him or be considered guilty. It had fallen into disuse after the Petition of Right was passed in 1628, but the Star Chamber resurrected the oath in the late 1630s to intimidate troublemakers like Lilburne. At every appearance before the Star Chamber, Lilburne refused to take the oath and "thundered out" against the procedure and the judges. He was whipped at the pillory and imprisoned for three years until the Long Parliament assumed control in London in 1640 and released him. Within a year Parliament passed a law abolishing both the Star Chamber and the oath ex officio.[21]

In 1670 another important trial occurred. William Penn and William Mead were tried for "unlawfully and tumultuously . . . assembl[ing] and congregat[ing]" by preaching a sermon after their Quaker church had been closed by the Conventicle Act. The trial opened with Penn demanding his rights:

> *Recorder:* What say you, William Penn and William Mead, are you Guilty, as you stand indicted, in manner and form, as aforesaid, or Not Guilty?
> *Penn:* It is impossible that we should be able to remember the Indictment verbatim, and therefore we desire a copy of it, as is customary on the like occasions.
> *Recorder:* You must first plead to the indictment, before you can have a copy of it.

*Penn:* I am unacquainted with the formality of the law, and therefore before I shall answer directly, I request two things of the court. 1. That no advantage may be taken against me, nor I deprived of any benefit, which I might otherwise have received. 2. That you will promise me a fair hearing, and liberty of making my defence.

Two days later the defendants came into court with their hats on. Court officers immediately took them off.

*Clerk:* Bring William Penn and William Mead to the bar.

*Mayor:* Sirrah, who bid you put off their hats? put on their hats again.

*Obser.:* Whereupon one of the officers putting the prisoners hats upon their heads [pursuant to the order of the court] brought them to the bar.

*Record.:* Do you know where you are?

*Penn:* Yes.

*Record.:* Do you know it is the king's court.

*Penn:* I know it to be a court, and I suppose it to be the king's court.

*Record.:* Do you not know there is respect due to the court?

*Penn:* Yes.

*Record.:* Why do you not pay it then?

*Penn:* I do so.

*Record.:* Why do you not pull off your hat then?

*Penn:* Because I do not believe that to be any respect.

*Record.:* Well, the court sets forty marks a piece upon your heads, as a fine for your contempt of the court.

*Penn:* I desire it might be observed that we came into the court with our hats off (that is, taken off) and if they have been put on since, it was by order from the bench; and therefore not we but the bench should be fined.

After this incident the trial began. Witnesses were called to show that a "tumultuous assembly" had taken place at Penn's instigation. Penn insisted he had broken no law but only assembled with his friends to pray.

*Penn:* I affirm I have broken no law, nor am I Guilty of the indictment that is laid to my charge; and to the end the bench, the jury, and myself, with these that hear us, may have a more direct understanding of this procedure, I desire you would let me know by what law it is you prosecute me, and upon what law you ground my indictment.

*Rec.:* Upon the common-law.

*Penn:* Where is that common-law?

*Rec.:* You must not think that I am able to run up so many years, and over so many adjudged cases, which we call common-law, to answer your curiosity.

*Penn:* This answer I am sure is very short of my question, for if it be common, it should not be so hard to produce.

*Rec.:* Sir, will you plead to your indictment?

*Penn:* Shall I plead to an Indictment that hath no foundation in law? If it contain that law you say I have broken, why should you decline to produce that law, since it will be impossible for the jury to determine, or agree to bring in their verdict, who have not the law produced, by which they should measure the truth of this indictment, and the guilt, or contrary of my fact?

*Rec.:* You are a saucy fellow, speak to the Indictment.[22]

The jury eventually found Penn guilty of preaching to an assembly but refused to say that the gathering was unlawful. After being sent back to deliberate again, they returned with a verdict of not guilty. The court was not satisfied with the verdict and fined each member of the jury and ordered them imprisoned until the fine was paid.

Bushell, the jury foreman, petitioned for a writ of habeas corpus and the case was heard in the Court of Kings Bench. The court discharged the prisoner on the ground that "finding against the evidence in court, or direction of the court . . . is no sufficient cause to fine; the jury answers all these cases. . . ."[23]

These cases were "disorderly" only in the sense that the defendants insisted on the rights they felt they possessed under the English Constitution. By pressing their points the defendants in the three cases brought about important changes in the procedural rights of English citizens which eventually became part of the American Constitution. The right of confrontation, found in the Sixth Amendment, is generally traced back to Raleigh's case. The abolition of the Star Chamber, the oath ex officio, and the protections against self-incrimination in the Fifth Amendment unquestionably arose from the trials of Lilburne and Dr. Bastwick. And the independence of the jury was firmly fixed by the acquittal of William Penn and the decision in Bushell's case.[24]

The English judicial system has generally expected the strictest conduct of its barristers and defendants. For example, Sir Thomas Erskine's famous exchange with Justice Buller in the case of the Dean of St. Asaph in 1784 was considered the height of impertinence and defiance by a lawyer. Yet it is quite restrained by today's standards. In that case, a trial for seditious libel, the jury returned a verdict of "guilty of publishing only."

*Erskine:* You find him guilty of publishing only?

*A Juror:* Guilty only of publishing.

*Buller, J.:* I believe that is a verdict not quite correct. You must explain that one way or the other. If you find him guilty of publishing, you must not say the word only.

*Erskine:* By that they mean to find there was no sedition. . . .

*Buller, J.:* Gentlemen, if you add the word "only" it will be negativing the innuendoes.

*Erskine:* I desire your Lordship sitting here as Judge to record the verdict as given by the Jury.

*Buller, J.:* You say he is guilty of publishing the pamphlet, and that the meaning of the innuendoes is as stated in the indictment.

*Juror:*  Certainly.

*Erskine:*  Is the word "only" to stand part of the verdict?

*Juror:*  Certainly.

*Erskine:*  Then, I insist it shall be recorded.

*Buller, J.:*  Then the verdict must be misunderstood; let me understand the Jury.

*Erskine:*  The Jury do understand their verdict.

*Buller, J.:*  Sir, I will not be interrupted.

*Erskine:*  I stand here as an advocate for a brother citizen, and I desire that the word "only" may be recorded.

*Buller, J.:*  SIT DOWN, SIR: REMEMBER YOUR DUTY, OR I SHALL BE OBLIGED TO PROCEED IN ANOTHER MANNER.

*Erskine:*  YOUR LORDSHIP MAY PROCEED IN WHAT MANNER YOU THINK FITS. I KNOW MY DUTY AS WELL AS YOUR LORDSHIP KNOWS YOURS. I SHALL NOT ALTER MY CONDUCT.[25]

The extraordinary respect afforded judges in England may have been based on their special class position in society. Defendants and lawyers deferred to judges primarily because they were members of the nobility, not because they were judges. The rules governing proper conduct in court incorporated many of the requirements of homage due to the higher classes and remained even after the ranks of the judiciary were opened beyond the nobility.

Although we think of the English courts as models of civility and decorum, English lawyers and judges on occasion have gone far beyond the dignified protests of Erskine and greatly exceeded the limits required by the rules of orderly justice. In one of the most notorious civil trials of the nineteenth century, the Tichborne case,[26] the presiding judge invited his personal friends and ladies of fashion to sit at the bench with him during the trial and gossiped and chatted with them throughout the proceedings. In a criminal case that followed the civil suit, the defendant's counsel upbraided witnesses, argued extensively with the judge, and used improper and insulting language in court. He was later disbarred for his actions. The Tichborne case suggests that the glare of publicity is very likely to bring out the worst in lawyers and judges even in a highly civilized nation.

## American Disorderly Trials

In the United States disorderly trials have occurred for all three of the causes referred to on page 25. Some have been similar to the continental cases in that they remained almost exclusively on the political level. In others, politics and procedure merged.

We now have some perspective on the social and political conditions out of which they grew; they show that broader political movements and conflicts find their way into the courts and that it is difficult if not impossible to insulate the courts from these forces.

## Political Cases

Disorderly trials have occurred in times of great political stress, when the courts have been used to enforce an unpopular policy of the government. During the abolitionist controversies of the 1840s and 1850s, for example, the courts were often the scene of disturbances and disorders. The Fugitive Slave Laws required that accused blacks be brought before the federal courts to determine whether or not they were runaway slaves. If so, they had to be returned to their owners. It was bad enough that slavery existed in the South but it was intolerable to many Northerners that their own courts had to support and sustain the institution in this way. The courts, as the instrument of the hated fugitive slave laws, thus became the focus and battleground of abolitionist agitation.

Soon after passage of the 1850 Fugitive Slave Law, which contained even harsher provisions than the previous law (passed in 1793), a young black named Shadrach was arrested in Boston as a fugitive slave. He was taken directly to the federal courtroom for an examination before U.S. Commissioner Curtis. Soon a large crowd gathered outside the courtroom, consisting mainly of Negroes who had been excluded from the court. Three prominent Boston lawyers, Ellis Gray Loring, Richard Henry Dana, Jr., and Robert H. Morris, acted as Shadrach's counsel. They requested and were granted a postponement for ten days and the commissioner ordered the courtroom cleared. According to a report in the *New York Weekly Tribune*:

> The Court room was then cleared, Shadrach remaining in the Court room in custody of United States Deputy Marshall. . . . just as they were leaving, the doors, which had been locked, were suddenly burst open by a mob of Negroes, the officers guarding then kicked, cuffed, and knocked about in every direction, and, notwithstanding the resistance of a posse of about twenty strong upon the inside, the prisoner was seized and carried off in triumph.[27]

Dana, who had returned to his office, described what he saw from his window across the street.

> I returned to my office, & was planning out with a friend, the probable next proceedings, when we heard a shout from the Court House, continued into a yell of triumph, & in an instant after, down the steps came two huge negroes, bearing the prisoner between them, with his clothes half torn off, & so stupified by the sudden rescue & the violence of his dragging off that he sat almost down, & I thought had fainted; but the

men seised [*sic*] him, & being powerful fellows, hurried him through the Square into Court st., where he found the use of feet, & they went off toward Cambridge, like a black squall, the crowd driving along with them & cheering as they went. It was all done in an instant, too quick to be believed, & so successful was it that not only was no negro arrested, but no attempt was made at pursuit.[28]

Another important fugitive slave case in Boston took place in May 1854. Anthony Burns of Virginia, the slave of a Colonel Charles Suttle, was seized in Boston on May 24. On Saturday, May 27, the courtroom was filled with what Richard Henry Dana (who acted as Burns's lawyer) called "hireling soldiers of the Standing Army of the U.S. nearly all of whom are foreigners." Three lines of police and two lines of soldiers guarded the building against repetition of the Shadrach rescue. Inside the courtroom was the marshal's "guard" which Dana described as a "gang of about 120 men and lowest villains in the community, keepers of brothels, bullies, blacklegs, convicts, fire-lights &c. . . ."[29] The lawyers objected to the courtroom atmosphere:

> *Mr. [Charles M.] Ellis:* We protest against the proceedings not on personal grounds, but because it is not right and fit. . . .
> This room has been packed with armed men, and it is not fit that an examination should proceed. We protest, also, against conducting this case, when all its avenues and apartments are filled with military, making it difficult for any friends of the prisoner to obtain access. It was but fit that every one here present should bear the semblance of humanity upon his countenance and the conduct of a man in his person. But though not denying that some friends enter as an act of courtesy where they have a right, the object seems to be, for some cause, that the countenances about, instead of reflecting the benignity that ought to be shed from a tribunal of justice, shall only state on it with hate.[30]

The judge rejected Ellis's protest, allowing the marshals to remain. Burns was found to be a runaway slave and was returned to his owner under the guard of the entire military force of Boston—3,000 soldiers and police.

The situation in other states was similar. Ohio had always been the most important avenue for slaves escaping from the South. Lying across the Ohio River from Kentucky, it was the most direct route to Canada, and many fugitives found its residents willing to give assistance. The first Ohio case under the 1850 law involved a runaway named Louis who was captured in Cincinnati in 1851. The young Rutherford B. Hayes, later to be President, defended Louis. Levi Coffin described the excitement of the courtroom rescue:

> Louis was crowded, and to gain more room, slipped his chair back a little way. Neither his master nor the marshal noticed the movement, as they were intently listening to the judge, and he slipped in his chair again, until he was back of them. I was standing close behind and saw every movement. Next he rose quietly to his feet and took a step back-

ward. Some abolitionist friendly to his cause, gave him an encouraging touch on his foot, and he stepped farther back. Then a good hat was placed on his head by some one behind, and he quietly and cautiously made his way around the south end of the room, into the crowd of colored people on the west side, and, through it, toward the door.[31]

A minister and his wife eventually smuggled Louis to Canada.[32]

During the turbulent days of the early 1930s the courts were subjected to great pressures similar to those of the abolitionist period. In 1933, farmers in the Midwest felt so outraged by the mortgage foreclosures that were depriving them of their homes that they marched into an Iowa courtroom, grabbed the presiding judge off the bench, and tarred and feathered him. The *New York Times* reported the incident as follows:

> LE MARS, IOWA, Apr. 27—District Judge Charles C. Bradley was dragged from his court room this afternoon by a crowd of more than 600 farmers. They slapped him, blindfolded him and carried him in a truck a mile from the city, where they put a rope around his neck and choked him until he was nearly unconscious. His face was smeared with grease and his trousers were stolen.
>
> The abduction followed Judge Bradley's refusal to swear he would sign no more mortgage foreclosures.
>
> The farmers had entered his court room to discuss with him hearings which are to determine the constitutionality of two new laws relating to mortgage foreclosures.
>
> The judge requested them to take off their hats, and to stop smoking cigarettes.
>
> "This is my court," he said.
>
> At his words the farmers, wearing bandanna handkerchiefs over their faces, arose, hauled him off the bench, slapped him and shook him, and finally carried him bodily out the court house onto the lawn.[33]

## Politics and Procedure

The more typical disorderly cases in the United States have been trials of political dissidents who have tried to explain their political message while also claiming violations of their procedural rights. Often the court would try to restrict the defendant's opportunity to use the trial as a political vehicle, which generally produced further contention in court.

In the first years of the nation, the polarization between the Federalists and Jeffersonian-Republicans produced a series of trials in which this pattern emerged. After passage of the Alien and Sedition Acts in 1798, Republican legislators and editors were indicted for criticizing and libeling the government and its leaders. One of the first trials involved Matthew Lyon, a Republican congressman from Vermont, who was indicted for publishing a pamphlet in which he accused President John Adams of swallowing up the public welfare "in a continuous grasp for power, in an unbounded thirst for ridiculous pomp, foolish adulation, and selfish avarice." Lyon tried to defend himself on the grounds of truth. He baited the presiding judge, Justice William Paterson of the United States Supreme Court, trying to get him to admit that as a dinner guest of the President he had personally "observed his ridiculous pomp and parade."[34]

The trial of Susan B. Anthony a century ago is an unusually vivid example of the merger of political and procedural complaints. Fifteen women, led by Miss Anthony, persuaded the voting registrars in Rochester, New York, to let them vote in November 1872, although New York allowed only men to vote. They claimed that the Fourteenth Amendent, passed in 1868, automatically gave women the franchise. A federal law, however, prohibited any person's voting without the legal right to do so. On Thanksgiving Day, November 28, 1872, federal marshals served warrants of arrest on each of the women who had voted.

The trial took place in Canandaigua, New York, in June 1873. Presiding was a newly appointed Justice of the United States Supreme Court, Ward Hunt. The government decided to get the trial over with as quickly as possible and not to allow Miss Anthony to use it as a forum for her views. Instead of putting her on the stand, the government read a transcript of her testimony at a preliminary hearing. Justice Hunt would not let her fire her lawyer and conduct the defense herself. Indeed, he would not even permit the defense to present any evidence to answer the government's case. He ruled that the question of whether the Fourteenth Amendment granted women the right to vote was purely a question of law on which he alone could rule. He told the jury:

> The question, gentlemen of the jury, in the form it finally takes, is wholly a question or questions of law, and I have decided as a question of law, in the first place, that under the Fourteenth Amendment, which Miss Anthony claims protects her, she was not protected in a right to vote. And I have decided also that her belief and the advice which she took does not protect her in the act which she committed. If I am right in this, the result must be a verdict on your part of guilty, and I therefore direct that you find a verdict of guilty.
>
> *Mr. Selden [defense attorney]:*   That is a direction no Court has power to make in a criminal case.
>
> *The Court:*   Take the verdict, Mr. Clerk.
>
> *The Clerk:*   Gentlemen of the jury, hearken to your verdict as the Court has recorded it. You say you find the defendant guilty of the offense whereof she stands indicted, and so say you all?
>
> *Mr. Selden:*   I don't know whether an exception is available, but I certainly must except to the refusal of the Court to submit those propositions, and especially to the direction of the Court that the jury should find a verdict of guilty. I claim that it is a power that is not given to any Court in a criminal case. Will the Clerk poll the jury?

*The Court:*   No. Gentlemen of the jury, you are discharged.[35]

On June 18, 1873, Miss Anthony appeared for sentencing.

*Mr. Justice Hunt:*   The prisoner will stand up. Has the prisoner anything to say why sentence shall not be pronounced?

*Miss Anthony:*   Yes, your Honor, I have many things to say; for in your ordered verdict of guilty, you have trampled under foot every vital principle of our government. My natural rights, my civil rights, my political rights, my judicial rights, are all alike ignored. Robbed of the fundamental privilege of citizenship, I am degraded from the status of a citizen to that of a subject; and not only myself individually, but all of my sex are, by your Honor's verdict, doomed to political subjection under this, so-called, form of government.

*Mr. Justice Hunt:*   The Court cannot listen to a rehearsal of arguments the prisoner's counsel has already consumed three hours in presenting.

*Miss Anthony:*   May it please your Honor, I am not arguing the question, but simply stating the reasons why sentence cannot in justice be pronounced against me. Your denial of my citizen's right to vote, is the denial of my right of consent as one of the governed, the denial of my right of representation as one of the taxed, the denial of my right to a trial by a jury of my peers as an offender against law, therefore the denial of my sacred rights to life, liberty, property and—

*Mr. Justice Hunt:*   The Court cannot allow the prisoner to go on.

*Miss Anthony:*   But your Honor will not deny me this one and only poor privilege of protest against this highhanded outrage upon my citizen's rights. May it please the Court to remember that since the day of my arrest last November, this is the first time that either myself or any person of my disfranchised class has been allowed a word of defense before judge or jury.

*Mr. Justice Hunt:*   The prisoner must sit down—the Court cannot allow it.

*Miss Anthony:*   All my prosecutors, from the Eighth ward corner grocery politician, who entered the complaint, to the United States Marshal, Commissioner, District Attorney, District Judge, your Honor on the bench, not one is my peer, but each and all are my political sovereigns; and had your Honor submitted my case to the jury, as was clearly your duty, even then I should have had just cause of protest, for not one of those men was my peer; but, native or foreign born, white or black, rich or poor, educated or ignorant, awake or asleep, sober or drunk, each and every man of them was my political superior; hence, in no sense, my peer. . . .

*Mr. Justice Hunt:*   The Court must insist—the prisoner has been tried according to the established forms of law.

*Miss Anthony:*   Yes, your Honor, but by forms of law all made by men, interpreted by men, administered by men, in favor of men, and against women; . . . the slaves who got their freedom must take it over, or under, or through the unjust forms of law, precisely so, now, must women, to get their right to a voice in this government, take it; and I have taken mine, and mean to take it at every possible opportunity.

*Mr. Justice Hunt:*   The Court orders the prisoner to sit down. It will not allow another word.

*Miss Anthony:* When I was brought before your Honor for trial, I hoped for a broad and liberal interpretation of the Constitution and its recent amendments, that should declare all United States citizens under its protecting aegis—that should declare equality of rights the national guaranty to all persons born or naturalized in the United States. But failing to get this justice—failing, even, to get a trial by a jury not of my peers—I ask not leniency at your hands—but rather the full rigors of the law.

*Mr. Justice Hunt:* The Court must insist—(Here Miss Anthony sat down.)

*Mr. Justice Hunt:* The prisoner will stand up. (Here Miss Anthony arose again.) The sentence of the Court is that you pay a fine of one hundred dollars and the costs of the prosecution.

*Miss Anthony:* May it please your Honor, I shall never pay a dollar of your unjust penalty.[36]

The government made no effort to collect the fine or to imprison Susan B. Anthony. The case was therefore never appealed to a higher court.

A series of disorderly trials also resulted from the growth of the American labor movement. In the 1870s members of the Molly Maguires, a secret terrorist organization composed of Irish miners in Pennsylvania, were tried for conspiracy and murder and their tension-filled trials were the sensation of the day.[37] In 1906, "Big Bill" Haywood, the head of the I.W.W., was tried in Boise, Idaho, for the murder of former governor Frank Steunenberg of that state, and Clarence Darrow successfully defended him in an often disorderly trial. (Darrow specialized in picking one member of the prosecution as a target for invective and sarcasm, and was so venomous in the Boise trial that the prosecutor's son threatened him with violence in the middle of proceedings.)[38]

Darrow was himself tried in 1912 for attempting to bribe a juror in another labor violence case, and his trial was called "the most violent trial in the history of Southern California."[39] The lawyers on both sides insulted and abused each other and even struck each other in court. Each lawyer was cited numerous times for contempt.

The series of trials resulting from the bombing of the 1916 Preparedness Day parade in San Francisco, in which Tom Mooney played the principal role, saw frequent disruptions.[40] In one of these trials, the following exchange took place between the judge and a defense attorney:

*The Court:* It's a significant fact that since the incarceration of these defendants there has been no dynamiting in this city.

*McNutt:* Yes, and there was none before in this city either.

*The Court:* I want to say so far as the prosecution is concerned that it has been hampered by the activities of the defense and the kind of activities that the defense has seen fit to resort to.

*McNutt:*   My answer to that is this; that these defendants, every one of them was framed against, and I have the proof.

*The Court:*   And every crook and every anarchist and every I.W.W. thinks as you do, Mr. McNutt. Every vicious anarchist and every vicious crook hollers "frameup."

*McNutt:*   I have the statement of some of the witnesses who indicted them.

*The Court:*   You ought to know all about perjury, Mr. McNutt.

*McNutt:*   I have been around here long enough to know all about it....

*The Court:*   You ought to know all about perjury and juries.

*McNutt:*   And judges included.

*The Court:*   Well, the motion is denied.[41]

During World War I, many members of the I.W.W. and other opponents of the war were indicted for violating the Espionage Act. Their trials saw frequent outbursts primarily because of the harsh sentences and biased statements of the judges. In Chicago, Judge Kenesaw Mountain Landis, later commissioner of organized baseball, did not let the Wobbly defendants make any statement before he imposed the highest possible sentences, and they reacted with angry protests.[42] In other cases the defendants sat silently through the entire trial and on being found guilty began singing the "Internationale."[43] Eugene V. Debs was also indicted under the Espionage Act for a speech he gave opposing the war. In his opening statement Debs's defense counsel, Seymour Stedman, said, "We ask you to judge Eugene V. Debs by his life, his deeds and his works. If you do that, we shall abide by your verdict." There was a small flurry of applause at that point and the judge began shouting, "Arrest that man and that woman! Arrest everybody you saw clapping their hands!"[44]

## The Frontier Tradition

The frontier tradition in America, in contrast to the English experience, produced a widespread skepticism about the need for decorum or civility by lawyers and defendants. The courtrooms in the frontier towns of the Midwest and the mining areas of the Rockies often witnessed riotous proceedings. Disappointed litigants were likely to draw their guns on hearing an unfavorable verdict, and convicted defendants would often have their friends ready to rescue them from the authorities by force. The rules of evidence and proper decorum were practically nonexistent and judges maintained what order they could by having the maximum fire-power available. This notion of frontier justice was not a figment of John Ford's imagination, for as late as 1885 lawyers in California were arguing that they should have the right to carry their guns into a federal court to protect themselves against

unfriendly witnesses. In one of the many court hearings involving the
case of Sarah Hill (described more fully below), her attorneys argued
that they should be allowed to be armed in court.

> *Mr. Justice [Stephen] Field [sitting on circuit]:*   I may add here, fur-
> ther, that any lawyer who so far forgets his profession as to come into a
> court of justice armed ought to be disbarred from practice.
>
> *Mr. Tyler:*   Witnesses are sometimes armed.
>
> *Judge Sawyer:*   Witnesses, it is true, may come into court armed; but,
> with the admonition we have given, and as there has been no evidence
> that witnesses have come before the examiner armed, we think it hardly
> advisable to anticipate any difficulty in that direction. We apprehend
> that witnesses will be likely hereafter to conduct themselves with pro-
> priety.
>
> *Mr. Tyler:*   I would say to his honor, Judge Field, that, although I thor-
> oughly concede everything he says, in certain instances, yet where a
> lawyer has information that a witness will come armed, he will very
> likely do as I myself have done—come armed, to protect himself. . . .
>
> *Mr. Justice Field:*   Then report the fact to the court; that is the proper
> way.
>
> *Mr. Tyler:*   That will not stop a bullet.[45]

This exchange took place in an action brought by William Sharon of
Nevada, a wealthy mine owner and U.S. senator, against Sarah Althea
Hill, who was claiming to be his wife, to have an allegedly forged
marriage contract canceled. Testimony in the case was taken before
a special examiner. Miss Hill regularly carried a gun to the proceedings and threatened the witnesses who testified against her.[46]

Miss Hill brought a second action in the California state courts to
have her marriage with Sharon declared legal and to obtain a divorce
and property settlement. She was successful in the second action and
was eventually awarded alimony, counsel fees, and half the defendant's
estate. After Sharon died, Miss Hill married David S. Terry, formerly
chief justice of the California Supreme Court, who was as belligerent
as his wife and as litigious in pressing her claims. Sharon's trustee
brought a new action in the federal courts to have the forged marriage
contract declared invalid. Eventually the federal circuit court found
against the Terrys on all counts, and as Justice Stephen Field was reading his opinion (which was gratuitously insulting to Mrs. Terry) the
following events occurred:

> *Mrs. Terry:*   Judge, are you going to take the responsibility of ordering
> me to give up that marriage contract?
>
> *Mr. Justice Field:*   Take your seat madam.
>
> *Mrs. Terry:*   How much did you get for that decision? You have been
> paid by Newlands.
>
> *Mr. Justice Field:*   Marshal, remove that woman from the courtroom
> and the Court will deal with her hereafter.

*Mrs. Terry:*   I won't go out and you can't put me out.

Marshal Franks proceeded to remove her—

*Mrs. Terry (striking him in the face):*   You dirty scrub. You dare not remove me from this court room.

*Judge Terry (rising from his chair):*   Don't touch my wife; get a written order.

*Marshal Franks:*   Judge, stand back, I have order enough, no written order is required.

*Judge Terry (as the Marshal took hold of Mrs. Terry's arm):*   No • • • damn man shall touch my wife (striking the Marshal a blow in the face). Here he endeavored to draw a bowie knife but was overpowered by the deputy marshals and forced to the floor while his wife was removed from the room, scratching and striking the officers, denouncing and threatening them and the judges, charging that they had stolen her jewelry and calling on one of her attorneys to give her her satchel in which she had a revolver.

   Judge Terry being allowed to rise, he drew a knife, exclaiming, "Let go, let go, you sons of • • • I will cut you to pieces; I will go to my wife." He was again overpowered, the knife taken from him and he also was removed from the courtroom.[47]

Both the Terrys were held in contempt.[48] Terry vowed to horsewhip Justice Field if he ever returned to California. A year later in 1889, they met by chance at a railroad station in Lathrop, California, and Terry knocked Field down with his fists. When Terry then reached for his bowie knife, a federal marshal guarding Field, David Neagle, drew his pistol and shot and killed Terry. Neagle was then arrested by the California authorities for murder, but a federal court ordered him released on the ground that he was a federal officer acting in discharge of a duty imposed on him by the laws of the United States.[49]

# Conclusion

The cases discussed in this chapter indicate the pervasiveness of disorderly trials in this and other societies. The cases also suggest that, viewed historically, there is no single cause of a disorderly trial. It is more likely that volatile defendants who politically oppose the government placing them on trial and feel strongly about highly emotional social issues will violate the governing rules on proper conduct in court. They may be alert and sensitive to what they view as the injustices of the policies or procedures that brought them before the bar. The fact that they are on center stage and their words and actions will be widely reported contributes to the likelihood of disorder.

   The cultural or political background of the society in which the court sits is also significant. Because of the professionalism of the

English judicial system and the class position of the judges, it has seen less disorder than the United States, where the frontier and a different legal tradition led to less respect for judicial robes. All this suggests that broad political and cultural forces over which individual lawyers or judges have little control may lead to a breakdown of orderly procedure in the courtroom.

# CHAPTER FOUR

# *Disorderly Trials of the Modern Era*

There have been four widely publicized disorderly trials in American courts since 1940: the Nazi sedition trial of 1944, the Communist conspiracy case in 1949, the Chicago conspiracy trials of 1969–70, and the New York Black Panther case of 1969–71.

The four cases shared certain salient characteristics: all the defendants represented highly unpopular political currents of the time; a large number of defendants and lawyers were involved in each case; the defendants were charged with conspiracy for their political activities (except for the Black Panther case); all were tried before judges who were accused of bias toward the defendants and their politics; all the trials took many months to finish; and the press reported extensively on what occurred in court.

The incidence and scope of the disorder in these cases were far greater than had previously been seen in an American court. As noted earlier, the Chicago and New York cases caused great concern about the problem of courtroom disruption and inspired this study. A detailed account of all four of these trials is therefore necessary.

## The Nazi Sedition Trial

Shortly after World War II began, the federal government brought charges against members of the German-American Bund and other fascist-type organizations (such as the Silver Shirts, the Silver Legion, and the American National Socialist party) for violations of the Espionage Act and the Selective Service Act. The indictments charged that the defendants and their organizations had counseled young men not to enter military service and had advised insubordination in the armed services through the distribution of anti-Semitic and hate-Roosevelt literature. The Supreme Court eventually reversed all their convictions.[1]

There was strong pressure to indict even more pro-Nazi groups for their opposition to the war effort. Francis Biddle, the attorney general at the time, reported in his autobiography that the President was insistent that more prosecutions be initiated; and an indictment was filed against twenty-six "native Fascists" in July 1942.

> The President was getting a good deal of mail complaining about the "softness" of his Attorney General. After two weeks, during which F.D.R.'s manner when I saw him said as plainly as words that he considered me out of step, he began to go for me in the Cabinet. His technique was always the same. When my turn came, as he went around the table, his habitual affability dropped. He did not ask me as usual, if I had anything to report. He looked at me, his face pulled tightly together. "When are you going to indict the seditionists?" he would ask; and the next week and every week after that, until the indictment was found, he would repeat the same question. Of course I felt uncomfortable. I told him that there was an immense amount of evidence; that I wanted the indictment to stick when it was challenged; and that we could not indict these men for their naked writings and spoken words without showing what effect they had on the war effort. His way of listening made my explanation sound unreal. At the Cabinet meeting a day or two after the return of an indictment he said, now in his most conciliatory manner, "I was glad to see, Francis, that the grand jury returned a true bill." I cannot remember any other instance of his putting pressure on me.[2]

Eventually a superseding indictment was brought early in January 1944 and prosecuted by O. John Rogge. Thirty defendants were named, including the leaders of the German-American Bund, the Silver Shirts, and other anti-Semitic organizations such as the Christian Mobilizers, the Knights of the White Camelia, and the National Copperheads. A group of propagandists was also indicted—editors and writers for small newsletters such as "Our Common Cause," "American Vigilante Bulletins," "The Revealor," "Liberation," and others. The government's theory was that the "native Fascists" were engaged in a conspiracy with the German National Socialist party to carry on "a systematic campaign of propaganda designed and intended to impair and undermine the loyalty and morale of the military and naval forces of the United States." In particular the defendants were accused of exchanging information with a German propaganda sheet called "World Service" even after the war began. In their literature the defendants were trying to show, among other things, that

> The Government of the United States, the Congress and public officials are controlled by Communists, International Jews, and plutocrats.

President Roosevelt is reprehensible, a warmonger, liar, unscrupulous, and a pawn of the Jews, Communists and Plutocrats.

The cause of the Axis Powers is the cause of justice and morality; they have committed no aggressive act against any nation and are fighting a solely defensive war against British Imperialism, American Capitalists, and the desire of American public officials to rule the world, hence any act of war against them is unjust and immoral on the part of the United States. . . .[3]

These actions were charged as violating the Smith Act, the Espionage Act, and the Selective Service Law.

The case began in April 1944 before Judge Edward C. Eicher with twenty-six lawyers representing thirty defendants. One defendant appeared pro se. Representatives from forty newspapers and magazines attended the trial.

From the beginning, the defendants engaged in every obstructive and delaying tactic they could devise. Before the trial began, two of the defendants filed a motion asking the court to summon Major General Walter C. Short and Rear Admiral Hubbard C. Kimmel as witnesses to prove that the government had ignored their pleas that a Japanese attack on Pearl Harbor was imminent. Other defendants demanded that Secretary of State Cordell Hull be called with all the records of diplomatic correspondence with the German government from 1933 to 1941. The defense also asked that Justices Frankfurter and Jackson as well as the presiding judge be called as witnesses to show the intent of the government in bringing the indictments.

On the first day of the trial:

When the roll call of the defendants was taken, Mrs. Lois de Lafayette Washburn jumped up and answered: "Here! de Lafayette, we are here! To defend what you gave us—our freedom from tyranny."[4]

Two days later one of the defendants who had not appeared the first day, Edward J. Smythe, was brought into the court by federal marshals. He shouted that he was innocently absent and that it was an "honor" to be present. He insisted that he never received notice of when the trial was to begin—"That's an old racket of the Roosevelt Administration, to steal the mail of patriotic Americans." He said that he had left the city to "rest" from "continuous hounding and persecution" of the F.B.I. and "pro-Communist organizations." According to the *New York Times*, "Throughout the questioning, Mr. Smythe's hearty air of indignation, his brisk denials, produced currents of laughter. When ruled out of order, his lawyer counseled him, saying 'Mr. Smythe you must obey his Honor.' "[5]

On the next day, after Judge Eicher merely identified the case and charges pending against the defendants, Smythe pointed his forefinger and shouted, "You've already convicted us in the light of that state-

ment you've made." Mrs. Lois de Lafayette Washburn arose and
bowed and then bowed some more. Judge Eicher then announced
that the defense would have ten peremptory challenges. Immediately,
the defendants shouted "unreasonable" and "unjust." The defense
sought to disqualify the entire civil and criminal venire for adverse
publicity, but the judge said he would rule on each prospective juror
individually. The defense lawyers submitted 600 questions to the judge
to ask the venire. They also objected to obtaining only ten peremptory
challenges and could not agree on how they should be exercised.

On May 1, Judge Eicher set into motion the first sanctions against
the lawyers for misbehavior. He cited defense attorney James J. Laughlin for contempt because of the following actions: a) a plea to President Roosevelt to stop the trial because it would brew racial and
class hatreds; b) in his affidavit to disqualify Judge Eicher on the
grounds of bias and prejudice, Laughlin alleged that the President
promised Eicher a position on the Eighth Circuit Court of Appeals or
the Supreme Court if the prosecution was successful; c) motions to
summon high government and business officials as witnesses.[6] Judge
Eicher did not pass on the contempt himself but assigned the hearing
to Associate Judge Jennings Bailey of the district court. In the contempt hearing Laughlin was fined fifty dollars. The court of appeals
affirmed his conviction.[7]

The defense attorneys devised a strategy of making objections *in
seriatim.* Each of the lawyers would make the same objections for each
of the clients in almost the same words. The judge fined one of the
lawyers fifty dollars when he persisted in pressing this technique after
the judge had ordered it to stop.

On May 15, the defense moved to have all of the defendants examined "for sanity." Several defense attorneys moved to disqualify
the jury. Then Smythe petitioned to become his own lawyer. The jury
was finally selected on May 16, exactly one month after the trial began.
Immediately, the defense made the following motions: to dismiss; to
ask the jury if it was "physically able" for the trial; to postpone the
trial until after the war; to sever the trials of some of the defendants;
to postpone until the Supreme Court reviewed *Keegan* v. *United
States,* a draft case involving Bund leaders; to send three defendants
to a mental hospital for examination. After denial of the last motion,
Smythe shouted, "I demand a mental test."

On May 17, Rogge began his opening statement. The *New York
Times* reported:

> Amid a tumult raised by defendants and their lawyers, O. John Rogge,
> the prosecutor, today outlined the Government's sedition case to the
> jury. . . . Many of the twenty-nine accused and their attorneys pre-
> vented him from speaking for thirty minutes by shouting objections and

execrations and raising an uproar, with the judge rapping for order and marshals stepping in to attempt to restore quiet. Smythe shouted: "I'm a Republican, not a Nazi."[8]

Even after defense attorneys agreed to defer objections until Rogge finished, they offered them repeatedly. At one point, laughter and booing broke out.

The defendants made their opening statements on the next day, each limited to a half-hour. One of the attorneys, Henry Klein, protested about the limitation: "But that's unfair, Your Honor!" He was fined $50. Klein then said, "I have a right to offer my objections." Judge Eicher raised the fine to $75, fixing bond at $150. "I think that's an insult," Klein charged. For that remark, Judge Eicher increased the fine to $100 and bond to $200. Against the judge's gaveling, Klein asked, "Now may I make an objection?" The fine was raised to $200; the bond to $400. At that point one of the defendants, Ellis Jones, broke in: "This is a persecution, not a prosecution."[9]

The first witness was put on the stand on May 23, 1944. Each question produced an objection from every one of the defense attorneys. Judge Eicher ruled that a single objection would protect all the defendants but the lawyers insisted on making them separately. When documentary evidence was submitted, each attorney examined it and passed it to the next attorney, and each tried to make a separate argument on its admissibility in endless and redundant speeches.

This pattern continued through the summer months. With some witnesses the judge limited each counsel to three minutes for cross-examination. Three of the lawyers were fined for dilatory cross-examination, repetitious tactics, or insisting on a line of questions already excluded.

Early in July, one of the attorneys, James Laughlin, filed a petition with the Speaker of the House of Representatives to have Judge Eicher impeached. The court of appeals later commented about the petition:

> The petition to the House of Representatives for respondent's impeachment, which petitioner publicly filed while the trial was pending, is in the record. It contains highly derogatory assertions, some of them fantastic, regarding respondent's alleged relation to the trial and his alleged conduct of the trial, and is in effect a public profession of contempt for respondent's character. An attorney who publishes such a document during the trial to which it relates should ask to be excused from the trial. His further participation would be useful neither to his client nor to the court and would seriously embarrass counsel, court, and defendants.[10]

Judge Eicher dismissed Laughlin from the case, denying him further right to participate in any phase of the trial, and told him to deliver all his documents to his succeeding attorney. Laughlin then sought a

writ of mandamus from the court of appeals to be reinstated. Three
of the five judges of the court sitting en banc upheld Judge Eicher
in the following words:

> Respondent [Judge Eicher] might, of course, have punished petitioner
> for this contempt. But petitioner had already been punished twice, once
> by respondent and once by another judge, for contemptuous conduct in
> this trial. Respondent turned from punishment to prevention. He might
> have instituted proceedings for petitioner's disbarment or suspension
> from practice. He chose a more lenient and more promptly effective
> course. He exercised only the elementary right of a court to protect its
> pending proceedings, which includes the right to dismiss from them an
> attorney who cannot or will not take part in them with a reasonable
> degree of propriety.[11]

The two dissenters, relying principally on Laughlin's freedom of
speech, felt that the judge lacked power to dismiss him. When Laughlin's client, Robert Noble, refused to accept the services of one of the
other attorneys in the case, Judge Eicher severed his case.

The dreary spectacle continued into the autumn. One of the attorneys was sentenced to ninety days in jail for absenting himself from
the trial for three weeks.[12] Another was held in contempt for his
"scurrilous and contemptuous" motion for a mistrial which accused
Judge Eicher of being too prejudiced in favor of President Roosevelt.
The succession of objections to documents and questions continued.
By the end of November, only 39 of the planned 106 witnesses for the
government had been called. On the night of November 30, 1944,
Judge Eicher died of a heart attack. A mistrial was then declared.

In the meantime, the Supreme Court decisions in the *Keegan* and
*Hartzel* cases had come down holding that Bund propaganda attacking
the government and the war did not violate the Espionage Act. Eventually the cases were dismissed for failure to prosecute.[13]

Francis Biddle thought that Judge Eicher was too lenient.

> Perhaps if the judge had been firmer from the beginning it might have
> been checked. But before long the lawyers were shouting in unison ob-
> jections to the admission of evidence that had already been ruled on. In
> vain Judge Eicher warned the defendants that he would not entertain
> repetitious arguments. . . . Turbulent scenes were the order of the day,
> and the courtroom was continually in an uproar, the judge fining the
> offending lawyers right and left for contempt in a vain attempt to keep
> order. Trivial technicalities continually interrupted and blocked normal
> procedure. The trial had become a dreary farce.[14]

The Sedition Trial saw greater disorder than any trial in American
history. Since the defendants were determined to disrupt the proceedings, and were evidently not concerned about contempt sanctions,
only their removal from the courtroom could have helped. This was
the model for the legal profession of what a "political trial" could
become.

# The Communist Smith Act Trial

In 1949 eleven Communist party leaders were tried in New York for violating the federal Smith Act. They were accused of conspiring to organize the Communist party and conspiring to teach and advocate the overthrow and destruction of the United States government by force and violence. The trial went on from January to October 1949, when a verdict of guilty was returned. Throughout the trial there was constant contention between the lawyers, defendants, and the trial judge, Harold R. Medina. They engaged in frequent arguments, exchanging insults and charges concerning the conduct of the trial.

Judge Medina was convinced that the defendants and lawyers were trying to duplicate the efforts of the participants in the 1944 sedition trial. Many of his comments and complaints to the lawyers indicate that he anticipated similar dilatory, obstructive tactics by them. When the trial ended Judge Medina held five of the lawyers and one defendant who represented himself in contempt, sentencing them from thirty days to six months in jail. He said in his certificate holding the lawyers in contempt:

> Before the trial had progressed very far. . . . I was reluctantly forced to the conclusion that the acts and statements to which I am about to refer were the result of an agreement between these defendants, deliberately entered into in a cold and calculating manner, to do and say these things for the purpose of: (1) causing such delay and confusion as to make it impossible to go on with the trial; (2) provoking incidents which they intended would result in a mistrial; and (3) impairing my health so that the trial could not continue.[15]

He also claimed that the lawyers

> insisted on objecting one after another to rulings of the Court, despite a ruling on the first day of the trial, repeated several times thereafter, that all objections and exceptions would inure to the benefit of each of their clients unless disclaimed;
> Persisted in making long, repetitious, and unsubstantial arguments, objections and protests, working in shifts, accompanied by shouting, sneering, and snickering;
> Urged one another on to badger the Court. . . .[16]

The Second Circuit concluded that there was no proof of any agreement among the lawyers to undermine the proceedings but nevertheless upheld the findings of contempt.[17] The Supreme Court affirmed on the ground that the lawyers' conduct was improper.[18] Justices Frankfurter, Black, and Douglas dissented with Justice Frankfurter commenting:

The conduct of the lawyers had its reflex in the judge. At frequent intervals in the course of the trial his comments plainly reveal personal feeling against the lawyers, however much the course of the trial may have
justified such feeling. On numerous occasions he expressed his belief
that the lawyers were trying to wear him down, to injure his health, to
provoke him into doing something that would show prejudice, or cause
a mistrial or reversal on appeal.[19]

At this point it is difficult to decide whether the obstructive behavior
at the trial arose out of the lawyers' individual, vigorous assertion of
their clients' cause or was planned beforehand to duplicate the events
of the Sedition Trial, or whether their conduct was the result of a
self-fulfilling prophecy, a consequence of Judge Medina's own behavior. Certainly, as many of the examples below show, there was
extensive contention between the judge and the lawyers. The lawyers
reacted and overreacted to what the judge said about them, which
soon became the main point of conflict.

In his contempt certificate Judge Medina charged that the lawyers
engaged in thirteen types of misbehavior. These fall into five general
categories: 1) willful delaying tactics, 2) objecting one after another
to rulings of the court, 3) persisting in making long, repetitious, and
unsubstantial arguments, 4) making disrespectful and insolent comments to the court and charging the judge with bias, connivance with
the government, or corruption, 5) disregarding rulings of the court. A
discussion of each of these categories follows. The quoted examples
are taken from Judge Medina's contempt certificate.

## Willful Delaying Tactics

The trial began on January 17, 1949, with the defense challenging
the jury selection system as administered in the Southern District of
New York. The attack continued until March 1, when Judge Medina
cut off further evidence on the point and rejected the challenge. He
later claimed that the defendants "had taken almost four weeks to put
in evidence which could have been adduced in no more than three
or four days." Judge Medina also said that the lawyers were trying to
delay proceedings by going into "peripheral issues," and restricted
their attempt to put in evidence on the Communist party's position on
racism, veterans' rights, and the problems of housewives in capitalist
society. He characterized their continuing objections as a "deliberate
effort for delay."

## Continuous Objection

Judge Medina made the same ruling as Judge Eicher, that an objection
from one lawyer preserved the point for all defendants. Nevertheless

the lawyers continued to press points individually, often in response to Judge Medina's comments. For instance, the court asked one of the defense witnesses a question which led to a series of objections by the lawyers:

> *The Court:* Mrs. Lightfoot, in this matter of the strategy of the workers, did you discuss the dictatorship of the proletariat, imperialism, and just and unjust wars, and things of that kind, or were they not mentioned?
>
> *Mr. Isserman:* I object to the question.
>
> *The Court:* Overruled.
>
> *The Witness:* Under topic 3—under topic C—
>
> *The Court:* You will answer that question yes or no or state that you cannot answer it.
>
> *Mr. Gladstein:* I object to the Court's tone and manner of badgering the witness.
>
> *The Court:* There is nothing about my tone, and you will please sit down.
>
> *Mr. Gladstein:* I desire to make an objection.
>
> *The Court:* Mr. Marshal, will you just—(to the reporter) Read the question to the witness. We will have no more monkey business here.
>
> *Mr. Gladstein:* I object to the ruling.
>
> *Mr. Isserman:* I object to the Court's remark.
>
> *The Court:* You will sit down, Mr. Gladstein.
>
> *Mr. Isserman:* And I want to register an objection to the Court's ruling.
>
> *The Court:* Very well.[20]

## Repetitious and Unsubstantial Argument

The defense not only made a series of objections to Judge Medina's rulings, but they then objected to the manner in which he overruled their objections and then to his comments or characterizations of their rebuttals. Thus a single objection might lead to a round robin of continuous colloquy. A typical example occurred on August 1.

> *The Court:* Do you remember the oath you took when you were sworn as a witness?
>
> *Mr. Isserman:* I object to that question.
>
> *The Witness:* Yes.
>
> *The Court:* Overruled.
>
> *Q.:* No, before you—
>
> *Mr. Gladstein:* May I object to the Court's—the inference from the Court's statement?
>
> *The Court:* Your objection is noted. It is overruled.
>
> *Mr. Gladstein:* Because the Court's statement has nothing to do with that.

*The Court:*   I will hear no argument.

*Mr. Gladstein:*   I want to note my objection on the record.

*The Court:*   You have noted it. Sit down.

*Mr. Gladstein:*   I object to that and ask your Honor to admonish the jury—

*The Court:*   Will you sit down or must I call an officer to put you down? I will have no more interruptions on cross-examination. Your field day is over.

*Mr. Gladstein:*   I resent your Honor's remarks as—

*The Court:*   Mr. Marshal, will you please—all right, I see you sat down by yourself.

*Mr. Isserman:*   May I object to your Honor's remarks and ask for a mistrial on the basis of your Honor's remarks?

*The Court:*   Denied.

*Defendant Dennis:*   Your Honor—

*The Court:*   I want no argument, Mr. Dennis.

*Defendant Dennis:*   May I make an inquiry of the Court?

*The Court:*   You may.

*Defendant Dennis:*   I would like to know whether the ruling and remarks of the Court are directed to the defendants and counsel as to prejudice our case before the jury?

*The Court:*   They are not. I have heard enough from Mr. Gladstein. I have heard enough interruptions and suggestions to witnesses and so on, and I will have no more interruptions of cross-examination. Now, that is final and that is over for this trial.

*Mr. Sacher:*   I wish to object to your Honor's remarks as being wholly improper and unjustified and designed to prejudice the jury against the defendants.

*The Court:*   Your motion is denied.[21]

## Charges of Bias and Prejudice

Attacks on the impartiality of the judge occurred throughout the trial. On February 2, Sacher, one of the defense lawyers, and the judge crossed swords. Mr. Sacher said to Judge Medina:

> I repeat, this is an Alice in Wonderland procedure. We always get the sentence first and then the trial. Now, if we would just get back to ordinary procedure with trial first and sentence afterwards, this might be a little bit more real. . . .[22]

On February 18, McCabe, another defense lawyer, remarked in the course of an argument:

> I would like to say to your Honor that I really have come to believe that the constant repetition by your Honor at intervals which are almost as regular as the tolling of Big Ben—and I mean nothing personal in the allusion—or the eruption of Old Faithful out in Yellowstone Park, or wherever it is—these come at stated periods. I, you, can pick 11:20

and 3:20 when these statements come that we are delaying; we are doing nothing; your Honor has seen nothing in the record. I say, I don't want—

*The Court:* What is the point of those times, of those particular times?

*Mr. McCabe:* 11:30 I think is the deadline for the afternoon papers, your Honor, and I think around 3:20 is the deadline—

*The Court:* Well, that is something I had no idea of, and I must say you have got an ingenious mind to suppose that something was said for such a purpose. I think you ought to be ashamed of yourself.[23]

## Disregard of Court Rulings

Judge Medina ruled that the lawyers should note their objections to questions without any comment unless he asked for it. This ruling was disregarded as the following example shows.

*Mr. Isserman:* I object to that as argumentative. It is not based on the facts in evidence as testified by this witness.

*The Court:* Mr. Isserman, do you remember my admonition, that when counsel objects, counsel is merely to state "I object"? You have violated it several times this morning. Did you forget?

*Mr. Isserman:* I am reminded of it now. It is a habit that goes back over 25 years. It is hard to give up that habit, which your Honor has undoubtedly engaged in yourself.

*The Court:* Every time you do that your action is contemptuous and direct, I think, wilful and deliberate disobedience of my command.

*Mr. Isserman:* I must object to your Honor's characterization of my conduct.

*The Court:* I have heard counsel for the defense here again and again give various excuses, say they have forgotten or it was inadvertent, and I have warned them again and again. I now say that such conduct must be and I find it to be wilfully and deliberately done and contemptuous.

*Mr. Isserman:* I must object to your Honor's finding.

*The Court:* Very well.[24]

At a later point in the trial, the following exchange occurred after the judge had sustained a government objection:

*Mr. Crocket:* May I point out—

*The Court:* I don't want further argument.

*Mr. Crockett:* I wanted to say—

*The Court:* I think you are in contempt now. Don't do it. I will not have any more. The time for that is over.

*Mr. Sacher:* I wish to object to your Honor's characterization of Mr. Crockett's conduct as contempt.

*The Court:* You may object. You have done enough of it yourself.

*Mr. Sacher:*   I wish to object to that characterization. I think the record will prove, I think your Honor has sought to prejudice this jury sufficiently against counsel.

*The Court:*   You are deliberately contemptuous again.

*Mr. Sacher:*   I am not. I wish to defend the rights of my clients and the right to advocate their cause, and I resent the constant obstruction of that effort on the part of the Court.

*The Court:*   There has been no obstruction of effort, but I will have order by the attorneys here, and I will enforce it with every power at my disposal.

*Mr. Crockett:*   May I ask if the Court is suggesting there has been any disorder by the attorneys?

*The Court:*   You insisted upon continuing arguing only a moment ago and I told you to stop.

*Mr. Crockett:*   I was not arguing.

*The Court:*   That is what you now say but every time you said it you kept it up. Let us stop now and go on with the question.[25]

Most of the disorders occurred because of actions of the attorneys and the judge and, unlike the Sedition Trial, the defendants were minor characters. There were, however, some incidents when the defendants jumped up to speak; one resulted in the revocation of bail for defendants Hall and Winston, on June 3, and their incarceration for the remainder of the trial.[26]

Defendant Gates was also cited for contempt on that day and jailed for thirty days for refusing to answer questions about the names of various people affiliated with the Communist party. On June 20, defendant Green was remanded for the balance of the trial because of outbursts. At various times, the judge commented that the defendants were improperly laughing, smirking, and giggling.

Eugene Dennis, a defendant who dismissed his counsel and appeared pro se, also was involved in numerous altercations with Judge Medina. He said to the judge on May 19:

> And it is highly reminiscent in many respects of the Reichstag fire trial and of the efforts of reactionaries in this and other countries to outlaw the Communist Party as a prelude to trying to drag our nation along the path of war and fascism. And however much you may think or agree or disagree with this I would strongly urge as a matter of most elementary justice and not to deprive the defense of some of the remnants of due process of law that we should be afforded an opportunity of a few days at least to prepare our motions, our argumentation.[27]

Five of the attorneys in the case actually served varying terms in jail for contempt (Sacher, Gladstein, and Isserman served six months, Crockett, now a Detroit municipal judge, served four months, and McCabe served thirty days). Thereafter disciplinary proceedings were instituted against Sacher and Isserman. Sacher was disbarred from the federal district court in the Southern District of New York but the disbarment was reversed by the Supreme Court as too severe a penalty since he had already served time in jail for contempt.[28] Isserman was suspended from the federal district court in New Jersey and then disbarred in the state courts.[29] At first he was excluded from practicing in the Supreme Court, but the decision was reversed.[30] After nine years he was reinstated in New Jersey.[31] In 1956, the United States District Court for the Southern District of New York disbarred Isserman, but its decision was reversed by the Second Circuit.[32] (Isserman is now practicing in New York.) A law review note commented that these proceedings were "the only cases found. . . . where a defense attorney was disbarred for [forensic misconduct] . . . and no case has been uncovered where the prosecutor was so disciplined."[33]

The reaction of the legal profession to the Communist Smith Act trial (*Dennis*) was swift. In 1950 the House of Delegates of the American Bar Association resolved that all lawyers be required to take a loyalty oath and recommended that they disclose any past or present membership in the Communist party.[34] A year later a resolution was passed recommending disbarment of all lawyers who were "members of the Communist party of the United States or who advocate Marxism-Leninism."[35] In 1955 a special A.B.A. committee recommended disbarment of lawyers who invoked the Fifth Amendment when questioned about their Communist affiliations.[36]

As a result of the contempt citations in the *Dennis* case and this reaction of the legal community, the "second string" Communists tried for Smith Act violations after 1949 had great difficulty obtaining counsel. Professor Fowler Harper of the Yale Law School reported, "After a hundred and fifty failures, they were forced to appeal to the idealism of a law school professor, not engaged in active practice to take on their case in addition to his heavy academic duties."[37]

Many observers insisted that the heavy penalties meted out to the lawyers in the *Dennis* case (in the form of jail sentences and disbarment proceedings) were due in part to the unpopularity of the clients. The lawyers were not as abusive or irrationally obstructive as some of those in the 1944 sedition trial. But supporters of Judge Medina insisted that the combination of acts—the repetitive argumentation, cumulative objection, and continuous accusations of bias—justified the penalties imposed. The *Sacher* case, the contempt charges against the five lawyers and one defendant, established the governing law on what is disruption and what power a judge has to control his courtroom.* The disciplinary actions subsequently taken show how far the bar could go in punishing lawyers who were found to misbehave in politi-

---

* For a discussion of recent interpretations of the *Sacher* case, see chapter 10.

cally oriented cases. While the tensions of the times have receded, the rules have remained to control the action of lawyers in a new period of political tension which produced new challenges in the courtroom.

## The Chicago Conspiracy Trial

The most notorious disorderly trial in recent years was the Chicago conspiracy trial of 1969–70. In that case, eight leading members of the Vietnam antiwar movement were indicted under the federal anti-riot statute of 1968 for conspiring, organizing, and inciting riots during the 1968 Democratic National Convention in Chicago. It appears from the evidence introduced at the trial that seven of the eight defendants[38]—David Dellinger, Abbie Hoffman, Jerry Rubin, Rennie Davis, Tom Hayden, Lee Weiner, and John Froines—had planned to hold massive demonstrations in the streets and parks of Chicago at the time of the 1968 convention to protest the continuation of the Vietnam war. After extensive negotiations with city officials, permits for large-scale demonstrations were refused. Nevertheless, rallies were held, which led to violent confrontations between the demonstrators and the Chicago police.

Subsequent investigations by a special committee of the National Violence Commission concluded that the disturbances that ensued were the result of a "police riot."[39] The Justice Department initiated its own investigations into the disorder. A federal grand jury was instructed by the chief judge of the district to examine violations of federal law by both the demontrators and the police. In March 1969, eight policemen were indicted under the 1870 Civil Rights Act for interfering with the civil rights of demonstrators and the eight individuals named above were indicted for conspiracy under the anti-riot act. All eight policemen were acquitted of the charges.

The trial drew considerable public notice because of the notoriety of the defendants and because this was the first use of a statute which was of doubtful constitutionality. From its inception numerous incidents occurred which attracted even more attention. In the week before the trial began, four of the attorneys who had appeared earlier in the case for specific pretrial motions telegrammed that they were withdrawing from further participation. On the motion of the United States attorney, Judge Julius Hoffman took the unusual step of issuing bench warrants to have all four arrested and brought before him. Five days later, after a storm of protest from lawyers and law professors, he vacated the order.

Additional contention arose because of the judge's refusal to postpone the trial until Charles Garry of California, who was engaged to act as Bobby Seale's lawyer, had recovered from a gall bladder operation. Seale insisted from the first days of the trial that he was unrepresented until Garry appeared. On September 26, he said to the court:

> If I am consistently denied this right of legal defense counsel of my choice who is effective by the judge of this Court, then I can only see the judge as a blatant racist of the United States Court.[40]

On the same day the court reprimanded Tom Hayden for giving a clenched fist salute to the jury and Abbie Hoffman for blowing them kisses. On September 30, the court discharged one juror after reading to her the contents of a threatening letter signed "The Black Panther," which had been sent to her home. On October 15, the defendants asked to celebrate Vietnam Moratorium Day and tried to drape the counsel table with American and N.L.F. flags. On October 22 the defendants tried to bring a birthday cake into the courtroom for Bobby Seale.[41]

The three particular incidents that gave rise to the greatest number of contempt citations were as follows:

## Gagging and Binding of Bobby Seale

The most serious disorders occurred over the problem of representation for Bobby Seale. After Charles Garry became unavailable, William Kunstler filed an appearance for Seale ostensibly in order to see him at the county jail. On the first day of the trial, he also filed a general appearance for four of the defendants, including Seale. On September 26 Seale rejected Kunstler as his lawyer and thereafter insisted on his right to defend himself. The court and Seale argued about this issue at almost every opportunity. On October 14, the following colloquy occurred:

> *Mr. Seale:*  I don't have counsel, Judge, I don't stand up because—
> *The Court:*  Mr. Kunstler filed his appearance for Mr. Seale. The record shows it orally and in writing, sir. . . .
> *Mr. Seale:*  Hey, you don't speak for me. I would like to speak on behalf of my own self and have my counsel handle my case in behalf of myself.
>    How come I can't speak in behalf of myself? I am my own legal counsel. I don't want these lawyers to represent me.
> *The Court:*  You have a lawyer of record and he has been of record here since the 24th.
> *Mr. Seale:*  I have been arguing that before the jury heard one shred of evidence. I don't want these lawyers because I can take my own legal defense and my lawyer is Charles Garry.

> *The Court:*   I direct you, sir, to remain quiet.
> *Mr. Seale:*   And just be railroaded?
> *The Court:*   Will you remain quiet?
> *Mr. Seale:*   I want to defend myself, do you mind, please?[42]

On October 20 Bobby Seale made a motion to act as his own lawyer. The U.S. attorney opposed the motion and Judge Hoffman ruled that Seale was represented by Kunstler and could not discharge him. The court of appeals later ruled that Judge Hoffman acted improperly in not inquiring whether Seale wanted Kunstler to represent him.[43]

The conflict escalated on October 28, when Seale again insisted on his right to represent himself.

> *Mr. Seale:*   . . . You are in contempt of people's constitutional rights. You are in contempt of the constitutional rights of the mass of the people of the United States. You are the one in contempt of people's constitutional rights. I am not in contempt of nothing. You are the one who is in contempt. The people of America need to admonish you and the whole Nixon administration.
> *Mr. Hayden:*   Let the record show the judge was laughing.
> *Mr. Seale:*   Yes, he is laughing.
> *The Court:*   Who made that remark?
> *Mr. Foran [prosecutor]:*   The defendant Hayden, your Honor, made the remark. . . .
> *The Court:*   You are not doing very well for yourself.
> *Mr. Seale:*   Yes, that's because you violated my constitutional rights, Judge Hoffman. That's because you violated them overtly, deliberately, in a very racist manner. Somebody ought to point out the law to you. . . .[44]

On the next day, October 29, Seale addressed a group of his followers in the courtroom before the judge appeared. As soon as the court was called into session, Richard Schultz, the assistant United States attorney, spoke:

> *Mr. Schultz:*   If the Court please, before you came into this courtroom, if the Court please, Bobby Seale stood up and addressed this group.
> *Mr. Seale:*   That's right, brother. I spoke on behalf of my constitutional rights. I have a right to speak on behalf of my constitutional rights. That's right.
> *Mr. Schultz:*   And he told those people in the audience, if the Court please—and I want this on the record. It happened this morning—that if he's attacked, they know what to do. He was talking to these people about an attack by them.
> *Mr. Seale:*   You're lying. Dirty liar. I told them to defend themselves. You are a rotten racist pig, fascist liar, that's what you are. You're a rotten liar. You are a fascist pig liar.
>   I said they had a right to defend themselves if they are attacked, and I hope that the record carries that, and I hope the record shows that tricky Dick Schultz, working for Richard Nixon and [his] administra-

tion all understand that tricky Dick Schultz is a liar, and we have a right to defend ourselves, and if you attack me I will defend myself.[45]

Seale was forceably put into his chair by the marshals. After he again insisted on his right to represent himself, the court took a brief recess. Seale was then taken out of the courtroom by the marshals and returned bound and gagged in his chair. The gag was not secure, and he could still speak through it. Kunstler described the scene for the record:

> *Mr. Kunstler:* I wanted to say the record should indicate that Mr. Seale is seated on a metal chair, each hand handcuffed to the leg of the chair on both the right and left sides so he cannot raise his hands, and a gag is tightly pressed into his mouth and tied at the rear, and that when he attempts to speak, a muffled sound comes out.
>
> *Mr. Seale (gagged):* You don't represent me. Sit down, Kunstler.
>
> *The Court:* Mr. Marshal, I don't think you have accomplished your purpose by that kind of a contrivance. We will have to take another recess.[46]

On the next day, October 30, 1969, Seale was again bound and gagged.

> *Mr. Weinglass:* If your Honor please, the buckles on the leather strap holding Mr. Seale's hand is digging into his hand and he appears to be trying to free his hand from that pressure. Could he be assisted?
>
> *The Court:* If the marshal has concluded that he needs assistance, of course.
>
> *Mr. Kunstler:* Your Honor, are we going to stop this medieval torture that is going on in this courtroom? I think this is a disgrace.
>
> *Mr. Rubin:* This guy is putting his elbow in Bobby's mouth and it wasn't necessary at all.
>
> *Mr. Kunstler:* This is no longer a court of order, your Honor; this is a medieval torture chamber. It is a disgrace. They are assaulting the other defendants also.[47]

The three days from October 28 through October 30 produced the most serious crisis in the trial. Of the 137 citations for contempt against the defendants, 47 occurred then. Seale was cited six times for his actions and the remaining defendants for their support of Seale and their protest against what was happening to him. One week later, on November 5, 1969, Seale was held in contempt by Judge Hoffman and severed from the trial. He was sentenced to forty-eight months in jail —three months for each of sixteen acts of misconduct. The court of appeals later held that four of the sixteen specifications dealing with Seale's attempt to defend himself were insufficient to justify contempt charges. After the case was reversed and sent back by the court of appeals for retrial before a different judge, the government decided not to reprosecute the contempt charges because it did not wish to disclose information concerning wiretaps of Seale.[48]

## Ralph Abernathy Incident

Two other triggering events that led to numerous contempt citations were the refusal to allow Reverend Ralph Abernathy to testify and the revocation of the bail of David Dellinger. On Friday, January 31, the defense indicated it was prepared to rest its case on Monday, February 2, after submitting some television film. Over the weekend, another witness, Ralph Abernathy, became available. On Monday morning, Kunstler asked to reopen the case to allow Abernathy to testify. Judge Hoffman refused the request.

> *The Court:* There have been several witnesses called here during this trial . . . whose testimony the Court ruled could not even be presented to the jury—singers, performers, and former office holders. I think in the light of the representations made by you unequivocally, sir, with no reference to Dr. Abernathy, I will deny your motion that we hold—
>
> *Mr. Kunstler:* . . . Your Honor. . . . I think what you have just said is about the most outrageous statement I have ever heard from a bench, and I am going to say my piece right now, and you can hold me in contempt right now if you wish to. You have violated every principle of fair play when you excluded Ramsey Clark from that witness stand. The New York Times, among others, has called it the ultimate outrage in American justice.
>
> *Voices:* Right on.
>
> *Mr. Kunstler:* I am outraged to be in this court before you. Now because I made a statement on Friday that I had only a cameraman, and I discovered on Saturday that Ralph Abernathy, who is the chairman of the Mobilization, is in town, and he can be here. . . . I am trembling because I am so outraged, I haven't been able to get this out before, and I am saying it now, and then I want you to put me in jail if you want to. You can do anything you want with me. . . . because I feel disgraced to be here.[49]

Kunstler was then ordered to make no reference to Abernathy before the jury.

> *Mr. Schultz:* Your Honor, may the defendants and their counsel then not make any reference in front of this jury that they wanted Dr. Abernathy to testify?
>
> *Mr. Kunstler:* No, no.
>
> *The Court:* I order you not to make such a statement.
>
> *Mr. Kunstler:* We are not going to abide by any such comment as that. Dr. Ralph Abernathy is going to come into this courtroom, and I am going to repeat my motion before that jury.
>
> *The Court:* I order you not to.

. *Mr. Kunstler:*  Then you will have to send me to jail, I am sorry. We have a right to state our objection to resting before the jury.
*The Court:*  Don't do it.[50]

After the jury was brought into the court, Abernathy arrived and Kunstler immediately asked that he be allowed to testify. The request was refused.

## Revocation of David Dellinger's Bail

At the same time controversy grew over a speech that Dellinger had made in Milwaukee, criticizing the judge's handling of the trial. On January 30, the judge said in open court:

> *The Court:*  I wanted to say to counsel for the defendants and the defendants, that it has been brought to my attention that there was a speech given in Milwaukee discussing this case by one of the defendants. I want to say that if such a speech as was given is brought to my attention again, I will give serious consideration to the termination of bail of the person who makes the speech. I think he would be a bad risk to continue on bail. The one who made it knows it. I won't go any further than this.
>
> Monday morning at ten o'clock.
>
> *Mr. Weinglass:*  If your Honor please, could the Court just identify the defendant who gave the speech?
> *The Court:*  No, I won't do it. I want them all—
> *Mr. Dellinger:*  I made the speech. Was there anything in the speech that suggested I won't show up for trial the next day or simply that I criticized your conduct of the trial?
> *The Court:*  I didn't ask you to rise, sir, and I am certainly not going to be interrogated.
> *Mr. Dellinger:*  Why are you threatening me with revocation of bail for exercising my freedom of speech? What has that got to do with it? I am here, aren't I?
> *A Voice:*  Right on.
> *Mr. Hoffman:*  We all give the same speech.[51]

Two days after the Abernathy incident, James D. Riordan, the Chicago deputy police chief, testified about Dellinger's action during the Chicago demonstrations:

> *Mr. Schultz:*  Did Dellinger say anything when this announcement was made?
> *The Witness:*  I did not hear him say anything.
> *Mr. Schultz:*  Did you see where he went?
> *The Witness:*  He left with the head of the group that were carrying the flags.
> *Mr. Dellinger:*  Oh, bullshit. That is an absolute lie.
> *The Court:*  Did you get that, Miss Reporter?

> *Mr. Dellinger:* Let's argue about what you stand for and what I stand for, but let's not make up things like that.
>
> *The Court:* All of those remarks were made in the presence of the Court and jury by Mr. Dellinger.
>
> *Mr. Kunstler:* Sometimes the human spirit can stand so much, and I think Mr. Dellinger reached the end of his.
>
> *The Court:* I have never heard in more than a half a century of the bar a man using profanity in this court or in a courtroom.
>
> *Mr. Hoffman:* I've never been in an obscene court, either.[52]

The court then revoked Dellinger's bail.

> *The Court:* I have some observations to make here, gentlemen.
>
> Time and again, as the record reveals, the defendant Dave Dellinger has disrupted sessions of this court with the use of vile and insulting language. Today again he used vile and obscene language which, of course, is revealed by the record.
>
> I propose to try to end the use of such language if possible, and such conduct, by terminating the bail of this defendant.[53] *

The six days from February 2 through February 7, at the very end of the trial, produced twenty-four of the 121 citations against the seven defendants other than Seale and an additional four citations against the lawyers.

## Lawyer Contempts

The contempt citations against the two lawyers in the case did not involve abusive language or obscene remarks. The government said in its appellate brief, "The attorneys present a far different case; they did not heap vituperation upon the judge as did their clients, but rather repeatedly contested rulings by the judge to the point of obstructing the trial."[54] Thus Weinglass was cited for refusing to sit down immediately after being ordered to do so, for asking questions on cross-examination beyond the scope of the direct examination, for repeating citations of legal authorities, for continuing an argument after the judge had ruled on it, and for making disrespectful remarks about the prosecution. He also was cited for making "invidious comparisons" between the court's treatment of the government's case and of the defense's.

Kunstler was cited for similar transgressions, such as refusing to sit down or continuing to argue. The court also cited him for going into the substance of a document not introduced in evidence and for arguing about the time of recess. In addition he defied specific orders of the court not to mention before the jury certain matters which the court had ruled on. Kunstler was given the maximum sentence of

---

* See the discussion on revocation of bail as punishment for disruption on pages 102–105.

six months for these transgressions and an additional six months for his intemperate remarks on the morning of the Abernathy affair. He also received four months for telling the court, "You brought this on [referring to fistfights between the marshals and spectators following the Dellinger affair]. This is your fault," and four months for accusing the government of using violence in the courtroom and of liking to strike women. He was also cited for referring to the gagging of Bobby Seale as "medieval torture" and for expressing his approval of dis-approving groans from the spectators.

## Total Contempt Citations

Aside from the cluster of disruptions described above, the trial proceeded without significant interruption for four and a half months. There were individual incidents from time to time, produced in part by the unconventional life style and political activism of the defendants: Rubin was cited twice for wearing judicial robes in court; Hoffman, for blowing kisses to the jury and asking the court, "How is your war stock doing"; Dellinger, for requesting a moment of silence on Moratorium Day; and all of the defendants were cited for inter-rupting the court or making comments on political subjects or the proceedings. At the very end of the trial, immediately after the jury was charged, Judge Hoffman handed down a total of 159 citations for contempt, 121 against the defendants other than Seale and 38 against the two lawyers.[55] The largest single category (36 citations) consisted of defendants refusing to rise at the beginning or close of a court session. In 27 cases they called the judge a name or accused him of prejudice or injustice or made sarcastic comments to him, mostly aris-ing from the incidents described above. In 10 cases they interrupted or insulted the prosecution, and in 11 cases they applauded or laughed in the courtroom.

On May 11, 1972, all the contempt convictions of the defendants and the lawyers were reversed by the Seventh Circuit Court of Appeals.[56] The appellate court held that the judge cannot wait until the end of the trial to punish the defendants and the lawyers.

> . . . the trial judge must disqualify himself if he waits to act until the conclusion of the trial. When the trial proceedings have terminated, the need for proceeding summarily is not present.[57]

The court also determined that Bobby Seale could not be punished summarily by the judge.[58]

The court of appeals sent the case back to the district court level for retrial of the contempt before a judge other than Judge Hoffman.[59] It also held that many of the contempt citations by Judge Hoffman against the lawyers were legally insufficient and had to be dismissed. These included most of the charges against Kunstler and Weinglass for continuing to argue with Judge Hoffman after he had made a ruling.

With respect to the substantive charges, the court of appeals on November 21, 1972, reversed the convictions of the five defendants who had been found guilty.[60] It held that the trial judge's examination of potential jurors on *voir dire* was unsatisfactory because he did not allow questions on the jurors' attitudes toward the Vietnam war or the youth culture, which may have curtailed the defendants' challenges for cause. The judge also acted improperly in not inquiring about the effect of pretrial publicity on the jurors. In addition, the court of appeals held that it was improper for the trial judge and court marshal to communicate with the jury, urging them to continue their deliberations after they said they had reached an impasse. The judge also improperly excluded certain documentary evidence on the defendants' plans for the Chicago demonstrations and rejected expert witnesses who should have been allowed to testify. Finally, the court said that prejudicial remarks by the trial judge and inflammatory statements by the prosecutor required reversal of the convictions. Subsequently the government decided not to retry the substantive charges.

# The New York Black Panther Case

On April 2, 1969, twenty-one members of the Black Panther party were indicted by a New York County grand jury for conspiring to bomb police stations, department stores, railroads, and the Bronx Botanical Gardens, and to murder various policemen.[61] There were three stages to the proceedings in this case: 1) a series of hearings on bail reduction and other matters relating to defendants' confinement were held from April 3 to December 18, 1969; 2) pretrial hearings were held from February 2 to July 30, 1970; 3) the trial proper, which began on September 8, 1970, and lasted until the defendants were acquitted on May 13, 1971.

## Bail Reduction and Confinement Hearings
## (April 3 to December 18, 1969)

Thirteen of the twenty-one defendants were arraigned on April 2, 1969. Judge Charles Marks, presiding, fixed bail at $100,000 for each of the defendants on the basis of the serious charges of terrorism alleged and the representation of the district attorney that "certain acts might be performed today, and if they were performed, it might result in the death of many hundreds of people in certain large department stores."[62] (Two younger defendants who were arrested later had bail set at $25,000 and $10,000. They were later severed from the case and given youthful offender treatment.) Judge John M. Murtagh, who presided at all later proceedings, held bail reduction hearings and motions on related matters on several dates. On November 17, the bail for two of the defendants was reduced to $50,000 but no one could raise the necessary bond until January 30, when a group of clergymen raised $100,000 bail for Afeni Shakur.

During many of the hearings, the defendants were not present. When they appeared in November and December they expressed their outrage at the high bail set by the court. On November 17, the defendants became incensed because bail was set at a lower level in federal court for four white radicals accused of bombing various federal buildings in New York City. These four—Samuel Melville, George Demmerle, Jane Alpert, and David Hughey—were charged with bombing eight buildings and two were arrested with bombs in their possession. Bail was initially set at $500,000 for each defendant but on November 15 federal Judge Marvin Frankel reduced it to $20,000 for Miss Alpert and Hughey and $150,000 for Melville. The Panther defendants thought that they were being treated differently because they were black. One of their attorneys explained their position, which led to a row:

> The defendants have been in this court a number of times and have sat patiently and quietly and have not uttered a word up until today, and it was only the occurrence in the Federal Court, where four white people who were charged with significantly more serious crimes had their bails drastically reduced on worse records, that has caused what I believe to be the disruption today. It's a denial of constitutional rights to black people that has caused the problem in this courtroom today. I ask the Court to disqualify itself from reviewing these bails.
> *The Court:*  Application denied.
> *A Defendant:*  Why don't you plug yourself in?
> *The Court:*  You will remain quiet.
> *A Defendant:*  I be quiet? You can put me in jail.
> *Another Defendant:*  Where is the equal justice? The Fourth Amendment says you cannot—
> *The Court:*  Do the defendants want to enter pleas?
> *A Defendant:*  You can take the indictment, you can take the entire Nixon administration and stick it up your ass. We're not willing to—
> *Another Defendant:*  This is toilet paper.
> *The Court:*  You be seated.
> *A Defendant:*  You think we got contempt for your court? You're absolutely right, Mister. It's nothing but a joke. It's a class institution that

upholds your class. You going to put me in jail? I've been in jail almost
a year. You're going to put me in jail, punk.

*The Court:*   Be seated.

*A Defendant:*   You white-haired rascist [*sic*] pig.

*Another Defendant:*   This is toilet paper.

*The Court:*   And you will be seated, too.

*Another Defendant:*   Why don't you shut up?[63]

After the uproar subsided, the court set December 18 for trial.

*Mr. Katz:*   We would need thirty days for motions and any possible
demurrers, your Honor.

*A Defendant:*   This is supposed to be justice.

*The Court:*   All right, December 18th.

*A Defendant:*   Why don't you make it Christmas? You trust in God,
you lying bastard. Why don't you make it Christmas?[64]

The defendants also complained about the fact that they were kept
separate in jail and could not communicate with each other in the
preparation of their defense.

## Pretrial (February 2 to July 30, 1970)

The pretrial motions began on February 2. On the first day there were
frequent interruptions of the proceedings:

*The Court:*   The defendants are assured that they will have a fair
trial.

   The motion [for a new judge] is denied.

*Defendant Moore:*   How can it be fair if Hogan picked you?

*The Court:*   You are represented by counsel—

*Defendant Moore:*   But I still got a voice and it is going to be heard
in this court whether you like it or not.[65]

The defendants insisted their families be allowed in:

*A Defendant:*   You got the whole press sitting up in front and our families are stuck out there.

*A Defendant:*   We want our family to hear what is going to happen to
us.

*Mr. Katz:*   Your Honor, in non-legal language that is the essence of my
motion—

*The Court:*   You will make your motion in writing.

*A Defendant:*   We refuse to listen. Our families can't hear what is happening with our lives. We don't have anything to do with you. It's a
very simple matter to deal with that. We are not asking you to tear
down that whole building.

   That sign up there should read "In Pig We Trust."[66]

The first order of business was a hearing on a motion to suppress evidence that had been seized by the police. One of the attorneys sought to introduce a document.

> *The Court:* Your application is denied at this time. You can do it at the appropriate time.
>
> *Defendant Moore:* That's a violation of his constitutional rights and due process of law. He has evidence to put in his behalf and you are going to deny him that right and the man is in court? Are you insane? Or is Hoffman your brother-in-law.
>
> *Defendant L. Shakur:* Carswell is his cousin.
>
> *Defendant Moore:* This is a racial joke. The man has evidence to present in his behalf and you are not going to let him. It's a violation of due process.[67]

There were frequent outbursts during testimony of the detectives who had seized the evidence sought to be suppressed.

> *Mr. Crain:* I would ask to strike that testimony and to ask that this weapon not be introduced in evidence.
>
>   This witness specifically stated he did not seize anything else, and then the testimony was resurrected by a leading question by the district attorney.
>
> *The Court:* Your motion is denied.
>
> *Defendant L. Shakur:* What you mean. He said there was nothing else in the house.
>
> *The Court:* The weapon is offered for identification, not in evidence.
>
> *Defendant Moore:* You are a liar.
>
> *The Court:* And it will be so marked.
>
> *Defendant Moore:* You want to know why black people don't dig this racist mother-fucken country. You can understand it. When you get on the car in your commuter train and go back out in your comfortable suburbs, and when them black people go up in there, they're going to have M14's for your ass. You don't like it, but I don't care. I don't care. You want to know my name again? Ask the stenographer.
>
> *The Court:* The record will reflect that on this occasion, Mr. Crain is laughing with this—
>
> *Defendant Moore:* Not only is Mr. Crain laughing, the people is laughing. All the people are laughing. You have everybody laughing. The press is laughing. I'm laughing, ha, ha, ha.
>
>   (Spectators applaud.)[68]

The court tried to identify the person responsible for the remarks:

> *The Court:* Mr. Lefcourt, what is his name?
>
> *Defendant Moore:* My name is Richard Moore.
>
> *The Court:* The record will so reflect.
>
> *Defendant L. Shakur:* What does that mean?
>
> *Defendant Moore:* Reflect what? Racism? It's already reflected there. If I had $100,000, I wouldn't even bail myself out. You serve to educate black people better than anybody in the world.

We've got a man sitting right there, his lawyer is over there, and you telling the man he can't get evidence to defend himself. And you talk about constitution.

What the hell you know about the constitution? The constitution gives a black man a right to bear arms. And we're going to bear them and we're going to use them.

(Spectators applaud.). . . .

*Defendant Moore.* . . . If you can't give black people justice in this courtroom, don't bring us in here.

All we ask for is justice. That's all we ask for. Four hundred and fifty mother fucken years, we ask for justice. And you got this punk calls us terrorists and you got the Gestapo in our community murdering us; because of punks like that we got guns.[69]

On the next day, a fistfight broke out in court between some of the defendants and the police after a spectator was dragged out of the courtroom.

On February 25, after three weeks of pretrial hearings, Judge Murtagh indefinitely recessed the proceedings.

*The Court:*   Yesterday the Court told counsel that it had a formula for firmly maintaining the dignity of this court without in anyway sacrificing the rights of the accused.

I stated that I did not intend to use the formula for a week or two. This was in order to accomplish the end short of using the formula.

It is obvious that other measures will not prevail. The continued misconduct of the defendants persuades me to use the formula without any further delay.

Frequently a formula is as effective as it is simple. If this formula proves to be effective as this Court believes it will be, it will be in large measure because of its utter simplicity.

The Court declares these hearings to be recessed indefinitely. That, in essence, is the formula.[70]

Judge Murtagh announced that he would resume hearings if the defendants gave "unequivocal assurance" that they would show "complete respect" to the court. Since only one of the defendants was released on bail at the time, Judge Murtagh's action meant that the defendants could be kept in jail indefinitely until they promised to behave.*

The recess was made in anticipation of the Supreme Court's decision in *Illinois* v. *Allen,* which was expected to tell judges how to deal with disorderly defendants. On March 31, 1970, the Supreme Court handed down its decision in *Allen.* The case permitted a trial judge to remove a defendant from the courtroom if he continued to misbehave. Armed with this additional power, Judge Murtagh resumed the hearings on April 7, without receiving the assurances he originally sought.

* See discussion on page 104 on this issue.

The problem of wiretaps, grand jury composition, and other matters were examined until the end of July with relatively little interruption. The judge continued to make disparaging remarks about the defense. On April 7, he said he had "misgivings" about William Crain's competence as a lawyer. He later upbraided Crain for interrupting him when he was talking to one of the defendants.

It was a distinct discourtesy to the Court and an affront to the Court, and a complete contempt of court. The Court had a distinct view of the situation. There was no excuse for your conduct, and the Court abhors your lack of respect for the Court.[71]

As for the defendants, the court remarked on July 30, "Since the ruling of the Supreme Court of the United States in *Illinois* v. *Allen* there has been a marked improvement in the conduct of the defendants."[72] However he criticized the lawyers for their delays in examining witnesses, their frequent arguments with the courts, and their refusal to control the defendants' behavior. On the last day of the pretrial hearings, he handed the defense attorney copies of the American College of Trial Lawyers report on disruption and said,

Throughout the hearings conducted to date there has been conduct by counsel obviously designed to promote disorder and to disrupt the proceedings. Statements have frequently been inflammatory; the tone of voice of one or another defense counsel has repeatedly been unwarranted and inappropriate; counsel by facial grimaces have repeatedly reflected not merely disagreement but disrespect for the judge presiding; counsel have repeatedly engaged in unwarranted sarcasm. In general, counsel have persistently engaged in conduct that is not in accordance with the traditions and standards of the American bar.[73]

## Trial (September 8, 1970, to May 13, 1971)

The trial of the thirteen defendants began on September 8, 1970, with the selection of a jury which took six weeks to complete. The trial proper began on October 20. There were few incidents of disruption involving the defendants, but the contention between the court and the lawyers continued. The following are typical incidents.

The court threatened the defense counsel with contempt proceedings for laughter ("You have been giggling and laughing throughout this testimony, and you are in contempt of court";[74] "Defense Counsel Lefcourt is smiling again, for the record. I direct you as a representative of the bar to conduct yourself like a gentleman"),[75] and for looking at a newspaper during a long interval when the jurors were examining exhibits (". . . while the jury was examining exhibits Mr. Crain was busy reading a newspaper and desisted only when admonished by the

Court. Now Mr. Crain, your lack of good taste is unbecoming a member of the bar.")[76]

The court was particularly sensitive to being interrupted by defense counsel.

> *The Court:*  I was starting to talk. May I have enough respect from you that I may address the jury? . . . The minimum a lawyer should bring to the bar is good manners.[77]
>
> *The Court:*  Once again you have interrupted me. Will you please be seated?
>
> (Counsel insists on making his objection notwithstanding the Court's order to be seated). . . .
>
> *The Court:*  Mr. Crain you are going to be seated this minute or I'm going to begin contempt proceedings. . . . You are in contempt of court.[78]

The judge also made disparaging remarks about the prosecuting attorney. In his opening statement the prosecutor did not mention the actual charges in the indictment.

> *The Court:*  Please Mr. District Attorney can we have the charge in each count. . . .
>
> *Mr. Bloom:*  I object to the Court coaching the District Attorney as to how—
>
> *The Court:*  Apparently it's necessary.[79]

The climax of the conflict between court and counsel came on December 14, when Judge Murtagh established rules for the conduct of the attorneys throughout the remainder of trial.

> The conduct of the defendants since the Supreme Court ruling that laid down guidelines has been in the main commendable. I wish I could say as much for counsel, but I am determined that from this point on you are going to conduct yourselves properly or the Court will have to take formal recognition without further delay of such misconduct.[80]

First, the court prohibited counsel from arguing in support of an objection or about a ruling of the court without explicit permission. ". . . I am expecting from this point on that there will be religious adherence to that practice. You are not to argue an objection except with the permission of the Court, and I tell you now that I do not intend, except in rarest instances, to grant such permission."[81] Furthermore, "I want absolutely no comparison again to be made between the Court's rulings with respect to matters affecting the district attorney and defense counsel. The making of such comparisons is clearly insolent and contemptuous."[82] Finally, "facial grimaces and expressions of contempt that are continually directed at the witness and the Court . . . do not serve the cause of your clients. They constitute misconduct. They are provocative."[83]

The court was evidently eager to demonstrate its determination to enforce these rules, and a contempt citation against William Crain was the immediate result. While Crain was cross-examining a witness, the prosecution objected to a question, and the court sustained him. Crain replied, "Your Honor, I'm simply inquiring into motive, which is fundamental in this case."[84] The court stopped the trial, questioned Crain about his understanding of the court's admonition not to argue objections, and then ruled that "it is therefore ordered and adjudged that you are guilty of contempt of court." The defendants commented:

*Mr. L. Shakur:* You're intimidating our lawyers.
*Defendant Hassan:* That's right.[85]

Shortly thereafter Crain told the court that he would not be intimidated.

*The Court:* Your statements are noble, counsel, but I remember—
*Defendant Hassan:* And the people are going to back him up.
*The Court:* I beg you to remember—
*Defendant Hassan:* Don't beg.
*The Court:* that as a member of the bar—
*Defendant Hassan:* He ain't no member of the bar.
*The Court:* —you have an obligation to act with respect to this court.
    (Various defendants speaking at the same time.)
*The Court:* All of the defendants will be removed from this Court.
*Mr. Crain:* The Court has an obligation to try—
*Defendant L. Shakur:* His first obligation is to his client.
*The Court:* I trust the reporter is making notes of this conduct.
*Defendant L. Shakur:* You put this on the record.
*Defendant Collier:* You're intimidating these counsel because of the fact you want to get even with us.[86]

Crain later apologized to the court and the contempt citation was withdrawn.

Another attorney, Sanford Katz, was cited for his "sarcasm." During the questioning of a police undercover agent about his grand jury testimony, the assistant district attorney, Phillips, objected that Katz was reading only a portion of the agent's answers. When Katz resumed his cross-examination, he read part of the officer's testimony and then remarked:

Before Mr. Phillips has another heart attack I'd better read the next question.[87]

The judge then cited Katz for contempt. Katz apologized but refused to promise he would never use sarcasm again. The judge later withdrew the citation. Following the acquittal of the defendants, no further disciplinary action was taken against any of the lawyers or defendants.

## Other Trials

A trial with no political overtones which saw many disorderly moments was the murder trial of Charles Manson and three women members of his "family." The four were tried from June, 1970, to March, 1971, for the murder of movie actress Sharon Tate and three friends and two other Los Angeles residents. The sensational nature of the crime and the outlandish life style of the defendants attracted considerable public attention. The frequent outbursts in the court contributed to extensive publicity about the case.

When the trial began in June, Manson asked that his court-appointed lawyer, Irving Kanarek, be dismissed and that he be permitted to act as his own attorney. Judge Charles H. Older refused his request on June 10. Manson then stood up and turned his back on the judge, and the other defendants did the same. They were removed from the courtroom. They returned later in the week and repeated their symbolic gesture, and were removed each time this happened.

The defendants engaged in other symbolic behavior during the trial. On June 14, they rose and stood with arms outstretched and heads hung down in imitation of Christ. When they refused to take their seats, they were again ordered from the court.

An uproar arose when the state's chief witness, Linda Kasabian appeared to testify on July 27. Even before she was sworn, Irving Kanarek leapt to his feet and in front of the jury objected to the witness's appearing at all: "Object, your Honor, on the grounds this witness is not competent and she is insane!"[88] The district attorney shouted in reply that Kanarek was not making a legal objection and that it was improper to make such remarks before the jury.

> *Bugliosi [assistant district attorney]:*   Wait a while, your Honor, move to strike that and I ask the court to find him in contempt of court for gross misconduct. This is unbelievable on his part.
>
> *Older:*   If you have anything to say, Mr. Kanarek, come to the bench.[89]

Over the next few days, Kanarek objected to almost every question the district attorney asked Mrs. Kasabian. Despite the fact that the judge ordered the lawyers not to mention Mrs. Kasabian's mental condition before the jury he continuously did so. On July 29, Kanarek was held in contempt for interrupting Mrs. Kasabian's testimony and sentenced to one night in jail.

> *Older:*   Mr. Kanarek, you have directly violated my order not to interrupt repeatedly. You did it again. I find you in contempt of court and

I sentence you to one night in the County Jail starting immediately after this court adjourns this afternoon until 7:00 A.M. tomorrow morning. The order will further provide that you are to be given free access to confer with your client, Mr. Manson, during the time you are in custody.[90]

Another defense attorney, Ronald Hughes, was fined seventy-five dollars or one night in jail for using an expletive to the prosecutor ("shit") during a bench conference the previous afternoon. He declined to pay the fine and spent the night in jail.

On August 3, President Richard Nixon made the following comment about the trial: "Here is a man who was guilty, directly or indirectly, of eight murders without reason." Many newspapers headlined his remarks: "MANSON GUILTY NIXON SAYS." Judge Older ordered the lawyers not to bring into court any newspapers that mentioned the President's statement. Nevertheless on the next day, Manson held up a newspaper with that headline to the jury. There was an immediate halt in the trial. The judge questioned the jurors about possible bias and then denied a motion for a mistrial. He then questioned the lawyers about where the newspaper came from, and defense attorney Dave Shinn admitted that he brought it into court. He was sentenced to three nights in jail on contempt charges for allowing Manson to get it.

On August 5, the three women defendants arose and chanted, "If President Nixon thinks we're guilty, why go on with the trial?" The judge told them firmly to sit down, and they sat down.

On October 1, the four defendants were barred from the courtroom for singing during the proceedings. Manson also shouted that he was not getting a fair trial. On the next day, Manson returned and told the judge, "You are doing a very poor job of showing the public justice." When Judge Older interrupted him, Manson began singing, "Old black magic will get you in its spell." After further comments to the judge, Manson was ordered from the court. The three women began to chant at the judge and they too were removed.

On Monday, October 5, the uproar continued. After testimony resumed, Manson asked permission to cross-examine.

> *The Court:* Any examination?
>
> *Mr. Fitzgerald:* No, your Honor.
>
> *Defendant Manson:* Yes. May I examine him, your Honor?
>
> *The Court:* No, you may not.
>
> *Defendant Manson:* You are going to use this courtroom to kill me?
>
> *The Court:* You may step down.
>
> *Defendant Manson:* Are you going to use this courtroom to kill me? Do you want me dead?
>
> *The Court:* Mr. Manson!

*Defendant Manson:* The minute I see you are going to kill me, you know what I am going to do.

*The Court:* What are you going to do?

*Defendant Manson:* You know. You have studied your books. You know who you are talking to.

*The Court:* If you don't stop, Mr. Manson—and I order you to stop now—I will have to have you removed as I did the other day.

*Defendant Manson:* Order me to be quiet while you kill me with your courtroom? Does that make much sense? Am I supposed to lay here and just let you kill me? I am a human being. I am going to fight for my life, one way or another. You should let me do it with words.

*The Court:* If you don't stop, I will have to have you removed.

*Defendant Manson:* I will have to have you removed if you don't stop. I have a little system of my own.[91]

When a new witness was called, Manson leapt over the counsel table with a pencil in his hand and tried to get to the judge. He was stopped by the bailiffs. The judge ordered him removed.

*The Court:* . . . The record will show that Mr. Manson came over the counsel table in the direction of the bench and was subdued by the bailiff, and I order him removed from the courtroom.

*Defendant Manson:* Don't let me get the jump on your boys, the jump on your boys. In the name of Christian justice someone should cut your head off.

*Defendant Atkins, Defendant Krenwinkel, Defendant Van Houten:* Noem be oro decaio, Noem be oro decaio, Noem be oro decaio.

*The Court:* I order you ladies to stop or I will order you to be removed also.

*Defendant Atkins, Defendant Krenwinkel, Defendant Van Houten:* Noem be oro decaio, Noem be oro decaio, Noem be oro decaio, Noem be oro decaio.

*The Court:* I order you ladies to stop or you will be removed.

*Defendant Atkins, Defendant Krenwinkel, Defendant Van Houten:* Noem be oro decaio, Noem be oro decaio, Noem be oro decaio.

*The Court:* If you don't stop I'll have you removed.

*Defendant Atkins, Defendant Krenwinkel, Defendant Van Houten:* Noem be oro decaio, Noem be oro decaio, Noem be oro decaio.

*The Court:* All right, remove the female defendants from the courtroom. I want the record to reflect that the female defendants repeated over and over again, despite the Court's order for them to stop, some phrase, what it was I did not understand.[92]

For the next two weeks the defendants refused to give the judge any asurances that they would behave properly. They were kept in small rooms near the court with loudspeakers available to hear what was happening. On October 23, they promised not to disrupt and returned to court. But on November 10, Manson criticized the judge for overruling his attorney. The judge ordered him to be quiet and threatened him with removal. Manson continued to speak in barely audible tones and the judge ordered him removed. The three other defendants were later removed for chanting as Manson was led out.

After the defense rested its case without putting any of the defendants on the stand, the three women insisted on testifying, presumably to take all the blame for the killings and exonerate Manson. There was a delay in the trial when the attorney for Leslie van Houten disappeared one weekend (floods and landslides hit an area he was camping in) and a new attorney had to be selected. Miss van Houten refused to accept her new attorney and demanded that a woman lawyer represent her. There were frequent shoving matches in court between the bailiffs and the defendant about the matter.

After the jury returned a verdict of guilty, it began to hear testimony on the penalty phase of the case. Manson again shouted at the judge numerous times and continued his feud with his lawyer. Once he was ejected from the trial for punching Kanarek. The trial finally ended on March 29, 1970, when the jury voted the death penalty against all the defendants.

There were other disorderly trials during the period of 1970–72. A group of nine anti-Vietnam war activists broke into the Dow Chemical offices in Washington, D.C., and in February, 1970, were tried for unlawful entry and malicious destruction of property. The D.C. Nine case saw frequent contention between the defendants, the lawyers, and the judge.[93] In Tacoma, Washington, seven young radicals were tried for violating the federal anti-riot act in charges growing out of a demonstration protesting the contempt sentences handed down by Judge Hoffman in Chicago. The seven were tried in November and December, 1970, but their trials ended in a mistrial declared on December 10. The court aborted the trial and held six of the seven in contempt when they refused to come to the courtroom at the commencement of the trial day.[94] Thereafter during the hearing on those charges four days later, six of the defendants were again cited for contempt for disruptions that occurred that day. Both contempt convictions were later reversed by the Ninth Circuit Court of Appeals: the first because the disruption occurred outside the judge's presence; the second because the contempt certificate was not specific enough. On retrial of the second contempt charges, the defendants pleaded nolo contendere and were sentenced to varying terms in jail.

There was fighting between spectators and the police in the courtroom during the Chicago trial of eleven University of Illinois students charged with causing a campus disturbance.[95] The trial of a Puerto Rican nationalist accused of trying to bomb an office building in New York City was also disrupted by spectators.[96] The trial of a group of Black Panthers in Los Angeles for attempted murder and assault against police officers also saw disorderly moments.[97] From January to March, 1972, two black inmates of Soledad prison—John Clutchette and Fleeta Drumgo—were tried in San Francisco for the murder of a prison guard. In pretrial hearings there were two incidents of riotous conduct in court involving spectators, and during the trial frequent clashes arose between the judge and defense lawyers. The defendants were acquitted.[98] There were also disturbances in murder trials in New York[99] and Cleveland[100] that received some newspaper attention.

## Conclusion

With hindsight, the reasons for the disorder in the four politically oriented trials described in this chapter seem obvious. The sheer numbers of defendants and defense lawyers involved—from fifty-six in the Nazi case to ten in the Chicago case—magnified the problems of maintaining order. In addition, the judges in some of the cases seemed particularly antagonistic to the defendants or their lawyers and did not establish a proper atmosphere for the proceedings. The fact that the political activities of the defendants were cited as a basis for the indictments (or, in the Black Panther case, as evidence of the charges) led to continuous political argument in the courtroom. The defendants were not likely to be impressed with the need for proper decorum in court since they were basically opposed to many of the institutions and values of American society. The fact that except for the Panthers, they were charged with conspiracy under statutes that affected their freedom of speech added to the defendant's feelings of anger. Finally, the cases were widely covered by the press, which gave the defendants an opportunity to convey their political message to a wide audience.

# CHAPTER FIVE

# Disorder and the "Political Trial"

Courtroom disorder has become associated in the public mind with what has been called a political trial, and for good reason. The Chicago conspiracy trial, the New York Black Panther case, the earlier Communist party case of 1949, and the sedition trial of 1944 all involved political activists who claimed that they were being prosecuted for their political beliefs. These defendants expressed outrage at what they felt was the unfairness of the proceedings, and exhibited undisguised contempt for the political institutions and officials that subjected them to their ordeal. They also tried to explain their political positions, expose what they saw as the government's aim, and educate the public politically. The prosecutors naturally resisted these efforts, and frequently sharp confrontations occurred—involving all participants in the trials. The result was the uproar described in the previous chapter.

There is, therefore, some correlation between courtroom disorder and political justice, however this term is defined. But not every trial that has political overtones has led to courtroom disruption, nor is courtroom disorder restricted to such political cases. Whether disorder occurs depends upon a number of factors which will be examined in this chapter.

## What is a "Political Trial"?

The most elusive concept pertinent to this study is the so-called "political trial." Lawyers who appeared before the Committee held diametrically opposed views of what the concept means. New York trial lawyer Louis Nizer told us that there is no such thing as a political

trial, a view shared by some commentators and judges.[1] William
Kunstler took an opposite view, saying that "a political trial is any
trial in which the defendant feels he is not getting a fair shake."
Kunstler felt that the term encompasses every court proceeding involving the sixty to eighty million poor, young, unpopular, or minority
members of this society. Supreme Court Justice William O. Douglas
has said that "political trials . . . frequently recur in our history . . . ,"[2]
while Chief Justice Warren E. Burger has disparaged use of the
term.[3]

Even among those who believe that political trials exist, there is
a wide range of definitions. Malcolm Burnstein, a civil liberties lawyer
from San Francisco, defines a political trial as one in which "public
opinions and public attitudes on one or more social questions will have
an affect on the decisions. . . . For example, in the trial of an unem-
ployed black man, the attitude of middle-class jurors toward the
defendant may be essentially their attitude to a stereotype of the
ghetto dwellers."[4] Professor Richard Uviller of the Columbia Law
School told our committee that a political trial is one in which the
"defendants and their counsel are using the trial process for political
ends; and are attempting to make the trial a political event." A professor of political science and law, Theodore Becker, has written that
the "perception of a direct threat to established political power is a
major difference between political trials and other trials."[5]

Speaking more broadly, the late Otto Kirchheimer, a highly regarded
scholar of political justice, defines a political trial as any proceeding
that can be used to shift political power.

> . . . both governments and private groups have tried to enlist the sup-
> port of the courts for upholding or shifting the balance of political
> power. With or without disguise, political issues are brought before the
> courts; they must be faced and weighed on the scales of law, much
> though the judges may be inclined to evade them. Political trials are
> inescapable.[6]

It is not hard to see why this diversity of opinion exists. When the
term "political trial" is used by defendants in a criminal proceeding or
by their lawyers or allies, they mean to accuse the authorities of using
the criminal law for illegitimate political purposes. The extreme examples in European history are the Moscow purge trials of the 1930s and
the Reichstag case in Nazi Germany, where totalitarian states tried to
eliminate their enemies in carefully staged show trials. In this context,
the term signifies a criminal action initiated by a government against
representatives of an opposing political group to suppress their political
activities or at least to shed unfavorable light on their efforts. This
motivation affects the entire proceeding and justifies, in the defendants'

view, a political response of exposing the government's purpose and explaining to their followers and the public at large why the government brought the suit.

Prosecuting authorities and some commentators naturally resist the notion that a political motivation lies behind any criminal indictments. In their view every prosecution must be treated the same way. The defendants cannot question the reasons for a prosecution so long as sufficient evidence to warrant an indictment has been presented to a grand jury. Moreover, it is totally improper to use the courtroom for explicit political agitation no matter what prompted the prosecution. A defendant's remedy is to move to have the indictment dismissed if it was improper, to persuade the jury to acquit, or to appeal the conviction to a higher court if it is contrary to existing law.[7]

One of the difficulties in unraveling this issue is that the term "political trial" has become so value-laden that its usefulness as an analytic concept has been undermined. The term obscures rather than clarifies the difficult area where law and politics merge. It has acquired such a pejorative cast that anyone using it is generally indicating that he disapproves of a particular indictment. To call the Chicago conspiracy case a "political trial" automatically suggests that the indictment was improperly brought and should have been dismissed or the defendants acquitted. Analyzing the problem in another way, the term "political trial" is suffering from what Harvard Law Professor Lon Fuller calls "metaphorical contamination."[8] The word "political" may contaminate all aspects of the problem: the defendants believe if any political considerations are present in a case, their response must be totally political, while prosecutors tend to deny the existence of political elements. Pro-government or anti-government antagonists then debate the use of the label and not the reality that the term is describing.

Our view is that political factors do play an important role in the legal process and that they have played a part in many of the disorderly trials we are examining. Political considerations affect the judicial system in three different areas:

1. The decision to prosecute may be motivated by political factors.

2. The outcome of a case may be affected by political attitudes or considerations.

3. The participants in a case, either before or during a trial, may behave in such a way as to maximize the political consequences or impact of the action.

Of course, these categories are not mutually exclusive: a trial may be politically motivated, the result may be determined by the politics of the time, and it may in turn affect the distribution of political power. Politics and law may interact at one or all of these levels. Nevertheless, each has its own special characteristics which require separate analysis.

## Politically Motivated Trials

The American Nazis in 1944, the Communists in 1948, and the Chicago conspiracy defendants in 1969 all claimed that they were prosecuted because of their political beliefs and actions and that their indictments reflected an effort by the government to suppress peaceful political activities. To the extent that these defendants believed that improper motivation lay behind their prosecution, they were less likely to sit quietly during their trials without making an effort to explain their views. In fact, their perception of a political motivation by the prosecution led to a political counterattack which produced courtroom disorder.

The problem is complicated by the fact that the statutes under which prosecutions of this type are initiated are sometimes directed at restricting the efforts of political outgroups and are therefore of doubtful constitutionality. For example, the Alien and Sedition Acts of 1798 were passed for the specific purpose of restraining political criticism of the John Adams administration by Jeffersonian-Republican editors and congressmen.[9]

Beginning in 1917, many states passed criminal syndicalism, sedition, and "anti-Red flag" laws, aimed chiefly at suppressing the I.W.W. and other allegedly radical groups. During 1919–20, about 1,400 people were arrested under these acts and about 300 imprisoned. From 1919 to 1924, the state authorities in California prosecuted 531 I.W.W. members, convicted 264, and sentenced 128 to prison, including Charlotte Anne Whitney, the niece of former Supreme Court Justice Stephen J. Field. A number of those trials had contentious episodes.[10]

Sometimes the statute involved is of more general application and a prosecutor has greater discretion in seeking indictments. Here also the law may be applied against specific political opponents of the government's policies. For example, prosecutions under the sedition or espionage laws or under various conspiracy charges have been applied against important political figures. During World War I the Espionage Act, which forbids interference with or discouragement of enlistment into the armed forces, was the basis for indictments of many opponents of the war. Leading members of the I.W.W., the Socialist party, and the Nonpartisan League in North Dakota were prosecuted for criticising American participation. Eugene Debs was sentenced to five years in jail for saying that the war "was instigated by the predatory capitalists in the United States," that it was "a crime against the people of the United States and the Nations of the world," and that the workers should engage in "continuous, active and public opposition to the war through mass demonstrations, mass petitions and all other means within our power."[11]

The Nazi sedition trial of 1944 arose after President Roosevelt insisted that the Justice Department prosecute certain members of the German-American Bund and other fascist-type organizations under the wartime sedition laws. From the vantage point of the 1970s the cases seem politically inspired, an effort by the Roosevelt administration to mobilize home-front sentiment against the Germans by equating vocal opposition to the war with sedition. The result was the trial described in chapter 4.

The Smith Act prosecution against Communist party leaders raise similar questions. By 1948, when the *Dennis* case was brought, the party had ceased to be a factor of major importance in the United States, The government apparently initiated the series of conspiracy prosecutions to justify its anti-Communist international policy.

It is difficult to avoid the conclusion that the Chicago conspiracy trial was also politically motivated. To try to show evenhandedness, the government sought and secured indictments against an equal number of policemen and demonstrators. The peace group defendants seem to have been specially selected to represent the varying components of what has been called the "New Left," and a great fanfare of publicity attended the return of the indictments in Chicago. These elements suggest that David Dellinger and the others were indicted not primarily because of legally objective factors but to make a political point: to demonstrate that the convention disturbances were not the result of police riots, as the Walker Commission Report to the National Commission on Violence had found, but were planned by antiwar organizations, student protestors, Black Panthers, and other dissident groups to undermine the political system and destroy law and order.

These cases show that a decision to prosecute leaders or representatives of political outgroups is often the result of action by both the legislative and executive arms of the government. The prosecutor may be executing laws passed by the legislature which are specifically aimed at controlling certain conduct by these organizations. When the defendants resist and challenge the indictment, they see themselves as challenging the policy of the entire government.

In these circumstances, the likelihood of court disorder increases significantly. The chances are strong that the defendants will vigorously express their opposition to the government in the courtroom. They view the proceeding as a trial not of the acts charged but of the legitimacy of the governmental policy behind the charges. Professor Geoffrey C. Hazard, Jr., of the Yale Law School has called the contention associated with these trials "defendants' counterclaims."

The counterclaims in a political trial are based on a maddening combination of transcendental political or ethical issues and procedural technicality. One counterclaim is that the regime—all of it or the part directly involved in the altercation—is illegitimate according to some theory of political justice so that the actions of its officials are not clothed with legal authority and therefore amount to naked coercion. A subsidiary count is that the court trying the case is part of the illegal system and that its proceeding is a juridical pretension and a farce as indeed it is if the premise is accepted.[12]

In some cases a single individual may have been singled out by the government for special treatment because of political considerations. For example, in 1938 the government tried to deport Harry Bridges, the head of the International Longshoremen's Union.[13] Bridges came to the United States from Australia in 1920; by the middle 1930s he was an important west coast labor leader with close ties to the Communists. In 1938 the government tried to deport him on the grounds that he was then a Communist. A hearing examiner, Dean James Landis of the Harvard Law School, upheld Bridges. Immediately afterward, a member of the House of Representatives introduced a special bill ordering Bridges out of the country. It never passed, and in 1940, Congress amended the Alien Registration Law to provide for deportation of any alien who was a member of or was affiliated with any subversive organization at any time after entering this country. The sponsor of the law proudly proclaimed that it was designed to deport Bridges.[14] However, the Supreme Court held in 1945 that the government had not proved the necessary affiliation with the Communist party to justify his deportation.[15]

After Bridges applied for citizenship, swearing that he had never been a party member, the government indicted him for taking a false oath and also initiated denaturalization proceedings. He was convicted in 1950, and the government tried unsuccessfully to have his bail revoked when the Korean war broke out, claiming that Bridges was a menace to national security because of his control of the waterfront workers.[16] In 1953 the Supreme Court reversed his conviction (on the ground that the statute of limitations had run out) and ordered a new denaturalization hearing.[17] In 1955 a federal district judge stated that the testimony of the government witnesses was "flimsy," "unacceptable," "unsubstantial," and "tinged and colored with discrepancies, animosities, vituperation, hates."[18] Bridges kept his citizenship and continued to live in this country.

A number of contempt citations grew out of the Bridges case, involving his attorneys. One of them, Vincent Hallinan, was convicted of contempt for stating to the jury, after the judge had ordered him to cease, that the charges against Bridges were the result of the government's warfare against his union and that the government witnesses were perjurers, "spies, turncoats, the very swills of humanity." He also refused to stop asking questions about wiretaps after the trial judge had ruled them out of order. The trial judge held another lawyer, George MacInnis, in contempt for saying to him, "You should cite your-self for misconduct" and "You ought to be ashamed of yourself."[19]

The history of the *Bridges* case shows that both the Roosevelt and Truman administrations were willing to use the legal process for political ends. Frank Murphy, who as a Justice was outraged at the *Bridges* case,* had authorized indictments when he was attorney gen-eral of Spanish Loyalists who were recruiting for the International Brigades. Roosevelt wanted to show Congress that his administration was enforcing the Neutrality Act, and the Loyalists seemed an ideal target to Murphy.[20] In another case, in 1941, Attorney General Francis Biddle invoked the newly passed Smith Act (later used against Com-munist leaders) to prosecute the Trotskyite leaders of a small Teamster Union local in Minneapolis. Since they were enemies of both the na-tional leaders of the Teamsters and the Communist party (then a firm supporter of Roosevelt) the administration stood to gain politically by the action.[21]

These instances indicate that the decision to prosecute political out-groups or their leaders involves complicated political factors and is not solely determined by a prosecutor's effort to apply the law evenhand-edly. The government has enormous discretion in initiating prosecu-tions, and the conspiracy, sedition, and national defense laws cover so wide a range of actions that they can justify a great variety of indict-ments against political fringe groups.

Politics may rear its head even when common crimes are involved. Of course no one can claim immunity from prosecution for murder or robbery either because he is a respected member of the government or a political radical. But a political figure is sometimes linked to a violent crime on very tenuous grounds. The stories of the Haymarket bombings, Tom Mooney, and Sacco and Vanzetti have been repeated too often to require retelling. In the first case, there was no credible evidence that the defendants played any part in the violent crimes that were committed other than speaking about anarchism and the class struggle. In the latter two cases, the prosecuting authorities ignored evidence that would have tended to exonerate the defendants, because they were undesirable radicals. As Max Lerner has commented, "The real crime [of the defendants] was opposition to the dominant economic interest around which the state was organized."[22]

Related to the problem of improper motivation behind a prosecution is the issue of police surveillance and entrapment—the instigation of crimes by the authorities. A necessity may exist for police observation

* *See* note 15.

of narcotics defendants, organized crime figures, and other types of criminals, but infiltration of political groups is of a totally different character.[23] For the purpose of this study such infiltration may add yet another aspect of betrayal or unfairness for defendants who are already antagonistic to the policies of the government. It may lead to outrage, which may vent itself during the trial, to the detriment of judicial order and of public confidence in the entire legal system. Some of the more contentious moments in both the Chicago conspiracy case and the New York Black Panther case, for example, occurred when police informers were testifying.

## Politically Determined Trials

It should come as no surprise to legal realists of the 1970s that prejudice of all kinds—social, racial, political—has a substantial impact on the judicial process. Not only does enormous latitude exist at the prosecutorial level, but judges and juries make hundreds of decisions every day that are dictated or affected by their political stance. In the South, many opportunities were taken to exploit the powers of discretion in the legal process in order to perpetuate an oppressive system against the black minority: Southern white judges and juries consistently voted to uphold the prevailing system of white supremacy in any case involving black people.[24] Nor is this unique to the South. As we have discussed in chapter 2, blacks are arrested more cavalierly than whites in the North as well, indicted more often, found guilty in a higher percentage of cases, and usually sentenced to longer terms.

Members of unpopular political groups have always been subject to the emotional hates and fears of judges and juries. The bias of Judge Joseph E. Gary in the Haymarket trials of 1886 and of Webster Thayer during the Sacco-Vanzetti case has been often cited.[25]

At the height of the McCarthy era in 1951, a Pennsylvania judge ordered a lawyer out of a case because he thought he was a Communist. The judge asked the lawyer:

> Hymen Schlesinger, have you ever been a member of the Communist Party.
> Are you a member of the Civil Rights Congress.
> Did you or did you not form the Civil Rights Congress, which is a Communist Front Organization, in your office—the Civil Rights Congress which is part of the movement to overthrow the Government of the United States by force and violence.

When the lawyer refused to answer these questions, the trial judge ruled:

We have formally adjudged you unfit to try a case in this Court as of today, morally unfit. You do not possess an allegiance to the United States.[26]

A Kentucky judge sentenced a sincere Jehovah's Witness who was found to be a conscientious objector by his draft board to five years in jail with these words: ". . . in cases of this kind [defendants who refuse a draft board order] deserve a five year sentence . . . [their offense] strikes at the very foundation and fundamentals . . . of our whole governmental system."[27]

Judge Jerome Frank wrote that "the personality of the judge is the pivotal factor in law administration" and that his "political, economic and moral biases" affect almost all of his decisions.[28] The great variation in sentencing from judge to judge is merely one way in which these biases show themselves. A judge's sympathy for or antipathy to a radical defendant appearing before him is very likely to enter into any decision he must make in the trial. And a defendant is likely to be attuned to these biases and react to them himself.

A jury is equally liable to the political pressures of the time. The foreman of the Sacco-Vanzetti jury said to a friend before he was called for duty: "Damn them! They ought to hang them. . . ."[29] One of the Spock trial jurors told Jessica Mitford: "I personally feel the government had a weak case. But if the defendants had been found not guilty—we'd have chaos!"[30] Members of the Chicago conspiracy trial jury indicated that their decision was certainly affected by the growing militancy of the antiwar protest movement.

In short, the politically insulated prosecutor, neutral court and jury, and normal trial are more ideal than reality, at least in this type of case. When political outgroups and vociferous dissenters are brought into the judicial system, it is very difficult for a judge or jury to ignore their own political ideas in passing on guilt or innocence.

Because of the possibility of prejudice in such cases, a court should inquire into a jury's political orientation. The court of appeals in the Chicago conspiracy case said:

Many elements of this case might have aroused the jurors' prejudices. One of the central themes was the protest against this nation's involvement in war in Vietnam. Defendants were leaders in such protest and claimed that their militancy did not go beyond constitutionally protected bounds. There were and are deep divisions in our society resulting from that war, gravely illustrated by this unprecedented confrontation at the convention of a major political party in 1968.[31]

The court recounted various milestones in the antiwar campaign and noted:

We have no doubt that defendants brought to trial in 1969 upon charges that their anti-war activities were carried beyond constitutional protection were entitled to a testing of their jurors for biased attitudes on this subject.[32]

Every trial lawyer knows the desirability of questioning prospective jurors on the *voir dire* to detect prejudices, to select potentially sympathetic jurors, and in jurisdictions where more extensive *voir dire* is allowed to begin to educate the jury with the defendant's point of view. Charles Garry, Bobby Seale's lawyer, has explained:

> You have to project your client's ideas in the legal context. The trial is an educational tool—for the jury, the judge, and the community. You start presenting your theory of the case to the jury during voir dire. Sometimes you can even educate the jury in this way. . . .
>
> And if you don't develop some sympathy with your client, you are doing him a disservice, no matter how good a lawyer you are, because the story of the political dissenter has to be projected in a way that the jury, the court, and the world will understand.[33]

## Political Agitation in the Courtroom

There is little likelihood of courtroom disorder arising merely from the effort to create sympathy from the judge or jury for a politically unpopular defendant. The difficulties arise when the defense (or in rare cases, the prosecution) goes further, trying to make a political point outside the courtroom rather than to win the case inside. An attempt to play to this audience can produce much of the contention associated with "political trials," however they are defined.

The problem may first arise when a defendant seeks to register a complaint against the indictment itself. If he feels that a prosecution is politically inspired—that the government is moving against him for political purposes—he will bring the complaint to his followers and the public and will generally do so where he can be seen—in the courtroom. Often he will assume a symbolic stance of outrage throughout the trial.

In other cases, defendants may deliberately disobey a law in part for the very purpose of using the court to convey their political message. In one case in our questionnaire material, described by the prosecutor involved, a group of Hawaiians was charged with criminal trespass.

> Defendants were charged with trespass on lands owned by the Bishop Estate. Defendants (32 in all) claimed that the land in question (Kalama Valley located on the island of Oahu) belonged to the Hawaiian People and not the Estate.
>
> All defendants belonged to an organization called "Kokua Hawaii."

The goals of this organization is to turn over various lands to Hawaiians.[34]

During the trial they engaged in frequent outbursts.

Making speeches in front of the Court prior to trial and during the re-
cesses. Disrupting the trial by yelling various slogans such as "Huli"
(means to turn over) and using the black-power clenched fist. The two
defense attorneys raised many irrelevant issues far afield from the question of trespass to bring home the point, i.e. people of Hawaiian ances-
try are being robbed of their land by the "Haole" (mainlander).
    Defendants would fail to show up at a scheduled hour, thereby caus-
ing delay and extending trial considerably. Defendants would yell at
me or jeer me when I would raise an objection. Defendants would
throw paper wads at me or threaten me in the hallway during recess
periods.

Often members of a small militant political group with no wide following feel that they must commit a symbolic and outrageous illegal
act to both portray their political complaints and draw media attention:
a draft board raid by antiwar demonstrators,[35] criminal trespass by
Hawaiian nationalists or college students, the seizing of a courthouse
in New Mexico by militant Spanish-Americans who claim the area
rightfully belongs to them.[36] Once the crime is committed, a trial necessarily follows. The trial itself illustrates and dramatizes the conflict between the government that is trying them (and had generally ignored
them previously) and the political movement they represent. The conflict that inspired the crime is generally continued in the trial. The trial
again attracts media attention which gives the defendants another
chance to convey a political message to the widest possible audience.
The more disorder that occurs, the more attention the trial will attract
and the more people will hear the message.
    An attack on the government is sometimes joined with protest
against an aspect of the procedure under which defendants are to be
tried. This may be a legal rule or process of long-standing, but its use
in a politically oriented trial may reveal some vice that was not previously apparent. Highly articulate political defendants also may be
more alert to the injustice of a rule or procedure, or to the arbitrariness
of a particular judge, and better able to focus public attention on it.
    Sometimes special rules are imposed when particular political de-
fendants are brought before the courts—as in the Black Panther case
when Justice Murtagh required written motions on reduction of bail
when ordinarily oral motions were acceptable. Since the defendants
were already angered by their indictment, they were especially attuned
to what they felt were additional injustices or inequities. Professor
Graham Hughes of the New York University Law School has written
in the paper he prepared for this committee:

Defendants charged with crimes with a radical political connection often meet judges who set impossibly high bail which in practice condemns them to long incarceration before a verdict is reached or even before trial begins. Impartial observers sometimes conclude that judicial conduct of trials of politically radical defendants sometimes falls short of the proper standard of impartiality. Defense attorneys may be harassed; the contempt power is wielded too generously; sentences may seem harsh and punitive in the worst sense.

The defendants in the Chicago conspiracy case complained about both the indictment and the refusal of Judge Hoffman to allow Seale to defend himself or Ramsey Clark to testify. And the Panther complaint about the indictment was combined with an attack on the high bail, which kept them incarcerated throughout the trial.

When the defendants go beyond their own case and consciously try to advance their political program in the courtroom—try to make their trial a "political event"—their tactics can very likely lead to a disruptive trial. It is understandable that they should react politically to an indictment that they consider politically inspired. But the courts have difficulty enough unraveling the particular facts of a case and, more important, administrating justice fairly, without being used as a forum for the broader social and political arguments of the day. The rules of evidence, the temperament of judges, the very dynamics of the trial situation do not lend themselves to this type of debate.

The many undesirable legal consequences of disruption were described in chapter 2. It is unclear, however, what the political consequences are. Sometimes the disorder may lead to desirable legal or social reform as in the early English cases described in chapter 3 and the Susan B. Anthony case in America. But disruption that is viewed by the bar and the public as a deliberate attempt to undermine the judicial system by radical political defendants is not likely to bring them any measure of political support. Professor Arthur Kinoy of the Rutgers Law School, who is sympathetic to radical causes, has written:

> Today in the United States such a myth [that the radical lawyer and the radical defendant are in fact the principal underminers of the system of "justice," of "democratic liberties,"] is facilitated by the distorted image of a political trial as primarily a contest between political lawyers and defendants and a "hard pressed," if "irascible," judge. The development of such a caricature of the radical lawyer or defendant in the present period would be disastrous. It would undermine the effectiveness of radical lawyers and radicals in general in participating in the organizing of powerful movements to oppose the transition measures of repression and reaction. And most serious of all it would blunt the radicalization of the millions in struggle, since it would mask the reality of who is the real enemy of the elementary liberties of the people.[37]

Thus, efforts in this direction are likely to be politically self-defeating.

# Conclusion

The problems of political justice are extraordinarily complex, and the proper analytic tools have not yet been developed to deal with them. The use of value-laden terms such as "political trial" do not contribute to their solution. On the other hand, whether we like it or not politics and law are not strangers. Statutes and prosecutions are often politically motivated. Judges and jurors do not always leave their political opinions at the courtroom door. Political groups often try to enlist the aid of the law to shift political power, and the political forces in a given society frequently take cues from decisions of legal institutions. When the political tensions of a society increase, they may spill over in these varied ways and, as we have seen, problems of courtroom disorder can then arise.

There is no guaranteed way to insulate the courts from political turmoil. An effective reform would ensure that vague and uncertain laws that infringe on First Amendment rights are not passed or invoked for political gain. As we elaborate in chapter 8, we believe that proof that prosecutorial discretion was abused for political purposes, or for any other illegitimate reason, should be a defense to the charges brought.

Aside from proof of such abuse, the lessons to be learned from cases that have political overtones or implications are more subtle. Judges and prosecutors should have a better understanding of the sense of unfairness or outrage that many representatives of political outgroups feel when the criminal law is invoked against them for what they view as their political opposition to the government. Such defendants are not likely to ignore all political considerations during their trial if they feel that politics brought them into the courtroom. But they should not be permitted to transform a court into a gladiatorial arena where they can trumpet their political program to their followers and the world at large.

We do not pretend that these suggestions are likely to eliminate all the disorders which have so troubled the legal community and the public. To some extent these disorders reflect more fundamental divisions which go deep into the structure of American society. If the political turmoil outside the court decreases, so will the problems of courtroom disruption.

# CHAPTER SIX

# *Regulating the Conduct of Defendants and Other Litigants*

At the core of the problem of trial disorder is the defendant, the central figure in any trial and the individual whose freedom and reputation are directly at stake. Most cases of disruption over the years have involved defendants. This is still true. The responses to the Committee's trial judges questionnaire showed that of 112 reported cases of disruption, 74, or almost two-thirds, were by criminal defendants, and 8 involved parties to civil actions. Of the 25 cases of disruption reported by United States attorneys and the district attorneys (which overlap the judges' responses), 17 involved defendants. In addition, many cases have engaged the interest of the public as well as the bar because they involved determined and colorful defendants, such as Bobby Seale, Abbie Hoffman, Jerry Rubin, and members of the S.D.S. and Black Panther party. It is therefore important to examine very closely the nature and causes of courtroom disruption by defendants and the remedies available to deal with the phenomenon.

## Remedies for Disruption— General Considerations

The first task in dealing with disorder by defendants is to define the conduct that may properly be classified as disruptive. The boundaries of such conduct are neither clear nor fixed. *Illinois* v. *Allen*[1] is the leading case, but the Supreme Court's decision provides little guidance. Nor do two recent reports concerned with maintaining order in the court. Neither the A.B.A. Project on Standards for Criminal Justice nor the

American College of Trial Lawyers attempts to define the type of conduct that may trigger the remedies authorized in *Allen*. In the only official attempt at such a definition, the First Department of the Appellate Division, New York, recently called "disruptive conduct"

> any intentional conduct by any person in the courtroom that substantially interferes with the dignity, order and decorum of judicial proceedings.[2]

This definition does not include all conduct that interferes with the administration of justice, but only that which "substantially interferes" with a judicial proceeding.

Strictly speaking, of course, every interruption of the smooth conduct of a trial, however slight, may be or seem to be disorderly and disruptive. Such interferences cover a wide range. Analysis of the questionnaires submitted by the Committee to trial judges, as well as the relatively few decided cases, suggests that there are five main types of disorder, which in particular circumstances may merit different treatment by the courts. These categories (which to some degree overlap) may be described as follows:

1. Passive disrespect. For example, a refusal to address the judge as "Your Honor" or to stand when he enters the courtroom.

2. Refusal to cooperate with the essential ground rules of the judicial proceedings. For example, a refusal to enter or leave the courtroom voluntarily.

3. The single obscenity or shout.

4. Repeated interruptions of the trial, ranging from embarrassing or insulting remarks to loud shouting, pounding, or cursing.

5. Physical violence in the courtroom, with or without weapons.

A defendant's refusal to obey a lawful order of the court, either temporarily or permanently, is not a separate category. It may arise in the context of one of the five categories listed above, and in such cases we deal with the underlying issue that led to the incalcitrance. On the other hand, refusal to obey a judge's order may be wholly unrelated to disorder; for example, if the defendant is ordered to answer a question on cross-examination, or to produce a document. Standing alone, a defendant's refusal to obey is not an aspect of "disorder," even though he may be subject to a contempt citation.[3]

Extended discussion is unnecessary to show that these forms of disorder, in varying degree, may threaten the integrity or decorum of the courtroom. To strip a trial judge of the power to cope with them would, we think, cripple his ability to assure a dignified proceeding and a fair trial.

From the questionnaire material we received and our analysis of the existing state of the law, including recent relevant Supreme Court decisions, we conclude that the five categories of misconduct should be dealt with as follows:

1. Passive disrespect should generally be ignored unless it substantially interferes with the proceedings.

2. A judge should ask why a defendant is refusing to cooperate with the essential ground rules of court proceedings. The defendant should be assured that his rights will be protected, and warned of the sanctions that he faces: exclusion from the courtroom or contempt. If he persists, sanctions should be imposed.

3. A single obscenity or shout should generally not be punished by contempt nor should it be ignored by the court. The judge should warn a defendant that if such action continues, it could lead to punishment or exclusion from the courtroom.

4. Repeated interruptions of a trial may be dealt with by exclusion or contempt after appropriate warnings have been given.

5. Physical violence in the courtroom cannot be tolerated and a court may deal with it by exclusion, physical restraint through handcuffs, or a contempt citation.

In *Illinois* v. *Allen,* the most important case in this area, the Supreme Court issued a forceful statement on behalf of courtroom dignity and decorum and ruled that a trial judge has wide discretion in maintaining order in his courtroom. The case involved a 1957 trial for robbery. Allen had refused appointed counsel and chose to represent himself. While doing so, he consistently berated the trial judge, speaking in a "most abusive and disrespectful manner." When the judge reacted by appointing counsel for him, Allen threatened that the judge was "going to be a corpse." Subsequently, Allen tore up a file and threw it on the courtroom floor. After warning Allen that he would be removed from the court if the misconduct continued, the judge excluded him. Twice Allen asked to return to court and was permitted to do so after he promised that he would not disrupt the trial. Each time, however, he was excluded in view of further misconduct. He was also physically restrained during a portion of the proceedings. Eventually Allen was convicted and sentenced to ten to thirty years in the penitentiary. Appellate review through the state courts failed.

Allen filed a petition for habeas corpus in federal court claiming that he had been denied his constitutional right under the Sixth and Fourteenth Amendments to confront the witnesses against him. The district court declined to grant the writ, but the court of appeals reversed, accepting Allen's contention that a defendant's right to attend his own trial is so "absolute" that, regardless of how unruly Allen's conduct was, he could never be held to have lost that right so long as he insisted on it. The Supreme Court reversed this ruling, agreeing with the district court that the right to be present at trial is not absolute and that Allen was properly excluded.

Justice Black's opinion for the Court is a sweeping statement that affords trial judges broad discretion. The opinion does not focus on the question of Allen's misconduct because on the trial record there was no doubt that he had been disorderly. Justice Black instead broadly reviewed the remedies available to trial judges when disorder occurs. He announced that exclusion is permissible if, after being warned, the defendant "nevertheless insists on conducting himself in a manner so disorderly, disruptive and disrespectful of the court that his trial cannot be carried on with him in the courtroom."[4] The opinion acknowledged that banishment of a defendant from his own trial is not "pleasant," but maintained that it "would degrade our country and our judicial system to permit our courts to be bullied, insulted, and humiliated and their orderly progress thwarted and obstructed by defendants."[5]

The Court also stated that shackling a disruptive defendant is permissible on the same degree of misconduct as would justify exclusion. After acknowledging that the use of physical restraints has shortcomings, it suggested criminal and civil contempt as alternatives.

Justice Brennan wrote a concurring opinion in which he stated that trial disruptions are a challenge to our "heritage of ordered liberty." He suggested additional remedies and safeguards in the case of misconduct by defendants. Justice Douglas entered an unlabeled opinion in which, after indicating that guidelines applicable to unruly defendants should be different in "political trials," recommended that the writ of habeas corpus requested by Allen be dismissed due to the staleness of the record.

The *Allen* decision provides a guide to the Supreme Court's attitude toward disorderly trials, and discusses the basic sanctions of exclusion, binding, and contempt. But it leaves many questions unanswered. It offers little assistance in determining what constitutes disruption; it does not spell out in any detail when trial judges may act to control their courtrooms; and it does not deal with other possible means of controlling disorder.[6]

Nor does the *Allen* case state whether the various acts of disorder mentioned earlier *should* be punished in the context of a particular trial. This is the issue that trial judges throughout the country face in a variety of factual circumstances. It cannot be answered by a mere recitation of the nature of the disruptive conduct. Only after a judge weighs all the pertinent considerations in a concrete setting will he be able to decide confidently whether to impose one of the *Allen* remedies or to take another course. The Supreme Court has lodged very broad discretion in the trial judge; it is imperative that this discretion be exercised with intelligence and sensitivity. As Whitney North Seymour, Sr., a former president of the American Bar Association, has commented, "There is no substitute for a trial judge who knows how to run his courtroom."

Each of the following considerations should bear on the way a trial judge reacts to a problem:

—Whether the disorder occurs frequently or over a period of time. Three verbal outbursts in one day obviously have a greater impact on a case, and therefore invite a severer judicial response, than the same outbursts spaced out over two weeks of trial.

—Whether the incident occurs before a jury so as to interfere with its ability to render an objective and impartial verdict.

—Whether the incident occurs at the time of sentencing or a plea of guilty, or takes place at the outset of a trial or during the presentation of evidence.

—Whether there are multiple defendants, especially when not all are misbehaving. In such a case a trial judge will want to consider the general impact of a particular remedy against one or more defendants.

—Whether a defendant is representing himself without a lawyer (pro se). This aspect of the problem is dealt with separately below.

—Whether there are indications of mental disturbance on the part of the disruptive individual, suggesting that he should be referred for a mental examination.

—Whether there are mitigating circumstances such as possible provocation by the prosecutor, or even the judge himself. This issue will be dealt with in the chapters relating to the prosecutor and judge.

It should not be forgotten that the pressures of a criminal trial or certain civil cases can be hard on the participants. If someone reacts to the situation with an emotional outburst, even one that is disruptive, this should be viewed by the court with understanding. One of the trial judges who responded to the Committee's questionnaire expressed what we believe is the correct attitude toward the tension that affects virtually every criminal defendant, and many parties to civil actions as well.

> I subscribe to the theory that all defendants in criminal cases tend to be anxious over the outcome of the trial, and in these cases where it can be reasonably expected that defendants will not comport themselves properly in the courtroom, the first thing to do is to listen and let the defendant explode and get it out of his system if he wants to talk. Secondly, let him know in a practical way that he will get a fair trial and proceed to do just that with the proper decorum of courtroom attitude, stressing that the courtroom should be a place of calm and dignity where all men can expect justice.[7]

We do not advocate that obstreperous defendants go unpunished when they plainly are acting in a manner that makes an orderly and proper trial impossible. Trial judges must possess and use their power if dignity and decorum are to be maintained. In the remainder of this chapter we shall discuss 1) the nature of the various remedies; 2) the occasions for invoking those remedies, with particular reference to the five categories of disorder discussed at pages 91–92; and 3) the special problem of a defendant who represents himself in court.

# Preventive Sanctions

The above discussion makes clear that the trial judge, with ample discretion to discourage and punish courtroom disruption, should carefully tailor his reaction to the particular incident before him. It also means that he should employ "a gradually escalating series of responses."[8]

## Pretrial Prevention

Several means are available by which a trial judge, prior to trial, may be able to reduce the likelihood of disturbance. The simplest technique is probably the most effective. At the outset of each case, at least those in which there is reason to believe that trouble is brewing, the judge should make known the ground rules that all participants will be expected to follow.[9] Although the A.B.A. Advisory Committee on the Judge's Function suggests that the code of criminal procedure or the published rules of court need not be explicitly referred to,[10] when a judge believes that a difficult trial is ahead, he should repeat or summarize all relevant rules. In such cases it may also be advisable to confer with the lawyers in the judge's chambers, answering questions and making clear the court's determination to assure an orderly proceeding. A South Carolina judge reported that he was able to avoid a potentially ugly incident by indicating a "firm observance" of court rules in such a pretrial conference.[11]

Another recommended pretrial technique is the severance of offenses and defendants.[12] The A.B.A. Advisory Committee endorses this method of coping with a situation in which one or more but not all of several codefendants appear likely to cause disorder. By severing his case the troublesome individual can be isolated and thus more easily contained. The court must of course also weigh the competing interests of efficiency and economy in judicial business, which suggest joinder not severance. But since disruptive conduct by a single defendant may seriously prejudice the others with judge and jury, we approve the use of this remedy in appropriate cases.[13]

## Warnings, Negotiation, and Related Remedies

In the *Allen* case Justice Black made clear that a defendant can be removed from his trial only after he has been warned that disorderly conduct will not be permitted.[14] Justice Brennan's concurring opinion elaborated the point: "Of course, no action against an unruly defendant is permissible except after he has been fully and fairly informed that his conduct is wrong and intolerable, and warned of the possible consequences of continued misbehavior."[15]

The *Allen* requirement of a warning is consistent with general judicial practice as well as with the ordinary legal assumption that an individual should not be punished without due notice that his conduct is improper and may be subject to sanctions.

To be effective a warning should be clear and follow the first instance of disruptive conduct, unless a judge is persuaded that an outburst is aberrational and unlikely to be repeated. If the disorder continues, a judge must exercise his discretion in determining whether to take one or more of the following actions: a) issuing a firmer warning; b) discussing the matter with the defendant and his lawyer; c) assigning further guards to the courtroom; and d) briefly adjourning the proceeding to allow a cooling off period. In addition, of course, if a defendant is acting in a violent manner, some immediate action must be taken to restrain him. Each of these remedies merits further comment.

In his warning, a judge should make evident to the defendant that his conduct is disruptive and will not be tolerated. He should also state explicitly that the *Allen* sanctions might be applied. It has been suggested[16] that a judge should warn the defendant that: 1) future occurrences of a like nature will result in expulsion from the trial for as long as his disruptive posture is maintained; 2) the trial will continue in his absence; 3) he will lose his right to see and hear the witnesses testify and the evidence introduced, and will lose his right to observe all other proceedings of the trial; and that 4) he will not be readmitted to the courtroom until he indicates expressly, and on the record, that he will behave. The judge should give his warning only after the jury, if there is one, is excused so as to insulate the fact-finding body from irrelevant and inevitably prejudicial comments on the defendant's behavior.[17]

A warning, however firm, may not work, or may not seem adequate to a particular incident. In that case, the patient judge may wish to reason with the defendant. One judge explained to us how he successfully dealt with a defendant's tirade that lasted fifteen or twenty minutes.

> First by listening without interruption until the defendant calmed down. Thereafter, speaking to the defendant in a calm voice and trying to convey the message that I understood his problem. Told him why I had to send him to a mental institution and that I wanted him to walk out of the courtroom as a man. He calmed down while the court spoke to him and did walk out of the courtroom with minimum security and in a calmer state.[18]

Another judge described how he dealt with frequent attempts at disruption, applause, occasional cheers and clenched fists, and sporadic abuse.

> All disturbances prior to the final one were not insurmountable problems. I stopped proceedings, sometimes excused the jury, talked things over in a mild but firm manner and we got along. I tried to be fair to the defendants and spectators and made it obvious, I believe, by seldom raising my voice and sometimes overlooking minor violations of rules. At the end of the trial I found four defendants guilty of contempt of Court.[19]

This excerpt indicates that even sensitive handling of disorder may not obviate the need for stricter sanctions.

In the normal case adding several guards could be expected to dampen or eliminate courtroom disorder as well as provide a ready means to cope with conduct that requires physical restraint. But the presence of guards in any number is an unsettling factor in a trial, and their use should be carefully justified. One court of appeals has said that

> any presence of guards other than an unobtrusive complement of security officers is bound to have some prejudicial effect, and can be justified only upon a showing of its necessity.[20]

Applying this or a similar standard, several courts have held that the use of guards was excessive.[21] Even when guards are properly deployed, "particular care must be taken to insure that the court does not take on the appearance of an armed camp."[22] The number of guards should therefore be limited and where possible nonuniformed personnel should be used.[23] In the New York Panther case, for example, the decision to station a uniformed guard behind each of the thirteen defendants throughout the trial may have been excessive. In any event, the guards should not be stationed where they can overhear communications between defendants and their lawyers.[24]

A brief recess has proven to be a valuable aid in simmering down an excited defendant and generally cooling off a potentially explosive situation. The easing of tempers may well reduce the likelihood of further disorder.[25]

Some courts have abused this useful technique by calling a recess and later basing a finding of contempt largely upon the "obstruction" it allegedly created.[26] This is an improper use of the contempt power, particularly when it is doubtful that without the recess the conduct of the defendant would have justified a contempt citation.

A different problem is presented when a case is recessed either while a defendant is incarcerated without bail or when the judge revokes a defendant's bail. The "recess" then becomes a variety of civil contempt—that is, confinement as a means of coercing a defendant to cease his disruptive behavior. This sanction raises separate problems which will be dealt with later in this chapter.

It may be that none of these methods will forestall continued disorder. The Supreme Court in the *Allen* case approved additional sanctions to cope with such conduct—criminal contempt, removal of the defendant from the courtroom, binding and gagging, and civil contempt. Although the Court did not explicitly draw the distinction, only criminal contempt is designed to *punish* a misbehaving defendant. The other three remedies are techniques for maintaining an ongoing trial by preventing the defendant from further disruption or inducing him to cease his disorderly behavior. We shall consider these preventive remedies in turn.

## Removal of the Defendant from the Courtroom

The precise holding of *Allen* was that the trial judge did not commit error in removing a disorderly defendant in the context of that case. Prior to *Allen* there was considerable disagreement over the appropriateness and even the constitutionality of the removal sanction.[27] The defendant's claim to be present is grounded in his right under the Sixth Amendment to confront and cross-examine witnesses against him. Indeed, the court of appeals ruling that was reversed by the Supreme Court in *Allen* stated this right of confrontation to be "absolute."

As others have recognized,[28] the decisions relied on by the *Allen* court involved different circumstances and therefore did not alone justify the Court's ruling. In *Diaz* v. *United States*[29] the defendant voluntarily absented himself from trial, and the Supreme Court had little difficulty in concluding that in these circumstances the defendant had no constitutional right to be present. To sustain the defendant's claim would enable him to "paralyze the proceedings of courts and juries and turn them into a solemn farce."[30] In the other principal case relied on in *Allen*,[31] a conviction was upheld even though the defendant had been denied the right to accompany the jury in its viewing of the scene of the crime. While the Supreme Court said that the viewing was "something separate from a trial in court," it observed that the Fourteenth Amendment grants a defendant the right to be present at any stage of the proceedings which has a "relation, reasonably substantial, to the fullness of his opportunity to defend" himself.[32] The *Allen* court, by contrast, approved exclusion from the trial itself, the stage at which the defendant's presence is most critical.

We think the *Allen* decision was necessary to assure the integrity of a trial. The Supreme Court did acknowledge the importance of the defendant's presence at trial by limiting carefully the occasions on which he can properly be removed. Removal is improper unless the defendant "insists on conducting himself in a manner so disorderly, disruptive and disrespectful of the court that his trial cannot be carried on with him in the courtroom."[33] Such a stringent test is desirable. A litigant's presence, especially in a criminal trial, is simply too important to be lost if another feasible remedy is at hand.

A judge should not only warn a defendant that he is engaging in contumacious behavior, but he should actually cite the defendant before proceeding with exclusion. Only if the contempt citation is ineffective, should the defendant actually be removed.

Many judges have not heretofore followed the pattern we recommend. For example, thirteen cases were reported to us in which a defendant was removed from a courtroom. (In one a defendant represented himself without a lawyer, about which we shall say more below.) All of the cases involved some form of verbal interruption of the trial—abuse, shouts, etc. In two of them the defendant also refused to cooperate in the proceedings, by attempting to act as his own counsel (and firing his attorney) in one, and by attempting to walk out of the courtroom in the other.

In only one of the six removal cases in which the defendant had a lawyer[34] did the trial judge use the contempt remedy, and even there the contempt citation was issued *after* the defendant was excluded— that is, when it no longer could be effective in inducing him to cease misbehaving.

None of the removal cases involved violence, but in another case, the trial judge dealt with incipient violence by warning the defendant that he might have to be removed.

> During voir dire defendant drew knife, threatened officers, stating that he wan't going to be "f . . . . . " because his skin was black. Shouting obscenities and curses. . . . after defendant delivered knife to his counsel, defendant was advised of his right to be present at the trial, but that if he continued his disturbance that he would be removed and placed in adjoining room with intercom to enable his hearing the procedure, that he could return at any time when he agreed to proper behavior.[35]

Recognizing the seriousness of the removal sanction, Justice Brennan, concurring in the *Allen* case, stated that

> when a defendant is excluded from his trial the court should make reasonable efforts to enable him to communicate with this attorney and, if possible, to keep apprised of the progress of his trial.[36]

Justice Brennan did not explain what he meant by "reasonable efforts." At the least, it would seem, an audio system should be set up so that a defendant can hear the proceedings from his cell. In such cases, he also should be given the opportunity to assist in his defense by conferring with his attorney at appropriate intervals. Whether audio techniques should be supplemented by visual ones is a more difficult question because of the expense of closed circuit television.

The A.B.A. Advisory Committee on the Judge's Function has expressed "serious doubts" about two-way audio and visual links, saying:

> Even the absent defendant can seriously interfere with his attorney's ability to follow the proceedings and participate effectively if he is tied to an open communications link with an obstreperous defendant.[37]

The A.B.A. committee concluded that a court is not obliged to provide "extraordinary measures" when a defendant, after warnings, makes his presence inconsistent with an orderly trial. We agree; for example, we do not think it is incumbent to provide an Eichmann-type isolation booth in the courtroom. But we also believe that the defendant should have as much communication with his lawyer as possible. An audio link to the defendant that does not enable him to interrupt the court proceeding is a practical resolution of the interests involved. This was the course followed by at least two of the trial judges reporting to us.[38] In neither case did there appear to be difficulty in arranging for microphones or other equipment. Nor was there any further disruption of the trial.

Trial judges should be alert to counteract possible jury prejudice when a defendant is excluded. A judge should warn a jury to disregard the misconduct and his response to it, explaining that they bear no relation to the defendant's guilt or innocence.[39] When the case goes to the jury at the end of trial, this cautionary statement should be repeated. After particularly disorderly incidents, where there is a strong likelihood of prejudice, a judge could poll the jury to determine whether prejudice has actually resulted. If there are alternate jurors, they should replace those who have evinced prejudice. Otherwise, the fact that the Supreme Court has approved juries of less than twelve,[40] may mean that jurors who have been affected could be excused and a case tried to a smaller number than twelve, although we have no record that this has been done in any case. When a judge forms the opinion that ineradicable prejudice has occurred, there is no alternative to a mistrial.[41]

## Binding and Gagging

The second preventive technique recognized by the *Allen* court for dealing with courtroom disruption is binding and gagging the defendant. Even while giving its approval, the Court expressed reservations:

> But even to contemplate such a technique, much less see it, arouses a feeling that no person should be tried while shackled and gagged ex-

cept as a last resort. Not only is it possible that the sight of shackles and gags might have a significant effect on the jury's feelings about the defendant, but the use of this technique is itself something of an affront to the very dignity and decorum of judicial proceedings that the judge is seeking to uphold. Moreover, one of the defendant's primary advantages of being present at the trial, his ability to communicate with his counsel, is greatly reduced when the defendant is in a condition of total physical restraint.[42]

The concern of the Court is mirrored in the views of other judges. While it has long been the law that a defendant may be handcuffed to prevent escape or keep him from violence, the additional element of gagging him raises serious problems. There has been almost uniform distaste for the idea of a defendant appearing bound and gagged at his own trial, particularly before a jury. Justice Holmes once observed that "any judge who has sat with juries knows that in spite of forms they are extremely likely to be impregnated by the 'environing atmosphere.'"[43] It is hard to imagine an environment more inconsistent with an orderly trial and, at the same time, more prejudicial to a criminal defendant, than his appearance trussed up and gagged throughout the trial.

Even though the *Allen* case sanctioned binding and gagging, we disapprove of it. We believe the remedy should not be used by trial judges, even as "a last resort." We have not seen or are we able to imagine a situation where binding and gagging is to be preferred to the alternatives of contempt and removal.[44]

It is true that there are instances, including seventeen reported to us in questionnaires, in which judges have bound and gagged disorderly defendants. The cases arose before the *Allen* case made clear that exclusion of the defendant is an acceptable remedy. In some of them it appears that the trial could not have otherwise continued in the defendant's presence. But six of the cases reported to us involved verbal interruptions of a trial, one of which included a defendant's ripping off his own shirt; one involved noncooperation with the court by failing to enter the courtroom (here no gag was used); and another an attempted escape. In only one of these cases did the judge use the contempt remedy against the defendant.

In eight other cases reported in the questionnaires, trial judges cooled off an excited and misbehaving defendant by reminding him and his lawyer that he might be bound and gagged.

While such warnings seem to have worked, we do not think they should be employed in view of our conclusion that it is inappropriate to bind and gag a defendant at his trial. If warnings are used, they should caution the defendant that he might be cited for contempt or removed from the courtroom.

A related question is under what circumstances if at all a judge should handcuff or shackle a defendant *without gagging him*. It is well established in cases dating back to the early common law, and followed today in all jurisdictions, that it is "an important component of a fair and impartial trial" to permit a prisoner to appear at his trial free from all shackles and other forms of restraint.[45] There are equally well established exceptions to this rule—defendants may be handcuffed to prevent their escape[46] or to prevent them from injuring other participants or officers of the court.[47] Handcuffs have also been used to assist in bringing a physically uncooperative defendant into the courtroom.[48]

Whether or not handcuffing without a gag should be used rests in a judge's sound discretion but a defendant should not be shackled in a degrading way. As in the case of gagging a defendant, discussed above, a form of manacling that places the defendant in an awkward physical posture is not only humiliating to him but degrades the judicial process. For example, we have doubts about the trial judge's action, as reported in the following California case:[49]

> During the testimony of a prosecution witness who testified that the defendant had admitted the murder, the defendant, a large, well-developed, male, negro, let out a raucous cry, picked up the heavy counsel table, and literally threw it at the bench, barely missing one of the clerks.
>
> The defendant was subdued by bailiffs, a recess was called, after which time the defendant was called in with his attorney and advised that it would be necessary to place him in chains and leg irons to prevent a recurrence. Defendant apologized to the court and there were no further displays of temper. The remainder of the trial the defendant was seated at the counsel table with leg and waist chains.

On the other hand, it was proper for a Missouri judge simply to have the defendant handcuffed in order to prevent the recurrence of a disturbance in which he "would not be seated, knocked books and papers off desk, directed obscenities at the court."[50] After the handcuffing there was apparently no further disturbance.

In approving a limited use of handcuffs without a gag or humiliating shackles, we reiterate that the alternatives of contempt and removal, or at least a warning of these sanctions, should first be fully tried. In addition, a trial judge should be cautious in applying handcuffs where he believes that prejudice is likely to result. This means of controlling a misbehaving defendant should be more readily applied, for instance, in a case tried without a jury.

## Civil Contempt and the Revocation of Bail

In the *Allen* case Justice Black, rather surprisingly, authorized the use of civil contempt as a remedy against a recalcitrant defendant. It was surprising because, so far as we can determine, the remedy has never been used for this purpose.[51] It must be recalled that civil unlike criminal contempt is not designed to punish an individual, but rather to coerce him through confinement to act or refrain from acting in a certain manner.[52] As stated in a leading case, civil contempt "is wholly remedial, serves only the purposes of the complainant, and is not intended as a deterrent to offenses against the public."[53] The defendant is always able to escape from confinement by taking the desired action; he has "the keys of [his] prison in [his] own pocket."[54]

Despite the absence of precedent for civil contempt in disorderly trials, Justice Black authorized its use as follows:

> Another aspect of the contempt remedy is the judge's power, when exercised consistently with state and federal law, to imprison an unruly defendant such as Allen for civil contempt and discontinue the trial until such time as the defendant promises to behave himself. This procedure is consistent with the defendant's right to be present at trial, and yet it avoids the serious shortcomings of the use of shackles and gags.[55]

Careful analysis of civil contempt is required not only because of the *Allen* dictum, but because another sanction, similar to civil contempt—revocation of bail coupled with an adjournment of trial—has been approved by the Supreme Court,[56] and is in current use, as indicated in the judges questionnaires.[57]

The effect of revoking bail pending a defendant's declaration that he will behave is identical to civil contempt in that the defendant by promising to behave can end his confinement. If the trial *proceeds* in the defendant's absence after bail is revoked, the remedy becomes the equivalent of exclusion. In other words, revocation of bail resembles civil contempt only if the trial is adjourned while a defendant "thinks it over."

Civil contempt and revocation of bail seem to be highly effective remedies to contain disorder. Assuming, as Justice Black was careful to note, that they are applied "consistently with state and federal law," they probably will work in all cases but those in which a defendant is wholly unamenable to persuasion. In such cases, the trial judge must consider the possibility that the defendant is mentally ill or is purposely, for his own reasons, seeking to postpone the trial. Justice Black was alert to the latter possibility, saying in *Allen,*

> It must be recognized, however, that a defendant might conceivably, as a matter of calculated strategy, elect to spend a prolonged period in confinement for contempt in the hope that adverse witnesses might be unavailable after a lapse of time. A court must guard against allowing a defendant to profit from his own wrong in this way.[58]

Sometimes a defendant appears to be acting "to profit from his own wrong in this way,"[59] but these are the exceptional situations. On most occasions in which civil contempt and bail revocation are used, or even threatened,[60] the defendant will come around, sometimes sooner, sometimes later.[61] In fact, the problem with these remedies is not that they might favor the defendant but that they are too harsh and easily can be abused.

This is so for several reasons. First, because an indeterminate sentence is ordinarily imposed in civil contempt. A defendant can theoretically remain in jail as long as he obdurately refuses to promise to behave. Second, while the defendant is entitled to a due process hearing, the constitutional and procedural protections for defendants in criminal trials, even the lesser requirements for criminal contempt, are not constitutionally required in civil contempt. Third, prolonged incarceration of a defendant may amount, at least in some cases, to a denial of his constitutional right to a speedy trial.

These problems have been faced to a limited extent. Some states have set a maximum period of incarceration for civil contempt (New York's is six months[62]), thus mitigating the first two objections to the remedy. But the practice in the states is far from uniform, and even six months is a long period of confinement for a defendant summarily put away. The speedy trial objection was raised in the New York Panther case, but the court rejected it because the delay was caused by the defendants' "persistently deplorable" conduct.[63] It is not necessary to decide whether the same result would follow from an indefinite postponement resulting in a longer delay than the three weeks which in fact occurred in the Panther case.[64] The critical fact for our purposes is that the risk exists.

These dangers suggest that civil contempt should be used with restraint. As Justice Harlan said in reversing a trial judge who revoked bail and remanded a defendant to custody for a single, brief incident of tardiness in appearing at trial:

> . . . this power must be exercised with circumspection. It may be invoked only when and to the extent justified by danger which the defendant's conduct presents or by danger of significant interference with the progress or order of the trial.[65]

Justice Harlan's warning indicates that a defendant should not be incarcerated under civil contempt for prolonged periods. In this light seven days would seem to be a maximum time limit in which to induce a defendant to behave.[66] This conclusion is supported by practical considerations. For example, it is ordinarily not feasible to sequester a jury for a long adjournment, and it would obviously be wasteful to discharge a jury after a case has been under way.

It has been argued that civil contempt should be used only when excluding the defendant from the trial is not authorized under the *Allen* requirement that the trial "cannot be carried on" with the defendant in the courtroom. It is true that when the *Allen* test is met and exclusion is authorized there is, strictly speaking, no need for civil contempt because the trial can proceed in the defendant's absence. This is a logical position but we believe it deprives a trial judge of needed flexibility in tailoring his responses to particular situations.

A judge should have the option of using civil contempt and an adjournment in cases of serious disorder, even where it would be proper to exclude a defendant from an ongoing trial. A short period of confinement may induce a defendant to cooperate and cease misbehaving. Then the trial can proceed in his presence—a highly desirable result. The trial can still be held in the defendant's absence if he persists in disruption.

While we think that civil contempt of a defendant, if used circumspectly, is a proper remedy for trial disruption, we take a different view of revocation of bail. This sanction should not be used. Although the effect may be the same as civil contempt if the trial is adjourned, bail revocation is surrounded by none of the latter's few procedural safeguards. Before civil contempt can be imposed, there must be a hearing and a specific order by the trial judge which is subject to appeal. By contrast, revocation of bail is entirely in the judge's discretion, and therefore open to abuse. Although bail revocation as a sanction has been used with approval, we believe that it is inconsistent with the spirit and perhaps the letter of the constitutional requirement of "reasonable bail" embodied in the Seventh Amendment.[67]

# Criminal Contempt as Punishment
# for Disorderly Conduct

The general rules authorizing criminal contempt are well established. Under federal law it includes any misbehavior in the court's presence which obstructs the administration of justice.[68] The Supreme Court has said that the criminal contempt power is needed to impose "silence, respect and decorum in [the court's] presence, and submission to [its] lawful mandates."[69] Thus, criminal contempt is appropriate to punish affronts to the authority of the court such as "acts threatening the judge or disrupting a hearing or obstructing court proceedings."[70]

In light of these precedents and the obvious needs of the judicial process, Justice Black approved criminal contempt as one appropriate sanction for courtroom disruption. In a passage in the *Allen* opinion he reviewed the strengths and weaknesses of this remedy. He first pointed out that "citing or threatening to cite a contumacious defendant for criminal contempt might in itself be sufficient to make a defendant stop interrupting a trial." But if a "defendant is determined to prevent any trial, the contempt remedy will not work and a court is still confronted with the identical dilemma that the Illinois court faced. . . ."[71]

The contempt remedy has shortcomings in addition to those referred to by Justice Black. As pointed out in a recent article,

> . . . imposing contempt charges, or threatening to do so, may prejudice the defendant if done in the presence of the jury much in the same manner that binding and gagging or excluding him may suggest the judge's disapproval.[72]

In view of these problems, it is not surprising that the Supreme Court has frequently cautioned in contempt cases that trial judges should use "the least possible power adequate to the end proposed."[73] We are reserving for full discussion in chapter 10 the procedural issues raised by the criminal contempt power. Here we shall concentrate on the conditions that justify its use and the severity and manner of the sentence or fine imposed.

It is often stated that four elements must exist in order to support a summary contempt conviction under the federal or equivalent state statutes.[74] There must be "misbehavior"; such misbehavior must be in the court's presence; it must "obstruct the administration of justice"; and there must be some sort of intent by the defendant to obstruct.[75]

Although the first two elements can be disposed of briefly, the other two raise questions that require some analysis.

## Misbehavior

Each of the five categories of misconduct mentioned at page 91 satisfies this element of contempt. Justice Black stated in *Illinois* v. *Allen*[76] that "it is essential to the proper administration of criminal justice that dignity, order, and decorum be the hallmarks of all court proceedings. . . ." Or, as recently put by the Court of Appeals for the Seventh Circuit, each participant must ensure that "a judicial proceeding is orderly, dignified, and confined to a rational search for truth in the context of defined legal issues."[77] Thus any action by a defendant, however slight, that interferes with the order or dignity of a court may properly be considered as "misbehavior."

## Proximity

In order for a contempt to be summarily punished the conduct must be in the court's presence.* He cannot rely on surmise and unproved assumptions. In the Tacoma Seven case, the trial judge cited one de-

---

* If the contempt is not in the court's presence, it still may be punished upon notice and hearing under Fed. R. Crim. Proc. 42(b). *See* page 230.

fendant for contempt for pounding on his door and five of the other defendants for refusing to come into the courtroom. The Ninth Circuit reversed.

> The defendants' refusal to come to the courtroom and Dowd's alleged misconduct at the door of the reception room were not punishable under Rule 42 (a) because they were not personally observed by the trial judge.[78]

## Obstruction

The Supreme Court has not finally clarified the meaning of "obstruction" under the contempt statute, and indeed it is not altogether plain that a person must "obstruct" judicial proceedings before he can be found in contempt. A large part of the difficulty can be traced to the statute itself. Section 401 of Title 18 of the United States Code and similar state laws authorize a court to punish such contempts of its authority as "(1) Misbehavior of any person in its presence or so near thereto as to obstruct the administration of justice."

This language does not make clear whether the requirement of an obstruction applies to both preceding clauses—that is, to misbehavior in the court's presence as well as misbehavior "so near thereto." The federal courts have uniformly construed it to apply to both clauses. The question is of considerable importance in determining whether passive disrespect of a court (failure to rise, etc.) and abusive language in the courtroom may be punished. Although these actions may not actually obstruct an ongoing judicial proceeding, they have been thought to be contemptuous,[79] and courts have had trouble in deciding whether they come within the contempt statute.[80]

The course of decision has been wavering. Two older cases ruled under a predecessor statute to Section 401 that conduct must "obstruct or halt the judicial process" before it amounts to contempt.[81] In those cases, the Supreme Court held that a witness may not be punished for contempt for perjuring himself on the stand because the falsehood does not constitute an "obstruction" in the performance of judicial duty. On the other hand, a later decision upheld a contempt citation against a witness who refused to answer questions on the mistaken ground that she was protected by the constitutional privilege against self-incrimination.[82] Finally, in 1962, the Court seemed to revert to its earlier approach by reversing the contempt of a lawyer for vigorous presentation of his client's case because he did not "in some way create an obstruction which blocks the judge in the performance of his judicial duty."[83]

In our judgment the key to these inconsistent holdings lies in the Supreme Court's deep and well-founded concern about the exercise of the power of summary contempt. Fearful of judicial arbitrariness, the

Court has tended, except in the self-incrimination case noted above, to construe the contempt statute narrowly. For example, in *In re Michael* the Court emphasized that the exercise of a broad contempt power by federal courts "would permit too great inroads on the procedural safeguards of the Bill of Rights, since contempts are summary in their nature. . . . It is in this Constitutional setting that we must resolve the issues involved."[84] Or as Justice Brennan has said, "[The] danger of abuse has required this Court closely to scrutinize these cases. . . ."[85]

To decide that certain conduct is punishable, however, does not mark the end of the inquiry for the trial judge. The more difficult question is whether to begin a contempt proceeding that can result in criminal punishment or rather to rely on the other more restrained means available to control misbehavior. As Justice Frankfurter has cautioned, judges must be alert to avoid an automatic conclusion that disrespect should be punished. "Trial courts . . . must be on guard against confusing offenses to their sensibilities with obstruction to the administration of justice."[86] In an effort to define the line between mere disrespect and obstruction, the Supreme Court held in another case:

> The fires which [the language] kindles must constitute an imminent, not merely a likely, threat to the administration of justice. The danger must not be remote or even probable; it must immediately imperil.[87]

A difficult issue is presented when a court attempts to impose a contempt penalty for disobedience of an order that later turns out to be erroneous. For example in the Bobby Seale case, the court of appeals found that the district judge erred in failing to inquire into the basis for Seale's dissatisfaction with his counsel of record other than Charles Garry. Seale argued that this error excused any possible contumaceous conduct on his part. The court of appeals disagreed, relying first on the rule that "the invalidity of a court order is not generally a defense in a criminal contempt proceeding alleging its disobedience."[88] Beyond that, with particular reference to disruptive courtroom conduct, the Seventh Circuit agreed with Justice Black's comment in *Illinois* v. *Allen* that courts are bound to make some errors, but these do not justify a defendant's introduction into the courtroom of "scurrilous or abusive language."[89] In *Allen* the defendant was insisting on Sixth Amendment rights, just as Seale was. It therefore appears that even an error regarding constitutional rights does not excuse contumaceous conduct.

## Intent

As in the case of the "obstruction" requirement, there has been considerable confusion about whether a conviction for contempt presupposes an intention on the part of the wrongdoer to interfere with the administration of justice or whether attention should be focused on the allegedly wrongful behavior to the exclusion of the accused's state of mind. Although we recognize that "intent" is sometimes said to be an essential element of any crime,[90] we think that in the context of contempt it is at best a distracting concept and at worst a misleading one.

Judicial decisions have been vacilating and even contradictory. The earliest discussion in the Supreme Court was in *In re Watts*,[91] a case of "indirect" contempt. There attorneys were cited by a federal court for falsely advising a state court concerning a pending federal court action, thereby obstructing the administration of justice and bringing the authority of the United States court into contempt. In reviewing the citations the Supreme Court asked the pertinent question:

> What evidence is there that these attorneys, or either of them, gave any advice or took any action in bad faith, not in the honest discharge of their duty as counsel, but with the *deliberate intent* to have the Federal court set at defiance and its orders treated with contempt?[92]

Finding no evidence of such deliberate intent, the Court reversed, noting that "the fearless discharge of their duty by the latter [attorneys] should not be shaken by liability to punishment for mere errors of judgment. . . ."[93]

The *Watts* decision did not resolve the intent issue. Some subsequent lower court cases either ignored or distinguished it. Thus, in one contempt case in which a lawyer allegedly communicated with a juror during a trial, the Ninth Circuit affirmed, holding that "it is not necessary to prove that the communication had or the acts done were accompanied with a wrongful intent."[94]

The Court of Appeals for the District of Columbia in 1956 adopted what amounted to a double standard. It distinguished between contempts involving "clearly blameworthy" conduct and those involving less serious conduct. Where the conduct is "clearly blameworthy" intent is not always a prerequisite for a conviction under §401 (1); where it is less serious, "there is not contempt unless there is some sort of wrongful intent."[95]

This double standard would obviously be difficult to apply in practice, and the District of Columbia circuit has retreated from it, saying more recently that "proof beyond a reasonable doubt that the alleged contemnor possessed the required intent must forerun a criminal conviction."[96]

We have said enough to indicate the absence of any clear judicial rule or principle regarding "intent" in contempt cases. This is not surprising in view of the enormous number and variety of mental states that are required for culpability in federal law generally. The Working Papers of the National Commission on Reform of Federal Criminal Laws found that "specifications of mental states form a staggering array."[97] The court of appeals in the Bobby Seale contempt action, aware of the confusion, rejected both the government's and Seale's suggested resolutions of the problem. The government had maintained that all that is needed to cause disruption is a volitional act, without regard to its known or intended consequences. This means that it is enough for a defendant to "know what he is doing so that his misconduct does not occur by accident, inadvertance or other innocent reason."[98] On the other side, Seale argued that the government must prove that he had a "vicious will" or a "culpable intent to obstruct justice" to support the contempt citation.[99]

The Seale court did not accept either polar position, taking instead as the proper standard for a contempt conviction "a volitional act done by one who *knows or should reasonably be aware* that his conduct is wrongful."[100] This is an objective standard that does not depend on a finding of subjective intent. At the same time, a person may not be convicted without a showing that he either knew or should have known that he was acting wrongfully. That he merely acted without accident or inadvertance should not be enough.

We think this is a sound approach. It incorporates a definition that should enable a trial judge to control his courtroom without subjecting those in it to unwarranted criminal punishment.[101] The *Seale* court cast its standard in terms of intent,[102] but the net effect of what it did was largely to eliminate the requirement of a "bad" mind by the accused. This is a salutary rule, similar in some respects to the First Amendment test of "reckless disregard," which was developed to determine when a person may be liable for defamation of a public official or public figure.[103]

The suggested standard does not mean that a "good faith" belief in the propriety of one's conduct will always be exonerating. In the *Seale* case the defendant tried to make a record for appellate review. The court of appeals did not reach the question whether he was acting in good faith in continuing to protest the ruling denying him a right to represent himself at trial. But it went on to say:

> . . . open defiance of the trial court's directives to desist or disruptive persistence beyond all bounds of propriety would not be justified merely because Seale may have entertained the belief that some protest was called for. Where there is such defiance or obstructive excess of persistence, belief in the necessity to register objections for the record may reduce the degree of culpability but does not exonerate.[104]

We agree with this analysis to the extent that it means that a person accused of contempt may be acting with subjective good faith and nevertheless go beyond the range of permissible courtroom conduct. On the other hand, where there is apparent good faith, a judge should be extremely careful before employing the contempt remedy, and should make ample use of warnings before taking action. In addition, the state of mind of the accused, as the Supreme Court recognized as long ago as 1925, should be considered in mitigation of the penalty imposed for contempt.[105]

# Effective Remedies for Particular Forms of Disorder

We turn now to the five types of disorderly conduct identified earlier in this chapter in order to suggest when criminal contempt or another sanction should be invoked.

## Passive Disrespect

Passive disrespect is a refusal to accord a judge the traditional and ceremonial respect, such as a refusal to address him as "Sir" or "Your Honor," to rise at the beginning or end of the court day, or to take off one's hat in the courtroom.

Witnesses who appeared before the Committee had different attitudes toward punishment of such conduct. Both judges and lawyers were divided. For example, one lawyer and one judge felt that it was important to enforce the ceremonial requirements, not only for their own sake but because a lowering of standards on these concededly minor infringements would invite more serious disturbances, to the detriment of the dignity of the court. Another judge viewed the failure to stand up and extend similar courtesies as "studied gestures of contempt."

Several lawyers and one federal judge took a different tack. They felt there was no real point in enforcing the ceremonial rules, and certainly not if it meant the punishment of a defendant. The judge said, "I don't believe that small passive disruption is of any significance." He went on to say:

> Some don't stand up out of ignorance. If you landed on them then you would merely embarrass them and probably force them into taking a defiant attitude. I think that these small problems should be handled much in the same way as you deal with children. There are just a lot of things you don't see. In that kind of situation I believe that it is just better not to see it.

In defining sanctionable conduct in the *Allen* case Justice Black bracketed the word "disrespectful" with "disorderly" and "disruptive"; he did not consider whether mere disrespect was punishable.[106] The only appellate court decisions that have discussed the question of punishment for passive disrespect have done so ambivalently. In the Chicago conspiracy case, the appellate court said that passive disrespect is not necessarily contemptuous. It wrote in *In re Dellinger*:

> Brief mention, however, must be made concerning those specifications which deal with the appellants' refusals to stand when court was convened and recessed. It is our opinion that such symbolic acts, when not coupled with further disturbance or disruption, might not rise to the level of an actual and material obstruction of the judicial process. In *United States ex rel. Robson* v. *Malone* [412 F.2d 848 (7th Cir. 1969)], we expressed "some doubt about the power of the court to require spectators to perform purely ceremonial or symbolic acts." While the per curiam opinion in *Malone* concluded that a court "may require such rising" and while we reaffirm that conclusion as to rising at the beginning of a session and end of a recess, we believe on remand some of the failures to rise here could be found non-obstructive. Such symbolic acts as cited here, when tested by the actual and material standard, do not necessarily alone amount to obstructions punishable as criminal contempt. Of course, where such an act is accompanied by some disturbance, disorder or interruption, an obstruction may exist.[107]

The *Malone* case referred to by the Seventh Circuit did not involve a disobedient defendant but two spectators in a courtroom. One refused to rise when a federal court opened in the morning even after the bailiff specifically requested her to do so. The judge directed the bailiff to take the woman into custody and stated that she was in summary contempt of court. The other spectator refused to rise when court adjourned for a recess. They were sentenced to jail terms of ten and thirty days. The court of appeals reversed because

> the record before us does not indicate that the two individual failures to rise were accompanied by any disturbance or that there were other circumstances by reason of which they tended to cause disorder, disturbance or interruption. . . .[108]

In effect, the court approved the sanction of exclusion for spectators who refuse to obey the ceremonial rules of court.

The problem of passive disrespect as it applies to spectators will be discussed in chapter 11. With respect to defendants, the judge in the celebrated Chicago conspiracy trial cited the defendants thirty-six times for contempt for not rising "in traditional manner" at the opening or close of the court day. We do not agree with this approach. Our conclusion is that on the first infraction a warning is necessary but neither exclusion nor the contempt sanction should be used. The mere repetition of the refusal to stand should not affect this result. The dignity and decorum of a courtroom does not turn on whether the defendant stands or addresses the judge as "Your Honor." There is, very simply, insuffiicent reason to exclude a defendant or to invoke the awesome power of contempt to cope with this petty form of disrespect.

Of course, if the "passive" conduct in fact amounts to a physical obstruction of the courtroom—for instance, if a defendant stands in the path of participants in the trial—a different problem is presented which will be dealt with below under the headings "Non-cooperation" and "Violence."

Judges should be, and apparently are, hardy enough to overlook minor affronts to their dignity. Of 1,056 judges responding to our questionnaire on how a judge should deal with passive insubordination by a defendant, 319 said it should be ignored and 216 said a warning or explanation should be given. Only 162 suggested contempt and 23 removal.

## Single Outburst

A defendant's isolated outburst or shout, whether or not it involves an obscenity, should not be punished by exclusion or criminal contempt. Since exclusion is a remedy designed to ensure that orderly proceedings continue, it seems excessive to deal with a single outburst. An appropriate warning should be given that continuous outbursts might lead to further sanctions.

So far as contempt is concerned, the Supreme Court recently had occasion to note that the expletive "M____ F____" directed at the trial judge "is of course reprehensible and cannot be tolerated."[109] But it did not reach the question whether that obscenity alone could be punished as contempt. In reversing a finding of contempt for a *different* outburst, in which the defendant said that the court had prejudged the case, the Court stated:

> There is no indication, and the State does not argue, that petitioner's statements were uttered in a boisterous tone or in any wise actually disrupted the court proceeding. Therefore, "The vehemence of the language used is not alone the measure of the power to punish for contempt. The fires which it kindles must constitute an imminent, not merely a likely, threat to the administration of justice. The danger must not be remote or even probable; it must immediately imperil. . . . The law of contempt is not made for the protection of judges who may be sensitive to the winds of public opinion. Judges are supposed to be men of fortitude, able to thrive in a hardy climate." *Craig* v. *Harney,* 331 U.S. 367, 376 . . . (1947).[110]

The lower courts have divided on this issue. Some have held that obscenities obstruct the proceedings and therefore can be punished as contempt.[111] Others have ruled that a single expletive in the emotional heat of a trial should not be punished. The latter view is supported by a decision reached by the Essex County Court in New Jersey in an incident involving LeRoi Jones.[112] During his trial for illegal possession of guns, Jones was cited for uttering "in an audible and disrespectful manner his disapproval of . . . [a] ruling by the Court by an epithet descriptive of excrement."[113] In reversing the contempt conviction on that count, the court said:

> While there is no reasonable doubt that the word was uttered by defendant, there is considerable doubt, particularly in light of the testimony of the witnesses for the prosecution on the subject, as to whether in the circumstances it was contumacious or obstructed or tended to obstruct the administration of justice.[114]

In agreeing with these latter decisions, we emphasize that a court need not permit a single obscenity or shout to pass unnoticed. As noted above, the court should immediately warn a defendant that further outbursts could lead to punishment, and if the circumstances warrant, inform him of the various remedies approved in the *Allen* decision. In some cases, a judge should consider whether the defendant's conduct indicates a disability suggesting that it would be appropriate to refer him to a doctor for a mental examination to ascertain his capacity to stand trial.

### Non-cooperation

The system of criminal justice depends upon voluntary compliance by the defendant with the basic rules of the trial. Even those accused of serious charges and facing long prison terms generally go along with the rules. One of the witnesses appearing before the Committee, Professor Richard Uviller of Columbia Law School, explained:

> There [is] on the part of defendants a remarkable passivity and acceptance of the judicial process, even by those who know that they will be convicted and sentenced to long prison terms or even death. This is especially remarkable since it has been so easy for a defendant to stop the whole proceeding by merely standing up when he should sit down, speaking when he should remain silent and in general not cooperating.

Nevertheless, the trial judges' questionnaires describe many cases in which cooperation was not forthcoming. In most of these, warnings or appropriate explanations by a judge were sufficient to obtain the defendants' compliance with the rules. Interestingly, contempt was found necessary in only one of these cases.

In a New Jersey case,[115] the judge wrote:

> Instances of defendants refusing to sit down without being forcibly seated, and thereafter a continuous period where defendants refused

to enter courtroom for trial and remained in jail. Defendant attempted
to leave courtroom and resisted officers, so that he had to be physically
subdued.

This occurred during voir dire examination of prospective jurors,
consuming many days. Three defendants on three separate indictments
were being tried jointly. The court ultimately severed two of the defendants and proceeded with one of the defendants, after which there
was no further difficulty.

Another type of refusal to abide by the basic ground rules occurs
where a defendant is dissatisfied with his lawyers and may seek to
defend himself.[116] A North Carolina judge described one such incident.[117]

Defendant was loud in denouncing counsel and refusing trial, standing
after being told to sit, and subsequently refused to answer any questions by the court.

Immediately excused all jurors. Advised defendant case was to be
tried, and that upon further disturbance I would order him bound and
gagged but proceed with trial (before U.S. Supreme Court ruling).
Directed court appointed counsel to continue representation.

Sometimes it appears that a defendant is refusing to proceed with
assigned counsel in an attempt to create reversible error by the judge
or to secure a mistrial. One trial judge commented on a case he
heard:[118]

Attempt by the defendant to frustrate and delay the trial in the case,
where the complaining witness was an 80-year-old woman. Further,
defendant attempted to create reversible error by refusing to proceed
with competent assigned counsel. His conduct continued for several
days.

Informed defendant of his rights: conferred with members of the defendant's family; protected defendant's right by directing assigned
counsel to remain and by advising defendant; granted a four-day adjournment for the opportunity to obtain new counsel with direction
that the original assigned counsel remain and assist the newly-retained
paid counsel.

These cases and others indicate that non-cooperation by defendants
ordinarily can be handled without use of the contempt power. Judges
should appreciate the strains on the individual defendant that can lead
to a stubborn and uncooperative attitude. But, as *Allen* states, the contempt remedy is an integral part of the trial judge's remedies and
"should be borne in mind."[119]

## Repeated Interruptions

Trial judges have used the *Allen* remedies for continued interruptions
of a trial. In our questionnaire material judges have imposed criminal
contempts against defendants for "shouts, abusive language to Court

and Jury" (thirty days);[120] for interrupting the attorneys (four days);[121] for protests against alleged "illegal" proceedings, including interruptions with "long rambling statements of protest and . . . irrelevant and verbose 'petitions' " (thirty days and $100 on each of three occasions);[122] for a "violent tantrum" (six months).[123]

On some occasions a trial judge imposed contempt penalties in conjunction with other remedies. For example, in one case,[124] after a defendant was brought into the courtroom, he "began to scream and shout." The judge "tried to calm him" and finally had him tied to a chair and threatened to gag him before the defendant behaved. A contempt sentence of six months was later imposed.[125]

In another case[126] contempt was combined with removal. After the closing argument each of two defendants "interrupted the State's Attorney by calling him obscene names, liar, etc., despite repeated warnings by the Court to desist." The judge removed the defendants and continued with the trial. Later he found them each guilty of contempt.

While contempt seems called for in many of these cases, in some of them trial judges seemed to impose excessive punishment. For example, for a single tantrum of "perhaps 10 to 15 minutes" after being found guilty of rape, a defendant summarily was held in contempt and sentenced to six months in jail.[127] In a similar case,[128] the defendants were sentenced to 120 and 150 days for calling the judge a "fascist" and stating in loud tones that they were "being railroaded."[129]

In both these cases less severe punishments and perhaps only a warning might have sufficed to achieve the ends of the court. This is borne out by the experience of other judges who showed greater restraint.

In the case of a defendant who was being tried for three counts of armed robbery, shooting with intent to kill, and auto theft, the trial judge showed unusual forbearance.[130] The disruption involved

> loud and obscene talk—fired lawyer 3 or 4 times—took 2 reporters to record his disruption for appellate court. Called the judge, his lawyer, the prosecutor, witnesses every name in the book.

The court dealt with the disturbance

> by not acknowledging the disruption by word or look. Requiring attorneys and witnesses to proceed as though it was not happening. Constant warning to the jury that they must determine the issue of guilt or innocence on the evidence and the law without regard to the conduct of the defendant.

There is no talismanic formula which will reveal when the contempt sanction should be applied and when it is unnecessary even in cases where it could properly be invoked. There is, in other words, no substitute for the insight of the individual judge. One judge, taking a rather punitive view after a trial in which a defendant had repeatedly disrupted the proceedings, put it this way: "Patience and fortitude, and contempt at end of trial."[131] The judge who restrained himself from employing the contempt remedy at the armed robbery trial took another view, which he summarized as follows:

> Now with Allen the Supreme Court has given us guidelines which will control the situation if patiently and prudently applied. Patience is the key word.

## Violence

There is no doubt that violence or the threat of violence by a defendant justifies the use of any of the *Allen* remedies including the contempt sanction, except perhaps where the conduct is the product of the defendant's emotional condition. The kidnapping and later killing of Judge Harold Haley in Marin County, California, in August 1970 is a shocking example of courtroom violence. In a notorious narcotics conspiracy case in New York City, two of the defendants engaged in various acts of violence which were punished by contempt.

> On one occasion Panico climbed into the jury box, walked along the inside of the rail from one end of the box to the other, pushing the jurors in the front row and screaming vilifications at them, the judge, and the other defendants. On another occasion, while the defendant Mirra was being cross-examined by the Assistant United States Attorney, Mirra picked up the witness chair and hurled it at the Assistant. The chair narrowly missed its target but struck the jury box and shattered.[132]

Similar cases were reported to us in the trial judges' questionnaires. In one case[133] the defendant "became wild and aggressive and attempted to attack the judge and other officers of court." He was summarily sentenced to five days in jail and a fifty dollar fine. In another case,[134] the defendant in a suit brought against him by the Missouri Highway Commission to enjoin a nuisance on his property assaulted the lawyers for the Commission, "knocked them down and chased them around." This court was more severe: after finding the defendant in contempt, it sentenced him to one year in jail and a $500 fine. Eventually the defendant served three months and paid a fine of $100, and submitted to a psychiatric examination at the request of the court.

In these cases lighter sentences were imposed on defendants for their violent behavior than for some of the merely verbal interruptions discussed above. In fact, in several cases of violence trial judges refrained altogether from invoking the contempt remedy although it doubtless would have been justified. In one such case the judge reported:[135]

> As soon as the guilty verdict [for armed robbery] was announced by the Clerk one of the defendants grabbed a chair and attempted to strike the Solicitor [Prosecutor] and the other defendant, as well as friends and relatives crowded inside the rail in an apparent effort to help the defendants escape as well as hurt the Court officials.

We express no opinion as to whether in the context of a particular trial the decision to eschew the contempt remedy is correct. Certainly it is within the discretion of the individual judge.

We do have reservations, however, about the possible use of a defendant's courtroom misconduct in connection with his trial for the substantive offense. For example, in one case reported to us, in which the defendant had been charged with aggravated battery with a gun, the trial judge wrote:

> The Defendant attacked complaining witness in presence of Court personnel as Court was beginning. Defendant was responsible and it lasted until the Sheriff had subdued the Defendant, approximately from five to ten minutes.
>
> The Defendant was not cited for contempt, *but the State's Attorney raised the question in his argument in aggravation of the conviction.* [Emphasis added.][136]

It is not clear what is meant by "argument in aggravation of the conviction," but whether it was argument on the defendant's guilt or innocence or on the appropriate sentence after conviction, we think it was improper. Whatever the appropriate remedy for courtroom disorder, it is plainly a distinct matter from guilt or innocence on the underlying criminal charge, and equally separate from the proper punishment for a conviction under the charge.

# Pro Se Representation and Disorderly Trials

Cases in which defendants choose to dispense with a lawyer and represent themselves—known as pro se cases—present special problems in the maintenance of order in the courtroom.

Pro se representation is a common phenomenon in the criminal courts.[137] The desire of defendants to defend themselves stems from varied motivations. Some believe they can do a better job than an assigned lawyer, or wish to speak personally to the judge or jury.[138] Others distrust lawyers and the legal process and wish to give vent to these hostile attitudes. It has also been suggested that some defendants harbor the hope that absence of counsel may afford a basis for reversal of a conviction regarded as inevitable.[139] Finally, some defendants may be mentally disturbed and irrationally persist in their own defense in ignorance of the value of defense counsel.

A substantial number of disorderly trials reported to us by the trial judges involved an aspect of pro se representation. In thirteen cases the defendant was representing himself, and in eleven others defendants tried to fire their lawyers so that they could act on their own. These cases covered a wide spectrum of crimes and types of trials. Some were typical criminal cases—murder, larceny, an attack on a prison guard. Others had political overtones—the burning of draft records and the disruption of a right-wing political parade. Some of them involved a single defendant; others several defendants. Some cases, such as Bobby Seale's and Lenny Bruce's, were notorious and received wide media coverage. Most were run of the mill and attracted no public attention. In all of them the trial judge had a difficult problem of judgment in deciding whether or not to allow the case to go to trial without a lawyer representing the defendant, and in determining how to handle disorderly situations when they arose.

Typical of these cases was a larceny case in Pennsylvania. The judge reported:

> When the defendant was brought into the court room for trial, he began to scream and shout—I tried to calm him—tried to get him to accept the appointment of counsel—finally I had him tied to a chair and I threatened to gag him. It took about ½ hour.[140]

Another disruptive trial was described as follows:

> Five defendants were indicted on three counts of armed robbery, one count of shooting with intent to wound and one count of larceny of a motor vehicle.
> At the very outset of the trial, his appointed attorney informed the court the defendant had fired him. Defendant yelled to the effect that he was a————lawyer. I quietly instructed his attorney he was to remain at the counsel table and protect the constitutional rights of the defendant.
> During the trial the defendant called me, the prosecutor, the police officers, witnesses and his attorney every name in the book and many I had not heard before. He fired his attorney at least three times a day.[141]

There is no doubt that most judges believe that disorder is more likely in cases in which a defendant chooses to represent himself. Of 1,056 responses to the questions on pro se representation in the judges questionnaire, 711 felt that pro se representation was more likely to lead to courtroom disruption than if counsel were retained to conduct the defense. Only 40 stated that it was less likely.[142] This explains the unhappiness of judges at the prospect of a pro se defense. Burton R. Laub graphically expresses this concern:

> Trying a case in criminal court with an unrepresented defendant is often like riding a tiger from which one dares not to dismount, and

many a trial judge supplements his crier's opening prayer with a mut-
tered supplication of his own, ". . . and, please, God, let there be no
unrepresented defendants in court today."[143]

The judges were asked to give reasons why they felt pro se representation was more likely to produce disruption. The responses were
as follows:

| *Number of Judges* | | *Number of Judges* | |
|---|---|---|---|
| 358 | pro se defendant unfamiliar with legal procedure and rules of evidence | 10 | same type of individual who would be likely to disrupt any trial |
| 45 | defendant is emotionally involved | 9 | defendant might commit unintentional disruptive acts |
| 43 | counsel would be able to quiet unruly defendant | 7 | defendant cannot appreciate full consequences of his action |
| 41 | defendant not subject to code of professional responsibility | 5 | difficulty of excluding defendant from courtroom when he is appearing pro se |
| 26 | the purpose of pro se defense is disruption | 144 | no answer |
| 12 | defendants who appear pro se have mental problems | | |
| 11 | gives defendant more opportunity to make speeches | | |

A number of judges elaborated on the principal reason for disruption
in pro se cases. A Colorado judge stated:

> [Disruption is] more likely because of the defendant's unfamiliarity
> with the rules of procedure and evidence. A defendant appearing pro
> se usually becomes frustrated and resentful when the Court has to sus-
> tain objections to improper questions and procedure.[144]

And a criminal court judge in New York stated:

> A defendant who is not an attorney and defends himself is too subjec-
> tively involved and therefore more likely to become emotional. He
> lacks an understanding of legal theory and logic and would have diffi-
> culty in understanding why evidence he seeks to introduce is excluded.
> This may lead him to indignant frustration.[145]

In view of the link between pro se representation and trial disorder,
it is important to examine the factual reasons and legal basis for allowing an accused person to defend himself, the recognized limitations on
this right, and the spectrum of remedies available to the judge seeking
to assure that a trial handled by the defendant is orderly.

## The Right to Pro Se Representation

The right to defend oneself without a lawyer is established in both the federal and state courts. On the federal level Section 1654 of the Judicial Code (Title 28) provides: "In all courts of the United States the parties may plead and conduct their own cases personally or by counsel. . . ." This provision had its origins in Section 35 of the Judiciary Act of 1789 and thus the right is coextensive with the existence of the federal judiciary.

The states have similar guarantees. No less than thirty-seven states provide in their constitutions for the right of a defendant to appear pro se.[146] Some of the state constitutions allow the accused to defend in person *and* by counsel; others grant the right to defend in person *or* by counsel; and others provide for the defendant's right to appear by himself, by counsel, or both. Where the right is not granted by the state constitution, generally a statute affords the same protection.

The reasons in favor of the right to a pro se defense were elaborated in a recent case.

> This right of an accused to defend himself, as we conceive it, rests on two bases. . . . He "must have the means of presenting his best defense," and to this end he "must have complete confidence in his counsel." Without such confidence a defendant may be better off representing himself. Moreover, even in cases where the accused is harming himself by insisting on conducting his own defense, respect for individual autonomy requires that he be allowed to go to jail under his own banner if he so desires and if he makes the choice "with eyes open."[147]

Despite these statements the Supreme Court has never held that a defendant in a criminal case has a constitutional right to defend himself. The Court has gone only so far as to say, in a decision upholding a conviction for murder in which the defendant pleaded guilty without the aid of a lawyer, that

> neither the historic conception of Due Process nor the vitality it derives from progressive standards of justice denies a person the right to defend himself or to confess guilt. . . . the Constitution . . . does not require that under all circumstances counsel be forced upon a defendant.[148]

Most of the lower federal courts have interpreted the right as constitutional in scope. For example:

> Under the Fifth Amendment, no person may be deprived of liberty without due process of law. Minimum requirements of due process in federal criminal trials are set forth in the Sixth Amendment. . . . Implicit in both amendments is the right of the accused personally to manage and conduct his own defense in a criminal case.[149]

A recent court of appeals decision held that whether or not the right is constitutionally mandated, it is a "fundamental right":

> In sum, whether or not the right of *pro se* representation has a constitutional foundation it is patently a statutory right, see §1654; this right was not only conferred by Congress in 1789 but has wide reverberation in organic state law and was recognized by Congress as a fundamental right. We conclude that this right must be recognized if it is timely asserted, and accompanied by a valid waiver of counsel, and if it is not itself waived, either expressly, or constructively, as by disruptive behavior during trial.[150]

Although the right to appear pro se may be "fundamental," it is well-established that it can be limited in some respects. For instance, trial judges have the power—indeed the duty—to ascertain carefully the defendant's intention to represent himself. This is usually justified on the ground that a decision to proceed pro se involves the "waiver" of the constitutional right to counsel, and accordingly a searching inquiry should be made to determine that it is "knowingly and intelligently" made.[151] For example, the Second Circuit, which has accepted the constitutional basis for pro se representation, nevertheless has stated that "there must be a record sufficient to establish to our satisfaction that the defendant knows what he is doing and his choice is made with eyes open."[152] The California Supreme Court, while also accepting the constitutional basis for pro se representation, has stressed the importance of a searching inquiry:

> [I]t is the very discrepancy between the legal skills of the layman and those of the licensed practitioner which fosters our deep concern to protect the right to the assistance of counsel against hasty and improvident waiver. . . . [I]n reviewing a trial judge's determination of a defendant's competence to represent himself, we will not accept a mere superficial inquiry.[153]

Other limitations have been imposed on a defendant's "right" to represent himself. For example, there may be circumstances where the interests of justice require that an individual be represented by an attorney because he is incompetent to represent himself.[154] That a defendant is mentally competent to stand trial does not necessarily mean that he is capable of defending himself.[155] The alertness and degree of intelligence a defendant needs to assist his lawyer are plainly less than those he would need to take on the burden of defense himself. As the District of Columbia Circuit has said:

> . . . there is a point of incompetency, where a defendant is able to understand the nature of the charges against him and to assist in the preparation of his defense, yet does not have the capacity to waive counsel and undertake representation of himself.[156]

In addition, a court may find in a joint trial that the interests of other defendants might be jeopardized by prejudicial statements of a defendant who is allowed to represent himself, and that severance is not practicable.[157]

The time at which a defendant seeks to act for himself is also important. Thus, a defendant ordinarily has a right to fire his appointed attorney before trial and take over the defense himself, even if the attorney committed no error and no prejudice can be shown.[158] On the other hand, in most jurisdictions a court may deny a defendant this right after the trial has begun. A Washington State court expressed the prevailing view:

> The right to defend one's self and the necessity of the defendant to have trust and confidence in his counsel are propositions which defendant can insist upon before trial is convened. However, when they are asserted during trial they are necessarily limited in extent by the necessity of having an orderly proceeding.[159]

One federal court has explained the interests a trial judge should consider:

> When the pro se right is claimed after trial has begun, the court exercises its discretion. It may weigh the inconvenience threatened by defendant's belated request against the possible prejudice from denial of defendant's request. In exercising discretion the judge may take into account the circumstances at the time, whether there has been prior disruptive behavior by defendant, whether the trial is an advanced stage. etc.[160]

The Second Circuit has also stated that a defendant "should not be allowed to manipulate his constitutional right to counsel in order to delay and disrupt the proceedings.[161] Accordingly, as Judge Friendly has pointed out, "Judges must be vigilant that requests for the appointment of a new attorney on the eve of trial should not become a vehicle for achieving delay."[162]

But it sometimes is error not to allow a defendant to take over his case. The Chicago conspiracy case is an illustration. There a large part of the disorder is traceable to Judge Hoffman's refusal to allow Bobby Seale to represent himself, a ruling later held to be erroneous on appeal. Seale sought to assume his own defense early in the trial. The court found he was already represented by counsel—William Kunstler—who had filed a general appearance on his behalf. Although Seale protested that he never consented to being represented by Kunstler, Judge Hoffman looked no further than the formal notice of appearance. The Seventh Circuit held that Judge Hoffman acted improperly in not inquiring further:

> [T]he trial court was put on notice when hearing the continuance motions on August 27 and September 9, and when conducting the pretrial proceedings on September 24, that Seale was dissatisfied with any counsel except Garry. Moreover, on September 26, at the earliest opportunity after the impanelling of the jury, Seale's pro se motion ad-

vised the court that he had relieved all other counsel of record for him in Garry's absence. Soon thereafter he attempted pro se to make an opening statement to the jury, thus reiterating his non-acceptance of these attorneys of record. Since Seale had amply indicated dissatisfaction with counsel, the trial court was under a duty to inquire into the subject. . . . Since the trial judge was bound to look into the basis of Seale's dissatisfaction with his lawyers of record apart from the hospitalized Mr. Garry, failure to do so was an abuse of discretion.[163]

The court of appeals indicated that Seale should have been allowed to represent himself, saying that

if the above facts regarding Kunstler's attorneyship were found true and Seale was found to be free of ulterior motivation, it would have been error for the trial court to force Kunstler's services upon Seale over his insistence on defending himself.[164]

We agree with this approach. Other courts have often said that a defendant has the right to take over the defense in the middle of the trial if no delay will occur and there is no likely prejudice to other defendants. The problem should be and generally has been handled by the courts in the same way as a defendant's request to replace his counsel with a different lawyer. If no delay or disruption occurs because of the substitution of lawyers, it should be allowed. But if unreasonable delay or other serious difficulty can be expected, then substitution may be denied.[165] What amounts to an unreasonable delay depends on the nature of the charge, whether codefendants are involved, and whether a jury is hearing the case. No mechanical rules can be established.

For two reasons, the Committee agrees with those who think that pro se representation should be discouraged. First, we do not believe that a layman is equipped, except in the rarest of cases, to handle a defense adequately. When the trial is particularly simple, or the defendant unusually intelligent and experienced, it may be otherwise. But in the overwhelming majority of cases, a lawyer can be of great assistance to the accused, and a trial judge acts responsibly when he tries to persuade the defendant to accept legal services.

Second, as the evidence shows, and as the trial judges surveyed point out (see pages 119–20), pro se cases do tend to become disorderly more frequently than those in which a lawyer handles the defense. As Chief Justice Burger has commented, "Laymen, foolishly trying to defend themselves, may understandably create awkward and embarrassing scenes."[166]

Although pro se representation should be discouraged, the possibility of trial disruption in such cases is an insufficient reason for rejecting the right altogether. In a case arising in the District of Columbia, the trial judge denied the right of seven defendants to act as their own lawyers on the ground that "there have been rumors that maybe some disruptive tactics [were] going to be employed."[167] However, the appellate court held that while disruptive tactics during the trial may be construed as a waiver of the right to appear pro se, the trial judge improperly assumed that such disorder would occur.

> In effect the unqualified right of self representation rests on an implied presumption that the court will be able to achieve reasonable coopera- tion. The possibility that reasonable cooperation may be withheld, and the right later waived, is not a reason for denying the right of self representation at the start.[168]

If a judge is concerned about possible disruption in a multi-defendant trial, his best tack may be to sever some of the defendants.

> In the last analysis, however, if the assertion of a pro se right makes a multi-defendant trial unmanageable, or unfair to the other defendants, the remedy lies in severance.
> But the joint trial that the prosecution seeks in the interest of effi- ciency cannot set aside the fundamental right of pro se representation. The trial judge must proceed by skill and suasion, by obtaining de- fendants' cooperation, not by denying their pro se rights.[169]

## Remedies for Assuring Order in Pro Se Cases

If a defendant insists on appearing pro se and meets the other require- ments of effective waiver and competence that are discussed above, a trial judge must be alert to ward off potentially disruptive situations and to deal with them sensibly when they arise. The first point to bear in mind, as the A.B.A. has stated, is that "a layman representing him- self cannot be held to the same standards of decorum or competence expected of a member of the bar."[170] A trial judge would be in error, therefore, if he failed to be flexible in responding to situations in the courtroom caused by pro se defendants.

A judge should be liberal in issuing warnings for improper state- ments, offering a certain amount of guidance and holding frequent bench conferences to explain to the layman-defendant the reasons for rulings on evidentiary matters. Moreover, although not all courts have followed this precept, we think that contempt should be imposed sparingly against a pro se defendant. This is not to say that a layman should be immunized from the court's control, but that a "defendant appearing pro se, who has more of a direct stake in the outcome (than a lawyer), must be allowed a great deal of leeway in venting his emo- tions in a zealous handling of the proceedings."[171] In this connection, it should be recalled that the Supreme Court has limited the authority of lower courts to mete out contempt citations to lawyers who are representing clients. As will be more fully discussed in the following

chapter, the Court has ruled that the "argument of a lawyer in presenting his client's case strenuously and persistently cannot amount to
contempt of court so long as the lawyer does not in some way create
an obstruction which blocks the judge in the performance of his judicial duty."[172] The rule should be even more evident in the case of a
layman acting as his own lawyer.[173]

The above approach is clearly called for when a pro se defendant is
not being actively disruptive. For example, in a Pennsylvania case[174]
a defendant on trial for armed robbery moved for the appointment of
new counsel to replace the voluntary defender. The judge relieved the
defender but refused to appoint substitute counsel. The following
colloquy ensued:

> *The Court:*   Now, Mr. Fletcher, do you have a pretrial motion to make
> at this time?
> *Leroy Fletcher:*   I will make them later.
> *The Court:*   You will make them now.
> *Leroy Fletcher:*   I will make them later.
> *The Court:*   It will be right now and not later.
> *Leroy Fletcher:*   I have nothing to say at this time, your Honor.
> *The Court:*   Very well. Your trial will start tomorrow morning with a
> jury. . . .
> *The Court:*   Mr. Fletcher, are there any witnesses you wish summoned
> in your behalf?
> *Leroy Fletcher:*   Nothing to say at this time.
> *The Court:*   You will say an answer of yes or no?
>
> *Leroy Fletcher:*   (No response.)
> *The Court:*   Answer me, yes or no?
> *Leroy Fletcher:*   (No response.)
> *The Court:*   I adjudge you in Contempt of Court and sentence you to
> one year in prison.[175]

The Supreme Court of Pennsylvania reversed the contempt, saying
that "we cannot expect a layman to interpret questions as if he were
an attorney. Certainly a layman who insists on representing himself. . . . cannot be held to the same level of competence as counsel,
nor can he be punished for not having legal knowledge at his fin-
gertips."[176]

Similarly, a California appellate court reversed a finding of contempt
against a pro se defendant, saying:

> It has frequently been held that even an attorney who is proceeding in
> good faith to urge on the court an erroneous view of the law cannot be
> held in contempt for so doing. . . . Here where a layman was attempt-
> ing, perhaps inadvisedly, to represent himself the same rule should
> apply with somewhat more latitude to be allowed to him because of his
> ignorance of the refinements of trial procedure.[177]

The court went on to conclude that the key question in determining whether the defendants was guilty of contempt was whether "this layman under the circumstances was acting contumaceously or other than in good faith."[178] This concern for the layman's motivation is consistent with rulings in other courts and with the finding of a judicial survey conducted by the *Georgetown Law Journal*. A majority of the judges responding believed that the disrupter's subjective state of mind should be taken into account in determining whether punishment is appropriate.[179]

An important remedial question is whether, and in what circumstances, a court should revoke permission for a defendant to proceed without the aid of a lawyer. The American Bar Association has suggested that when a layman is unable or unwilling to conduct an orderly defense, it is preferable to revoke such permission, after appropriate warnings, rather than to cite the defendant for contempt. It is certainly true, as the A.B.A. says, that contempt is usually inappropriate because the misconduct of a pro se defendant "will frequently be a blend of ignorance, emotional involvement, and mounting recognition of the inadequacy of the defense."[180] Nevertheless, we have concern about the possibility of moving too quickly to terminate the layman's right to represent himself.

Just as the *Allen* case held that a defendant's right to be present at his trial may be forfeited, so also the right to appear pro se can be lost by disruptive behavior.[181] Nevertheless, trial judges should insist on a substantial showing of disorderliness before acting to disqualify a defendant from acting on his own behalf. In addition, the judge should consider in each case whether the more appropriate remedy for disorder is a contempt citation. If the disorder engendered by a pro se defendant seems to result from incompetence or inexperience, revocation of the right to appear pro se would be proper. On the other hand, if the disorder suggests intentional obstruction of the proceeding or involves violence, a contempt citation is the preferable remedy.

It remains to consider in the pro se context the other *Allen* remedies of removal, binding and gagging, and civil contempt. Removal is inappropriate in pro se cases because the premise of that sanction is that the trial will go forward in the absence of the defendant. Obviously this remedy and binding and gagging are not possible if the defendant is conducting his own defense. Accordingly, removal is unavailable until the judge, in proper cases, terminates the pro se defense and appoints a lawyer; afterward, the rules governing this sanction should be the same as in the ordinary trial at which a lawyer is present.

Civil contempt and the related remedy of bail revocation are possible sanctions in pro se trials. As indicated earlier civil contempt may be used, for short periods and with the reservations already stated, to try to persuade a disorderly defendant representing himself to behave properly. Bail revocation is, in our judgment, an improper technique for controlling the conduct of pro se as well as other defendants.

A large majority of judges that were polled recommended that a standby counsel be appointed to assist laymen intent on representing themselves. It is well established that a court may appoint such advisory counsel,[182] but at the same time there is no requirement that this be done.[183] The standby counsel should respond to questions from the accused, and also call the attention of the court to matters favorable to the accused and overlooked by him. But it is not his responsibility to examine witnesses or otherwise take an active part in the trial. Nor should the standby counsel, except to the extent necessary, interfere with the defendant's treatment of the case or say anything that might embarrass the defendant because of his inexperience in the judicial forum.

Despite this circumscribed responsibility, the standby counsel is important. His availability to assist the defendant means that the rights of the accused will receive protection. These rights, as the A.B.A. has stressed, are "a matter of public interest even if the accused has rejected professional assistance."[184] In addition, experience has shown that the presence of standby counsel will often persuade a defendant to abandon a pro se defense and rely on representation by the standby. Similarly, if the occasion should arise when permission to proceed pro se is revoked, the standby is available to act.

Chief Justice Burger, concerned that the Sixth Amendment right of a pro se defendant will be violated if an attorney unfamiliar with the case assumes control of the defense after the exclusion of the defendant, has recommended that courts *always* appoint standby counsel.[185] In our view, such counsel should be appointed, at the very least, in all cases expected to be long or complicated or in which there are multiple defendants.[186]

## Trial Participation by Defendants Represented by a Lawyer

A question closely related to pro se representation which arises frequently concerns defendants who are represented by a lawyer but nevertheless wish to participate in conducting the case. Except in a few states[187] where a defendant may make a personal statement to the jury that is not subject to cross-examination, it is established that a defendant has no legal right to participate in his defense.[188] Thus, a judge may refuse to allow a defendant to cross-examine witnesses or to address the bench or jury.[189]

The reasons for this rule are ordinarily stated in highly general terms.

For example, in one federal case the court said that its purpose was to

> maintain order, prevent unnecessary consumption of time or other un-
> due delay, to maintain the dignity and decorum of the court and to
> accomplish a variety of other ends essential to the due administration
> of justice.[190]

A more specific but no more persuasive reason for denying a defendant the right to participate in his trial was stated by Learned Hand
in the 1948 Communist conspiracy case. The trial judge had refused
to permit Benjamin Davis, a leader of the party, to fire his lawyer at
the end of the trial and sum up to the jury himself. In affirming this
ruling, Judge Hand said that a defendant should not be permitted "to
make a flaming address to the jury which would have reverberations
not only inside but outside the courtroom."[191] We believe that the possible impact of the defendant's statement on the public is an inadequate ground to deny him the right to speak in his own defense.

In recognition of the weakness of the view that denies a litigant a
right both to have counsel and to actively participate in his trial, a
number of courts have exercised their discretion to permit hybrid
representation. A California court summed up this view by saying that
a litigant should not be permitted to examine witnesses, interpose
objections, or argue a point of fact or law, "unless the court on a substantial showing determines that . . . the cause of justice will thereby
be served and the orderly and expeditious conduct of the court's
business will not thereby be substantially hindered, hampered or
delayed."[192]

In one federal case, the trial judge permitted defendant to act as
co-counsel for all purposes:

> A careful reading of the record convinces us that appointed counsel was
> able, diligent and faithful, and that his participation in the trial cer-
> tainly did not prejudice Juelich. Indeed, Juelich himself was freely per-
> mitted to assign additional grounds for his motion to vacate, to testify
> at length in his own behalf, to ask questions of the witnesses, and to
> argue his contentions. He thus had the benefit both of his counsel's
> services and of his own direct participation in the hearing.[193]

In other cases, a defendant has been allowed to cross-examine.

> The court then appointed counsel but made it clear that this counsel
> would participate in the trial only to the extent that appellant desired.
> Appellant said that he wanted counsel to fully represent him, except he
> himself was to have the right, after his counsel had cross-examined wit-
> nesses, to himself further cross-examine them. The court permitted this
> unusual arrangement, the appellant expressed his complete agreement
> with it, it was followed throughout the trial, and the appellant made no
> complaint about its operation. He was thus allowed to represent himself
> to the extent that he desired to do so.[194]

In other cases, the defendant was allowed to make any statement he wished to the court outside the presence of the jury,[195] and in a Smith Act case involving Communist party leaders in Pennsylvania, the judge permitted the defendants to open and close to the jury.[196] In such cases the prosecutor may wish to state to the jury that the defendant is speaking as a lawyer and that his assertions of fact are therefore not entitled to the same weight as sworn witnesses. We see no constitutional or other objection to such comment by the prosecutor.[197]

In the 1972 trial of Angela Davis in San Jose, California, for conspiracy and murder growing out of the San Marin County courthouse shooting in August 1970, she was permitted to act as cocounsel. She questioned some of the prospective jurors during the *voir dire,* argued parts of some of the pretrial motions, and made an opening statement to the jury. Apparently her participation did not interfere with the flow of the proceedings in any way.

Viewed as a whole it is rare that defendants with lawyers have been permitted an opportunity to participate in trials, and the practice has been described as "undesirable."[198] But there is no question that a trial judge has the discretion to allow a litigant to participate to any extent that is thought necessary. We see no reason of principle to deny litigants this opportunity so long as no duplication occurs and there is no delay or disruption of the proceedings.

In determining whether to allow a litigant to participate, a trial judge should of course take into account the views of defense counsel. He should give weight, for example, to an objection that a statement by the defendant may interfere with the lawyer's trial strategy.

# CHAPTER SEVEN

# *Regulating the Conduct of Defense Attorneys*

A large percentage of the public and many members of the legal profession associate courtroom disruption primarily with the misconduct
of defense lawyers, rather than defendants, prosecutors, or judges. A
1971 article in a national magazine written by a Yale law professor
begins by stating:

> A highly visible and audible section of the defense bar (with the un-
> intended cooperation of a few judges) seems to have set out to demon-
> strate, by turning trials into combinations of political rally and five-ring
> circus, that the adversary system of criminal justice . . . is unworkable.[1]

The American College of Trial Lawyers Report focuses primarily on
the transgressions of defense lawyers, and many speeches by judges
and others on the problems of disruption are devoted to what should
be done about lawyers' conduct, often without mention of others who
might be responsible.[2]

One reason for this emphasis is that the defense attorney has tremendous responsibility for making the legal process operate properly.
In addition, the legal profession is largely self-disciplined. Accordingly,
misconduct by its members produces, as it should, great concern in
leaders of the bar. But unless proper perspective is achieved on the
extent and degree of that kind of courtroom disorder, there is danger
that the profession will overreact to this problem and establish rules
and procedures that may threaten the independence and vigor of
the bar.

The incidence of courtroom disorder by defense attorneys is small.[3]
The 1,602 returns of the trial judges questionnaire produced only eight
cases of defense lawyer misconduct out of 112 reported cases of disruption. Even in these some of the misconduct was minor. In one case
from Colorado, the judge reported:

> Defense counsel called detective a "liar" out of presence of jury. Admonished by me. In open court counsel refused to accept a ruling until warned to sit down.[4]

A California judge reported on two separate cases:

> Repeated (for 11 weeks) bickering between lawyers—loud laughing, paper rustling to drown out answers of witnesses, slamming books on table, etc.
> Repeated admonition in chambers and finally citations for contempt.[5]

In the second case:

> Repeated interruption of court's statements, misstatements to jury, failure to obey procedural rules of court.
> Repeated admonition and threat of sanctions.[6]

The United States attorneys reported no cases of lawyer misconduct to us and the district attorneys reported misconduct by only two lawyers.

The number of reported cases of lawyer misconduct that led to a contempt citation or disciplinary action by a bar association is small. From 1960 to 1972, a period of twelve years, there were seventeen cases reported in which such sanctions were upheld by appellate courts in the fifty states and the federal system. Considering that there may be about 100,000 criminal jury trials each year and hundreds of thousands of non-jury trials and civil cases, the amount of punished misconduct by lawyers is not significant.

For the most part these incidents, like the cases described above, involved a different type of misbehavior from that of defendants. It is extremely rare for a lawyer to commit physical acts of violence in the court, or for him to refuse to come into the courtroom, or to shout, curse, or interrupt the proceedings by embarrassing or insulting remarks. The type of lawyer misbehavior that has been punished by contempt or other sanctions almost always involves forensic misconduct—verbal arguments with the judge, failure to obey court orders or the basic procedural rules of the judicial process, for example by repeating arguments or questions that have already been rejected by the court or trying to introduce evidence that has been ruled inadmissible.

These actions disrupt a trial not by producing anger and contention or lowering the dignity of the proceedings, but by making it more difficult for a trial to be completed in accordance with established rules of the legal process. The judicial system rests in part on mutual trust between lawyers, prosecutors, and judges. Each is given important privileges and great latitude in performing his task and does so with a minimum of supervision or policing by the others. In most cases documents are handed over, witnesses produced, and information exchanged without the need for compulsory process. Lay people are often surprised at the extent of good faith that exists between prosecutor and defense lawyer in criminal matters or between opposing counsel in a civil case.

The actual conduct of a trial depends on such trust and on mutual recognition of the importance of each role in the process. Rules of procedure show what is expected of each party and each does his job on the assumption that the others will follow these procedures.[7] The process has its problems. It has always been difficult to balance the need for vigorous advocacy by a lawyer with the need for defined procedures that try to channel the arguments and evidence as efficiently as possible. Unnecessary contention by a lawyer or a prosecutor as well as a judge's inability to guide the presentation of a case properly means that the process is in danger of breaking down not only to the derogation of the rights of litigants but also to the detriment of the society that depends so much on a fair, dispute-settling judicial system.

# The Responsibilities of a Lawyer

Just as a trial involves a difficult balancing operation among the efforts of prosecutor, defense attorney, and judge, each must himself reconcile different responsibilities and duties. A defense lawyer must be concerned with three distinct obligations: to his client, to the court, and to the larger society that the courts are serving.

## Responsibility to the Client

The defense lawyer's primary role, as laid out by the American Bar Association's Standards Relating to the Prosecution Function and the Defense Function, is that of "champion of his client."

> Part 1. General Standards. . . . [The Defense Function]
> 1.1(b) The basic duty the lawyer for the accused owes to the administration of justice is to serve as the accused's counselor and advocate, with courage, devotion and to the utmost of his learning and ability, and according to law.[8]

The lawyer acts as the defendants' counselor in the broadest sense, advising him not only in the law but with respect to all aspects of problems facing him—what the probable consequences of certain trial strategies would be, whether or not it would be advisable to plead guilty. The A.B.A. Standards state:

> Another function of the lawyer is as his client's "learned friend," his counsel in the literal sense. The defense lawyer often may be the only

person to whom the defendant can turn in total confidence, once a proper relationship exists, to explain fully his position, which may be incriminating, even though he is in law not guilty of the crime charged. The defendant needs counsel not only to evaluate the risks and advantages of alternative courses of action, such as trial or plea, but also to provide a broad and comprehensive approach to his predicament which will take the most advantage of the protections and benefits which the law affords him.[9]

Devoted service does not mean that the lawyer must do whatever his client wants him to do. The A.B.A. Standards explain:

> From time to time over the past one hundred years or more, in both England and America, an occasional voice is raised advocating what has come to be known as the "alter ego" theory of advocacy. The thesis depicts defense counsel as an agent, permitted, and perhaps even obliged, to do for the accused everything he would do for himself if only he possessed the necessary skills and training in the law; in short, that the lawyer is always to execute the directives of the client. This spurious view has been totally and unequivocally rejected for over one hundred years under canons governing English barristers and is similarly rejected by canons of the American Bar Association and other reputable professional organizations. It would be difficult to imagine anything which would more gravely demean the advocate or undermine the integrity of our system of justice than the idea that a defense lawyer should be simply a conduit for his client's desires.[10]

This issue is important for the problem of courtroom misconduct. If a client insists on his attorney's insulting the prosecutor or judge, asking improper questions, making irrelevant speeches, or introducing extraneous matters into the proceedings, the lawyer must reject those instructions. A lawyer may not excuse his own professional misconduct on the ground that his client demanded it.

Although a lawyer's task is to use his professional skills as ably as he can in the courtroom on behalf of those he defends, that does not mean that there is an identity between the lawyer and the client or the client's cause. Many members of the public often identify the two and assume that every lawyer defending a Communist or a Black Panther or a Ku Klux Klan member follows the same political ideology as his client. Many lawyers representing alleged Communists in the early 1950s found that they were subject to professional pressure and loss of business. Civil rights attorneys in the South during the early 1960s faced not only harassment by local courts and bar groups but threats of violence against themselves and their families.[11] Such a development helps neither the client nor the administration of justice. Nor does it contribute to order in the courts, since it makes it more difficult for defendants to obtain counsel.

Conversely, lawyers who do identify with their client or his cause are not, by that token, undesirable members of the bar and therefore subject to sanction or public censure. It has been claimed that one reason for the allegedly increased contention or misconduct in the courts by defense attorneys is that many lawyers representing public interest or radical clients have too strong an emotional bond with them and lack the detachment necessary to perform the lawyer's function. They may react too angrily to adverse rulings or urge improper defenses in their sympathetic efforts to win the case. The A.B.A. Standards lend some support to this position when they suggest that "emotional detachment" is a desirable feature of a defense lawyer.

> As in other contexts of human endeavor, the intermediary brings to the controversy an emotional detachment which permits him to make a more dispassionate appraisal. He translates the desired course of action into those steps which the form and procedure of the system permit and professional judgment dictates. He channels the controversy into the established mode of legal procedure and deals with the other participants in the process—the prosecutor, the judge—on the level of professional understanding of the rules and their respective roles. When the lawyer loses that detachment by too closely identifying with his client, a large measure of the lawyer's value is lost; indeed he then suffers some of the same disabilities as an accused acting as his own counsel.[12]

There is a question whether there has been any change in the lawyer's attitude toward his client. One Yale Law School professor has been quoted as stating that there is no essential difference in this regard between the new community service lawyer and the private attorney. "When I was in Davis, Polk in Wall Street, and we represented U.S. Steel, we used to identify with them just like all get out." Prosecutors who emotionally identify with their client—the state— have seldom been criticized for doing so.

Many young lawyers have joined public interest law firms because of their strong attachment to social justice and economic equality. They are performing a vital task in our society by representing members of disadvantaged groups.[13] Many of them may come to feel that they are representing a cause or a movement rather than an individual. A recent study prepared under the auspices of the American Bar Foundation discusses this problem.

> The lawyer cannot avoid seeing his role and even his skills in terms of the clients he serves. This is true for the public interest lawyer, the public lawyer, and the traditional private lawyer. It is a function of his loyalty and his training. To the extent that the public interest lawyer serves clients he has not previously served, the needs of these clients, the nature of their problems, and the demands that they make are bound to affect—extend—his view of his role. The lawyer in the public interest law firm and in the public interest section of the traditional law firm is necessarily reshaping his view of his role. . . .
> The public interest clients "educate" the lawyer. He is exposed to new problems. He learns a new language. And he may develop a sensitivity to the needs of those clients.
> . . . As the public interest lawyer builds up and provides service for a

regular clientele, thoughtfulness leads him to see that particular problems are common to many clients; inevitably he begins to serve as a
lawyer for the situation.[14]

Certainly any increase of this sensitivity which may help a lawyer
better understand the needs of his clients is a positive development.
As a general proposition, any understanding or sympathy that an
attorney may have for his client that allows him to do a better job
without violating his professional duties or that adds to a client's confidence in him is beneficial to the system. Sir Thomas Erskine, the
great English barrister, said in 1792 during his defense of Thomas
Paine for seditious libel:

> If an advocate entertains sentiments injurious to the defence he is en-
> gaged in, he is not only justified, but bound in duty, to conceal them;
> so, on the other hand, if his own genuine sentiments, or any thing con-
> nected with his character or situation, can add strength to his profes-
> sional assistance, he is bound to throw them into the scale.[15]

We have previously pointed out that some courtroom disorder results from a defendant's dissatisfaction with his court-assigned lawyer.
If more competent criminal attorneys were available and were paid
enough to accept such assignments, this problem might be greatly
reduced. A client who has confidence in his attorney and feels he is
being properly represented is more likely to listen to his lawyer's
recommendations or respond to his suggestions on how he should
behave himself in the courtroom. If a defendant is represented by
someone in whom he does not have faith, the danger of trial disruption is greatly increased.

Whatever the nature of "emotional attachment" between lawyer
and client, it is basically irrelevant to the issue of professional responsibility. A lawyer may freely choose to represent only those he
loves or those he hates, or those who pay him the most money. He may
think of himself as representing an individual, a group, or a cause.
A client may choose an attorney for his competence or his politics or
his good looks. But inside the courtroom the lawyer has a defined role
that he must follow regardless of his emotional feeling toward the
client or his cause.

## Responsibility to the Court

Bar associations have continuously tried to define the professional re-
sponsibilities of attorneys inside and outside the courtroom. The
Canons of Professional Ethics were adopted by the American Bar
Association in 1908 and by almost all state bar associations in succeed-
ing years. An overhaul of these rules was completed in 1969 when the
A.B.A. adopted a new Code of Professional Responsibility.[16] In addi-

tion, every major bar association has a committee on professional ethics which passes on specific questions that are presented to it. The opinions of these committees are considered authoritative decisions on what a lawyer should or should not do within their respective jurisdictions.[17]

Despite all the attention devoted to forensic conduct, there is comparatively little discussion about what a lawyer may or may not do in the courtroom. The Code of Professional Responsibility has only one disciplinary rule dealing with trial conduct.* The A.B.A. Standards on the Defense Function also contain rules relevant to courtroom conduct.

There are a number of points worth noting about DR 7-106 and the A.B.A. Standards. In the first place, many of the matters covered are obvious propositions that are not central to a lawyer's responsibility to the court.

Secondly, some of the rules—those relating to the presentation of irrelevant matters or inadmissible evidence in court—are often violated. Many trial lawyers try to present such evidence to a jury if they think it will be beneficial to their client. They are frequently admonished by a judge but seldom if ever disciplined for doing so.

Thirdly, the rules do not tell a lawyer much about what he may or may not do in court. They emphasize that a lawyer must be courteous

---

* DR 7-106 Trial Conduct.

(A) A lawyer shall not disregard or advise his client to disregard a standing rule of a tribunal or a ruling of a tribunal made in the course of a proceeding, but he may take appropriate steps in good faith to test the validity of such rule or ruling.

(B) In presenting a matter to a tribunal, a lawyer shall disclose:

(1) Legal authority in the controlling jurisdiction known to him to be directly adverse to the position of his client and which is not disclosed by opposing counsel.

(2) Unless privileged or irrelevant, the identities of the clients he represents and of the persons who employed him.

(C) In appearing in his professional capacity before a tribunal, a lawyer shall not:

(1) State or allude to any matter that he has no reasonable basis to believe is relevant to the case or that will not be supported by admissible evidence.

(2) Ask any question that he has no reasonable basis to believe is relevant to the case and that is intended to degrade a witness or other person.

(3) Assert his personal knowledge of the facts in issue, except when testifying as a witness.

(4) Assert his personal opinion as to the justness of a cause, as to the credibility of a witness, as to the culpability of a civil litigant, or as to the guilt or innocence of an accused; but he may argue, on his analysis of the evidence, for any position or conclusion with respect to the matters stated herein.

(5) Fail to comply with known local customs of courtesy or practice of the bar or a particular tribunal without giving to opposing counsel timely notice of his intent not to comply.

(6) Engage in undignified or discourteous conduct which is degrading to a tribunal.

(7) Intentionally or habitually violate any established rule of procedure or of evidence.

and dignified and obey local customs or established rules or procedure without defining what they might be. There is no attempt to establish or define or point to universal rules of conduct for all lawyers in all courts. Nor do local court rules define such proper conduct. They generally tell a lawyer when he must file certain papers and what the form of his brief should be. But they do not tell him how to behave once he enters the courtroom.

Some jurisdictions have propounded specific rules for the proper conduct of a lawyer in court. The rules approved by the Conference of California Judges are printed below.*

Some of these rules are common-sense, others are quite petty. They are suggested rules of etiquette rather than definitive rules of conduct, and therefore should be considered an ideal standard of how a lawyer should behave in court rather than a minimum code of conduct whose violation may lead to a contempt citation or disciplinary action.

In a 1971 case decided by the Michigan Court of Appeals, a trial judge had laid down strict rules on proper procedure to be followed in his court. They included the following requirements:

1. Neither counsel shall interrupt the judge while the judge is speaking;
2. No motions will be made in the presence of the jury, except to strike testimony or to instruct the jury to disregard or for other good cause;

* Section 3. CONDUCT OF ATTORNEYS:

(a) Attorneys should arise and remain standing while addressing the court or a jury, except in the case of an objection or statement of only a few words.

(b) Attorneys should address the court from their position behind the counsel table or from a lectern.

(c) Attorneys should examine witnesses from their position behind the counsel table, and may properly, at their option, be seated or standing. Where a lectern is provided, counsel desiring to stand should stand at the lectern. With the court's permission, it is proper to approach witnesses who are hard of hearing or when handling exhibits, or to stand at the blackboard when questioning concerning a map or diagram. This suggestion should be observed in all proceedings, including default and probate matters.

(d) Attorneys should not, in addressing the jury, crowd the jury box nor address the jury in a loud voice or in an undignified manner. When a lectern is provided, attorneys should address the jury from the lectern. . . .

(f) Attorneys should be impersonal toward the Court and should address the Court in the third person, as "The Court will remember the testimony," not, "You will remember." When the judge is on the bench, he may be addressed as "Your Honor," but he should never be addressed as "You" or "Judge." Counsel should invite, not "direct," the Court's attention. The proper form of an opening statement or argument should be "May it please the Court," not, "If the Court please."

(g) The trial attorney should refrain from interrupting the Court or opposing counsel until the statement being made is fully completed, except when absolutely necessary to protect his client's right on the record, and should respectfully await the completion of the Court's statement or opinion before undertaking to point out objectionable matters. When objection is made to a question asked by him, he should refrain from asking the witness another question until the court has had opportunity to rule upon the objection.

(h) All objections and arguments should be made to the Court rather than to opposing counsel.

3. No motion for mistrial shall be made in the presence of the jury;
4. No facetious question will be asked or facetious remark will be made;
5. Neither counsel shall address each other, or the jury except, of course, upon argument at the conclusion of the case;
6. Any counsel who wishes to object to testimony shall state that he objects and then state succinctly the reason for the objection. Grounds for the objection must be stated with perspicuity.
7. After the court has ruled on any matter, neither counsel shall argue that same matter or again object to the same matter.

A lawyer was cited and convicted for 106 separate violations of these rules. But the Michigan Court of Appeals reversed all the convictions.

> There is no room in our system of justice for inflexible rules of conduct. In applying the generally observed norms of conduct, a judge must make a balanced value judgment case-by-case. This cannot be avoided by a mechanical approach, with rigid commandments, inflexible administration and automatic contempt citations for those who stray across the line.[18]

The fact is that proper rules of professional courtroom conduct are for the most part undefined. Most courts go on the assumption that lawyers should know what they may properly do. Justice White of the Supreme Court expressed the prevailing point of view in a case involving out-of-court conduct by a lawyer.

> . . . members of a bar can be assumed to know that certain kinds of conduct, generally condemned by responsible men, will be grounds for disbarment. . . . all responsible attorneys would recognize [certain conduct] as improper for a member of the profession.[19]

The vagueness of this standard has been noted in a Kentucky case involving the suspension of a lawyer for in-court behavior. The state court of appeals pointed out that the operative words in the canons and rules were vague and uncertain.

> If the canons of ethics adopted for the legal profession were tested under the "void for vagueness" doctrine which has spelled the doom of various breach of peace and disorderly conduct laws throughout the country it is doubtful that they would survive this case. What is "fair and honorable," "a respectful attitude," "candor and fairness," or "chicane" must depend very largely on the subjective point of view of the person or persons making a judgment after the fact. Obviously we do not all have the same sense of propriety. It is interesting to note, for example, the chairman of the trial committee's comment that "you all live in a legal jungle down here."

The court then pointed out that the lawyers in the lower criminal courts—"jungle-fighters" in the words of the court—have a different notion of what constitutes proper conduct from other members of the profession.

> It may well be that the standard of decorum usually prevailing in the sedate precincts of chancery should also be observed by the jungle-fighters in the pit of police and criminal courts, but it would be some-what less than realistic to assume that the advocate who practices exclusively in one of these two worlds will have the same conception of what is expected of him as the lawyer who confines his practice to the other. We do not mean to suggest that there should be two different sets of rules. On the contrary, there can be only one. But when the rules are loosely couched in terms of high principle, as are the canons, there is room for differences of opinion, hence the distinct possibility that they do not provide sufficiently explicit "no trespassing" signs for those who may approach the invisible line of proscription.[20]

One law professor told us that the "canons are as much use to a practicing attorney in the courtroom as a valentine card would be to a heart surgeon in the operating room."[21]

In some ways it is paradoxical that a profession that insists on the need for definitive rules to regulate other people's conduct has generally failed to establish rules to regulate the conduct of its own members in court. But as the Michigan Court of Appeals indicated in the case noted above, there is something to be said in favor of the absence of defined rules. Many lawyers have different styles of presenting a case. They may question witnesses, submit their evidence, cross-examine, or argue to the judge in a variety of ways. Telling a lawyer exactly how he must perform in court may impose too great a restriction on his performance. Situations may arise that require unorthodox responses. A lawyer should be given some leeway in the vital task he is performing in defense of those charged with a criminal offense. Dean Albert M. Sacks of the Harvard Law School told us: "If you tell me exactly how a professor should conduct his classes, I'll tell you exactly how a lawyer must act in the courtroom."

What these considerations mean for our purposes is that a lawyer's responsibility to the court is defined in the most general way: he must be courteous, dignified, and honest while he vigorously defends his client. He must not be disruptive or disorderly. He must obey the orders of the court. We shall see below how these requirements are applied in the actual trial.

## Responsibility to the Public Interest

American lawyers are more concerned and involved with great social and political issues than are lawyers in almost any other country. In England, for example, the organized bar (composed of about 2,000 barristers) resembles a club and is "remote from the concerns and passions of ordinary life."[22] A distinguished English solicitor, Lord Goodman, has said that "the [English] Bar has a coy terror of the human race."[23] This may be the reason for its admirable decorum and the fact that so few lawyers are ever disciplined for misbehavior in court.[24]

By contrast, American lawyers are more passionate about many of the important cases that they argue. Anthony Lewis explains:

> Because the function of the American lawyer is different, he cannot be expected to have the same degree of detachment. Perhaps in theory one ought to be able to argue a case about the fourteenth amendment and capital punishment with the same detachment as one about a commercial contract. But in the real world, lawyers who are engaged in great social and political issues must be more committed than would be appropriate in the Strand. I do not regret that. I feel as Professor Benjamin Kaplan of Harvard evidently did after a year in London observing that legal system. "The American scene is disordered," he wrote, "but it it is lively."[25]

In addition, the legal profession has come to recognize a new definition of its responsibility to the public interest, and more and more attorneys are devoting either full time or part time to what has been called *pro bono publico* work. Thousands of lawyers have engaged in public service in legal aid, neighborhood legal services, or civil rights causes, which have sharpened the lawyer's awareness of his own responsibility to promote equal justice to the poor and disadvantaged. This development involves not just the small group of lawyers who make *pro bono* work their chief occupation but many lawyers in the private sector who have been devoting part time to such work. Justice William J. Brennan, Jr., said at the Harvard Law School in 1967:

> An institutional framework designed for the service of the law's traditional clients, with their ready access to legal services, cannot now satisfy the profession's responsibility to the client born of more recent social upheavals, a task that implicates quite different and practical considerations. The profession must, indeed, purge itself of the inbred precepts of another day, rethink its code of practice and reshape its internal mechanisms for meeting its public responsibilities. Else the dangerous cleavage between a public sector of the Bar devoted to the developing issues of society and a private sector—the practicing Bar —which ignores them will only widen.[26]

The recognition of the profession's responsibility to the public interest has produced certain arguments about a lawyer's traditional standards of conduct. It has been suggested that in certain cases a lawyer's larger responsibility to society or the public interest may indeed require him to violate his professional obligations. That claim has been advanced in many different contexts. Lawyers who represent large corporate clients in antitrust matters or environmental suits or in negotiations with certain South African countries have been criticized for taking too narrow a view of what they should or should not do for their clients and for not demanding that the clients change their policies. Legal Aid lawyers representing the poor have been criticized for trying to strike the best bargain for their clients instead of attacking the injustices of a system that offers them such unpalatable choices. And lawyers representing defendants in so-called political cases have been criticized for not offering political explanations in court for the indictments that brought the accused before the bar.

But regardless of what position a lawyer takes on political issues as a citizen, in the courtroom there are rules that he must follow as a lawyer—however ill-defined they might be. Those rules are themselves an embodiment of an important public interest—the need for orderly procedures to ensure swift and equal justice. That public interest must in the end prevail over any other inconsistent political ideas.

The role of the lawyer concerned about social change is to defend his client with all the skill he possesses. If he is in sympathy with his client's cause, he serves it best by serving the client best and by letting the client do the political work outside the courtroom.

# The Nature of a Lawyer's Responsibility for His Client's Actions

In addition to the responsibility that a lawyer has *to* his client, it has been suggested that a lawyer has a defined responsibility *for* his client, that a lawyer must use his efforts to dissuade or prevent a defendant from acting improperly in court. In addition to making sure that his own conduct is proper, it is said, a lawyer must do everything necessary to make his client behave. For failing to do so, the lawyer may himself be disciplined even if his own behavior is exemplary. This presents an issue of considerable importance.

The rules of the Appellate Divisions of the First and Second Departments in New York City, which have been referred to earlier, seem to contain such a requirement: "The attorney shall use his best efforts to dissuade his client and witnesses from causing disorder or disruption in the courtroom."[27]

This approach corresponds to a suggestion made by the American College of Trial Lawyers which would require a lawyer "to advise any client appearing in a courtroom of the kind of behavior expected and required of him there, and to prevent him, so far as lies within the lawyer's power, from creating disorder and disruption in the courtroom."[28]

The Appellate Division rule seems to add a new dimension to the professional responsibilities of lawyers.[29] We have concluded that the cause of orderly justice requires that a lawyer seek to influence his client *in private* not to disrupt the courtroom. But it is neither necessary nor desirable to require an attorney to take active steps in court to restrain potentially disruptive conduct by his client. We endorse the Appellate Division rule so long as it is interpreted in this manner.

Some judges have assumed that defense attorneys have an absolute obligation to take visible steps to keep their clients in line. For example, Judge Julius Hoffman twice cited William Kunstler for contempt in part because he did not help to keep order in court. At the end of the trial Judge Hoffman berated Kunstler in the following words:

> And for you. . . . to have sat through the Bobby Seale incident . . . and not lifted an arm off your chair, not lifted your hands, not lifted an arm, not spoken a word. . . . not a word from you to him. . . . You have never, never, made an attempt to say something like this to him, "Bobby, hush, Cool it. Sit down now." You let him go on.[30]

While the court of appeals in the *Dellinger* case disagreed and ruled that a lawyer has no obligation to take such steps, other courts have held that a lawyer has a duty "to assist the court in the proper administration of justice."[31] Since he has a "solemn duty . . . to encourage respect for the law and for the courts and the judges thereof,"[32] he must do what is necessary to restrain his client from disrupting a trial. Orderly proceedings are so important to the judicial system that every participant in the process, it is argued, must do everything that he can to ensure that decorum is maintained.

As a practical matter, the lawyer has enormous influence with his client, who will generally do what he tells him. Judge Jon Newman explains:

> Upon the lawyer falls a limited but, in a few instances, critical responsibility. He must do what he can to keep his client under control. Some have argued that a lawyer's caution to his client will be ineffective. that a defendant undeterred by threat of contempt penalties will not respect his lawyer's admonition. That may be true in some cases, but surely not in all.
>
> There inheres in the attorney-client relationship a large opportunity for lawyer guidance. The client with any faith in his counsel, may well be far more anxious to do what his lawyer says than what the judge says. In a contentious trial, the judge is perceived as an adversary: the attorney may be the only one in the courtroom on the defendant's side. Many defendants will be extremely reluctant to incur their lawyer's displeasure by disruptive behavior.[33]

It is often said that a lawyer is an "officer of the court." Some commentators and judges infer that for this reason he must act as a disciplinary agent for his client and take steps to restrain him in court.

The Supreme Court has acknowledged that the courts have shown "confusion and difficulty. . . . in explaining what is meant" by the term "officer of the court."[34] It has been held to mean that minimum education and training requirements can be imposed by the state before a person can practice law.[35] His fees may be regulated by the courts.[36] He is obliged to accept clients when ordered to do so by a court.[37]

But a lawyer is not subject to summary punishment of a court for misconduct which does not take place in the court's presence. In a 1956 case, an attorney was held in contempt under 18 U.S.C. 401 (2), which forbids "misbehavior of any [court] officer in their official transactions." The District of Columbia Court of Appeals held that it was improper for a lawyer to send questionnaires to members of a federal grand jury investigating his client's activities. Since an attorney was an "officer of the court" and the mailing complained of was an "official transaction," the federal court of appeals upheld the summary punishment of the lawyer. The Supreme Court reversed, saying:

> It has been stated many times that lawyers are "officers of the court."
> . . . [But] nothing that was said in *Ex parte Garland* or in any other
> case decided by this Court places attorneys in the same category as
> marshals, bailiffs, court clerks or judges. Unlike these officials a lawyer
> is engaged in a private profession important though it be to our system
> of justice. In general he makes his own decisions, follows his own best
> judgment, collects his own fees and runs his own business.[38]

We conclude, from a careful examination of the relevant case law, that the term "officer of the court" is an expression of the close supervision and control which the courts can and should exercise over members of their bars, of the special privileges lawyers receive, and the importance of the right to practice law. The term "officer of the court" also indicates that high standards of professional responsibility and conduct are expected of an attorney. But using the metaphor does not tell us what those standards are. The lawyer is not a bailiff or a marshal or an "officer" in the sense of a policeman or other disciplinary agent. If an obligation is to be imposed on him to control his client in court, it must be because such an obligation is a logical extension of the accepted norms of conduct imposed upon members of the profession, not because the term "officer" has been indiscriminately applied to his position.

Many others claim that there should be absolutely no requirement of lawyer control over his client's actions in court. A lawyer is obliged to represent his client with total fidelity. A federal district court has stressed the "importance of the attorney's undivided allegiance and faithful service to one accused of crime. . . .[39] If the attorney is viewed by the client as the only one "on his side," should that trust be jeopardized or undermined by requiring him to act as another arm of the court in publicly restraining his client?

This position has received support from the court of appeals in the *Dellinger* case, arising out of the Chicago conspiracy trial.

> [A]nother frequent charge against the attorneys is that they failed to aid the court in maintaining order. While this charge was often coupled with the additional assertion that they actively encouraged their clients in their disruptions, for purposes of remand it is necessary to distinguish between the two situations. An attorney has no affirmative obligation to restrain his client under pain of the contempt sanction, although we do not express an opinion as to the breach of professional ethics that may be involved in this situation. Indeed, compelling an attorney to control the conduct of his client under the threat of the contempt sanction might well destroy the confidence in the attorney-client relationship which is necessary to a proper and adequate defense.[40]

One reason for not holding a lawyer responsible for his client's action is that the trial judge has been given ample weapons to punish or control disruptive conduct by a defendant. Under the *Allen* case, he may cite for contempt, bind and gag a defendant, or remove him from the courtroom. With this variety of effective sanctions, there is no need to add still another instrument of control—the defense lawyer.

Moreover, if a lawyer must control his client, he may later face disciplinary proceedings if the client is disorderly in court. One lawyer has written that

> no amount of apologizing or disclaiming will remove a lawyer's obvious complicity when he fails to take appropriate action to control his client's obscenities and insults. Trial counsel should be the first warned by the court that punishment for both counsel and client will follow if the improprieties are persisted in, and defense counsel should be held responsible not only for his own but his client's conduct.[41]

This approach is inconsistent with the independence of the attorney and his duty to follow professional standards irrespective of a client's demands. If a lawyer cannot excuse his actions by relying on his client's directives, a court or disciplining agency cannot insist on converse responsibility; that is, it should not attribute a client's conduct to the lawyer by requiring him to restrain the client in court and punishing him if he fails to do so.

Practically, the requirement that a lawyer openly restrain his client could be used to stifle effective representation of minority groups. Lawyers who represent radical or dissident groups, even if they engaged in no personal misconduct, could be censured or disciplined because of their clients' actions. The upshot would be that radicals who do not intend to disrupt would have a more difficult task securing effective and sympathetic counsel. More important, nonradical lawyers would be discouraged from appearing in such cases since they would not want to be placed in a position of being disciplined because they could not control their clients. And, as shown in the preceding chapter, when the defendant appears pro se, the incidence of courtroom disruption is likely to increase.

Finally, the problem of establishing proper guidelines of control are enormously difficult. This is the principal ground on which Melvin Kodas and Robert Joost of the American Trial Lawyers Association have critized the American College of Trial Lawyers' proposed recommendation that "a trial judge has power to punish summarily for contempt any lawyer who in his presence wilfully contributes to disorder or disruption in the courtroom." Their position is reported in *Trial Magazine* as follows:

> Consider the proposed element "wilfully contributes to disorder or disruption in the courtroom" and ponder its meaning.
> "Wilfully" is not defined. Does "wilfully" mean purposely or intentionally? Or knowingly? Or recklessly? Or all three? . . .
> "Contributes" is not defined. If defendants start shouting in the midst of a criminal prosecution does the lawyer "contribute to disruption":
> (a) if he joins them in shouting; or
> (b) if he says "right on" while they shout; or
> (c) if he smiles as they shout; or
> (d) if he leaves the courtroom while they shout; or
> (e) if he looks on helplessly while they shout?
> Must the so-called contribution amount to an actual cause of the disruption? Or a proximate cause? Or no cause at all.[42]

Similarly, the Appellate Division rule specifying that a lawyer "must use his best efforts to dissuade his client and witnesses from causing disorder or disruption in the courtroom" creates serious problems of interpretation. If a lawyer leaves the courtroom or looks helplessly on while his clients shout, is he violating the rule? Must he take active steps to prove he is using his "best efforts" to dissuade his client from causing disorder?

We think it possible to formulate a reasonable and workable set of principles without placing lawyers in undue jeopardy. Most of the objections to lawyer control of his client focus on the problems incident to restraining a defendant in open court. But before the parties enter the courtroom the lawyer can exercise an important function. Thus we endorse the principle that a lawyer might be required to help "to dissuade his client . . . from causing disorder and disruption in the courtroom" if the requirement is interpreted in the following way:

1. A lawyer should be expected to tell his client what the consequences of disorderly conduct would be, including the sanctions available to the judge. He should also advise him of the probable prejudice to his case if he disrupts the proceedings. Such a requirement flows directly from the duty of candor which the lawyer owes his client. The Code of Professional Responsibility requires that a lawyer "should exert his best efforts to insure that decisions of his client are made only after his client has been informed of relevant considerations. . . . A lawyer should advise his client of the possible effect of each legal alternative."[43]

2. A lawyer should also seek to influence or dissuade his client from improper courtroom behavior. But, whatever advice a lawyer gives or persuasion he applies to ensure that a client acts properly in court must be done in the privacy of the attorney-client privilege. It need not be proclaimed openly to the world. An illustration is the following exchange between Michael Tigar, a defense counsel, and the court in the Tacoma Seven trial.

> *The Court [Judge George H. Boldt]:* Mr. Tigar, this gentleman is one of the Deputy Marshals. Tell him what you have.
>
> *Mr. Hanson (deputy marshal):* I watched Jeffrey Dowd place this on the wall and asked him to take it off and he gave me the finger, and on the elevator and on the walls we have seen them. They don't come off when they dry.
>
> *The Court:* Mr. Dowd is your client, Mr. Tigar, and I expect you to take appropriate action to see that this does not occur.
>
> *Mr. Tigar:* Your Honor, the only evidence we have is this one label and I take the position I am the man's lawyer and I have an obligation to explain your Honor's wishes and I have an obligation to explain what the law is but I don't believe that I have the obligation to control his conduct or behavior, even assuming that I wanted to or that I could. He is his own man and he will take the consequences.

Mr. Tigar explained further:

> *Mr. Tigar:* My thinking is I represent two defendants in these proceedings, Jeff Dowd and Roger Lippman, and we will have conversations throughout the course of the trial about their legal liability and obligation for things they have done. Those conversations are covered by the lawyer-client privilege. My job is to advise those defendants about consequences of actions they may contemplate taking and actions they may have taken in the past.
>
> *The Court:* I take it you will do that now in connection with this incident?

*Mr. Tigar:*   Judge, the conversations I may have with them you may be assured will be in accord with my consideration of my responsibilities. I cannot talk to you about my professional client-attorney relationship.

*The Court:*   I only ask you to advise them about this type of conduct and what it may lead to.

*Mr. Tigar:*   I will inform them of your Honor's views, certainly.

*The Court:*   If you will do that, that is all I am asking you to do.[44]

A criminal lawyer should no more be obliged to announce that he has cautioned his client against disruption than an antitrust lawyer should be obliged to announce that he has cautioned his corporate client against price-fixing. Moreover, from a practical point of view, a client is more likely to listen to advice that is given in confidence than to public announcements designed to protect the lawyer's record.

3. A trial judge should accept an attorney's representation that he is doing what is appropriate to dissuade his client from causing disruption without asking exactly what he has said or done and without requiring public manifestation of control. In many situations—such as the production of documents in discovery proceedings—a court will accept an attorney's representation without further inquiry. If great responsibility is placed on an attorney in this and other situations, there must be corresponding trust that he will fulfill his duties to court, profession, and client to the best of his ability.

4. A lawyer who encourages courtroom misconduct in any manner should be punished under rules that establish his own responsibility for maintaining courtroom decorum. If he nods encouragement or advises a client to disrupt, he may properly be disciplined.[45] However, silence alone by a lawyer while disruption is occurring in a courtroom should not be considered "encouragement." Courts or disciplinary agencies should be extremely wary about pressing charges against lawyers simply because their clients were disorderly during a trial and they did nothing about it in open court.

Judge Jon Newman has written the following about this problem:

> In those few instances where the lawyer declines to try to influence his client's courtroom conduct, disciplinary remedies should be invoked. At a minimum, a lawyer who openly acknowledges that he will not try to caution his client should be denied the privilege of appearing in a trial courtroom for some period of time.[46]

We agree that a lawyer should try to influence his client to behave properly in court. But he should not have to prove he has done so or "openly acknowledge" how or in what way he has performed that task. And he need not control the client openly or upbraid him publicly to prove that he is satisfying his professional responsibilities. The distinction between influence and control is crucial and should not be blurred. All a judge should expect from a lawyer is a respectful representation that he has performed his professional responsibilities.

# Punishable Misconduct in the Courtroom by Defense Attorneys

Lawyer misconduct in the courtroom which may properly be punished or which may justify preventive remedies by the court falls into three general categories:* 1) disrespectful remarks to the court, the prosecutor, or other parties; 2) refusal to obey proper court procedures or a proper order of the court; 3) excessive or repetitive argumentation or other willful delay of proceedings.

## Disrespectful Remarks

The legal profession has long declared the basic principle that a lawyer must be "respectful, courteous and above board in his relations with a judge or hearing officer before whom he appears."[47] Legal commentators seldom discuss why it is necessary to be respectful to a judge, and some lawyers have questioned whether obeisance to the judicial office is required for the proper administration of justice.

We believe that the necessity for respect is inherent in the very nature of the judicial process. A judge should be accorded every reasonable deference commensurate with his authority. He must be treated with respect to ensure that his decisions are based on reasoned principles instead of emotional reactions to insult. He must be treated with respect so that the legal process functions smoothly. As Chief Justice Burger has said, "When men shout and shriek or call names, we witness the end of rational thought process if not the beginning of blows and conflict."[48]

Since the defense attorney and the prosecutor address the court in the overwhelming majority of instances, their comments must be couched in respectful terms. They may say almost anything to a judge that they feel is necessary to plead their case—that he is wrong in his evaluation of the facts or in his application of the law or that he is

---

* Much of the analysis on punishable misconduct by defendants in chapter 6 applies also to attorneys. Obviously, any physical violence by an attorney as well as any loud shouting, pounding, or cursing can be punished as contempt. However, this type of conduct is so rare among lawyers that there is little point in discussing it as a distinct problem.

prejudiced and biased. But they must do so in a courteous and respectful manner, not only because the system requires it but to better serve
their client.

It is for this reason that comments of a lawyer that would be overlooked if the defendant or a witness made them may be properly
punished by a court. A defendant's insulting outburst is often understandable—he is under great pressure in a criminal trial since his
life or liberty is at stake, and he often is confused by judicial procedures. Thus, as we have suggested, some leeway should be given to a
single emotional explosion by a defendant. But none of these mitigating
factors exists for a defense lawyer.

Both direct insults and disrespectful comments by a lawyer can be
punishable. One of the attorneys in *United States* v. *Hoffa* was convicted of contempt for saying that the court was conducting a "drum
head court martial" and "a star chamber proceeding." He said the
court's rulings "smacked of Stalinism, Hitlerism, Mussoliniism, and all
these isms," and accused the court of "being used as a tool by the
Government" and "as an adjunct to the prosecutor to hide evidence."[49]

In another case, involving west coast labor leader Harry Bridges, one
of his lawyers objected to the judge's asking a defense witness whether
he had recently been "subjected to medical treatment." The witness
had said that his memory was bad, and the judge inquired whether
this was due to medical reasons. The defense lawyers became incensed
because the judge had not permitted them to ask prosecution witnesses
whether they were insane. One of Bridges's lawyers, who told the
judge he should "cite yourself for misconduct" and "ought to be
ashamed of yourself," was held in contempt.[50]

In recent years courts have become more tolerant of isolated instances of disrespect, often noting that insulting language that does
not obstruct the trial should not be punished as contempt. For instance,
the court of appeals in the Chicago conspiracy case wrote:

> . . . it has frequently been held, and considerable scholarly comment
> supports the view, that mere disrespect or affront to the judge's sense of
> dignity will not sustain a citation for contempt. The line between insult
> and obstruction, however, is not clearly delineated, and at some point
> disrespect and insult become actual and material obstruction. . . .
> "The fires which [the language] kindles must constitute an imminent,
> not merely a likely, threat to the administration of justice. The danger
> must not be remote or even probable; it must immediately imperil." . . .
> A showing of imminent prejudice to a fair and dispassionate proceed-
> ing is, therefore, necessary to support a contempt based upon mere
> disrespect or insult.[51]

This means that the effect of the words on the judge or on others
present may determine whether it is an obstruction of the proceeding

or not. This in turn may be influenced by the tone of the remarks, whether any physical action accompanies them, and how much of a delay follows.[52]

In the D.C. Nine case in Washington, a lawyer, Philip Hirschkop, spoke strongly to a judge who was conducting a hearing on whether the defendant could appear pro se:

> As to the self-representation, okay, you made your mind up. The problem is that you made it up before you ever came to this courtroom. . . .
>
> I get the feeling we are wasting our time here. I can go back to my office and do other things rather than take part in a pro forma hearing.
>
> I fully believe, and with all due respect to the Court as a person, that you made up your mind about everything except the length of the sentence.[53]

The district judge passing on the contempt citation held these remarks to be improper but not obstructive.

> [The Court] does find that certain of his spoken words add up not only to misbehavior but also were wilfully and designedly spoken. But neither all nor any part of what Hirschkop did or said actually obstructed the district judge in the performance of his duty.[54]

In some cases, an insulting remark may be provoked by the trial judge. In a Wisconsin case the lawyer objected to certain questions asked by the judge about efforts to intimidate a witness in a divorce action. The judge said the questions were proper.

> *Mr. O'Brien:*  Well, there's so much about the proceedings of this Court that I don't consider proper, that we are just in a mess.
>
> *The Court:*  You mean that?
>
> *Mr. O'Brien:*  Yes.
>
> *The Court:*  What, for instance, do you particularly refer to, Mr. O'Brien?
>
> *Mr. O'Brien:*  Oh, the last thing you did; the last thing you did.
>
> *The Court:*  Mr. O'Brien, it's just because you do not know any of the principles of law applicable to the cases, or you don't make any pretense of learning them.
>
> *Mr. O'Brien:*  I'll never learn it from you.
>
> *The Court:*  You'll never learn it from anybody, because you've not got enough brains to learn anything from anybody.
>
> *Mr. O'Brien:*  I wonder what's the matter with your brains; you've been staggering around here for three years, an object of charity.[55]

Although the lawyer was held in contempt, we have substantial doubts that he should have been punished. The judge in his own insulting remarks had so far departed from his role as impartial arbiter that it seems unfair to punish the lawyer for replying in kind.

We agree with the trial judge who responded to our questionnaire as follows:

So far as attorneys are concerned, nothing should be done to limit even the most aggressive defense, provided that that which is done is not directed to obstruction of the proceedings. A "normal" amount of "judge baiting" is permissible, as a stock in trade of the lawyer. Only when these limits are *continually* transgressed should the contempt power be used (it should be used sparingly and only under the direst provocation for in a contempt proceeding the judge usually turns out to be the defendant). Patience, a most difficult attribute in these days of demand for instant justice must be cultivated by the judge to an unusual degree.[56]

An attorney may accuse a judge of bias or impartiality if he does so through proper procedures, such as a motion to have the judge excuse himself. The complaint should not be considered insulting or contemptuous conduct even if it is expressed in strong language. In one case, the defendant was a civil rights lawyer who had filed a motion for change of venue in a state contempt action against another lawyer, accusing the judge of bias. The judge, he said, was "acting as police officer, chief prosecution witness, adverse witness for the defense, grand jury, chief prosecutor and judge," and was "intimidating and harassing," seriously hampering the efforts of defense counsel.

This was held by the trial judge to violate the Virginia Code, which authorized summary punishment of a person who misbehaves in the presence of the court so as to obstruct justice, or who uses "vile, contemptuous or insulting language"[57] to or about a judge in respect of his official acts.

The Supreme Court reversed on the grounds that due process and the Sixth Amendment protect a lawyer's right to file for a change of venue for his client based on a judge's alleged bias. The language used, even if it was insulting and reflected poorly upon the court, "was inherent in the issue of bias raised, an issue which we have seen had to be raised. . . ."[58]

## Disobedience of Proper Court Procedures or Orders

A lawyer may not disobey a valid rule of procedure or a proper order of the court. This requirement is basic to the orderly proceeding of a trial. Courts have evolved rules on the admission of evidence, on the proper scope of direct and cross-examination of witnesses, and on the methods of arguing a legal point. Often lawyers and judges disagree about the proper interpretation of the rules, and a lawyer may press his point and explain what he is trying to do in order to preserve a record for appeal. But at some point he must stop. The Seventh Circuit explained in the Chicago conspiracy case:

> . . . failure to heed the directive of the court to desist from arguing, to sit down, or to remain quiet may indeed constitute an actual material obstruction to the administration of justice. . . .

As governor of the trial, the trial judge must have the authority necessary to ensure the orderly and expeditious progress of the proceedings.
His directives in exercise of this authority must be obeyed; otherwise
the clear result would be courtroom chaos. Wholly arbitrary limits on
argument will, if prejudicial, merit reversal of the substantive case, but
that hardly can excuse open defiance of the court's commands. . . .
   We do not say that automaton-like, reflexive obedience to the court's
orders is necessary to avoid a contempt citation. The law does not expect unhuman responsiveness. A certain amount of leeway must be
allowed. But where the directive is clear, the judge's insistence on
obedience is not undercut by his further rejoinder, and the party directed understands what is being asked of him, he must obey.[59]

Lawyers sometimes persist in questioning after they have made their
record for appeal in the face of a direct judicial order to stop. In a
case involving revocation of the citizenship of union leader Harry
Bridges, his attorney tried to show that the government had engaged
in illegal wiretapping. The judge ruled that all questions on wiretapping were irrelevant. But the attorney persisted. A federal court of
appeals upheld a contempt citation against him in these words:

We think appellant went far beyond the necessity of making a record
and that his conduct shows a deliberate and studied design to ignore
the rulings of the Court in order to get before the jury the excluded
matter. A sufficient record was made long before appellant desisted.[60]

Two of the most serious charges against William Kunstler in the
Chicago conspiracy case were for directly disobeying an order of the
trial judge not to mention certain matters before the jury. He was told
by the court not to move to have Mayor Daley declared a hostile witness while the jury was present. He did so. He was also ordered not
to mention the defense's desire to call Reverend Ralph Abernathy as
a defense witness after the judge ruled he could not testify. Again he
disobeyed the order.

An attorney must actually take the action forbidden by the judge
before he can be punished. If he expresses an intent to do so but does
not follow through, the Supreme Court has held that he has not obstructed the proceedings.[61]

Furthermore, not every order of the court must be obeyed. Sometimes a court may so totally exceed the bounds of proper procedure
that a lawyer has the right to protest despite the court's order to keep
silent. In the Dr. Bernard Finch murder trial in Los Angeles in 1959,
the jury had been deliberating about three weeks when the judge
recalled them to the courtroom for further instructions. He began to
comment on the testimony of certain witnesses. When the judge began
his remarks, Finch's lawyer, Grant Cooper, objected:

*The Court:* To my mind the testimony given by the [Prosecution]
witness John Cody [who had testified, in effect, that he had been employed by the defendants in the murder case to kill Finch's wife] re-

garding the purpose for which he was employed by the defendants was
more believable than the testimony of the two defendants on that
subject.

*Mr. Cooper [petitioner herein]:*   If your Honor please—

*The Court:*   Now Mr. Cooper, I don't want a word out of either one of
you.

*Mr. Cooper:*   If your Honor please, as a lawyer I have a right to address this court.

*The Court:*   You don't have a right to say a word when the jury is
down here in the process of their deliberations, and I instruct you . . .
to keep seated and wait until the jury is out to make your objections.

*Mr. Cooper:*   If your Honor please, I feel your Honor has no right to
invade the province of the jury.

*The Court:*   Mr. Cooper, I hold you directly in contempt.[62]

The California Supreme Court reversed the finding of contempt.

> It is also well nigh unheard of for the trial judge, after the jury has
> deliberated for three weeks in a capital (or any other case), to recall
> them and express to them his opinion that the defendants testified
> falsely and prosecution witnesses told the truth. This recall of the jury
> was by the judge on his own initiative, i.e., it was not at the request of
> jurors for further instructions. . . .
>     It is clear that under the circumstances of the case at bench peti-
> tioner, if not required to make, was at least justified in presenting,
> immediate objection to the hereinabove described procedure followed
> by the judge.[63]

The situation is not comparable to one in which someone violates
an injunction outside of court and then seeks to defend himself against
a contempt citation on the ground that the injunction was invalid. The
Supreme Court has held that it is improper to challenge an injunction
by violating it; the appropriate remedy is to try to dissolve the injunction in the trial court or to appeal the order to a higher court.[64] Anyone complaining that the injunction is illegal "could not bypass orderly
judicial review of the injunction before disobeying it."[65]

The courtroom setting is markedly different. A lawyer cannot immediately appeal a judge's directive to stop arguing a point, or to keep
certain matters from the jury. With respect to these orders, no immediate "orderly judicial review" is possible.[66] In addition, a judge's
mistaken ruling may seriously jeopardize the lawyer's case (in the
Finch case described above a hung jury resulted), which may not be
correctible on appeal. Thus, a lawyer may feel he must challenge a
judge's orders immediately despite a warning not to raise the point
further.

Even if a lawyer goes beyond the rules, and tries to present matters
to the jury which are not properly before it, his actions may not be
punishable if he acted in a good faith attempt to argue his case. In a

Chicago case involving charges of extortion, the defense lawyer violated an express stipulation of the judge not to mention certain points in open court concerning a tape recording of conversations between the defendant and a government informer. He did so, on the belief that he was not going beyond the stipulation; objection was made, and the lawyer promptly corrected the matter for the jury.

> The statements made by the appellant in his closing argument were improper. But the government's prompt objection, the trial court's immediate ruling and comment, and appellant's subsequent statement to the jury, appear to have remedied that impropriety in so far as the case on trial was concerned. As we view the record, it discloses the appellant erred in his conclusions as to the possible permissibly arguable inferences. No doubt, as a member of the bar, he owed the court a more careful appraisal of the record, in the light of the effect of the stipulation, before advancing the argument he attempted. But in our judgment, his failure in this respect is too tenuous a basis to support a finding of contempt.[67]

The decision indicates that the courts will give a lawyer every latitude in presenting his case.

## Repetitive or Excessive Argumentation

It is obvious that there must be some end to a lawyer's argument. He may make any point he wishes so long as he does so courteously and in good faith. He may argue the question fully and preserve his record for appeal. But if he continues after all these conditions are met, he is obstructing the proceedings and can be properly punished for contempt.

In a federal action in California involving the forgery of government checks, the prosecution examined its chief witness in the morning, and ended its questioning of witnesses just before the noon recess. The defense attorney began his cross-examination and then asked that the case be recessed at noon so that he could examine certain documents and talk to some witnesses before resuming his cross-examination. When the judge insisted on the defense lawyer's continuing his questioning, the lawyer objected:

> *Mr. Osborne:*  . . . I would like to take a recess to get organized. . . .
> *Mr. Osborne:* I have a number of documents to look through in respect to my examinations. . . .
> When the Court noted that counsel should have previously examined his exhibits and again directed counsel to continue, counsel replied:
> *Mr. Osborne:*  I think I am entitled to rely upon the normal court hours. . . .
> The Court repeated its direction and counsel stated:
> *Mr. Osborne:*  Your Honor, I would again request a recess.
> Again told to proceed, counsel replied:

*Mr. Osborne:*   Your Honor, it's time for the recess.

*The Court:*   No, it's not, counsel.

*Mr. Osborne:*   I know you are running this Court, your Honor. However I think counsel are entitled to go out to lunch at the normal hour. I have an appointment in my office. The jury is hungry. I don't want to try my case to an uncomfortable jury. And I don't think you should take out a personal thing on me.

After another direction to proceed counsel stated:

*Mr. Osborne:*   I would like to sit down and review some documents so that it's not necessary to ramble. . . .

*Mr. Osborne:*   That's no option, your Honor, not when a man is charged with a serious crime. He is entitled to counsel who has time to sit down and prepare a case adequately.[68]

At some point in his colloquy with the judge requesting a recess, Mr. Osborne passed the point of proper argumentation and could be punished.

On the other hand, for a lawyer to argue novel constitutional questions is not disruptive even if presentation and consideration of the issues may consume much judicial time. And for a lawyer to protest a judge's ruling and otherwise to press his client's cause is not disorderly even if it annoys the judge hearing the action. We will discuss in chapter 9 how action by a judge refusing to hear such arguments may itself be disruptive of the proceedings.

In a case involving forgery of endorsements on certain government checks, the issue arose of whether the defendant was apprised, on his arrest, of his right to remain silent and not to answer certain questions. The judge claimed that the question had already been asked on direct examination and that the defense lawyer could not bring it up on cross-examination.

*Mr. Phelan:*   This is cross-examination, your Honor. Is it error for me to ask him the question again?

*The Court:*   It certainly is error for you to take up the time of the Court and the jury asking questions which are favorable to you and which the witness has already answered.

*Mr. Phelan:*   In other words, I am precluded from proper cross-examination?

*The Court:*   You are precluded from repeating the same questions that were already answered.

*Mr. Phelan:*   I submit I am precluded from cross-examination. I have no further questions.

*The Court:*   You are not precluded from cross-examination. This witness has previously testified that he gave the defendant no warning at all.

*Mr. Phelan:*   I need nothing further, your Honor.

*The Court:*   Very well, don't try to say you are precluded from cross-examination.

*Mr. Phelan:*   I said it, your Honor, and I believe it.[69]

The trial judge then held the lawyer in contempt, but an appeals court reversed the finding, stating that there was nothing "arrogant, hostile or defiant in the words" used by the lawyer.

The distinction between permissible and excessive argumentation may rest both on the tone of the lawyer's remarks and the length of time consumed by him in continuing to argue. The precise point when argumentation becomes defiance and obstruction of proceedings occurs is often difficult to pin down.

There are other types of aggressive conduct by a lawyer that may not be punished. For example, a lawyer may properly interrupt another case in progress to make an "emergency" motion with respect to his own case:

> All judges know that occasions arise when an attorney, in the interests of justice, must interrupt the court while he is engaged in hearing a cause . . . [a] trial judge has no right to refuse to hear [an emergency motion].[70]

Similarly, if a judge charges a lawyer with unprofessional conduct and the lawyer demands the right to be heard in response, this cannot be cited as contempt.[71] In addition, a lawyer may properly object to antagonistic or irascible comments by the judge.[72]

In an attempt to reconcile the interests involved, the court of appeals in the *Dellinger* case stated what we think is a sensible and practical view of the problem:

> If a trial judge prejudicially denies counsel an adequate opportunity to argue a point, appellate courts will reverse, and that alone will deter most judges from arbitrarily cutting off argument. . . .
>
> And where the judge is arbitrary or affords counsel inadequate opportunity to argue his position, counsel must be given substantial leeway in pressing his contention, for it is through such colloquy that the judge may recognize his mistake and prevent error from infecting the record. It is, after all, the full intellectual exchange of ideas and positions that best facilitates the resolution of disputes. However, this is not to say that attorneys may press their positions beyond the court's insistent direction to desist. On the contrary, the necessity for orderly administration of justice compels the view that the judge must have the power to set limits on argument. We simply encourage judges to exercise tolerance in determining those limits and to distinguish carefully between hesitating, begrudging obedience and open defiance.[73]

# Remedies

Much of what we said in the previous chapter on defendants applies also to the problem of the appropriate sanction to be applied against errant lawyers in the courtroom. The judge must weigh a series of factors which may bear on what sanction should be imposed: whether the dereliction is a single episode or is repeated over the course of proceedings; whether the incident occurs before a jury; whether there are mitigating circumstances, such as possible provocation by the prosecutor or the youth and inexperience of the attorney. We repeat our suggestion that contempt or other severe sanctions should be sparingly and carefully used and that the judge should ordinarily impose the "least severe sanction appropriate to correct the abuse and to deter repetition."

It is also extremely important that the pretrial or preventive techniques suggested earlier be followed. A judge should inform all parties of the substantive ground rules that they are expected to follow. In addition, lawyers must be given a clear warning after the first instance of misconduct that they have overstepped the limits of proper presentation or argument.[74] They should be told again what is expected of them, and allowed to defend or justify their actions if they think they were correct or to apologize if they recognize they were wrong.

In almost all cases these techniques should be enough to bring the lawyer back to the mark. Most lawyers realize that they do not serve their clients well by antagonizing the judge hearing the case. If a warning does not suffice, a judge may consider the possibility of a contempt citation or use other preventive measures discussed below.

## Punishment

### CRIMINAL AND CIVIL CONTEMPT

In certain circumstances contempt is the appropriate punishment for courtroom misconduct by attorneys. Judges should be reasonable but firm with members of the bar, whose conduct is held to a higher standard of proper decorum than that of defendants. Thus a single insulting outburst might serve as the basis for a contempt citation against a lawyer.

But judges should be hesitant to cite for contempt when the lawyer has, to a minor extent, overstepped proper procedures or has engaged in repetitive or excessive argumentation. In the emotional heat of a trial, a lawyer may exceed the bounds of proper presentation out of zeal for his client. Every latitude should be given lawyers trying to argue their cases.

The crucial inquiry is whether a lawyer is doing his job as an advocate in good faith or whether he is gratuitously obstructive or insulting. When he does the former he is given every doubt. But when he is outside those limits, he can be more swiftly punished than a defendant or a spectator who engages in similar conduct.

In addition, a judge may hold a lawyer in civil contempt until he promises to behave in a proper manner. However, the penalty imposed should not be excessive. For example, an order specifying that a lawyer pay fifty dollars an hour until he behaves properly might accumulate into an enormous fine over a long trial and would seriously jeopardize his capacity to represent his client.[75] The penalty should be commensurate with the offense and should not be openended. Similarly, as with defendants, a penalty of seven full or partial days in jail should be the maximum that is imposed.*

## DISCIPLINE BY BAR ASSOCIATIONS

The traditional method of control over lawyers who violate their professional responsibilities is through action by local disciplinary agencies of the bar. In most states, a complaint against a lawyer for either in or out-of-court conduct can be filed with the local grievance committee of the bar by a judge, other lawyers, or private citizens. The committee investigates the charges and decides whether it should lodge a formal complaint against the lawyer.

A formal hearing is held on the charges before that committee or another disciplinary group of the local bar. If a committee decides that discipline is required, it files its report in the local court, which decides after argument by the lawyer whether or not to impose sanctions. All proceedings are secret until the court issues a final decision against the lawyer. Punishment can range from reprimand to censure to suspension of the right to practice to disbarment.

There have been many criticisms voiced over existing disciplinary procedures. A Special Committee on Evaluation of Disciplinary Enforcement of the American Bar Association, headed by former Justice Tom C. Clark, has reported that the existing procedures are inadequate, cumbersome, and slow. It recommended streamlining and centralization under a statewide agency with a professional staff which would speed up and coordinate all efforts to control lawyer ethics and conduct.

Although we have made no independent study of this problem, we agree that swifter disciplinary action is desirable for professional misconduct, particularly for improper behavior in court. However, there are often good reasons for delay. Our parent body, the Association of the Bar of the City of New York, has a policy that no disciplinary action should be taken against an attorney while a case involving his alleged misconduct is still pending in the courts. This rule avoids duplication in fact-finding and allows the local grievance committee to act with full knowledge of what the courts have determined. A lawyer may be cited for contempt but an appeals court may later

* See the discussion on page 104.

exonerate him completely. There is no point in a grievance committee filing a formal charge or holding hearings when the courts are still considering the matter.[76]

Some courts have drawn a distinction between the contempt sanction by a judge and disciplinary action by the bar:

> A contempt proceeding for misbehavior in court is designed to vindicate the authority of the court; on the other hand the object of a disciplinary proceeding is to deal with the fitness of the court's officer to continue in that office, to preserve and protect the court and the public from the official ministration of persons unfit or unworthy to hold such office.[77]

But the Supreme Court has made clear that disciplinary proceedings must be conducted, like other criminal actions, with due process safeguards, since they "are adversary proceedings of a quasi-criminal nature."[78] Depriving a person of his livelihood is a far more severe sanction than a fifty dollar contempt fine or even thirty days in jail. Thus the decision to invoke disciplinary proceedings should be made at least as carefully as the decision to cite for contempt.

Seldom does a single act of forensic misconduct by a lawyer not amounting to a crime serve as the basis for serious disciplinary action by the bar.[79] A leading expert on legal ethics, Henry S. Drinker, has written:

> Ordinarily the occasion for disbarment should be the demonstration, by a continued course of conduct, of an attitude wholly inconsistent with the recognition of proper professional standards.[80]

This has been the almost invariable practice. In almost every one of the reported cases of lawyer misconduct which led to a conviction for contempt, there is no subsequent record of suspension or disbarment proceedings.

The only apparent exceptions involved the lawyers in the Communist conspiracy case and a civil rights lawyer from Kentucky. In the former case Abraham Isserman, one of the defense lawyers, was disbarred in the New Jersey state courts but later reinstated. He was also suspended from practicing for two years in the United States District Court for the Southern District of New York. The Supreme Court on its own motion and by a four to four vote disbarred Isserman, following his disbarment in New Jersey,[81] holding that the burden was on him to show that he should not be stricken from the roll of attorneys. But the Court later decided that a majority was necessary to disbar and reversed its earlier decision.[82]

Justice Jackson wrote on behalf of the justices who voted in favor of Isserman: "We do not recall any previous instance, though not venturing to assert that there is none, where a lawyer has been disbarred by any court of the United States or of a state merely because he had been convicted of a contempt."[83] He went on to say:

If the purpose of disciplinary proceedings be correction of the delin-
quent, the courts defeat the purpose by ruining him whom they would
reform. If the purpose be to deter others, disbarment is belated and
superfluous, for what lawyer would not find deterrent enough in the jail
sentence, the two-year suspension from the bar of the United States
District Court, and the disapproval of his profession? If the disbarment
rests, not on these specific proven offenses, but on atmospheric considerations of general undesirability and Communistic leanings or affiliation, these have not been charged and he has had no chance to meet
them.[84]

The second principal case where a serious penalty was imposed for
misconduct in a single case involved a Kentucky lawyer, Daniel T.
Taylor III, who represented many minority group members, civil
liberties organizations, and civil rights activists, Taylor was suspended
from practice for six months because of his actions in a murder trial,
in which two young blacks were accused of killing a policeman (the
trial ended in a hung jury). Taylor had accused the presiding judge
in open court of calling him a "dirty son of a bitch." At the later disciplinary hearing, the judge denied he had done so, although Taylor
presented one spectator at the trial who said the judge's lips formed
the words. During the same trial Taylor announced to the jury that
he was being threatened with contempt charges by the judge and had
been punished by him previously. On the basis of these charges, a
trial committee of the state bar association recommended that Taylor
be suspended for one year. On appeal the Board of Governors recommended that the penalty be increased to five years. (While the case
was on appeal, Taylor was sentenced to four and a half years for
contempt for his actions in a later murder trial, described at page
233 below.) The state court of appeals finally imposed a six month
suspension with the following comments:

> It is common knowledge that in certain widely publicized trials of re-
> cent years a new breed of lawyers has instituted the studied technique
> of baiting the trial judge in order to convey to the public an impression
> that its courts are instruments of discrimination and injustice. Frequent
> contempt citations are the hallmark of that technique. It will not be
> tolerated in this jurisdiction. The representation of unpopular clients or
> points of view does not clothe the lawyer with a special immunity from
> his obligations as an officer of the court.

The court noted that Taylor had been held in contempt in other cases
but these were not relied upon by the bar association.

> As it is, however, the serious charges are largely confined to one trial,
> which could not constitute a fair basis for a determination that Taylor is
> a deliberate and persistent violator so as to merit disbarment or a sub-
> stantial period of suspension, and certainly he should not be made a
> scapegoat for the sins of others.[85]

These are apparently the only cases in which lawyers were severely penalized by the bar for forensic misconduct in a single case. Within the past few years complaints of improper behavior in the courtroom have been filed against other attorneys who represented radical or unpopular clients.

In a case in Washington, D.C., Philip Hirschkop, a lawyer representing certain antiwar radicals who broke into a Dow Chemical office in the District, was censured for his conduct during that trial.[86] (He had also been cited for contempt in that case but all the charges were later dismissed. See discussion at page 151.) In another case, a lawyer who had represented a number of radicals and minority group members in California faced disciplinary proceedings because of his conduct in a murder case that was tried in early 1970, involving some Mexican-Americans who allegedly attacked a policeman.[87]

We have not investigated the charges involved in these proceedings and are in no position to pass on the validity of the complaints. But we must stress the danger that Justice Jackson warned of in the *Isserman* case: that charges can be brought against attorneys representing unpopular clients "based on atmospheric considerations of general undesirability and Communistic [or radical] leanings or affiliation," rather than specific proven offenses. If charges are brought against radical lawyers for behavior that is ignored in negligence lawyers or other criminal lawyers, then bar associations are engaging in discriminatory prosecution which is as much a violation of the equal protection clause of the Constitution as prosecutorial abuse of discretion in other contexts.

Public confidence in the courts and the bar requires that disciplinary action be taken against lawyers who are unfit to practice because of criminal activity, moral derelictions, or misconduct in the courtroom. If the misbehavior becomes a matter of public notoriety there is more reason that swift action be taken to maintain that confidence. But the sanction must be invoked with an even hand, and with no thought of picking out certain lawyers for special treatment because of the unpopularity of their clients.

As a general matter, we think it is undesirable, as Mr. Drinker suggests, to initiate disciplinary action against a lawyer for his behavior in a single hotly contested case. Many of the political cases which we discussed earlier involved volatile defendants and emotional issues. If a lawyer exceeded the bounds of proper behavior in a single case, the most appropriate remedy may be contempt before a different judge from the one who heard the case. If his actions were consistently outrageous throughout the trial with no mitigating circumstances, disciplinary action (though not disbarment) may then properly be taken. Or if a lawyer's misbehavior occurs in more than one trial, it may show his unfitness to practice.

## SUSPENSION OF THE RIGHT TO PRACTICE

Both the American Trial Lawyers Report and the A.B.A. Standards on Trial Disruption recommend a novel punishment for lawyers— suspension from practice—which might be imposed by a judge. The remedy would be applied not in the traditional manner, through a complaint before a bar disciplinary committee, but directly and summarily by a judge in lieu of a contempt citation. The Trial Lawyers Report states:

> In lieu of imposing a traditional fine or imprisonment (for not more than six months), a judge, if permitted by law, may impose any of the following lesser sanctions, which are necessarily implicit in the power to impose imprisonment: . . .
> (b) Suspension for 6 months or less of his right to appear in any case in the particular court where the contempt is committed; or
> (c) Suspension for 6 months or less of his right to appear in any court of the jurisdiction where the contempt was committed.[88]

The A.B.A. Standards also include among their recommendations for deterring and correcting misconduct of attorneys the "suspension for a limited time of the right to practice in the court where the misconduct occurred."[89]

Both reports justify this sanction on the ground that a judge could hold a lawyer in contempt and send him to jail for six months. He should, therefore, have the power to impose a lesser punishment that would protect the court from disruption. The Trial Lawyers Report explains:

> Sending a lawyer to jail would not only prevent his participation in the particular case where the contempt was committed; it would prevent him from appearing in any case in any court while the sentence was in effect. Logically, therefore, a judge should be able to suspend a lawyer's right to appear in any court in the nation, state or federal, for as long a period as he could imprison the lawyer.[90]

We disagree. We do not think that the suspension sanction, a hybrid between criminal contempt and disciplinary action by the bar, should be adopted.

There are several reasons for this. Initially the same judge should no more have the power to suspend a lawyer from practice than to punish him for contempt (see chapter 10). But even if a suspension hearing were held before a different judge, substantial procedural problems exist. There is no indication what burden of proof would be imposed or what standards should be established to justify suspension. Should a judge consider only the action in a single case or can he take into account other misconduct? Would the proceedings be conducted under the secrecy traditionally associated with disciplinary action against lawyers?

Furthermore, there are substantial legal problems with the proposal.

Courts have no inherent authority to impose suspension without specific legislative authorization.[91] The idea that suspension is a "lesser-included-penalty" than contempt is fallacious. Each penalty is different in kind and consequence from another and each must be weighed on its own merits. For instance, although a court could send a lawyer to jail for contempt for six months, this does not mean it could order him not to make political speeches for that period. Sending him to jail would "prevent him from [making political speeches] while the sentence was in effect," as the Trial Lawyers state. But it does not follow that "a judge should be able to suspend a lawyer's right to [make such speeches] for as long a period as he could imprison the lawyer." The right to speak is protected by the First Amendment. The right to practice law is a privilege protected by the Constitution as well.

> The attorney and counselor being, by the solemn judicial act of the court, clothed with his office, does not hold it as a matter of grace and favor. The right which it confers upon him to appear for suitors, and to argue causes, is something more than a mere indulgence, revocable at the pleasure of the court, or at the command of the Legislature.[92]

The two traditional sanctions—contempt imposed by a court or disciplinary action by a bar association—have well-established standards and procedural safeguards (subject to the criticisms contained in chapter 10). Adopting a new sanction which has no basis in existing law is not necessary in view of the few documented instances of lawyer misconduct. The right to practice law should not be tampered with through novel proposals that contain serious constitutional problems.

## Preventive Measures

In addition to the penalties mentioned above, two preventive measures have been suggested for lawyer misconduct in the court. The first would provide for removal of the attorney from a case; the second would bar certain lawyers from appearing in court at all.

### REMOVAL

Just as a particularly obstreperous defendant may be removed from the courtroom in order to allow the trial to continue, a lawyer who misbehaves to the point that continuation of the trial is made virtually impossible could also be dismissed from the case. Both the Trial Lawyers Report and the A.B.A. Standards provide for such a sanction. The A.B.A. Advisory Committee on the Judge's Function states:

> It is also clear that if he engages in such unruly conduct as would require removal of a defendant, the attorney may be removed from the case.[93]

And the Trial Lawyers comment:

> If a judge has inherent power to remove a disruptive defendant from
> the courtroom . . . he should have inherent power to deal with a dis-
> ruptive lawyer in much the same way—by excluding him from further
> participation in the case.[94]

The case law clearly establishes that a trial judge has the power to
remove an attorney to protect the integrity of the proceedings. The
leading case arose out of the Nazi sedition trial in which one counsel
for the defendants, James J. Laughlin, was dismissed from the case.
He had filed a petition of impeachment against the trial judge, containing what the court described as scurrilous and fantastic charges,
and had repeated some of the charges in open court. The trial judge
also criticized his day-to-day courtroom tactics, some of which are
described in chapter 4. Finally the judge dismissed him from the case.
The court of appeals in a three-to-two en banc decision upheld the
trial judge.

> Respondent might, of course, have punished petitioner for this con-
> tempt. But petitioner had already been punished twice, once by re-
> spondent and once by another judge, for contemptuous conduct in this
> trial. Respondent turned from punishment to prevention. He might
> have instituted proceedings for petitioner's disbarment or suspension
> from practice. He chose a more lenient and more promptly effective
> course. He exercised only the elementary right of a court to protect its
> pending proceedings, which includes the right to dismiss from them an
> attorney who cannot or will not take part in them with a reasonable de-
> gree of propriety.[95]

Although two of the judges dissented, because they felt removal
was not called for by the facts, they recognized the power of a judge
to remove an attorney for disrupting a trial in certain circumstances.
The dissenters even noted other circumstances where this power might
be exercised, "for example, where an attorney in disorderly manner
continuously interrupts and interferes with the progress of a trial."[96]
They felt, however, that the filing of the petition of impeachment was
not a sufficient basis for removal.

When a judge should exercise the power of removal is a matter of
his reasonable discretion.[97] As in the case of a disruptive defendant,
the power should not be employed until an attorney has been warned
of the possible consequences of continued misbehavior. In addition, no
attorney should be removed from a case until he has either been cited
for contempt or engaged in clearly contemptuous conduct that seriously interferes with the proceedings. The right of a client to have
counsel of his choice requires that every opportunity be given the attorney to apologize to the court and correct his actions before this remedy
should be used.

## BARRING OUT-OF-STATE LAWYERS

In addition to removing an attorney, the Trial Lawyers and the A.B.A. Advisory Committee recommend that stricter rules be imposed on an out-of-state lawyer who seeks to appear in an action when he is not admitted to practice in that jurisdiction. The A.B.A. recommends that the trial judge may:

> (a)  deny such permission if the attorney has been held in contempt of court or otherwise formally disciplined for courtroom misconduct, or if it appears by reliable information that he has engaged in courtroom misconduct sufficient to warrant disciplinary action;
> (b)  grant such permission on condition that
>     (i)  the petitioning attorney associate with him as co-counsel a local attorney admitted to practice in the jurisdiction,
>     (ii)  the local attorney will assume full responsibility for the defense if the petitioning attorney becomes unable or unwilling to perform his duties. . . .[98]

We recognize the importance of out-of-state attorneys' having knowledge of local rules and, where needed, associating a local attorney for that purpose. Certainly the state's interest in ensuring that its court proceedings are conducted with full knowledge of local requirements is a legitimate one. Nevertheless, we have substantial doubts about the constitutional validity of the proposed remedies and even more doubts as to their wisdom.

The federal courts have recognized that an attorney has a right to practice his profession and that the states can deny that right only on a showing that he fails to meet a standard rationally connected with his fitness to practice. In a case involving the admission of allegedly Communist lawyers to the bar, the Supreme Court wrote in *Schware* v. *Board of Bar Examiners:*

> A State cannot exclude a person from the practice of law or from any other occupation in a manner or for reasons that contravene the Due Process or Equal Protection Clauses of the Fourteenth Amendment. . . . A State can require high standards of qualification. . . . but any qualification must have a rational connection with the applicant's fitness or capacity to practice law. . . . Even in applying permissible standards, officers of a State cannot exclude an applicant when there is no basis for their finding that he fails to meet these standards, or when their action is invidiously discriminatory.[99]

The interest of the attorney in practicing his profession is not substantially lessened by the mere fact that he is seeking to practice in an out-of-state case. State boundaries mean less today than they ever have. An attorney's clients do business in many states, travel freely between states, and may find themselves in legal difficulties, either civil or criminal, almost anywhere. A national law practice has become common and often necessary in many specialized areas of law, such as

federal tax problems, antitrust and securities questions, and other matters. Many trial lawyers have a nationwide reputation and are called
upon to practice in many states. The success of an attorney's practice
may depend as much upon open access to the courts of all states as
upon access to the courts of his home state.

From the client's point of view, it is highly important for individuals
subject to the criminal law to be able to choose their own lawyers. So
much is at stake in a criminal trial that a client should be free to call
on any lawyer of his choosing for assistance. Where necessary, local
counsel should be associated with an out-of-state lawyer to familarize
him with local practice. But the foreign lawyer should be allowed to
take the leading role in presenting the case, if the client wishes.

Many states have laws prohibiting the practice of law by an out-of-
state attorney within their borders unless he had been admitted *pro
hac vice* for an individual case.[100] These laws would apply to the ren-
dering of advice over short periods of time—even two weeks.[101] But the
trend of the federal cases has been to recognize the right of lawyers to
advise on federal matters and appear in federal courts no matter what
the state law says. The Second Circuit Court of Appeals wrote in 1955:

> [W]e hold that under the privileges and immunities clause of the Con-
> stitution no state can prohibit a citizen with a federal claim or defense
> from engaging an out-of-state lawyer to collaborate with an in-state
> lawyer and give legal advice concerning it within the state. . . . We are
> persuaded . . . that where a right has been conferred on citizens by
> federal law, the constitutional guarantee against its abridgement must
> be read to include what is necessary and appropriate for its assertion.
> In an age of increased specialization and high mobility of the bar, this
> must comprehend the right to bring to the assistance of an attorney ad-
> mitted in the resident state a lawyer licensed by "public act" of any
> other state who is thought best fitted for the task, and to allow him to
> serve in whatever manner is most effective, subject only to valid rules
> of courts as to practice before them.[102]

In another case, a federal court of appeals struck down a restrictive
rule of the federal district court in Mississippi prohibiting out-of-state
counsel from appearing except under stringent conditions. It ordered
that the district judge permit "non-local counsel chosen by the parties. . . . [to] take the lead in the direction and argument of the case."[103]

In a leading case in the Third Circuit, the court of appeals held:

> To hold that defendants in a criminal trial may not be defended by out-
> of-the-district counsel elected by them is to vitiate the guarantees of the
> Sixth Amendment.[104]

In a later case arising in New Jersey, out-of-state attorneys had
argued a murder case on appeal which resulted in a new trial being
ordered by the state supreme court. When the attorneys then returned

to the trial court, the local judge would not let them appear in the new trial. They brought suit in the federal courts, which upheld the clients' right to have them represent them.

> While admission pro hac vice is stated in the rule to be in the discretion of the court, the rights and duties of an outside lawyer, once so admitted, appear to be the same as those of a local lawyer. We think that admission pro hac vice, as the rule seems to indicate, is for the entire "cause" and that counsel so admitted in a capital case cannot be arbitrarily and capriciously removed without depriving their clients of rights conferred by the constitution.[105]

While the state's need for an orderly trial is important, the right of an individual to counsel of his choice cannot be denied unless some compelling state regulatory interest can be demonstrated. The state's interest must be asserted in a reasonable manner and in our view only through the least drastic means required to protect the integrity of the court proceedings—such as requiring the association of local counsel.

We conclude that a court cannot and should not bar an out-of-state lawyer from appearing if 1) he is willing to have local counsel associate himself with the case to familiarize the foreign lawyer with local practice, and to obtain service of papers, and 2) the out-of-state lawyer has no present disability or limitation on his right to practice in his own state.

# CHAPTER EIGHT

# *Regulating the Conduct*
# *of the Prosecutor*

The prosecutor stands at a critical point in the system of criminal justice. His office is a public trust and he acts as the official representative of the state or federal government in enforcing the law. It is the responsibility of his office to decide whether to bring a charge against an accused, and if so, which one; he plays an important role throughout the pretrial proceedings and the trial itself; and his actions may decisively determine the outcome of the case.

The special role of the prosecutor is summarized in the Code of Professional Responsibility: "The responsibility of a public prosecutor differs from that of the usual advocate; his duty is to seek justice, not merely to convict. . . ."[1] Or, as stated by the American Bar Association:

> Although the prosecutor operates within the adversary system, it is fundamental that his obligation is to protect the innocent as well as to convict the guilty, to guard the rights of the accused as well as to enforce the rights of the public. . . . [t]he character, quality and efficiency of the whole system is shaped in great measure by the manner in which he exercises his broad discretionary powers.[2]

Because of his pivotal position, the prosecutor can have great influence on whether a trial proceeds in an orderly or disorderly manner. The prosecutor himself may misbehave and thereby cause disorder in the courtroom. In such cases it is proper to consider sanctions against him because the prosecutor, like other lawyers, is subject to discipline for "conduct prohibited by applicable codes and sanctions."[3] In addition, the bearing and actions of the prosecutor can affect the behavior of other participants in the trial, particularly the defendant and defense counsel.

As courtroom disorder became a public issue because of several celebrated trials in the late 1960s, attention focused primarily on criminal defendants and their lawyers. Neither the A.B.A. Standards for dealing with trial disruption nor the rules adopted by the Appellate Division for the First and Second Judicial Departments in New York separately discusses problems relating to the prosecutor. The report of the American College of Trial Lawyers touches on the subject briefly and in general terms, making it plain that prosecutors should be held to high standards of deportment, "standards at least as high, perhaps higher, than those which govern defense counsel."[4]

## Misuse of the Discretion to Prosecute

There is little doubt that the enormous range of discretion held by prosecuting authorities in the United States allows them to use the law for political and other improper ends. Supreme Court Justice Robert H. Jackson acknowledged this possibility when he was attorney general of the United States:

> The prosecutor has more control over life, liberty, and reputation than any other person in America. His discretion is tremendous. He can have citizens investigated and, if he is that kind of person, he can have this done to the tune of public statements and veiled or unveiled intimations. Or the prosecutor may choose a more subtle course and simply have a citizen's friends interviewed. . . . He may dismiss the case before trial, in which case the defense never has a chance to be heard. . . . [A] prosecutor stands a fair chance of finding at least a technical violation of some act on the part of almost anyone. . . . It is in this realm—in which the prosecutor picks some person whom he dislikes or desires to embarrass, or selects some group of unpopular persons and then looks for an offense, that the greatest danger of abuse of prosecuting power lies.[5]

Under the federal system and in most states a grand jury must return an indictment for felonies. In theory the grand jury acts as a shield against prosecutorial overreaching. As a practical matter, however, it seldom disagrees with a district attorney; in the overwhelming majority of cases it will vote as the prosecutor directs. The Wickersham Commission reported in 1931 that the grand jury was acting as a "rubber stamp" of the prosecutor, and many recent studies confirm this judgement.[6] Recent changes in the criminal procedure laws in New York and other states have made it easier for a prosecutor to begin criminal proceedings on his own.[7] Thus there are few procedural impediments blocking a prosecutor from initiating a criminal action.

Prosecutorial abuse is related to courtroom disorder in two ways. Initially, it is a form of official behavior that itself is inconsistent with the integrity of the system of criminal justice. More directly, as we discussed in chapter 5, when prosecutions are sought for political or other improper ends, those accused are inevitably going to experience a sense of anger and frustration which could have explosive results during judicial proceedings.

The reason prosecutors have such wide discretion is threefold:

1. A wide range of penal laws, often not widely known, affect the day-to-day lives of citizens. These include prohibitions against intoxication, against certain types of sexual behavior by adults, against almost any form of gambling, and more recently against certain drug offenses. The tax laws prohibit any intentional falsification of returns, however small. Licenses or permits are necessary for many business activities and the failure to secure the right document may lead to criminal charges. Sunday blue laws are in force in most states, as well as many outdated laws trying to regulate the morals of the people. Bad check and non-support laws exist in every jurisdiction with heavy criminal sanctions possible. In the business field laws against securities violation, price-fixing, market-sharing, conflict of interest, or trading with the enemy are in force. The fact that many millions of Americans are unclear about what conduct is forbidden and may regularly violate such laws—in part because they do not feel that their conduct is morally reprehensible—gives a prosecutor the opportunity to apply the criminal codes selectively.

2. Some criminal statutes are so loosely written, vague, and ambiguous on the one hand, or so complex and incomprehensible on the other, that it is often difficult or impossible to determine what behavior they cover. For this reason state laws have been held unconstitutional by the Supreme Court on the ground that "men of intelligence must necessarily guess as to its meaning."[8] One commentator has noted:

> Draftsmanship has seldom been adequate to clearly set out the specific elements of a crime. This condition may [enable] district attorneys to reach into the depths of antiquated law to find a code section under which a particularly unpopular defendant may be prosecuted.[9]

3. Legal prohibitions exist against many types of inchoate crimes (attempts, solicitation, or aiding and abetting). Under the federal criminal law, national security offenses, such as obstructing recruiting into the armed forces, causing insubordination, or aiding deserters also give prosecutors weapons to use against political enemies. When one adds the possibility of prosecuting for conspiracy to violate these laws, the opportunity for abuse increases manifold.

The fact that prosecutors are often chosen through the political process either as successful candidates for election or as the appointees of candidates whose campaigns they brought to victory has been cited as another reason for possible abuse.[10] In contrast, the British and European prosecutor is more often a professional civil servant owing his allegiance to and under the responsibility of the judiciary rather than the executive department.[11]

In practice this distinction may be more apparent than real. Most American prosecutors have conscientiously performed the functions of their office without being improperly tempted by higher political office. And some of the best prosecutors have been those with political ambitions which may have inspired them to do their best work in the office. Furthermore, political considerations have sometimes played a role in English and European prosecutions.[12]

There are circumstances in which the wide discretion granted prosecutors to bring criminal charges should be examined by the courts. In this connection it is important to define carefully "abuse of prosecutorial discretion" as well as to consider the appropriate remedies for such abuse.

The decided cases do not reveal a clear pattern, but there are two types of case in which an abuse of discretion has been recognized. The first is racial or other invidious discrimination against an entire class, similar to that described in the leading case of *Yick Wo* v. *Hopkins*. There a San Francisco ordinance prohibiting laundries to operate in wooden buildings was applied only against Chinese laundrymen. The Supreme Court declared this illegal.

> Though the law itself be fair on its face and impartial in appearance, yet, if it is applied and administered by public authority with an evil eye and an unequal hand, so as practically to make unjust and illegal discriminations between persons in similar circumstances, material to their rights, the denial of equal justice is still within the prohibition of the Constitution.[13]

The *Yick Wo* ruling involved *administrative* discrimination in the awarding of laundry licenses. Many courts have declined to apply *Yick Wo* to criminal enforcement,[14] but other courts have done so.[15] The Supreme Court has indicated on two occasions that "systematic or intentional discrimination"[16] is improper.

A recent California case illustrates the proposition. In *People* v. *Winter*,[17] gambling charges against a group of black defendants were dismissed by a municipal court judge on the ground that the police department was engaged in discriminatory enforcement. The judge said:

> . . . I also take great exception to what I term a discriminatory pattern of enforcement of the gambling laws of this city. It is my opinion they are enforced mostly against members of the Negro race. If I were to take the Chief's figures as they speak of this, it would lead me to believe that Negroes, who constitute 10% of the population of this city, are responsible for 90% of the gambling in this city. I refuse to believe that

as the truth. I refuse to believe that the people who make their money off of gambling in this city are making it from the penny-ante gambling that goes on in Negro homes and Negro districts. . . . gambling is going on in all sections of our city: (and in all) private clubs; it is going on in fraternal organizations; it is going on in every fight stadium on fight night in the first few rows of the ringside.[18]

On appeal the superior court reversed the dismissal because no proof was offered to show the discrimination charged. But it also said:

Beyond doubt, where the laws have been enforced in a discriminatory manner, with the intent and purpose to deny the equal protection of the law to any persons or group of persons, a discriminatory enforcement of a statute fair on its face when established by adequate proof may invalidate an otherwise proper conviction.[19]

The improper classification need not be by race or sex or some other suspect grouping. As in cases invoking the equal protection clause of the Constitution, any invidious selection may be attacked. In a New York case the defendant had been convicted of violating the state's Sunday closing laws. He admitted the crime but claimed that many other stores in Utica stayed open on Sunday in violation of the statute, but only his discount drugstore and one other cut-rate store were prosecuted. The appellate division remanded the case to the trial court to give the defendant an opportunity to prove selective enforcement:

The claim of discriminatory enforcement does not go to the question of the guilt or innocence of the defendant, which is within the province of the jury. The question is rather whether in a community in which there is general disregard of a particular law with the acquiescence of the public authorities, the authorities should be allowed sporadically to select a single defendant or a single class of defendants for prosecution *because of personal animosity or some other illegitimate reason.* The wrong sought to be prevented is a wrong by the public authorities. To allow such arbitrary and discriminatory enforcement of a generally disregarded law is to place in the hands of the police and the prosecutor a power of the type frequently invoked in countries ruled by a dictator. . . .[20]

It is irrelevant whether the prosecution resulted from an initial decision by the police to arrest members of the class or from a decision by the district attorney to bring such criminal charges.[21] A district attorney can wipe out discriminatory arrests by refusing to proceed with a case. To the extent that he decides to press criminal charges with knowledge of the circumstances, he is endorsing the police in such actions and becomes a participant in the discriminatory tactics.

A second type of prosecutorial abuse has been recognized in cases involving freedom of expression. The Supreme Court in 1971 held unconstitutional on due process and First Amendment grounds an ordinance making it a criminal offense for "three or more persons to assemble . . . on any of its sidewalks . . . and there conduct themselves in a manner annoying to persons passing by. . . ."[22] Justice Stewart, speaking for the Court, stated that this

> contains an obvious invitation to discriminatory enforcement against those whose association together is "annoying" because their ideas, their life style or their physical appearance is resented by the majority of their fellow citizens.[23]

An egregious example of improper use of the prosecutorial office to dampen rights of free expression is a tax case that was instituted against a lawyer who was active in the National Lawyers Guild, a group of liberal and left-wing lawyers. A special agent of the Internal Revenue Service investigated the tax returns of the lawyer and recommended criminal action. The agent's written report made clear that the lawyer's political expressions were an important factor in his recommendation. The report stated that the F.B.I. and the police "have reason to believe Mr. Lenske is a Communist,"[24] and that Lenske and another lawyer had called a meeting for the purpose of forming a local chapter of the Lawyers Guild. It also included a long letter to the editor from Lenske, in which he expressed the thought that in "Cuba, Laos, China" this country's actions had been in violation of our own laws and treaties, and in violation of international law.

As a result of the special agent's recommendation, prosecution was brought against Lenske for filing a fraudulent tax return having overstated his deductions in certain tax years by taking too high a depreciation on certain items. He was found guilty by the trial court, but the court of appeals reversed on the ground that there was no basis for a criminal prosecution:

> We are not aware of any precedent for a conviction of tax fraud by the net worth method in which the question of whether any tax was due was a closed question and an important factor in the case was the amount of depreciation which the prosecution might properly assign to the defendant on a large number of miscellaneous properties owned by the defendant. We find it hard to imagine a case in which such a conviction would be defensible. In the instant case the Special Agent testified on cross examination that he had never recommended a criminal prosecution on the basis that items of depreciation were fraud items.[25]

One of the concurring judges would have reversed the conviction because of improper prosecutorial motivation behind it:

> I regard what I have recited above as a scandal of the first magnitude in the administration of the tax laws of the United States. It discloses nothing less than a witch-hunt, a crusade by the key agent of the United States in this prosecution, to rid our society of unorthodox thinkers and actors by using federal income tax laws and federal courts to put them in the penitentiary.[26]

In a more recent case brought in the federal court in Hawaii, four persons who objected to supplying information for the 1970 census were tried and found guilty for refusing to answer census questions. They appealed on the ground that others had also refused to comply with the census requirement but they alone were prosecuted because they had taken a public stand urging non-cooperation and were known as "hard-core resisters." They supplied the names of six other persons who had refused to answer questions but were not prosecuted. A federal court of appeals upheld their defense.

> The fact alone [that six others had refused cooperation] strongly suggests a questionable emphasis upon the census resisters. When one also considers that background reports were compiled only on persons who had publicly attacked the census, the inference of discriminatory selection becomes almost compelling. An enforcement procedure that focuses upon the vocal offender is inherently suspect, since it is vulnerable to the charge that those chosen for prosecution are being punished for their expression of ideas, a constitutionally protected right.[27]

The Committee endorses the view that prosecutorial abuse consists of discriminatory enforcement against a particular class of persons or arbitrary enforcement of either a generally disregarded law or a law not usually invoked against the conduct complained about. The authorities should not be allowed, in the words of the *Utica Daw's* case, "sporadically to select a single defendant or a single class of defendants for prosecution because of personal animosity or some other illegitimate reason."[28]

In many of the cases described above, prosecutorial abuse was linked to enforcement of a law that had lain dormant and was never previously applied to the conduct in question. Prosecution in such circumstances is not ordinarily an abuse of discretion.

A law may not be enforced because of laxity, because the prosecuting authorities did not know of it, or regarded it of low priority. Sometimes conditions change so that a law unused for a time will be applied. Thus, the criminal provisions of the Rivers and Harbors Act of 1899 have recently been invoked against polluters of navigable rivers after many years of non-use due to a lack of concern about water pollution. Without a showing of purposeful discrimination the first defendant after the hiatus could not properly claim that he should not be prosecuted. In 1952, the authorities in the District of Columbia invoked a law prohibiting racial discrimination by restaurants, despite the fact that no prosecutions had taken place since 1872. Nevertheless, the Supreme Court upheld the prosecution saying:

> Cases of hardship are put where criminal laws so long in disuse as to be no longer known to exist are enforced against innocent parties. But that condition does not bear on the continuing validity of the law; it is only an ameliorating factor in enforcement.[29]

Similarly, tax laws are frequently invoked to punish alleged gangsters or other undesirables when it is impossible to prosecute them on other charges. Except in the Lenske situation where clear First Amendment rights were involved, such an approach is proper, since the tax laws are regularly applied against fraudulent filers. Professor Arthur Bonfield explains:

> In such a situation, a generally enforced statute intended to be widely applied may be used to penalize individuals for other unprovable or even unpunishable activities. But since the articulated acts for which the individual is punished are in fact generally proscribed and penalized no real abuse of administrative discretion is presented.[30]

Prosecutions under a statute long in disuse will involve an abuse of discretion only in cases, such as those previously discussed, where the selectivity is based on First Amendment considerations, racial or other invidious classifications, or a decision "purposely to 'persecute' a particular individual or individuals,"[31] as in the *Utica Daw's* case.[32]

The identification of prosecutorial abuse in certain classes of cases presents squarely the issue of the proper remedy for such misconduct. One of the consultants to the Committee, Professor Graham Hughes, discussed the contention that, in cases where an unjust and unequal enforcement policy has been countenanced by the law, "the usual moral arguments in favor of cooperating with judicial processes have been overborne by countervailing arguments of justice and fairness." He suggested the possibility of civil disobedience in the courtroom as a response to evidence of arbitrary caprice on the part of the judicial system. His argument was presented with particular reference to the claims of black citizens.

This line of analysis did not lead Professor Hughes to sanction disruption in the courts. Nor do we. It is understandable that defendants who have grounds for believing that they have been singled out for prosecution will be outraged. Indeed, it is arguable, in Professor Hughes's terms, that "lawyers have a peculiar and inescapable duty to press this point of view upon the community and the legislatures." Nevertheless, the integrity of the system requires that a complaint about prosecutorial abuse of discretion be dealt with in an orderly manner and that judges be given the opportunity to pass on the issue in an unemotional and rational atmosphere.

The proper and most effective remedy for abuse of prosecutorial discretion in the categories we have described is to allow the defendant an affirmative defense to the criminal charge. As the court said in the *Utica Daw's* case:

> A heavy burden rests on the defendant to establish conscious, intentional discrimination, but if it succeeds in sustaining that burden, the defendant will be entitled to a dismissal of the prosecution as a matter

of law. We believe this to be the necessary consequence of the principle of equal protection of the laws proclaimed in both the Federal and State Constitutions. The Constitution not only forbids discriminatory laws (making distinctions without rational basis . . .) but it also forbids the discriminatory enforcement of nondiscriminatory laws. . . .[33]

Dismissal of a charge for discriminatory enforcement has occurred in a number of cases, some of which have been previously discussed. In other situations state prosecutions have been enjoined because of charges of discriminatory enforcement. In one case a state court enjoined discriminatory enforcement of an ordinance prohibiting certain sidewalk obstructions.[34] In another case, a showing of discriminatory enforcement was the basis for denying a city enforcement of its zoning ordinance.[35]

On almost every occasion where prosecutorial abuse has been raised it was presented to the trial court before or after trial outside the presence of the jury.[36] Nevertheless, it would be equally appropriate for the issue to be presented to the jury. The Supreme Court has expressed a presumption in favor of a jury trial on at least some factual issues relating to arbitrary exercise of official power, such as entrapment.[37]

One desirable way of dividing the responsibility between judge and jury would be to permit the judge to make an initial determination of whether a prima facie case of discriminatory enforcement has been shown. If sufficient evidence is presented, the ultimate question can then be submitted to the jury by the defense, which bears the burden of proving purposeful discrimination. A precedent for this procedure can be found in the issue of admitting into evidence a confession alleged to have been coerced. Although the judge must make an initial finding on the question of voluntariness, many states provide that the issue then becomes one for the jury's consideration.[38]

Other means exist to combat prosecutorial discretion in addition to dismissal of criminal charges. One straightforward remedy is to lodge a prompt complaint with a prosecutor's superiors. While this might seem futile, it has sometimes worked. At the height of the McCarthy era one employee of the State Department, Val R. Lorwin, admitted to security officers that he had been a member of the Socialist party during the 1930s, but denied under oath that he had any Communist ties. A government informer testified that Lorwin told him that he had been a Communist. The Justice Department thought the case warranted grand jury investigation but no indictment for perjury unless more evidence was unearthed. The assistant United States attorney in charge of the case, however, went ahead on his own and secured an indictment by presenting the informer to a grand jury and promising that the F.B.I. would produce corroborating testimony. After the matter was brought to the prosecutor's superiors in the Justice Department, they agreed to dismiss the indictment, and discharged the overeager assistant U.S. attorney.[39]

Another possible remedy lies in the sentencing discretion of the trial judge. In cases where the defendant has not carried the "heavy burden" of proving a clear abuse, the judge may at the time of sentence properly take into account any improper motive by the prosecutor. This means that when there is credible evidence that a prosecution has been improper, but not enough to warrant dismissal, a judge may mitigate the sentence if he believes that substantial justice requires it. Further, while disruption during a trial should not be excused, prosecutorial abuse can be judicially considered in mitigation of a contempt citation.

As stated earlier, the dangers to a tranquil courtroom are intensified when selective, discriminatory prosecution is brought for political or other improper ends. Although relatively few cases have dealt with the problem, they are an indication of its importance. If defendants feel they have a legal defense to the charges against them when they can show purposeful discrimination, it should reduce their incentive for courtroom tactics to protest and dramatize the grievance. The low visibility of the problem merely permits continuation of abuse. We agree with Professor Kenneth Culp Davis that the courts should

> take a fresh look at the tradition that prevents them from reviewing the prosecuting function. . . . The reasons for a judicial check of prosecutors' discretion are stronger than for such a check of other administrative discretion that is now traditionally reviewable. Important interests are at stake. Abuses are common. The questions involved are appropriate for judicial determination. And much injustice could be corrected.[40]

## Mass Trials and Conspiracy Charges

A prosecutor's decision to join several defendants in a single criminal trial typically presents serious problems concerning the right to a fair trial for those accused. Less widely recognized but of considerable importance to the present inquiry is the fact that mass trials aggravate the potential for a disruptive trial.

There are many possibilities for prejudice to defendants: the demeanor or reputation of one defendant may adversely affect another, the evidence introduced by one defendant may be harmful to another, the jury may have difficulty differentiating guilt among the defendants, etc. Recognizing this problem, the Supreme Court has held that in joint trials the confession of one codefendant implicating another cannot be introduced in evidence if the codefendant does not testify.[41]

The Court has acknowledged that "joint trials do conserve state funds, diminish inconvenience to witnesses and public authorities, and avoid delays in bringing those accused of crime to trial."[42] But it has recognized that the cost may be excessive by approving the following statement from a New York conspiracy case:

> We secure greater speed, economy and convenience in the administration of the law at the price of fundamental principles of constitutional liberty. That price is too high.[43]

The potential for prejudice is greatest in conspiracy cases, for each conspirator is deemed to act as the agent of all the others, resulting in the admission of evidence not permitted in an ordinary criminal prosecution. Moreover, the mere fact that coconspirators are tried together cannot help but suggest to the jury that they were jointly implicated in something. Justice Robert H. Jackson's famous remarks about the conspiracy doctrine still have validity today.

> The modern crime of conspiracy is so vague that it almost defies definition. Despite certain elementary and essential elements, it also, chameleon-like, takes on a special coloration from each of the many independent offenses on which it may be overlaid. It is always predominantly mental in composition because it consists primarily of a meeting of minds and an intent. . . .
> [T]he conspiracy doctrine will incriminate persons on the fringe of offending who would not be guilty of aiding and abetting or of becoming an accessory, for those charges only lie when an act which is a crime has actually been committed. . . .
> Strictly, the prosecution should first establish prima facie the conspiracy and identify the conspirators, after which evidence of acts and declarations of each in the course of its execution are admissible against all. But the order of proof of so sprawling a charge is difficult for a judge to control. As a practical matter, the accused often is confronted with a hodgepodge of acts and statements by others which he may never have authorized or intended or even known about, but which help to persuade the jury of existence of the conspiracy itself. In other words, a conspiracy often is proved by evidence that is admissible only upon assumption that conspiracy existed. . . .[44]

The relationship between mass trials and courtroom disruption has received insufficient attention. All four of the contemporary trials analyzed in earlier chapters which involved considerable disruption— Nazi sedition, Communist party, Chicago conspiracy, and New York Black Panther—had many defendants and lawyers. There are many other examples of disruption in trials with more than one defendant. The returns to our questionnaire to judges revealed thirteen such disorderly proceedings, five of which resulted in contempt citations.

The reasons for the relationship between mass trials and disorder are not difficult to perceive. One or more defendants may believe they are unjustly joined with the others. Several defendants usually means several lawyers, with resulting confusion and loss of centralized control of the case. And if there is disorder, the numerous defendants may reinforce and encourage one another. All of these factors were present in the Chicago conspiracy case, and many of them in the other trials that we have analyzed for this report. The government prosecutor in the Nazi sedition case, O. John Rogge, believes that the government erred there in bringing thirty defendants into court at the same time. "You can't avoid trouble if you bring that large a group of political dissidents into court whipping up enthusiasm for each other." Rogge believes that smaller groups of defendants should have been tried together. Even if there was duplication in trial preparation, probably, as things turned out, less total time would have been consumed.[45]

Several remedies have been proposed for the indiscriminate and often prejudicial use of conspiracy and other mass trials. One is to alleviate the procedural disadvantages to defendants through modification of the law of evidence, thereby reducing the risk of guilt by association. On the whole this has proved unsuccessful,[46] and the courts have generally relied on limiting and clarifying instructions to juries in order to obviate possible prejudice from mass trials.[47]

Another remedy is to give defendants an absolute right to separate trials. This is the practice in a few states, but most jurisdictions are liberal in permitting prosecutors to join defendants. Federal Rule of Criminal Procedure 8(b), for example, which is identical or similar to many state rules, provides:

> Two or more defendants may be charged in the same indictment or information if they are alleged to have participated in the same act or transaction or in the same series of acts or transactions constituting an offense or offenses. Such defendants may be charged in one or more counts together or separately and all of the defendants need not be charged in each count.

The courts have had considerable difficulty in applying the above language to the variety of fact situations that have arisen, and they have developed complex rules for determining whether or not joinder of offenses is permissible.[48]

Federal and state rules also provide for relief from prejudicial joinder, but do so in terms so vague that there is insufficient guidance for courts. Severance is entirely discretionary,[49] and is so rarely granted that one observer has noted that the rule "might as well be entitled 'No Relief from Prejudicial Joinder' as now construed. . . ."[50] The principal reason for the reluctance to grant severance—like the decision to join defendants initially—is the desire to avoid the delay and expense of multiple trials, but the effect may be a prejudicial and disorderly proceeding.

Another method has been proposed for remedying the threat to fairness of conspiracy prosecutions while maintaining conspiracy as one way to attack groups organized for criminal objectives.[51] Under it the government, at a closed hearing before a judge, would be required 1) to make a convincing showing of a conspiratorial agreement, and 2) to bring forward admissible evidence for proof at trial. Only if it were able to do this could the case proceed to the jury. In addition, the court would have the authority to direct a special verdict or order a severance as to any defendant against whom the evidence appeared substantially less or different from the evidence against the others. Finally, in cases where there has been a completed crime involving group criminality, the government must choose between prosecuting for conspiracy and prosecuting for the substantive crime, the choice of either alternative barring the other. This proposal, while worthy of study, has not been implemented.

Historically, in the words of Learned Hand, conspiracy has been the "darling of the prosecutor's nursery."[52] The vagueness and complexity of the joinder rules when added to the openended nature of conspiracy enables a prosecutor who lacks judgment and sensitivity to charge a broad conspiracy involving several substantive offenses. As events have shown this can easily lead to courtroom disorder. The Committee believes that prosecutors, before proceeding with mass trials, should take strictly into account not only the possibly prejudicial consequences of conspiracy indictments but the potential harm to courtroom order that they invite.

# Courtroom Misconduct by Prosecutors

Prosecutorial misconduct in the courtroom has a long history, although its form tends to differ from the misconduct of criminal defendants and their lawyers. There is no reported case of courtroom violence by prosecutors and instances of verbal abuse by a prosecutor against a trial judge are very rare and do not appear in any cases that we have discovered.[53] On the other hand, prosecutors sometimes argue points of law excessively and, more frequently, make arrogant or provocative comments in the course of a trial which tend to prejudice the defendant. For example, in a recent Texas case, when a defendant on the stand complained that he had been manhandled by the police, the district attorney responded by saying, "Too bad they didn't kill you."[54] There are also many cases in which prosecutors made racial and religious slurs, and employed other emotional appeals, although this is now less frequent than in the past.

The issue in most of these cases is whether the prosecutorial statements were sufficiently prejudicial to require reversal of a conviction. But such statements also inflame the atmosphere in a way that can pro-

voke responses by defendants and their lawyers, thereby seriously
escalating the level of trial disorder. Contrary to what may be the
general impression, a high proportion of appeals in criminal cases involve a claim of improper conduct by the prosecutor. One appellate
judge has estimated that at least 60 percent of the cases coming before
his court involve such a claim.[55]

## The Nature and Significance of Prosecutorial Misconduct

The courts have pretty well outlined the basic forms of improper statements by a prosecutor, which usually involve attempts to influence the
jury through use of inadmissible evidence or inflammatory remarks
about the defendant or his lawyer. Prosecutors have been known to
comment on the failure of the defendant to testify or to assert facts that
have not been presented in evidence. Prosecutors have suggested that
evidence exists which they have been unable to introduce, or expressed
their personal belief in the defendant's guilt. They have also raised the
possibility of executive pardon for the defendant and have argued that
erroneous convictions can always be reversed on appeal.[56] All of these
statements are improper in a criminal trial.

What most clearly emerges from the decided cases is their unpre-
dictability; no consistent pattern is evident. Even if the alleged misconduct in one case seems similar to the alleged misconduct in another,
the procedural context is invariable different. The force of precedent is
therefore slight. The courts seem to enjoy almost total freedom to reach
any result on any given set of facts.

Overt appeals to racial, national, and religious prejudice were once
fairly common. The courts reversed convictions when prosecutors had
argued that blacks should not be judged by the same law as whites,[57]
and that Southern gentlemen would not condemn anyone for trying to
keep a Negro in his place.[58] It was also reversible error, in an attempted
murder prosecution before an all-white jury, to cross-examine the
defendant by saying, "Then you struck him because he was a white
man."[59] Yet an admonition and an instruction to the jury to disregard
were held sufficient to cure the error when the prosecutor made the
following appeal in a prosecution for the unlawful sale of liquor:

> There is lots of drinking going on up around Liberty Hill. If you want
> to stop it, give this nigger the limit. . . . I want you gentlemen to send
> the word by these people from Liberty Hill out there in the court room
> that this nigger is stuck and there must be no more liquor drinking at
> their Saturday night socials or any other time up there.[60]

Moreover, when a prosecutor argued that a verdict of guilty would
"throw a chill down the spine of every Negro in Gregg County and
thereby stop some of these Negro killings," an appellate court in 1941

described the statement as a "mild effort at oratory" and said, "[W]e find nothing to condemn."[61]

Although such explicit racist remarks are now rarely encountered, the most frequent form of prosecutorial misconduct is still abuse of the defendant. It has been held reversible error to call the defendant "doubly vicious because he demanded his full constitutional rights,"[62] a "cheap, scaly, slimy crook,"[63] a "leech off society,"[64] a user of "Al Capone tactics of intimidation,"[65] and a "junkie, rat, and 'sculptor' with a knife."[66]

It was found improper for the prosecutor in the Chicago conspiracy trial to refer to the defendants in his final argument to the jury as

> "evil men," "liars and obscene haters," "profligate extremists," and "violent anarchists." He suggested one defendant was doing well as it got dark because "predators always operate better when it gets close to dark."[67]

Courts have found no error, however, in cases in which the defendant was called "animalistic,"[68] "lowdown, degenerate and filthy,"[69] "a mad dog,"[70] "a rattlesnake,"[71] "a trafficker in human misery,"[72] "a blackhearted traitor,"[73] "a hired gunfighter,"[74] "a creature of the jungle,"[75] " a type of worm,"[76] or " a brute, a beast, an animal, a mad dog who does not deserve to live."[77]

Prosecutorial abuse of the defense attorney is a frequent ground of reversal. The Seventh Circuit Court of Appeals found various remarks of the prosecutor in the Chicago conspiracy case to be improper and "below the standards applicable to a representative of the United States." They included the following:

> In objecting to a question put by Mr. Weinglass, the United States Attorney added: "We are not in some kind of kindergarten." After Mr. Weinglass offered his explanation, the United States Attorney said: "This crybaby stuff he goes through, your Honor, every time he asks a wrong question is just. . . ."[78]

> When Mr. Kunstler requested a half hour's variation in the schedule to accommodate a witness, the United States Attorney said: "Your Honor, that was a half hour of trial time. They haven't put a witness on yet that they got on and off in a half hour. Who are they kidding? This is just a showboat.[79]

Extreme examples are: the California case in which a prosecutor said that the defense attorney had for thirty-three years represented "highway robbers, murderers, men of the underworld and he is now defending Alpine. Do you not see back of this case, ladies and gentlemen, the operation of the underworld?";[80] and the 1970 Illinois case in which a prosecutor said that the defense attorney could qualify as an S.S. trooper.[81] In another 1970 Illinois decision, by contrast, an appellate court found it harmless error for the prosecutor to assert that he knew from years of personal experience that the defense counsel was trying to free the defendant by trickery.[82]

The varieties of prosecutorial misbehavior are such that it is not possible to define them in advance. Nevertheless, the impact of such statements may be great in a criminal trial, and they have been condemned by the Supreme Court. The classic statement is by Justice Sutherland, writing in 1935:

> The United States Attorney is the representative not of an ordinary party to a controversy, but of a sovereignty whose obligation to govern impartially is as compelling as its obligation to govern at all; and whose interest, therefore, in a criminal prosecution is not that it shall win a case, but that justice shall be done. As such, he is in a peculiar and very definite sense the servant of the law, the twofold aim of which is that guilt shall not escape or innocence suffer. He may prosecute with earnestness and vigor—indeed, he should do so. But, while he may strike hard blows, he is not at liberty to strike foul ones. It is as much his duty to refrain from improper methods calculated to produce a wrongful conviction as it is to use every legitimate means to bring about a just one.[83]

Despite this and similar strong statements, courts have been slow to implement the proposition fully. Part of the reason is the existence of other Supreme Court comments that provide a basis for disregarding instances of prosecutorial misconduct. As early as 1897 the Court said:

> There is no doubt that, in the heat of argument, counsel do occasionally make remarks that are not justified by the testimony, and which are, or may be, prejudicial to the accused. . . . If every remark made by counsel outside of the testimony were grounds for a reversal, comparatively few verdicts would stand, since in the ardor of advocacy, and in the excitement of trial, even the most experienced counsel are occasionally carried away by this temptation.[84]

Other judicial statements depart even further from the ideal stated in Justice Sutherland's opinion.[85]

## The Standard for Evaluating Prosecutorial Misconduct

The unclear pattern of decision and the rhetoric on both sides presents the crucial issue of the attitude with which a prosecutor should approach his courtroom responsibility, and more broadly the standard by which courts should appraise questionable prosecutorial comments.

Some courts have concluded that the prosecutor should be held to a stricter standard of courtroom conduct than the defense attorney;[86] others have employed the same standard for prosecutors and defense lawyers,[87] and the American College of Trial Lawyers has elided the issue by asserting that prosecutors should meet "standards at least as high, perhaps higher, than those which govern defense counsel."[88]

We conclude that the prosecutor should be held to a stricter standard than a defense attorney. In considering this matter, we are heavily influenced by the fact that a prosecutor's abuse of a criminal defendant can be more damaging to both the substance and appearance of justice than any injudicious statement by a defense attorney. Comments by a defense attorney "have little weight as compared with similar statements of the district attorney. . . . A statement of the prosecutor . . . is weighed with the authority of his office."[89]

The most obvious effect of prosecutorial abuse is of course on a fair trial through the impact on a jury. Professor Albert Alschuler of the Texas Law School, a consultant to the Committee, explains:

> When a defense attorney resorts to what Professor Paul Freund calls "the infantile-regressive mode of expression," he knows, if he has any sense, that he is likely to alienate the jury trying his client. The attorney may have decided to appeal to a larger audience (perhaps Walter Cronkite's) or just to go down with his colors flying. A prosecutor, of course, may also find that his misconduct will create resentment and hurt his chances with the jury. Nevertheless, while a defense attorney sometimes suffers from association with his client, a prosecutor usually benefits from his association with the cause of law enforcement. The assistant district attorney is the representative of an elected, presumably popular public official, and the mere fact that he is a state employee may create a sense of trust and an expectation of fairness that a defense attorney would find difficult to match through the most strenuous exertion of his charm.[90]

Apart from its effect on a particular jury, prosecutorial misconduct may also have serious consequences for the administration of justice. The Wickersham Commission observed in 1931 that, unlike police abuse, prosecutorial misconduct occurs "in the publicity of a court room" where it is easily observed by the press and the public. Because this "lawless enforcement of the law" is perpetrated by "officials most definitely responsible for law observance," the natural result is a serious questioning of the entire legal process.[91]

This resentment is likely to become especially intense when the defendant belongs to a racial minority or unpopular political group. Such people tend to view official misconduct as evidence that they cannot expect fair treatment from the courts. In addition, rehabilitative efforts are hindered when a defendant "feels deeply and justly that society in the person of its chief representatives has behaved tyrannically and brutally."[92]

Whether or not the prosecutor is held to a higher standard than the defense attorney, prosecutors who attempt to secure a decision on emotional grounds rather than on a rational appraisal of the evidence should be condemned. As early as 1889, the Pennsylvania Supreme Court said that "heated zeal" was not excusable on the part of the prosecutor, who should act as "an impartial officer" rather than a "partisan."[93] In a like vein, the Sixth Circuit more recently declared:

> Above and beyond all technical procedural rules . . . is the public inter-
> est in the maintenance of the nation's courts as fair and impartial forums
> where neither bias nor prejudice rules, and appeals to passion find no
> place. . . .[94]

Excessive appeals to passion are necessarily disruptive to the proceedings. They produce increased contention in court and distract the judge and jury from considering the evidence and reaching a fair verdict. They can be more disruptive of a trial than a defense lawyer's improper argumentation and refusal to obey a judge's orders. They are a serious threat to the cause of orderly justice.

## Remedies for Courtroom Misbehavior by Prosecutors

Despite the wide range of improper trial conduct by public prosecutors, it is difficult to fashion appropriate sanctions. This is true because of the traditional impediments to punishment of public officials, accentuated in this instance by the close working relationship that often develops between prosecutors and judges, the reluctance to employ a remedy that might lead to freeing an apparently guilty criminal defendant, and the absence of guidelines or experience in relation to some of the remedies that have been proposed.

### DIRECT REMEDIES

**Contempt of court.** Contempt is theoretically available against prosecutors in the same way that it has been used from time to time to control the in-court conduct of private attorneys. But contempt citations have in fact not been used for this purpose.

Two thorough studies of cases going back at least twenty-five years have failed to uncover a single instance in which a prosecutor was punished for contemptuous courtroom behavior.[95] Two cases were found in which trial courts held prosecutors in contempt for their courtroom statements, but both decisions were reversed on appeal.[96] There are other cases in which appellate courts have suggested that a prosecutor should have been held in contempt, but these have customarily come to nothing.[97]

The complete reluctance of courts until now to impose the contempt sanction should not be permitted to continue. We find no reason in principle why prosecutors should be immunized from contempt citations for flagrant or disrespectful conduct that obstructs the judicial process. This can only encourage prosecutor-initiated misconduct which must adversely affect the quality of justice. We recommend that trial judges use the contempt remedy to punish prosecutors at least as readily as they would defense counsel who misbehave in court. If anything, as we have pointed out above, prosecutors should be held to a stricter standard in view of their public position and their potential impact on juries and the fairness of a trial.

This does not mean that contempt should be imposed for trivial or isolated missteps; on the contrary, citations should be confined to cases of repeated misconduct in which judicial reprimands have not sufficed. A prosecutor should be scrupulously warned that his conduct is impermissible, and punishable if it continues, and the safeguards that we discuss in chapter 10 should be available to prosecutors as well as other lawyers.

**Discipline by the legal profession.** A second potential remedy against prosecutors—censure, disbarment, and suspension initiated by a complaint of a bar association—has been as dormant as the contempt power. As we have seen in chapter 7 such disciplinary measures are rarely invoked against defense attorneys for courtroom misconduct. A 1954 study found only one case in which a prosecutor was disciplined for forensic misconduct.[98] In that case, the prosecutor had criticized a decision of the state supreme court in open court, accusing it of relying on evidence not in the record. He was mistaken in his charge and the court later reprimanded him and suspended him from practice for thirty days.

Grievance committees of state or local bar associations have been overwhelmingly unsympathetic to disciplinary actions against public prosecutors.[99] Of course, prosecutors have been disciplined for accepting bribes, perjury, embezzling government funds, and other criminal conduct. Even in these situations, courts have been reluctant to subject them to the rules applicable to other attorneys, and have avoided severe sanctions. In one instance, although the court recognized that a prosecutor's actions might merit disbarment, the sanction was inappropriate on the questionable ground that it would forfeit the office of county attorney and deprive the people of the services of their elected representative.[100] The court was content to reprimand the individual involved. On other occasions, courts have suspended prosecutors from the practice of law, but ruled that this was not applicable to the performance of prosecutorial duties.[101]

We disagree with this approach. When prosecutors engage in prejudicial conduct of the type previously described, the appropriate grievance committees of the bar should be diligent in investigating and acting on the matter. Bar associations should encourage defense lawyers and judges to report cases of prosecutorial misconduct and should follow up on these cases as vigorously as possible. Further, if a prosecutor has been declared a danger to the bar he should not be allowed to represent the state in any further proceedings.

The need for professional discipline of this kind is obvious when one considers the alternative remedies. Relying on the prosecutor's superiors to punish him for these actions runs counter to the understandable reluctance of district attorneys to punish their own personnel for overzealous performance of their duties. Appellate review of the case in which prosecutors' misconduct occurred may lead to a reversal of the conviction but does not directly discipline the prosecutor himself. Since every bar association has insisted that a prosecutor is, first and foremost, a lawyer, it follows that control by the profession should be invoked when he violates the standards established to guide his courtroom performance.

## INDIRECT REMEDY

**Appellate reversal.** Because other remedies have not been used effectively the most frequent method for dealing with prosecutorial misconduct until now has been appellate reversal of a conviction obtained in a case where such conduct occurred. On the surface, the prosecutor himself is not punished if a conviction he secured by improper methods is overturned. But the reversal does serve as some check of his behavior. He himself has the burden of a retrial; he is told to "go back and do it right." Moreover, prosecutors tend to be concerned about their rate of valid convictions. A prosecutor's superiors know when the behavior of an assistant district attorney leads to a reversal since they read appellate opinions. Also, since he is a lawyer, a prosecutor may find a judicial rebuke especially stinging and professionally harmful.

Perhaps most important, appellate reversal gives a court the opportunity to elaborate the standards required of the prosecutor's office. Since prosecutors are rarely if ever held in contempt or disciplined by the legal profession for their derelictions, review of criminal convictions may be the only chance that a court has to determine whether or not a prosecutor acted properly and to announce what is expected of him.

There is often a noticeable reluctance by courts to discipline a prosecutor by letting a defendant go free if there is strong evidence of guilt. Judge Learned Hand wrote in 1939:

> That was plainly an improper remark, and if a reversal would do no more than show our disapproval, we might reverse. Unhappily, it would accomplish little towards punishing the offender, and would upset the conviction of a plainly guilty man. . . . [I]t seems to us that a reversal would be an immoderate penalty.[102]

Reflecting Judge Hand's approach, the courts have established a series of obstacles to appellate reversal of cases involving prosecutorial misconduct.

*Harmless error.* Many courts have expressed strong disapproval of improper remarks by a district attorney but have nevertheless upheld a conviction on the ground that it constituted "harmless error." This may mean that in the court's view the action of the prosecutor was technically incorrect but not serious enough to jeopardize the defendant's right to a fair trial. Or it may mean that the prosecutor's action was serious but that the court was strongly persuaded of the defendant's guilt and did not want to reverse the conviction.

It is difficult to discern a pattern in the application of the harmless error doctrine. In some cases the courts refuse to reverse if the jury deliberated a long time,[103] but in others they have said that lengthy deliberations showed that the case was a close one and the prosecutor's misconduct may have adversely affected the verdict.[104] If the jury acquitted some of the defendants[105] or found a defendant not guilty of some charges[106] or gave less than a maximum sentence,[107] some courts have concluded that the prosecutor's errors must have been harmless.

Judge Jerome Frank expressed strong disapproval of the way in which the harmless error doctrine was being used:

> This court has several times used vigorous language in denouncing government counsel for such conduct as that of the United States Attorney here. But, each time, it has said that, nevertheless, it would not reverse. Such an attitude of helpless piety is, I think, undesirable. . . . If we continue to do nothing practical to prevent such conduct, we should cease to disapprove it. . . . Government counsel, employing such tactics, are the kind who, eager to win victories, will gladly pay the small price of a ritualistic verbal spanking. The practice of this court—recalling the bitter tear shed by the Walrus as he ate the oysters—breeds a deplorably cynical attitude toward the judiciary.[108]

We believe that the doctrine of harmless error should never be applied to serious misconduct of the prosecutor that may have affected a jury verdict. In particular, the courts should not employ the doctrine solely because of a belief that the defendant was guilty. In a closely analogous context the Supreme Court has, we believe, indicated the correct approach to this issue. In 1967 it held that when a prosecutor had made an improper comment to the jury about the failure of a defendant to take the stand in his own defense, the "harmless error" rules could not be invoked by the state courts to justify an affirmance of the conviction, unless it was clear "beyond a reasonable doubt that the error complained of did not contribute to the verdict obtained."[109]

This standard should be applied in all cases of serious prosecutorial misconduct in both state and federal courts. It is difficult to determine the psychological effect of a prosecutor's improper remarks on the jury or how it weighed the evidence against the defendant. Sanctioning such conduct can only encourage prosecutors to use similar methods in the future, and winking at lawlessness by the prosecution can only promote a cynical public attitude toward the administration of justice.

*Need for proper objection.* A second obstacle which has been raised to appellate reversal of cases in which prosecutorial misconduct has occurred is that proper objection must be made. The Supreme Court has said:

> Counsel for the defense cannot as a rule remain silent, interpose no objections, and after a verdict has been returned seize for the first time on the point that the comments . . . were improper and prejudicial.[110]

The primary basis for the objection rule is one of judicial economy. If the prosecutor says something improper, the theory is that a trial judge can correct it if his attention is called to it by the defense. This is a far more efficient process than appellate reversal and a new trial.

But this approach overlooks certain practical problems. If a defense counsel objects frequently to what the prosecutor is saying, the jury may resent the interruption. Frequent objections also may focus the jury's attention on the improper statement.

Rule 52(b) of the Federal Rules of Criminal Procedure provides that "plain errors or defects affecting substantial rights may be noticed although they were not brought to the attention of the court." Certainly, serious prosecutorial misconduct should fall within the ambit of Rule 52(b). The trial judge therefore should assume some responsibility for correcting the situation even without objection by the defense.

In our view the interest in ensuring that the state authorities act properly outweighs considerations of judicial economy. Objection by the defense should not be a necessary predicate for presenting improper prosecutorial conduct to an appeal court. It offers too easy a shield for those whose actions already are overly protected.

*Provocation by the defense attorney.* A final obstacle to appellate review of prosecutorial misconduct is the notion that if such misconduct was provoked by the defense counsel, it cannot be the basis for reversal. Although provocation by a prosecutor or a judge does not generally excuse a defendant's contemptuous behavior or that of his lawyer, many courts conclude that a prosecutor's misbehavior need not be punished by appellate reversal if the defense induced it.[111]

We believe that the defense of provocation has been misapplied by appellate courts and should be permitted only in very special circumstances. Obviously a prosecutor should be permitted a limited response to correct defense misstatements. For example, a prosecutor cannot usually comment about a defendant's criminal background except to impeach him if he appears as a witness. But a prosecutor should be able to comment if a defense lawyer erroneously states the facts on this issue. Similarly, the prosecution should be permitted a limited response to correct defense misconduct or misstatements. Unfortunately, defense excesses have been allowed to justify serious retaliation by prosecutors.[112]

All of these obstacles make it difficult for appellate courts to review prosecutorial misconduct. Since such review has been the chief means of checking the problem, it is important that the obstacles be minimized so that the courts can establish proper standards for the prosecutor.

## LONG-TERM REFORM

We must also think of eliminating courtroom misconduct by prosecutors through reform of the office itself. The Wickersham Commission wrote in 1931:

> The system of prosecutors elected for short terms, with assistants chosen on the basis of political patronage, with no assured tenure yet charged with wide undefined powers, is ideally adapted to misgovernment.[113]

The rapid turnover among prosecutors combined with the overwhelming case loads, the lack of training, and sometimes an allegiance to political figures make it difficult to achieve the professionalism which the prosecution office requires. The European system, under which prosecutors are trained for the job and are responsible to the courts rather than to local political forces, seems to promote a more efficient and professional prosecutor. At the very least, legislatures should consider a system that gives prosecutors long-term tenure to allow for continuity and development of expertise in the office.

# CHAPTER NINE

# *The Responsibility of Judges*

## The Judge's Task in Maintaining Order

Justice Felix Frankfurter wrote in the *Sacher* case:

> In administering the criminal law, judges wield the most awesome surgical instruments of society. A criminal trial, it has been well said, should have the atmosphere of the operating room. The presiding judge determines the atmosphere. He is not an umpire who enforces the rules of a game, or merely a moderator between contestants. If he is adequate to his functions, the moral authority which he radiates will impose the indispensable standards of dignity and austerity upon all those who participate in a criminal trial.[1]

This comment points out that ultimately the problem of courtroom disorder is one which the trial judge must solve. His decisions are crucial for determining whether a trial will be disrupted or whether rational and civilized proceedings occur.

In discussing the responsibility of judges, we distinguish between what a judge should do to prevent disruption and what he should refrain from doing that might bring it about. In other words, there are times when a judge may be the principal agent in creating disorder in the court or in aggravating potentially disruptive conditions. Although these situations are comparatively rare, the manner in which a judge may contribute to disorder must be examined, as well as the sanctions or remedies that can meet this problem. In the larger number of cases, what is important is how the judge reacts to potentially disruptive conduct of the other participants—defendants, lawyers, prosecutors, and spectators—to ensure that the proceedings move along smoothly.

A judge has many distinct roles in the courtroom, some of which can conflict, or at least interfere, with each other.

A judge is, in the first place, a judge. He has what Professor Albert Alschuler has called the "naturally reflective role" of deciding focused disputes between contending parties, including those between the government and an individual charged with a criminal offense. He either supervises jury determination of the dispute or the criminal charge or makes the final decision himself. Along the way he must decide many procedural disputes concerning the admissibility of evidence, the relevance of certain issues, or the propriety of certain questions asked by the parties. This role is, by its nature, passive and deliberative.

His second role is that of "traffic policeman." He must keep the process moving, not only to ensure that the jury's attention is focused on the pertinent issues and that the government or the parties obtain prompt justice, but also to protect the interests of other litigants or defendants waiting in the wings to be heard. Because of the increased business of the courts, this role has become more and more important.

The judge's third role is that of examplar of justice. He personifies the abstract elements of the legal process—the need for fairness, understanding, and evenhanded application of the law. By what he is and what he does, he must create appropriate conditions so that the parties accept the immediate outcome of a case and the people generally appreciate the need for, and the virtues of, the judicial system.

This last function is the most difficult and subtle, and the one most important for ensuring civilized and orderly proceedings. Many of the judges who responded to our questionnaire tried to explain this crucial task. One judge, who handled many proceedings involving prison inmates (who, he said, tend to be particularly contentious in court), commented:

> My experience, particularly with penitentiary inmates, in connection with both the trial of criminal cases and the trial of post-conviction cases, has convinced me that even those inmates who are most suspicious and hostile in attitude will usually respond quite readily and appropriately if convincingly shown that the presiding judge is disposed carefully to consider all of their rights and to make rulings favorable to them, when appropriate, without reluctance.[2]

Another judge, who handled a difficult political case which involved the destruction of draft records, wrote:

> The trial judge must be firmly in charge. He must create the impression that he is fair by being fair. An excited voice, a display of alarm could set the spectators off. In this case spectators were young and I believe my many years as a father, as a judge, and as a presiding officer in numerous capacities for years stood me in good stead in maintaining order. He should try and understand the position of the defendants and convey to the defendants and spectators that he does, within such limitations as bind him.[3]

The need to move cases along, particularly in the lower criminal courts, has come to overshadow the other roles, often at the cost of orderly justice, thus eroding confidence in the courts. But if a judge conscientiously performs all three tasks, the chances of courtroom disorder are greatly minimized except for those cases in which a party determines to disrupt the trial no matter what happens in court. Since our investigations indicate that most disruption is caused by defendants in ordinary criminal cases, who are concerned and fearful about the ordeal they are facing, a judge's attempt to relieve those fears and to show his willingness to protect a defendant's rights will go a long way toward eliminating one of the chief causes of disruption.

What is most important is the general atmosphere created by the trial judge: is it one of respect for the rights of the defendants and litigants, for the responsibility of the prosecutor or lawyer, and for the high and important task that each performs? Or is it one of arbitrary or prejudiced rulings, tyrannical overreaching, partisan behavior, or the refusal to allow reasoned argument? The tone set by the judge gives the parties the cue as to whether they are engaging in serious, rational proceedings or something resembling a street brawl.

How to create the proper atmosphere is a subtle and difficult job. Every lawyer knows of judges who run their courtrooms quietly, efficiently, and with a recognition of the rights and responsibilities of all. These are generally judges who can maintain proper decorum with a glance or a word instead of with shouts and maximum use of the contempt power.

The A.B.A. Standards on the Prosecution Function and the Defense Function comment:

> The consensus of trial lawyers whose views were obtained by the Committee is that far too many American judges have tended to allow their courtrooms to "get out of hand," thus encouraging bad manners, excessive and unregulated zeal and other habits which prolong trials, confuse jurors and generally demean the profession and the courts. Interestingly, the lawyers of the widest experience in hotly contested criminal cases share a conviction that a "tightly run" courtroom is to be preferred over one which is lax. The latter, in this view, tends to lower the level of conduct to that of the least professional and most ill-mannered lawyer.[4]

# Preventive Techniques

A judge's responsibility for ensuring that the proceedings are orderly and just requires that he must anticipate potentially disruptive behavior by other parties in the trial and take steps to forestall it. His function goes beyond punishing or bringing charges against those who misbehave. Through a combination of pretrial meetings, establishing ground rules and creating the right atmosphere in the courtroom, he can go a long way toward eliminating any justification for disorderly conduct.

## Pretrial Techniques

The trial judges' questionnaires suggested a series of steps that should be taken even before the trial begins. As we discussed in chapter 6, pretrial conferences should be held with the defense attorney and the prosecutor. Candid lines of communication must be opened between counsel and court so that problems can be discussed in a low-key, frank, and common-sense way.

A trial judge in Oklahoma commented:

> The prior planning and courtroom demeanor of the judge are two very important factors. Pre-trial conference with the parties' counsel should very clearly lay out ground rules and what action the Court will take should such be necessary. Such conference should be made a part of the record.[5]

One of the matters that should be settled is the question of counsel. It must be clearly established from the start what counsel represents what defendant for what purpose. Much of the later disturbance in the Chicago conspiracy trial arose because it was never made clear who was representing Bobby Seale.

Furthermore, local counsel should be involved in the case as far as possible. One federal judge noted:

> Care should be taken that local attorneys participate in a meaningful way, by appointment if necessary, so a back-up lawyer will be available in case a contumacious lawyer has to be sent to the showers. When these arrangements are clearly appreciated, difficulty will be minimized.[6]

A realistic and fair trial schedule must be established, which permits ample time for preparation and gives counsel some leeway to meet prior commitments. The court should be prepared to allow some modification to meet unforeseen developments (illness of counsel, unavailability of witnesses, etc.) with due regard for the inconvenience caused opposing counsel.

In the pretrial conferences, the judge should also consider the possibility of severing defendants or charges if he feels they increased the likelihood of disruption. As we discussed in chapter 8, there are no hard and fast rules concerning severance. The judge should order severance even on his own motion if he thinks it is desirable or necessary for the cause of orderly justice.

## Trial Techniques

The most important step that a judge can take is to convey to the defendant the assurance that the trial will be conducted in a fair and impartial way. This point was emphasized in a number of responses from the trial judges.

> Trial disturbances should be avoided if possible. If the litigants and the attorneys were made to understand clearly and fully that the presiding judge has the disposition, the knowledge, and the ability to conduct the trial in a totally fair, impartial, and unbiased manner, there *should* be far fewer instances of violent, improper, and disruptive conduct on the part of litigants and their attorneys.[7]

The judge should also consider the possibility of some relaxation of the ordinary rules of procedure to meet a potentially explosive situation. For example, although defendants are not ordinarily given the right to argue as cocounsel and address the jury directly, there may be some occasions when it is desirable to permit this. One factor that may have contributed to the tranquillity of the Angela Davis trial was the judge's permitting her to act as cocounsel and explain her position to the jury.* In another potentially disruptive trial involving black militants in Kansas,[8] the trial judge permitted the defendants and lawyers to discuss the background of racial conflict and black-white tension in America. He explained:

> Rules have to be relaxed when you come into conflict with a philosophy of life that is entirely different than that which the normal judicial process runs on. And I think that rules can be relaxed without endangering our judicial system, and I don't think that rules are necessarily synonymous with justice. . . .
>
> [I]n the opening statement of defense counsel, I agreed that he could vary the usual type of opening statement in that he was able to expound upon the meaning of black power, the meaning of militancy, the difference that he saw between Negro, colored and black. He was allowed to go into the history of the black people of the United States.
>
> And I remember vividly, for example, that he was pointing out to the jury that at one time in this country it was the objective of the black man to be like the white man and act in the white man's community. And he told the jury, for example, that this didn't have anything to do with the evidence but it took the edge off the trial. . . .[9]

Since the defendants were also concerned about their rights being traded away by their lawyers at bench conferences, the judge permitted them to listen to what was going on.

* See discussion in chapter 6.

I agreed that at every conference between counsel and the court, at least one representative of the defendants would be present, and there were generally at least two present at every meeting.[10]

But the trial judge should always show that he is firmly in control. Laxity is not the same as flexibility in running a courtroom. If a judge permits violation of the basic dignity of the court and the ground rules of courtroom decorum, he is inviting disorder.[11]

While some procedural rules might be relaxed, others should be strengthened. Many trial judges in potentially disorderly trials have limited the lawyers' method of objection.[12] While a lawyer must give a reason for objection, it is sometimes joined with unnecessary comments which delay the proceedings. The trial judge who handled the Kansas case described above commented:

> I set out certain orders which were agreed upon by the defense attorney and objected to by the county attorney. And those orders were as follows and this one came after the first two weeks of trial; that was that the attorneys thereafter could only announce "I object."
>
> If they objected to any evidence or any of the testimony of witnesses, they could no longer give a reason for that objection, because you will find, and you know, I am sure, that most objections in this kind of a trial are speeches and not objections, and that cuts that out.[13]

The same kind of order was established in the Manson trial when defense counsel objected to almost every phase of the prosecution case.

A number of judges also emphasized the importance of not overreacting to transitory outbursts. A trial is likely to put severe emotional pressure on a defendant and an early impulsive reaction to the experience should be treated with understanding by the judge. One judge wrote:

> [A judge should possess] a fine sense for the worth and rights, sui generis, of all participants vindicated in an atmosphere calm enough to permit rational, fair judgment on the issues before the forum, always using common sense enough to make allowances for transitory outbursts by emotionally overwrought persons, as distinguished from a calculated attempt to disrupt the proceedings or make political capital out of them. This is easier to say than do.[14]

When a judge foresees disruptive conduct, he may take a series of measures short of imposing the sanctions described in chapters 6, 7, and 8. Calling a recess to cool the temper of an aggrieved party may eliminate the need to hold him in contempt or remove him from the courtroom. The A.B.A. Standards on Disruption make the following comment:

> It should be recognized, however, that mechanical and indiscriminate use of these [sanctions] will not assure a satisfactory result. Sometimes restraint by the judge, e.g., a timely recess, will lead quickly to restora-

tion of normalcy; yet too much restraint may be construed as a sign of
weakness, which itself may be provocative. At other times prompt imposition of sanctions may be the appropriate answer. Whenever misconduct occurs the important questions for the judge is not whether he
has power or discretion to deal with it but what action is appropriate.[15]

The judge should also be prepared to use his influence to correct
prejudicial remarks by the prosecutor or defense counsel. For example,
if the prosecutor comments on a defendant's refusal to testify or makes
an appeal to a jury's prejudice, the judge should not wait for an objection but act promptly to counter any misimpression.

The court should be prepared to issue rules covering the behavior of
spectators and members of the working press. These should be made
before trial and clearly spelled out to all participants. They should
recognize the importance of permitting the defendants to have friends
and relatives in the court. Many of the early disturbances in the New
York Black Panther case grew out of the defendants' concern that their
relatives were not allowed in court.

A potentially disruptive trial that was defused by sensible pretrial
planning and the issuance of appropriate rules for spectators is described by a federal judge in Kansas:

> At my request, the defendant and his attorney attended a conference in
> my chambers, which included the United States Attorney and the
> United States Marshal. I announced the entry of the standing order, a
> copy of which is enclosed, and suggested that its provisions be made
> known to those who might attend the trial.*
> On the opening day of the trial the marshal, reinforced by deputies,
> advised all who entered the courthouse of the provisions of the order,
> a copy of which was posted near the door. . . . although more persons
> appeared than could be accommodated in the courtroom, there was no
> disturbance in the building beyond a few expressions of resentment.
> During the voir dire examination of the jury panel, there was one out-
> burst of derisive laughter at the answer of one venireman. I announced
> immediately that any repetition would result in clearing the courtroom,
> and there were no more such incidents.[16]

Once again we must emphasize that there can be no hard and fast
rules for dealing with potentially disruptive situations. The judge
should anticipate problems, try to lay down ground rules as far in ad-

---

* The standing order issued by the judge was as follows:

"IT IS ORDERED, that throughout any day during which this Court is in
session at Kansas City, Kansas:

1. No person shall stand or loiter in the rooms, halls, corridors or entry-ways
of the first floor of the United States Courthouse or on any stairway leading
thereto; . . .

4. Spectators shall be allowed to sit only in that portion of a courtroom allocated
by the Marshal for spectator seating. No spectator shall be admitted to a courtroom unless spectator seating space is then available; . . .

6. The United States Marshal is directed to enforce this Order and to take into
custody any person violating its provisions. Such persons shall be brought before
the Court without unnecessary delay."

vance as possible, involve and inform the defendant or litigant so that he does not feel his fate is being decided without his participation, and above all convey the feeling that he will protect the rights of all concerned. He should be flexible when there is reason to bend the rules, but firm in his determination to protect the dignity of the proceedings. As the case proceeds, he must be prepared to tighten his control if the lawyers object too often and too lengthily, or if there are other unnecessary diversions. And he must use his good judgment to vary these recommendations if the situation requires it.

At some point the judge must be prepared to impose the sanctions described in previous chapters: a contempt citation, removal of the defendant or lawyer, or perhaps binding. The sanction must be effective, but the judge should be careful that it does not aggravate the situation in the courtroom. The A.B.A. Standards express a sensible approach:

> In imposing sanctions for courtroom misconduct, the trial judge should be alert to the fact that an inappropriately severe sanction may be self-defeating, as may any appearance of passion or pettiness, because it will bring "discredit to a court as certainly as the conduct it penalizes," and thus provide a basis for further displays of disrespect or defiance. In addition the standard recognizes that the appropriate use of a sanction requires consideration of its effect on the orderly conduct of the trial. Removal of a defense lawyer, for example, may well frustrate prosecution of the case, serving the purpose of his willful obstruction.[17]

# Forms of Judicial Misbehavior

Many of the lawyers we have spoken to complained about the misuse of judicial power. What troubles them is not the judge's power to decide the controversy before him or to sentence after a verdict is returned, but his exercise of authority in the courtroom—the Olympian distance of many judges from the parties, the tyrannical overbearing of a few, and the readiness of certain judges to punish for contempt those who cross them. One federal judge who appeared before our committee commented:

> Our court system comes from the English system. As a result judges have been given a large amount of power. This evidently derives from the English class system. There you had a stratified society where the judges represented the higher classes. Perhaps in that kind of society you can accept this. We have a very different society. I think it is healthy to reevaluate the powers given to judges. In addition I don't believe that a judge needs to use the full range of his powers to achieve the desired end. I'm not sure why a judge, who has such tremendous powers, needs to take the pure English position.

Professor Herman Schwartz of the State University at Buffalo Law
School and an experienced trial lawyer has written:

> Glaring down from their elevated perches, insulting, abrupt, rude,
> sarcastic, patronizing, intimidating, vindictive, insisting on not merely
> respect but almost abject servility—such judges are frequently encoun-
> tered in American trial courts, particularly in the lowest criminal and
> juvenile courts which account for most of our criminal business. Indeed,
> the lower the court, the worse the behavior.[18]

We cannot say whether such judges are "frequently encountered," as
Professor Schwartz states, but our own investigations indicate that it
occurs often enough to warrant concern. Since the judge is the per-
sonification of justice to most of the public, his misconduct is qualita-
tively more dangerous to the system than that of any other party. It is
therefore necessary to consider the types of judicial misbehavior that
create or contribute to disorder.

These fall into three classifications: arbitrary, biased, or vindictive
remarks or rulings; bickering with counsel; and interference with
proper presentation of a case by the attorney.

## Arbitrary, Biased, or Vindictive Remarks or Rulings

Some recent reports have painted the picture of the tyrannical judge.
There have been a number of cases in which a judge has acted as if he
were an arm of the prosecution, berating the defendant or his counsel
or sharply questioning defense witnesses. A newspaper account of
Judge Charles Carr, a federal judge in Los Angeles, describes one day
in his court:

> As the attorney for the first defendant, a convicted bank robber, began
> his plea for a reduction of the 25-year sentence Carr had handed down,
> the 69-year-old judge snorted: "It's just too bad they did away with the
> death penalty." When the attorney questioned Carr on a point of pro-
> cedure a moment later, the judge said: "Let's don't get me off in some
> position where some great liberal on the appellate court is going to find
> some way to get this man free . . . so-called liberals; I call 'em pseudo-
> liberals."[19]

In one narcotics case the judge insisted on calling and questioning
two witnesses that neither party had put on the stand. It was clear that
he did not believe what they said. The appeals court reversed the conviction in that case with these words by Judge Learned Hand:

> [T]he judge was exhibiting a prosecutor's zeal, inconsistent with that
> detachment and aloofness which courts have again and again de-
> manded, particularly in criminal trials. Despite every allowance he must
> not take on the role of a partisan; he must not enter the lists; he must

not by his ardor induce the jury to join in a hue and cry against the accused. Prosecution and judgment are two quite separate functions in the administration of justice; they must not merge.[20]

In the Chicago conspiracy case, the Seventh Circuit Court of Appeals reversed the conviction of the five defendants found guilty, in part because of the prejudicial behavior of Judge Julius Hoffman described in this and other chapters. The court said that many of Judge Hoffman's remarks before the jury were

> deprecatory of the defense counsel and their case. These comments were often touched with sarcasm, implying rather than saying outright that the defense counsel was inept, bumptuous or untrustworthy, or that his case lacked merit. . . . Sometimes the comment was not associated with the ruling in ordinary course; sometimes gratuitously added to an otherwise proper ruling; nearly always unnecessary. Taken individually any one was not very significant and might be disregarded as a harmless attempt at humor. But cumulatively, they must have telegraphed to the jury the judge's contempt for the defense.[21]

Some of Judge Hoffman's remarks cited by the appeals court were the following:

> After a ruling on hearsay grounds, Mr. Kunstler said in an attempt at argument, "I just don't understand it." The judge replied: "You will have to see a lawyer, Mr. Kunstler, if you don't understand it."
> On an occasion when Mr. Weinglass was arguing that he had asked appropriate questions for the purpose of impeachment, the court responded: "I would like to preside over a class in evidence, but I haven't the time today." In a similar situation when Mr. Kunstler acknowledged having difficulty, the judge said: "I will be glad privately to tell you how to do it. I haven't any right in a public trial to give you a course in evidence."[22]

In a criminal court action in New York City, the judge made the following remarks about the Legal Aid attorney appearing before him:

> *Mr. McCarthy:* Your Honor, at this time I'd also renew my Motion to Suppress as to the rest.
> *The Court:* Don't talk about a Motion to Suppress. There is no suppression. It's a question of fact whether she had it or whether she didn't. There's no suppression here. . . .
> *Mr. McCarthy:* Judge, I just want to make the record perfectly clear.
> *The Court:* The record is very clear. You weren't entitled to a motion in the first place when she had a hearing already. You are not entitled to a hearing. Nobody should have ordered a hearing. There was nothing to suppress. There was no search. You have to establish a search. And I am sick and tired of Legal Aid boondoggling this way and you do it all the time.[23]

Community legal service attorneys in New York City filed formal complaints against three judges who, they claimed, showed consistent hostility against legal services lawyers or poor clients generally.[24] Some lower court judges in Boston have shown a bias against underprivileged defendants appearing before them. In the district court in Boston, one judge remarked to a zealous defense counsel who cited the most recent Supreme Court cases on point: "We don't follow those Supreme Court decisions here."[25] An article on the criminal courts in Washington, D.C., recounted numerous incidents of prejudicial remarks by judges in the District and surrounding suburbs.[26]

Judges have also asked defense attorneys whether they were not taught better in their first year of law school,[27] called their actions "shyster stuff,"[28] or referred to their cross-examination of a witness as "just ridiculous."[29] Professor Alschuler has offered other illustrations:

> —the judge who, at a pre-trial conference in a torts case, told a lawyer who had refused to stipulate the amount of damages, "I'm going to screw you every way I can short of reversible error."
> —the judge who, at the conclusion of a court appearance by two defendants, shouted "Take those Puerto Rican animals out of here."
> —the judge who left the bench during testimony and wandered about the courtroom whittling on a pine board.
> —the judge who threw coffee in a lawyer's face in a courthouse corridor.[30]

The discriminatory behavior of many judges from the deep South before and during the civil rights drives of the early 1960s has also been well documented.[31]

By citing these examples, we do not suggest that any substantial proportion of the judiciary behaves in a tyrannical and arbitrary manner. But some do, and their misbehavior is a more serious threat to order and justice in the courts than that of prosecutors, lawyers, defendants, or spectators. A district attorney from New Jersey wrote in answer to our questionnaire to prosecutors:

> Disturbances seem to occur only, or principally, where judges are impatient, injudicious and animated by an overblown sense of their own pride and dignity. . . .[32]

For a judge to make a prejudicial or humiliating remark about the defendant or his lawyer may not lead to counterstatements and serious disorder by the abused party. However, it can and has done so. Even if this does not occur, such remarks are disruptive in that they may distract and improperly influence the jury. They may at least lead to continuous objections and serious contention between the attorney and the judge which will interfere with a trial. In any event, such actions undermine the people's confidence in and respect for the courts which are a necessary prerequisite for an orderly system of justice.

## Bickering with Counsel

The A.B.A. Standards on the Judge's Role in Dealing with Trial Disruptions make clear that the judge must exercise self-restraint in the court and should be an "examplar of dignity." Standard B.1 states in part:

> When it becomes necessary during the trial for him to comment upon the conduct of witnesses, spectators, counsel, or others, or upon the testimony, he should do so in a firm, dignified and restrained manner, avoiding repartee, limiting his comments and rulings to what is reasonably required for the orderly progress of the trial, and refraining from unnecessary disparagement of persons or issues.

For a judge to engage in petty arguments with counsel, in bickering, sarcasm, and irrelevant colloquy, must interfere with the proceedings and create the wrong kind of atmosphere in court. Although Judge Harold R. Medina was under great pressure in the *Dennis* case, Justice Frankfurter thought that there was too much repartee:

> Truth compels the observation, painful as it is to make it, that the fifteen volumes of oral testimony in the principal trial record numerous episodes involving the judge and defense counsel that are more suggestive of an undisciplined debating society than of the hush and solemnity of a court of justice. Too often counsel were encouraged to vie with the court in dialectic, in repartee and banter, in talk so copious as inevitably to arrest the momentum of the trial and to weaken the restraints of respect that a judge should engender in lawyers. . . .[33]

Justice Frankfurter cited numerous cases of this type of behavior, of which the following is an example:

> *Mr. Gladstein:* Your Honor, I would like to finish my statement for the record. I wish the record to show my objection to the tone and the manner in which the Court delivered that command as unbecoming a Court, and I object to it. I also—
> *The Court:* There is nothing unbecoming about it. I am through being fooled with in this case.
> *Mr. Gladstein:* Now, if your Honor please—
> *The Court:* If you don't like it you can lump it. Put that down.
> *Mr. Isserman:* I object to your Honor's remark and characterization of the conduct of counsel, and I ask that your Honor strike that remark.
> *The Court:* Oh yes, yes, I have heard all that. Now I am sick of it.[34]

It is obvious that banter and repartee lower the dignity of the court. They also elicit responses from the attorneys that may increase contention during the trial or at least introduce extraneous matters that will delay the proceedings. An Oklahoma court has said: "Trial courts should proceed with dignity, rule impartially, and say as little as possible in the trial of criminal cases."[35] This is particularly true of matters that have nothing to do with the proceedings.

## Interfering with Presentation by Counsel

Another cause of frequent contention in court which has the effect of disrupting the proceedings is a judge's cutting off an attorney before he has had an opportunity to make his argument or present the points he thinks necessary in the case. In a perjury case in Illinois, an appellate court found that the judge improperly restricted the lawyer for the defendant from the beginning of the trial:

> Commencing with the first witness, the court shut off Aimen's questions (which we consider to have been proper ones) characterizing them as "ridiculous"; general objections of the State's Attorney (in the form of "I object") were frequently and consistently sustained without any specification of grounds even when requested by Aimen; on occasions, the court foreclosed answers to Aimen's questioning without there having been any objection by the State's Attorney. The general atmosphere of the trial was so strained and heated that at one point the court said to Aimen, "I don't want you to have a heart attack."[36]

The Illinois court reversed a finding of contempt against the lawyer since it concluded that he had been provoked into improper comments by the judge.

Some of the contempt citations against attorneys Weinglass and Kunstler in the Chicago conspiracy case were found to be legally insufficient by the court of appeals because the judge prematurely cut off argument. For example:

> *Mr. Kunstler:*   You haven't even heard the motion.
> *Mr. Rubin:*   You haven't heard it yet.
> *The Court:*   For a mistrial.
> *Mr. Kunstler:*   Yes, but I would like to argue it.
> *The Court:*   Oh, there is no grounds for a mistrial.
> *Mr. Kunstler:*   Your Honor knows you have referred to the question of the defendants taking the stand. You have committed the cardinal error of a court with reference—
> *The Court:*   I ask you to sit down, sir.
> *Mr. Kunstler:*   But your Honor—
> *The Court:*   I direct the marshal to have this man sit down.
> *Mr. Kunstler:*   Every time I make a motion am I going to be thrown in my seat when I argue it?
> *The Court:*   You may sit down.
> *Mr. Dellinger:*   Force and violence.
> *Mr. Kunstler:*   If that is the ruling of the Court that we cannot argue without being thrown in our seats.[37]

Cutting off a lawyer's argument before he has had full opportunity to speak will not expedite the proceedings. It generally leads to continued wrangling about the judge's action, and increased agitation and bad will. While the judge can and should end the argument about a particular matter at some point, he should be prepared to tolerate wide limits in the attorney's presentation.

Since we have defined disruption as any substantial interference with courtroom proceedings, a judge's improper restriction on a lawyer's presentation should be considered disruptive. As we have said before, a trial involves the performance of certain well-defined roles by each constituent—judge, defense lawyer, prosecutor. Each must be given the opportunity to perform his role and each expects the others to recognize the boundaries of that role. When these expectations are seriously violated, the result can only be an upsetting of the trial dynamic with feelings of affront or resentment in the injured party.

# Controls on the Conduct of Judges

What can be done about judges who engage in the activities described above? The situation with misbehaving judges is quite different from that with misbehaving defendants, defense lawyers, prosecutors, or spectators. Since the judge has been given the authority to control all the other participants in the court, there is no one immediately available to control him if he acts improperly or arbitrarily. The legal system has had difficulty in determining the proper way to handle erring judges, and most sanctions or remedies against them are long after the fact and tend to be ineffectual.

The potential sanctions include: 1) appellate review; 2) impeachment; 3) statutory disciplinary procedures; 4) professional discipline by bar groups; 5) peremptory challenge. Their value and shortcomings will be discussed below.

## Appellate Review

The traditional view is that courtroom misbehavior by a trial judge can be corrected by an appellate tribunal. Judge Augustus Hand wrote in the *Sacher* case:

> The chief defense which appellants make for their obstructive tactics and imprudent charges is that the judge provoked them by making what they consider indefensible rulings in the case. The validity of these rulings is not before us on this appeal. But it must be borne in mind that

when counsel differ as to the rulings of a judge, they acquire no privilege to charge him with bad faith and misconduct, and to obstruct the trial. Their only remedy is by an appeal.[38]

Judge Hand's comment is the typical response of the courts to charges of misconduct by a trial judge: 1) such misconduct never justifies counterattack by the other parties; 2) any misconduct can be corrected on appeal.

Appellate courts regularly review charges of judicial misbehavior to determine whether due process was afforded the defendant or litigant. Many cases, including the Chicago conspiracy case, have been reversed because the appeals court thought a judge made a prejudicial remark or improper ruling restricting a defendant's case. While some courts may decide that certain misconduct was inconsequential and therefore constituted "harmless error," there are a surprising number of cases in which convictions are overturned because of improper behavior by the judge, despite strong evidence of guilt. A New Jersey court wrote in 1970:

> [W]e are not to reach a conclusion of harmless error because we may believe that the defendant in fact was guilty as charged. . . . [C]ourts of justice act upon the belief that if guilty, a party will be so found after a fair trial. . . . [N]o matter how . . . evident the guilt, an accused has an absolute constitutional right to a fair trial before an impartial judge and an unprejudiced jury.[39]

For the most part, appellate courts have conscientiously reviewed charges of judicial misconduct in cases that have come before them, and have done so more thoroughly than in cases of alleged prosecutorial misconduct. They will generally not tolerate abusive judicial misconduct and maintain what Professor Alschuler calls a "sensible, sensitive, and fair-minded attitude."[40]

Nevertheless, there are certain problems in relying on appellate review. Often an appellate court will not specifically focus on the judicial conduct it finds improper. It may reverse a case with the general comment that the trial judge did not act with the requisite impartiality. It will cite references to the record that are not published with the opinion. It may even omit the name of the erring trial judge from the official report. Secondly, appellate review is ineffectual where it is most needed: in the lower criminal courts where there is not an adequate written record for review and where judgments are rarely reviewed on appeal. In fact, some of the worst lower court judges may feel free to act as they do because of the absence of a real threat of review.

A third problem is that the cold written record does not reflect the facial gestures or general demeanor of the trial judge which might indicate hostility to the defendant or litigant. One experienced trial lawyer has written:

> Most judges do their utmost to maintain a poker face, unperturbable mind, and noncommittal attitude during a contested trial although driven by every instinct to take sides. But, judges are human and their emotions are controlled by the same human feelings as all people. No judge, normally endowed, can sit patiently on the bench during a spirited trial and remain completely indifferent. Human nature, outside the laboratory just doesn't work that way. The judge will react to the happenings just as any other person would and his facial expressions will convey thoughts to the minds of the jurors. It is this silent language on the part of the trial judge which frequently controls the thinking of the jury.[41]

Until it is feasible to keep a film record of what happened in a trial, there is the possibility that many prejudicial acts of the judge or improper acts of other parties will not be preserved. An alert lawyer must try to make a verbal record of any such action of the judge, being careful not to antagonize him even further by doing so.

Fourthly, appellate review takes time. To complete appellate review on the first level for the Chicago conspiracy case took from February 1970 when the trial ended until November 1972. While that case was unusual, the average time for disposition of an appeal in the federal system is over eight months from the time the record is completed in the district court. In many state systems the interval is longer, and in many cases there is a second appeal to a higher court. From the point of view of an aggrieved party—either a defendant or his lawyer who is complaining about a trial judge's misconduct—this interval is painfully long.

A final objection to the adequacy of appellate review is that the trial judge is not really disciplined by the reversal of his case. But judges do not like to be reversed on appeal and almost all will take seriously what an appellate court says about their actions. Of course, reversal is in no way comparable to a contempt citation which may lead to imprisonment or a fine. Professor Herman Schwartz commented about the Chicago trial:

> The two Hoffmans played to each other in Chicago, except that Julius had all the power and almost none of the restraints, though Abbie may have had the better lines. Although some judges see themselves as martyrs, it is still the defendants who face prison terms in a contest where the prosecution has most of the advantages, not the least of which is money, and experienced investigative resources; Abbie Hoffman may go to jail for five years, but Julius Hoffman went to Florida with a stop at the White House for breakfast where he met "my banker," former Treasury Secretary David Kennedy.[42]

Even though many of Judge Hoffman's actions were later found improper, the "punishment" he received from the court of appeals was a mild reprimand.

Professor Alschuler writes that some trial court judges do not care what an appellate court does. He points to some glaring examples:

> [T]he arrogance of some judges yields to no man and no law. These are the judges who seem to be most frequently involved in extreme cases of courtroom misconduct. Once, when a California appellate court reversed a conviction on grounds of judicial misconduct, it noted that on four previous occasions it had called the trial judge's attention to the impropriety of his behavior. "Anything we may say will have no effect on his future course of action," the court concluded. The court's prediction quickly proved accurate; within six months, the court was again required to reverse a conviction because of the judge's courtroom behavior.[43]

This is not to say that appellate review is not an appropriate way to check a trial judge's improper behavior. Indeed for some mistakes, it may be the only way. No one would assert that impeachment is a proper sanction for a judge who cuts off a lawyer's argument in one case. But for continued or egregious misconduct, other sanctions are necessary.

## Impeachment

At the other end of the spectrum from appellate reversal is the sanction of impeachment. Almost every observer has noted that impeachment is highly ineffective for handling courtroom misconduct. It is so heavy a club—calling for removal of the judge—and involves so cumbersome a procedure—one house of the legislature must vote to bring charges and the other house convict by a two-thirds vote—that it is rarely invoked for any kind of judicial derelictions and even less often for in-court behavior.

While complete figures for state impeachments are not available, the history of the federal impeachment power with respect to judges can be shown in the chart on page 209. Although there were fourteen federal judges accused of improper courtroom conduct and two were impeached, neither was convicted of the charges against him. (One judge, who was also charged with financial irregularity, resigned before charges were considered by the Senate.)

The first judge impeached was Samuel Chase, a Supreme Court justice, who was charged with his tyrannical behavior while acting as a circuit justice during the period of 1789–1800. Chase engaged in such an overbearing and vigorous enforcement of the Alien and Sedition

IMPEACHMENT OF FEDERAL JUDGES SINCE 1789

| | TOTAL CHARGES FILED IN HOUSE OF REP. | JUDGES RESIGNED BEFORE CHARGES HEARD | NO BILL OF IMPEACH-MENT PASSED | IMPEACHED BY HOUSE OF REP. | RESIGNED BEFORE SENATE HEARD CHARGES | FOUND NOT GUILTY BY SENATE | FOUND GUILTY BY SENATE |
|---|---|---|---|---|---|---|---|
| TOTAL | 56 | 22 | 25 | 9 | 1 | 4 | 4 |
| *Basis of charges* | | | | | | | |
| Bribery and financial irregularity | 38 | 22 | 11 | 5 | (English) 1 | (Swayne) (Lauerbach) 2 | (Archibald) (Ritter) 2 |
| Treason | 1 | — | — | 1 | — | — | (Humphreys) 1 |
| Drunkenness | 3 | — | 2 | 1 | — | — | (Pickering) 1 |
| Arbitrary rulings, misuse of contempt power | 7 | — | 6 | 1 | — | (Peck) 1 | — |
| Abusive conduct in court | 7 | — | 6 | 1 | — | (Chase) 1 | — |

Acts against supporters of Thomas Jefferson that the Jeffersonian-Republicans determined to remove him at their first opportunity. Chase was "a terror on the bench," and "bullied counsel, browbeat witnesses, ruled juries," and pressed his political views in court. He "brought down the laughter of the spectators on defense counsel."[44] Nevertheless it was not his courtroom conduct that led to his impeachment in 1804. The Jeffersonians took the position that the impeachment provisions of the Constitution could be invoked for any misbehavior or lack of "good conduct" deemed sufficient by the House. Thus Congress had the power to remove any judge it chose for political or other reasons. But the Senate refused to convict Chase, establishing the principle that there must be some type of crime to warrant removal through impeachment.

The federal judge who resigned after charges of courtroom misconduct led to impeachment by the House was George W. English. In addition to his abusive conduct in court, there were also charges of financial irregularity. New York lawyer John Ferrick described these:

> The first article accused him of having disbarred several attorneys without notice or hearing, and of using his power to summon people in order to harass, threaten and oppress. The second article cited him for managing the bankruptcy affairs of his court for the personal benefit of himself and a certain referee. The third charged unlawful and intentional favoritism in the appointment of receivers and other practices, including his acceptance of a cash "gift" from one of his appointees. The fourth article alleged corrupt practices in the handling of the funds in a particular bank which agreed, in turn, to employ his son. The last article alleged several instances wherein the judge had displayed unlawful, intentional and corrupt favoritism in his appointments, rulings and decrees.[45]

Before he was tried, English submitted his resignation to President Coolidge and the proceedings were terminated.

The other judges against whom claims of courtroom misconduct were charged escaped impeachment:

> Since those early years of the past century, the House has consistently refused to impeach for misuse of judicial authority: when it was charged, in 1804, that Judge Richard Peters of Pennsylvania engaged in on-the-bench misconduct in the trial of Sedition cases; in 1822, that Judge Charles Tait of Alabama engaged in "tyrannical conduct" toward members of the Bar; in 1825, that Judge Buckner Thurston was "rude, insolent, and undignified" while presiding on the circuit court for the District of Columbia; in 1833, that Judge Benjamin Johnson of the territory of Arkansas displayed favoritism of counsel, irritability, rudeness, and habitual intemperance; in 1908, that Judge Lebbus R. Wilfley of the United States Court in China maintained a "dictatorial attitude" on the bench; and, in 1935, when Congressman (later Senator) Dirksen charged that Judge Samuel Alschuler sat on a case and openly favored the Pullman Company, which was represented by the son of former governor Edward Dunne with whom the Judge had long political ties.[46]

There are many reasons for the infrequent use of the impeachment power to deal with abusive judges. Congress (or a state legislature) is responsible for bringing and hearing the charges. It would take an extraordinary case to warrant interference with their legislative functions to allow them to sit as a court of impeachment. Such proceedings are expensive—two recent impeachment trials in Florida cost $250,000 —and the procedure is necessarily slow—some state legislatures meet only once every two years. The procedures under which a judge is tried are also uncertain and unfair to the accused judge.

In addition, legislators may be affected more by political considerations than by the evidence presented to them. Many of the impeachment votes in the Senate corresponded to party affiliation. Finally, the Constitution provides for impeachment only for "high crimes and misdemeanors." There is some question whether abusive misconduct in court can be considered a crime. Professor Alschuler argues that it should be, since it amounts to contempt of the institution.

> Disruptive courtroom behavior by litigants and attorneys is commonly viewed as contempt of court, a criminal act, and there is no reason why a trial judge's misconduct should be considered any differently. Although it is conventional to refer to the trial judge as "the court," the man and the institution are plainly not the same. Indeed, one federal statute defines contempt of court, in part, as the "misbehavior of any of [the court's] officers in their official transactions." Another form of contempt under this statute is the "misbehavior of any person in [the court's] presence or so near thereto as to obstruct the administration of justice." Abusive judicial behavior could easily fit within these definitions, and in my view, contemptuous behavior by a trial judge might reasonably be classified as a high crime or misdemeanor.[47]

But the issue is uncertain and has never been decided.

There were reasons why the founding fathers chose so cumbersome a procedure. The easier it is to remove a judge, the less he is his own master. The independence of the judiciary is a virtue which the Constitution sets higher than control and discipline of judges. Some balance must be struck between allowing a judge to perform his task with a minimum of interference and insisting on some check on any overreaching on his part. But the traditional methods have tipped the balance in favor of his independence. The chief means of restraint has been his own conscience.

## Statutory Disciplinary Procedures

Within the past fifteen years at least twenty-five states have established new methods for disciplining judges for misconduct, including courtroom misbehavior. In most of these states disciplinary boards or courts have been set up, consisting either of other judges or of judges,

lawyers, and lay persons. Two examples are New York's Court on the
Judiciary and the California Commission on Judicial Qualifications.

The New York State Constitution was amended in 1947 to provide
for the New York Court on the Judiciary. It has six members: the chief
judge and the senior associate judge of the New York Court of Appeals
and one judge from each of the four departments of the Appellate
Division of the New York Supreme Court. The court has disciplinary
jurisdiction over all appellate judges and judges of the major New
York trial courts (about 400 judges in all). Lower court judges in city,
village, and town courts are subject to discipline by the various departments of the appellate division. The Court on the Judiciary was given
the power, upon the vote of four of its six members, to remove a judge
from office. It has also assumed the power to reprimand judges if it
feels removal is too severe a sanction.

The Court on the Judiciary has never removed a judge for his courtroom conduct, although it did censure two judges for publicly insulting
each other from the bench.[48] Until the end of 1972 it had been formally
convened in only four cases since its inception.[49]

California has a far more elaborate system. The nine-man commission on Judicial Qualifications is composed of five judges, two lawyers,
and two laymen. Their staff investigates complaints, closing out those
that are clearly without merit. It may communicate with the accused
judge to learn his side of the story.

The judge's response may show the Commission that no further
action is necessary. Sometimes the mere fact that a judge is asked to
respond to the charges may have a beneficial effect. Jack E. Frankel,
the Commission's executive secretary, explained to Professor Alschuler:
"Sometimes there may be reason to accept the plea, I didn't do it but
I'll see it doesn't happen again."[50] Some judges may expressly agree not
to engage in certain conduct again. In some cases the Commission may
warn the judge that formal proceedings will be brought if he does not
desist from the conduct complained of.

At some point, a formal hearing may be required. Witnesses may be
presented by both sides and the usual procedural rules of evidence are
observed, including the right to cross-examine opposing witnesses. At
the conclusion of the hearing, the Commission decides whether to
recommend that the California Supreme Court censure the judge or
remove him from office. Only at that point does the proceeding become
a matter of public record. If the Commission recommends removal, the
judge is disqualified from office until the Supreme Court acts.

The Commission has investigated about 100 complaints a year since
its inception in 1961. In the first four years of its existence, its investigations led to the resignation of twenty-six out of a total of 500 sitting
California judges.

Three cases became matters of public record—all of them involving charges of courtroom misconduct. In the first, which occurred in 1964, the Commission recommended that Judge Charles F. Stevens be removed from office. There were complaints before the Commission, not only about conflict of interest and dishonesty, but many witnesses testified that Judge Stevens had ridiculed and belittled police officers and prosecutors who had appeared in his courtroom. At the time of the charge the California Supreme Court did not have the power which it was later given to censure judges for improper behavior. The Court rejected the recommendation of removal without giving any reasons.

In 1970, the supreme court censured Judge Gerald S. Chargin on the Commission's recommendations. During a hearing involving a fifteen-year-old Mexican-American, Judge Chargin had referred to the youth's family and to Mexican-Americans generally as "miserable, lousy, rotten people." He had also stated in open court that "maybe Hitler was right" in seeking to destroy "the animals" in society.

A year later, in 1971, the California Supreme Court again followed a Commission recommendation and censured Judge Barnard B. Glickfeld for courtroom misconduct. During a chambers conference he had referred to a young woman who was the complainant in an assault case as "a horse's ass." Later, in the courtroom, he said that he did not want any police officer to sit near the "alleged victim . . . and I am using the term figuratively." When the prosecutor objected that some of the judge's remarks had been unfair, he replied, "That is the way it is going to be. And I don't want to hear about what a fair remark is. There are lots of things that are not fair."[51]

Many of the complaints about judges in California relate to their courtroom behavior. The executive secretary of the Commission states:

> If all forms of rude, abusive, screaming, arrogant, impatient, and tyrannical behavior are lumped together, courtroom misconduct probably constitutes the second most common complaint that we receive.[52]

The commission plan set up by California is the model which most other states have adopted. Eighteen other states have similar mechanisms as well as the District of Columbia. The District plan, established in 1970, deals only with so-called Article I judges sitting on local courts established pursuant to Congress's legislative authority over the District. Article III judges (regular federal judges appointed pursuant to Article III of the Constitution) cannot be removed except by impeachment. Only one member of the D.C. Commission is a judge, two are lawyers, and two other lay persons.

There have been proposals to establish a "Commission on Judicial Disabilities and Tenure" to supervise the federal judiciary as well.[53] In 1969 Senator Joseph Tydings of Maryland introduced a bill to circumvent the impeachment provisions of the Constitution and establish an efficient procedure to remove a federal judge. Under that plan, any person could file a complaint against a sitting judge. A staff under the control of the Commission, consisting of five federal judges, would investigate charges, hold hearings, and decide whether the judge's conduct was consistent with the requirements of "good behavior" in the Constitution. If four judges agreed that the judge was behaving improperly, it would report its findings to the Judicial Conference of the United States, which is comprised of the chief judge and one district judge from each judicial circuit plus the chief judge of the Court of Claims and of the Court of Customs and Patent Appeals. The Judicial Conference would hear argument, receive additional evidence, and then decide whether the judge should be removed from office.

Many arguments have been advanced against and in support of this plan, and its constitutionality is far from clear.[54] The proposal has not advanced very far in Congress.[55]

Nevertheless, the commission plan is the most feasible method yet proposed for dealing with misconduct by judges. Since it does not rely on the legislature for hearing charges, it avoids the great disadvantages of the impeachment process. A judicial commission with a permanent staff can serve as an effective conduit for complaints about the judiciary. Since the proceedings are secret until discipline is imposed, spurious charges can be weeded out.

It would also seem important that intermediate sanctions be available to a commission. This has not been the case in most states.* For the most part, judicial commissions or tribunals have not been given authority to suspend a judge for a short period or to impose a fine or cite him for contempt of the court as an institution. The argument against these sanctions is that they would so discredit the judge that he would be unable to run his court effectively. But it is difficult to distinguish a fine or contempt citation as any different in this regard from a formal reprimand, which has been authorized in many instances. With a greater range of sanctions, disciplinary commissions would possess the means to effectively supervise the judiciary while protecting their independence.

## Professional Discipline

Since judges are lawyers, bar associations can in theory investigate and initiate disciplinary action against judges who violate the code of Professional Responsibility or the Canons of Judicial Ethics. Two states (Missouri and Wisconsin) have given bar associations explicit authority

* See appendix J for an analysis of relevant state laws on disciplining judges.

to institute such action.[56] Many state courts have held that even without explicit authority, they could take action against judges in their capacity as disciplinary tribunals over members of the bar. Chief Justice Weintraub of the New Jersey Supreme Court stated in a leading case:

> In terms of rational connection with fitness at the bar, behavior of an attorney in judicial office cannot be insulated from the demands of professional ethics. On the contrary, the judge's role is so intimate a part of the process of justice that misbehavior as a judge must inevitably reflect upon qualification for membership at the bar.[57]

Massachusetts has taken the same position,[58] but there is authority to the contrary. Some courts have held that only explicitly granted authority to discipline judges can be utilized. For example, the Nevada Supreme Court stated in 1955:

> Our constitution and statutes have conferred upon this court no disciplinary authority over judges while acting as judges. As we have noted, it is not within the power of this court to remove or suspend a judge from office. A district judge owes his office not to appointment by this court but to election by the people. For what he does in his official capacity he is responsible to the public as its duly chosen officer and not to this court as our appointed officer. By the same token this court (aside from its function of judicial review and from that advisory encouragement normally expected of sound and effective leadership) cannot be said to be responsible for what a judge does in his official capacity. That responsibility rightly lies with the public which has placed him in office and chooses to retain him there.[59]

For the most part the cases that have discussed the point involved out-of-court behavior by the judge: signing false affidavits, bribery charges, fixing traffic tickets, having an interest in litigation before him, and so on. In some rare instance in-court conduct was involved.[60] No recent case has been found in which professional discipline was imposed for abusive or prejudicial conduct in court.

There is the further question of the effect of disciplinary proceedings upon the judge's term of office. If he is disbarred as an attorney, can he continue to act as a judge? If not, would this approach violate the constitutional independence of the judiciary and circumvent the protections granted judges against removal from office?

There are only a few cases discussing the problem. The Oregon Supreme Court held in 1965 that the requirement that anyone running for election to judicial office must be an attorney in good standing was no bar to a disciplinary proceeding against a then sitting judge:

> Any objection that, as a result of disciplinary action, a judge may be disqualified from seeking re-election is irrelevant. Any lawyer, if disbarred, is disqualified from seeking election or re-election to the bench. Disciplinary jurisdiction obviously cannot be made to turn upon a lawyer's desire to be a candidate for the bench in the future.[61]

The court intimated that a judge would presumably have to resign if he was disbarred as a lawyer:

> A more serious, but equally speculative, challenge to our jurisdiction is based upon an assumption that disciplinary action may indirectly result in the loss by the judge during his term of office of his qualification to serve the balance thereof. The constitutional question whether maintenance of membership in the bar is necessary for continuance in judicial office has never been decided in this state. If the time should ever come when a lawyer serving as a judge should be so wanting in scruples that he must be disbarred and so lacking in sensitivity that he would attempt, after disbarment, to remain in office during the balance of his term, that will be the time to decide whether or not maintenance of membership in the bar can constitutionally be made a condition of tenure in office.[62]

There appear to be no definite decisions on this point, and we take no position on the constitutional issue involved. We merely note that there is no constitutional problem about lesser sanctions than disbarment, such as censure or reprimand, if a judge misbehaves.

Disciplinary proceedings should not be overlooked by bar associations concerned about the behavior of trial judges in their jurisdictions. The authority of bar associations to initiate actions seems established by the case law. The mere possibility that supervisory courts acting on the basis of such charges could censure or reprimand a judge for particularly egregious behavior may act as a check on their conduct. It is understandable that members of the bar might be reluctant to bring disciplinary charges against a judge before whom they might have to appear in the future. But disciplinary panels should take their responsibilities more seriously in checking on the behavior of all lawyers in court—judges and prosecutors as well as defense attorneys.

## Peremptory Challenge

California and two other states have established a new method for controlling a trial judge's misconduct: litigants are permitted to challenge one judge without having to prove he may be biased or prejudiced. He is then disqualified from the case, as a potential juror would be if challenged peremptorily. Thus if a particular judge is thought to be highhanded or tyrannical or just unsympathetic, he may be passed over for another judge with little controversy or embarrassment and no questions asked.

The defense bars in the states that have established this system seem to believe it works.[63] Judges who find themselves passed over again and again because of their courtroom conduct will have an incentive for improving their behavior. And defendants and litigants feel that they have a better chance to obtain justice.

# Conclusion

The problem of abusive or tyrannical judges can be partially solved by a more careful selection process. One of the judges whose conduct has been described in previous pages was not reappointed when his actions were made known to the relevant authorities. But in some cases judges are appointed for life or elected for long terms, and the opportunity for reappointment does not arise. In most cases it is difficult to predict how a lawyer will behave if put on the bench. Nevertheless some better screening procedure is in order before a judge assumes his awesome power. Purely political considerations should not be decisive in the selection process.

It is clear that some procedure for judicial commissions to investigate judges is needed to supplement the traditional methods of control. Appellate review and impeachment alone cannot correct the situation. The A.B.A. Standards miss the mark when they state:

> Under present practices, virtually the only sanctions available when a judge occasionally fails in his responsibility are: correction of his decisions and, perhaps, censure by an appellate court, public criticism through the news media and possibly censure by the organized bar, and, if he serves a definite term, eventual termination of his services by the electing or appointing authority. While none or all of these may appear wholly satisfactory, adoption of alternative measures must be approached with considerable caution. Mechanisms which diminish the independence of the entire judiciary could have more harmful consequences than the occasional transgressions of a few judges. On the other hand, ineffective mechanisms merely raise false hopes.[64]

The sanction that should be imposed on an erring judge depends on the extent and frequency of his misconduct. As we stated earlier, appellate review is sufficient for errors of judgment in stopping argument, engaging in undignified repartee, or a single biased remark. But a pattern of consistent prejudicial conduct and arrogant behavior requires a greater response.

# CHAPTER TEN

# *The Contempt Power*

In this study we have considered many possible remedies for court-room misconduct. The most potent of these is contempt of court, which applies the sting and the sanctions of the criminal law to those who are convinced of serious misbehavior.* Not only may a person be imprisoned or fined for violating the rules governing courtroom behavior, but these sanctions can be imposed "summarily," that is, instantly by a single judge without the normal procedural requirements for meting out criminal punishment.

Because of the severity of the contempt remedy and the judge's power to act summarily, the Supreme Court has closely reviewed cases in which defendants or their lawyers have been held in contempt, and in recent years it has progressively expanded the procedural and constitutional protections of those accused of the crime.

The Judiciary Act of 1789 provided from the beginning that the federal courts "shall have power . . . to punish by fine or imprisonment, at the discretion of said courts, all contempts of authority in any case of hearing before the same."[1] The language was extremely broad, with a limitation only as to mode of punishment, and in 1831 Congress narrowed the federal contempt power to three categories: misbehavior in the presence of the court or so near thereto as to obstruct justice; misbehavior of court officers in their official transactions; and disobedience of or resistance to a court's lawful writ, process, order, or decree.[2] The current federal statute perpetuates these categories.[3]

State contempt statutes have largely been patterned after the federal law, and the discretion of state judges to exercise the contempt power

---

* It is now established that criminal contempt is a crime in the ordinary sense: it is a violation of law punishable by fine or imprisonment or both. As Justice Holmes once said:

> These contempts are infractions of the law, visited with punishment as such. If such acts are not criminal, we are in error as to the most fundamental characteristic of crimes as that word has been understood in English speech. [Gompers v. United States, 233 U.S. 604, 610 (1914)]

is of course subject to the constitutional requirements imposed by the Supreme Court.

In this chapter we shall first consider the principal procedural issues concerning contempt as it affects the judicial power to control and punish courtroom misbehavior. (We shall do so in the context of the federal scheme, but the same issues exist in most state courts.) Thereafter, we shall examine the summary contempt power and present our reasons for concluding that it is an anomalous and unfair procedure not needed by trial judges to control trials and discourage misconduct.

## Procedural Requirements

The procedural guarantees to which an accused is entitled in contempt cases, as much as the substantive definition of contempt discussed in chapter 6, determine whether courtroom integrity can be maintained without sacrifice of standards of fundamental fairness.

Rule 42 of the Federal Rules of Criminal Procedure provides two distinct procedures for trying and punishing contemptuous behavior: "summary disposition" and "disposition upon notice and hearing."[4] The key distinction is that a judge may punish a contempt summarily —that is, without a hearing or other procedural protections for the accused—only if "it was committed in the actual presence of the court." Misbehavior in the courtroom will ordinarily but not always fall in this category, sometimes called "direct contempts."

Most procedural questions in recent cases of misconduct have arisen under summary contempt. There are several approaches that the judge can follow in a case where warnings and other lesser sanctions fail to work and the contempt remedy seems appropriate:

1. Rule 42(a) permits a trial judge to use the summary contempt power to punish the alleged wrongdoer a) on the spot or b) at the end of trial. We shall discuss our reasons for concluding that it is not proper to wait until the end of trial to impose summary contempt. In the section entitled "The Summary Contempt Power" we discuss our reasons for concluding that this power should be eliminated altogether.

2. The case can be heard upon the notice and hearing provided for under Rule 42(b). This rule permits the trial judge to hear the case himself a) during the trial or b) after the trial, or he can c) refer the matter to be heard by another judge at the end of trial. For the reasons outlined below, we think that the judge should always refer the matter to another judge.

## Procedures for Summary Contempt

It is particularly important to consider closely the means by which the summary contempt power is exercised. As Retired Justice Tom C. Clark, sitting in the court of appeals, stated: "The procedural safeguards . . . must be strictly adhered to lest the drastic power authorized escape the permissible limits of reason and fairness."[5]

The only contempts that can be heard summarily are those that take place "in the actual presence of the court." If misbehavior takes place in the corridors or outside the courthouse, summary contempt is inappropriate. If it takes place inside a courtroom but the judge is not present to view it, he cannot punish summarily.

If the misbehavior occurs in the judge's presence, current law permits him to punish immediately with no indictment,[6] no notice, no evidentiary hearing, no opportunity for argument, and, except where a sentence of more than six months is involved, without a jury. Some courts have held that a judge must issue a prior warning that certain acts are considered contemptuous and will be punished if repeated, but this is not required for the more serious forms of disorder. No particular form of words must be used by the judge. He may simply say, "I find you in contempt."

The difficult problems relating to the summary contempt power involve: the certification of the facts; the right to a jury trial; the disqualification of the judge; and the use of summary procedures at the end of trial.

### CERTIFICATION OF THE FACTS

Rule 42(a) requires that the order entered by the district judge "recite the facts," that is, "the conduct constituting the contempt." The judge must also certify that he "saw or heard" this conduct and that it was committed in his "actual presence."

The certificate is of considerable importance. Because the defendant has been convicted without notice or hearing, there is no trial record underlying the conviction. The facts recited in the certificate are thus necessary to give the defendant notice of the crime alleged and to allow appellate review. As stated in a Third Circuit opinion, "[T]his requirement is more than a formality—it is essential to disclosure of the basis of decision with sufficient particularity to permit informed appellate review."[7] Obviously, such review is possible only if the facts are stated in enough detail to permit a clear determination of whether the conduct on which the conviction rests was contemptuous and of the sort to justify summary conviction. This means that the judge must recite specific facts; conclusory language and general citations to the record are not sufficient.

The Tacoma Seven case, in which there was trial disruption, was reversed in 1971 because of a faulty certificate. The court of appeals found the following description of the courtroom misconduct by the trial judge to be too general:

> Standing, vocal and obviously prearranged demonstrations by spectators, sometimes led by one or more defendants and joined in by all, shouting epithets, sometimes threats of violence and profanity, and other improper language accompanied by a variety of disorderly movements and actions, interruptions by one or more or all defendants in qualification of the jury, exercise of challenges, opening statement for the plaintiff, examination of witnesses, offering of exhibits, making and hearing of objections, rulings and statements of the Judge, and in various other phases of trial proceedings.[8]

In the same case, a second certificate specifying another contempt of court was also held to be inadequate. It said:

> Stern's defiance of the directions, orders and warnings by the court in continuing her remarks precipitated loud, boisterous and violent actions and language in which the Judge saw and heard defendant Stern and each defendant other than Lerner personally participate. Riotous conduct and an incipient riot occurred in the courtroom. [After] the Judge left the courtroom . . . at least for a half hour or more scuffling and loud and boisterous language in the courtroom could be heard in the Judge's office. . . . During the misconduct above specified, proceedings in the court were at a standstill and could not be resumed for more than an hour.[9]

The appellate court found the second certificate to be invalid for several reasons. First, because the contempt convictions it describes rested in part on conduct that occurred outside the court's presence—Stern stopped speaking about a half-hour *after* the judge left the courtroom. Second, the certificate was too general; language such as "loud, boisterous and violent actions and language" is too conclusory. Third, the certificate contained no citations to particular passages in the transcript. The court held that incorporation by reference to the entire transcript did not cure the deficiency, even though the entire transcript was only three pages long.

> Much that the judge saw and heard may not be reflected in the transcript. The trial judge recognized this: he sought to incorporate in the second certificate not only the reporter's transcript but also the reporter's recordings and the audio and video tapes. . . .
> Even this, however, is insufficient. If these records reflected contumacious conduct we could still not be sure that the judge saw or heard that particular conduct, as he must have to justify conviction under Rule 42(a). We can be sure that this prerequisite to conviction under Rule 42(a) is satisfied only if the judge himself states or unmistakably refers to the particular facts upon which he relies and certifies that he personally witnesses them. And that is true, of course, even as to conduct that is reflected in the reporter's transcript. . . .

The judge was faced with a tumultuous, confused, and confusing situation. It might have been difficult for him to immediately draw a certificate specifically describing the improper conduct of each defendant. But this does not justify the procedure followed.[10]

While the court of appeals stated, half-apologetically, in its opinion that this approach "may seem overly technical," we do not think so. A specification is important in cases of summary contempt; it would be wrong to permit general statements to deprive a defendant of meaningful appellate review.

## RIGHT TO A JURY TRIAL

It was not until 1968 that the Supreme Court ruled that criminal contempts were "crimes" for the purpose of determining a right to trial by jury. Earlier, relying on the "unique character" of criminal contempts under the Constitution, the Court had consistently held that defendants in contempt cases were entitled to neither an indictment by grand jury nor a trial by petit jury.[11] This line of cases was finally overruled in *Bloom* v. *Illinois*, where the Court said that "there is no substantial difference between serious contempts and other serious crimes," and that "in contempt cases an even more compelling argument can be made for providing a right to jury trial as a protection against the arbitrary exercise of official power."[12] If a jury trial is required in a given case, of course the "summary" procedure under Rule 42(a) cannot be followed.

Contempt cases are now subject to the general rule that jury trials are required in all but "petty" cases.[13] In contempt cases, as with other crimes, the criterion of seriousness is the penalty involved. Ordinarily, the maximum penalty in the statute is determinative,[14] but since Congress has not included a maximum penalty in the contempt statute (§401), the penalty *actually imposed* is the standard. If this exceeds six months' imprisonment, the contempt is serious, not petty, and a jury trial is required.[15]

An important question not yet decided by the Supreme Court is whether separate acts of disorder at a trial may be punished as separate contempts and the sentences accumulated beyond the six month maximum, without providing the jury trial contemplated in the *Bloom* case. The government took this position in the contempt cases arising out of the Chicago conspiracy trial, but the Seventh Circuit held that when a judge waits until the end of trial to impose punishment, as Judge Hoffman did, the aggregate sentence meted out to a particular defendant should govern.[16]

This decision seems plainly correct. Serious potential for abuse exists in the absence of aggregation because, as the Seventh Circuit pointed out, any judge could review the record to single out "discrete" instances of contempt, impose up to six-month consecutive sentences for each instance and thereby imprison the contemnor for a theoretically unlimited term. He would, in effect, have the power to decide whether the safeguard of a jury should be interposed wholly apart from the total punishment he metes out.[17]

The same court in the Bobby Seale case also suggested that a judge, if so inclined, could punish one outrageously contemptuous act with more than six months by spreading the penalty over other less serious contempts. Indeed, the court of appeals intimated that something like this was actually done in the *Seale* case, by saying that "the uniform three-month sentence for each specified act of contempt could leave the impression that no special attempt was made to make the penalty proportionate to the offense for which it was imposed."[18]

Although accepting the need to aggregate sentences when a trial judge waits until the end of trial, the Seventh Circuit held that when a judge acts *immediately* to punish misbehavior under the summary contempt power aggregation is not required. The court relied on a warning advanced by Professor Paul Freund that imposition of a six month contempt sentence early in a trial could exhaust the judge's summary contempt power and leave him helpless to deal with later trial misconduct.[19] The court also stated that in summary proceedings occurring immediately after the misbehavior the potentiality for abuse in spreading out a number of contempts to avoid a jury trial is not so great.[20]

In light of the strong policies enunciated by the Supreme Court in favor of a jury trial in serious criminal cases, we do not agree that aggregation should be required only at the end of trial. The opportunity for abuse is also present when summary contempt is imposed at once; a judge can tailor the punishment levied for each infraction to the six month maximum and nevertheless conclude the trial with punishments ranging far beyond six months. We believe that whenever the total punishment for contempt exceeds that period, only a jury can impose it.

It is unavailing to rely on appellate review to oversee the trial judge's determination of the discreteness of separate contempts and the proper penalty for each. Granting that there is authority for such appellate scrutiny,[21] the standards for review are wholly amorphous. Moreover, because a cold record cannot convey the feel of a courtroom situation, appellate courts inevitably rely on the judge who witnessed the events to determine what is a "discrete" contempt and the proper punishment for each infraction. The matter thus remains in the hands of the trial judge, to the exclusion of the jury.

Considerations of cost and efficiency also have been presented as a reason for not aggregating the penalties for contempt and therefore requiring a jury. But the Supreme Court has already dealt with this point by stating:

> Perhaps to some extent we sacrifice efficiency, expedition, and economy, but the choice in favor of jury trial has been made, and retained, in the Constitution. We see no sound reason in logic or policy not to apply it in the area of criminal contempt.[22]

A practical problem presented by the six month rule, whether or not aggregation is required, is how to determine whether to convene a jury before the punishment is actually meted out. During a trial it is impossible to know how many contempts will finally be imposed and what punishment will be inflicted for each. If a trial judge exceeds the six month limit, he must refer the matter for a Rule 42 (b) hearing after trial. At that point two solutions are possible. The first is for the United States attorney to decide before the hearing that he will not seek a sentence of more than six months. (This was the approach taken by the government in the *Dellinger* case after the Seventh Circuit reversed the contempt convictions imposed by Judge Hoffman.) The other solution, which was suggested in the *Seale* case, is for the judge, after preliminarily reviewing the transcript of the allegedly contemptuous conduct, to announce that he would not hand down a punishment of more than six months on that record.[23] In both cases the need for a jury would be obviated.

## DISQUALIFICATION OF THE TRIAL JUDGE

Due process of law requires an impartial judge in all criminal cases. This problem is particularly acute in contempt cases, where the actions or words of an individual accused of contempt often antagonize the sitting judge, raising questions about his suitability to act on the charge.

The importance of the constitutional requirement of an impartial judge was graphically illustrated in a non-summary contempt case. A Michigan judge as a one-man grand jury later tried for contempt witnesses who refused to answer his questions. The Supreme Court reversed the contempt convictions, holding that a judge who sat as a one-man grand jury was part of the accusatory process, and therefore "cannot be, in the very nature of things, wholly disinterested in the conviction or acquittal of those accused."[24] The Court went on to say:

> Fair trials are too important a part of our free society to let prosecuting judges be trial judges of the charges they prefer.[25]

The same principle has been applied in a succession of summary contempt cases. The leading case, *Cooke* v. *United States*, involved a lawyer convicted for writing a "personal" letter to a judge that charged him with "prejudice and bias" regarding four pending cases. The Court ruled that it was error for the judge who was personally attacked to sit on the contempt charge.

> The power of contempt . . . is a delicate one and care is needed to avoid arbitrary or oppressive conclusions. This rule of caution is more mandatory where the contempt charged has in it the element of personal criticism or attack upon the judge. The judge must banish the slightest personal impulse to reprisal, but he should not bend backward and injure the authority of the court by too great leniency. The substitution of another judge would avoid either tendency but it is not always possible. Of course where acts of contempt are palpably aggravated by a personal attack upon the judge in order to drive the judge out of the case for ulterior reasons, the scheme should not be permitted to succeed. But attempts of this kind are rare. All of such cases, however, present difficult questions for the judge. All we can say upon the whole matter is that where conditions do not make it impracticable or where the delay may not injure public or private right, a judge called upon to act in a case of contempt by personal attack upon him, may, without flinching from his duty, properly ask that one of his fellow judges take his place.[26]

The *Cooke* doctrine was extended in *Offutt* v. *United States,* where a federal judge engaged in a dispute with defense counsel and displayed considerable personal animosity. At the close of trial the judge summarily held the counsel guilty of criminal contempt for "contumaceous and unethical conduct." The Supreme Court reversed, holding that in the federal courts a contempt citation should be tried before another judge whenever a trial judge becomes "personally embroiled" with the accused.

> The vital point is that in sitting in judgment on such a misbehaving lawyer the judge should not himself give vent to personal spleen or respond to personal grievance. These are subtle matters, for they concern the ingredients of what constitutes justice. Therefore, justice must satisfy the appearance of justice.[27]

More recently, *Mayberry* v. *Pennsylvania* added a further dimension to the requirement that trial judges step aside in certain contempt actions.[28] Mayberry and two codefendants were tried for prison breach and holding hostages. They chose to defend themselves, and the court appointed standby counsel to assist them. During the trial Mayberry's conduct was egregiously contemptuous and included repeated personal insults to the judge. Among other things, Mayberry called him a "dirty sonofabitch," "dirty tyrannical old dog," "stumbling dog," and "fool." The judge was charged with running a "Spanish Inquisition" and told to "Go to hell" and "Keep your mouth shut."[29]

Near the end of the trial, Mayberry had to be removed from the courtroom because of his disruptive behavior. The jury found all defendants guilty, and the trial judge, before imposing sentence on the verdict, found Mayberry guilty of eleven separate contempts in a summary proceeding. He denied Mayberry's request to be heard, either in defense or in mitigation, and sentenced him to one to two years on each count of contempt, a total of eleven to twenty-two years. The Supreme Court of Pennsylvania affirmed with one judge dissenting.

The United States Supreme Court unanimously reversed, in an opinion by Justice Douglas, holding that the judge should have disqualified himself from deciding the contempt charges. It rested its analysis on the judgment that personal insults create a likelihood of prejudice, and therefore a trial judge should be disqualified whenever the defendant's conduct is personally insulting toward him, whether or not he has shown an actual lack of impartiality. This rule significantly expands the class of cases in which disqualification is required because a defendant need no longer demonstrate that the judge is biased, but rather may point to his own insulting behavior. In this way protection is increased against "subtle and unmanifested forms of prejudice" on the part of trial judges.[30]

The inevitable consequence of the Mayberry decision is to eliminate summary contempt in cases falling within the disqualification standard and to require another judge to hold a due process hearing under Rule 42 (b).

We think the result in *Mayberry* is salutary. We do not think its holding should be confined, however, to when the defendant has been "personally insulting" to the trial judge but should be applied to all cases of alleged contempt in the courtroom. By requiring disqualification in only a limited and vaguely defined class of cases, it presents a difficult factual question. Further, the *Mayberry* case permits the trial judge to make the initial determination of whether the defendant has been insulting; this judgment will tend to be upheld on appeal as "within his discretion."

The Court's test in *Mayberry* is paradoxical. As a defendant becomes less insulting and his guilt therefore less certain, his right to the procedural safeguard of a plainly unbiased judge becomes less sure. It is a questionable assumption, moreover, that personal insults create a possibility of bias while disobedience to a judge's rulings or orders or insults hurtled at the judicial system itself—prominent in political cases of the kind we have often discussed—do not. As the Court said in the *Sacher* case, "It is almost inevitable that any contempt of court committed in the presence of a judge during a trial will be an offense against his dignity and authority."[31]

## SUMMARY PROCEDURES AT THE END OF TRIAL

Summary procedures have ordinarily been used to punish contempts immediately upon their occurrence in open court in order to vindicate the court's authority promptly in the face of disorder. On occasion, however, judges have imposed contempt summarily *at the end of trial* for alleged misconduct during the proceedings. This occurred, for example, in the Communist conspiracy trial and the Chicago conspiracy case.

It was not until *Sacher* v. *United States*,[32] that the Supreme Court, over strong dissents, upheld summary procedures used in this way. The *Sacher* case grew out of the 1949 Smith Act case against the leaders of the Communist party, discussed in chapter 4. The contempts were lodged against their lawyers for, among other things, personal attacks on the trial judge. In sustaining the contempt charges the Supreme Court ruled that an evidentiary hearing was unnecessary when the judge had personally observed every element of the crime. In addition, by delaying, the judge removed the possibility that the contempt charges against the lawyers would prejudice the jury against the defendants.

Our analysis persuades us that the *Sacher* case, while never over-ruled, has been seriously weakened by later decisions in the Supreme Court, and further that there is no justification in principle for using summary contempt as a delayed action fuse.

The first decision to look in a new direction was *Offutt* v. *United States*,[33] which was identical to *Sacher* except that in *Offutt* the trial judge had become "personally embroiled" with the petitioner, while in *Sacher* there was disagreement among the justices on that score. In *Offutt*, the Supreme Court reversed a summary contempt order entered after trial, ruling that when the trial is over, the policy of preserving order could not justify summary contempt if the judge had become personally involved. In *United States* v. *Meyer*, the Court of Appeals for the District of Columbia concluded that *Offutt* was "an overruling, sub silentio, of *Sacher*" unless *Offutt* "is limited to situations in which there is evidence of actual embroilment on the part of the trial judge."[34] But that possible distinction seems weakened if not pre-cluded by the *Mayberry* case, where the Court reversed the summary contempt although the trial judge "was not an activist seeking combat . . . he was the target of petitioner's insolence."[35]

The court in the *Meyer* case concluded that a trial judge could not impose summary contempt after the trial was over through the follow-ing process of reasoning:

1. The *Cooke* case justified the summary contempt power on two bases: a) that it would be a waste of judicial resources to have another judge hold a contempt hearing since the trial judge had already viewed all the elements of the crime involved; and b) summary contempt was necessary to preserve order in the court. The Supreme Court intimated that both policies must be applicable to justify summary disposition by the trial judge.

2. The *Sacher* case suggested that only the first policy enunciated in *Cooke*—the waste of resources argument—was sufficient to justify summary contempt either during or after trial.

3. *Offutt* held that the waste of resources argument is inapplicable when a trial judge has become embroiled in a personal dispute with the person held in contempt since he no longer is a competent fact-finder. Nor was the need to preserve order relevant since the trial was already over when the contempt finding was made.

4. *Mayberry* reaffirmed the *Offutt* case and went beyond it by holding that insulting behavior toward a judge disqualifies him automatically because of the possibility of his personal animosity toward the defendant. Thus, the same considerations relevant in *Offutt* preclude an insulted judge from waiting until the end of the trial to punish for contempt.

5. The net effect of *Mayberry* is that whenever a judge is personally embroiled or insulted, he cannot use summary contempt unless it is necessary to preserve order while the trial is in progress. Thus he can never wait until the end of trial to impose summary punishment himself.

In the *Meyer* case itself, a lawyer's remark that the judge had made up his mind "about everything except the length of the sentence" was held to be sufficiently personal to invoke the *Mayberry* doctrine. The *Meyer* court did not reach the question of whether a judge who is not personally embroiled or insulted can wait until the trial is over.[36] This ruling was followed by the Seventh Circuit Court of Appeals in the *Dellinger* case. It concluded that the *Mayberry* case required that a new judge hear the contempts involving both the defendants and the lawyers.[37]

But even apart from the more recent cases, we do not think that the summary contempt power after trial can be successfully defended in principle.

Justice Jackson offered two reasons in the *Sacher* case to justify giving a judge the flexibility to wait until the end of trial before imposing a contempt sanction summarily. The first is:

> To summon a lawyer before the bench and pronounce him guilty of contempt is not unlikely to prejudice his client. It might be done out of the presence of the jury, but we have held that a contempt judgment must be public. Only the naive and inexperienced would assume that news of such action will not reach the jurors. If the court were required also then to pronounce sentence, a construction quite as consistent with the text of the Rule as petitioner's present contention, it would add to the prejudice.[38]

The difficulty with this argument is that it goes too far. Any sharp exchange between a judge and lawyer leading to an admonition to the lawyer is likely to affect the jury. This is a frequent occurrence, as any experienced trial lawyer knows. A warning to the jury that it is not to consider comments or sanctions against a lawyer in determining the guilt or innocence of the client is all that has ever been thought necessary. It is not possible to justify the extraordinary summary contempt power against a lawyer merely as a protective device for the client.

Justice Jackson stated his second argument in defense of summary contempt at trial's end as follows:

> If we were to hold that summary punishment can be imposed only instantly upon the event, it would be an incentive to pronounce, while smarting under the irritation of the contemptuous act, what should be a well-considered judgment. We think it less likely that unfair condemnation of counsel will occur if the more deliberate course be permitted.[39]

Justice Jackson's second reason is hardly a justification for allowing the judge to wait until the end of the trial to punish for contempt. Rather it is a reason for depriving him of the power altogether. The *Mayberry* case shows that it is just as possible for a judge to nurture the alleged wrongs done to him during the trial and then to maximize the penalties when he sentences at the conclusion of the proceedings.

It must be recalled that the principal argument offered to justify summary contempt is the need to maintain order in the courtroom. But this reason does not apply if the judge waits until the end of the trial and then imposes a heavy penalty for what the participants did earlier. This is precisely what occurred in the Chicago conspiracy trial and the Communist Smith Act case. As Justice Frankfurter said in dissent in the *Sacher* case:

> Summary punishment of contempt is concededly an exception to the requirements of Due Process. Necessity dictates the departure. Necessity must bound its limits. In this case the course of events to the very end of the trial shows that summary measures were not necessary to enable the trial to go on. Departure from established judicial practice, which makes it unfitting for a judge who is personally involved to sit in his own case, was therefore unwarranted. Neither self-respect nor the good name of the law required it. . . . It is a disservice to the law to sanction the imposition of punishment by a judge personally involved and therefore not unreasonably to be deemed to be seeking retribution, however unconsciously, at a time when a hearing before a judge undisturbed by any personal relation is equally convenient.[40]

As we have said previously, any violation of a judge's orders or of court decorum has a potential for inducing judicial bias, since the rules violated are the judge's own. Accordingly, it is difficult to escape the view that trial judges should be disqualified in *all* cases of direct contempt where immediate punishment is deferred, whether or not the contempt is "insulting." As stated in the *Harvard Law Review*:

> [This] is an easy test to apply and has none of the drawbacks or dangers of attempting to distinguish between contempts according to their pro-

pensity for creating bias. It elevates the criminal contempt defendant to the level of other criminal defendants, who run no risks of facing a prejudiced judge. There is little reason to justify any departure from this norm. Once the trial is over, the judge has no further interest in maintaining his control over the defendant. He has no protectable interest in deciding the charges himself; the crime is against the state.[41]

## Disposition by Notice and Hearing

A contempt action may be instituted under non-summary procedures, that is, under Rule 42(b), either by the judge sitting at the time of the alleged contempt or by another judge to whom the case is referred. In either case the notice of the charge must provide "the essential facts constituting the criminal contempt." There is no talismanic formula required for the necessary notice. The purpose of the rule is to give the defendant a fair opportunity to defend himself, and therefore the notice should contain enough particulars to inform him of the nature of the contempt. In addition, the notice must state the time and place of the hearing and allow a reasonable time to prepare a defense.

Rule 42(b) deals explicitly with the problem of disqualification. It provides that if the contempt charged "involves disrespect to or criticism of a judge, that judge is disqualified from presiding at the trial or hearing except with the defendant's consent." As discussed in the preceding section, this is identical to the rule that the Supreme Court has adopted as a constitutional standard to govern disqualifications in summary contempts.

The same standard should apply to contempt cases in which a jury is required because of a sentence of more than six months. It might be argued that since a jury and not the judge determines guilt a biased judge might not threaten the fairness of the contempt trial. But this assumes too limited a view of the judicial function. A judge's attitude can easily influence and in some cases dominate a jury's deliberations, especially since jury members will know that the judge personally witnessed the events at issue. In addition, the judge always controls the sentencing apparatus—crucial to many contempt cases where the issue is not whether a contempt has occurred but whether there are events in justification or mitigation to consider in deciding what sanction to apply.[42]

At the hearing on a contempt charge under Rule 42(b) the presumption of innocence applies, as in other criminal cases, and all elements of the offense must be proved beyond a reasonable doubt.[43] The trial transcript is ordinarily the basic item of evidence, and this may be augmented by witnesses called by the government, subject to defense cross-examination. The defendant of course has a due process right to enter a defense against the contempt charges. This includes, as the Supreme Court has long recognized, "the assistance of counsel, if requested, and the right to call witnesses to give testimony, relevant either to the issue of complete exculpation or in extenuation of the offense and in mitigation of the penalty to be imposed."[44]

The Court of Appeals for the District of Columbia has stressed the importance of permitting a defendant to introduce evidence at the hearing bearing on his demeanor. At one hearing in the *Offutt* case, the question was whether a defense counsel who had been cited for contempt was guilty of remarks that were "insolent, insulting and offensive."[45] The hearing was before a district judge other than the one who was sitting at the time of the alleged contempt (the latter had been disqualified).[46] The judge declined to accept an offer of proof that the lawyer's remarks were not disrespectful but were made in good faith in response to a trial judge who had "exhibited anger, temper and an antagonistic attitude toward appellant and his client."[47] The court of appeals held that the proffer of proof should have been received, saying:

> Ordinarily where the conduct alleged to be criminally contemptuous occurs during a trial the presiding judge sees and hears all that bears upon the issue of contempt. No additional testimony is needed in the usual summary proceedings. . . . But here a different judge sat. The transcript alone did not make available to him all relevant and material evidence. . . .
>
> [D]emeanor might have an important bearing on whether appellant was guilty of "gross discourtesy" to the court, or whether his remarks were "insolent, insulting and offensive." Evidence as to tone and inflection of voice and manner of behavior might give character to the printed word. And if after receiving the evidence the court believed Offutt guilty of contempt, the evidence might induce the court to mitigate the punishment.[48]

In hearings on a contempt citation when the trial judge does not sit, either because he is disqualified or for another reason, he may be regarded as a prospective witness, although we have found no reported case in which a judge has actually testified in such a situation. The court in *Offutt*, while saying that the hearing judge may decline to place the trial judge on the stand in his sound discretion to "control the scope of testimony and the number of witnesses," did not exclude the possibility.[49] The Court of Appeals for the Seventh Circuit in the Bobby Seale case also suggested the possibility of not permitting the original trial judge to be called as a witness, observing that in the rare case where the record does not adequately establish the facts, "live witnesses such as other court officers and bystanders could be called to testify."[50]

We understand the caution with which these courts have approached the possibility of requiring a judge to testify about a contempt that allegedly took place in his presence and in which he may have been involved. But we do not think this presents a serious problem. In the exceptional case where a trial judge's testimony would be important and there is no adequate substitute available, there is no indignity or loss of prestige to the bench in requiring the judge to testify and be cross-examined. As the *Harvard Law Review* has concluded, "Whatever personal discomfort judges may suffer [in appearing as a witness], the state's interest in respect for its judicial officers may well be better served in the long run by procedures which insure their scrupulous fairness."[51]

There is no reason to avoid calling a prosecutor to the stand when he has firsthand knowledge that can be useful in a hearing on a contempt charge.


# The Summary Contempt Power

The power of a trial judge to punish contumaceous behavior in his courtroom by summary process is of long vintage, has been approved by the United States Supreme Court, and has been justified widely as a necessary weapon in the judicial arsenal. Nevertheless, we do not think it should be perpetuated. It was recognized early that any procedure that permits a single judge to exact criminal punishment without notice of charges or an opportunity of the defendant to be heard is "arbitrary in its nature and liable to abuse."[52] We agree with the conclusion reached by Justice Black fifteen years ago:

> The power of a judge to inflict punishment for criminal contempt by means of a summary proceeding stands as an anomaly in the law. In my judgment the time has come for a fundamental and searching reconsideration of the validity of this power which has aptly been characterized by a State Supreme Court as "perhaps, nearest akin to despotic power of any power existing under our form of government."[53]

After reconsidering the justification and effect of summary contempt, we have concluded that it performs no essential role in controlling misbehavior, that alternative means are available to assure order in the court—including the civil contempt power—and that the arbitrary power it affords trial judges should be terminated. Courtroom misbehavior should be subject to punishment only after notice and fair hearing before a judge other than the one who presided during the incident giving rise to the contempt citation.

The essential vice of the summary contempt power is that it enables a judge to combine in one person a variety of functions in a criminal case. As stated by Justice Black in what is probably the most extensive judicial assault on the summary power:

> When the responsibilities of lawmaker, prosecutor, judge, jury and disciplinarian are thrust upon a judge he is obviously incapable of holding the scales of justice perfectly fair and true and reflecting impartially on the guilt or innocence of the accused. He truly becomes the judge of his own cause. The defendant charged with criminal contempt is thus denied what I had always thought to be an indispensable element of due process of law—an objective, scrupulously impartial tribunal to determine whether he is guilty or innocent of the charges filed against him. . . . To this end no man can be a judge in his case and no man is permitted to try cases where he has an interest in the outcome. . . . Fair trials are too important a part of our free society to let prosecuting judges be trial judges of the charges they prefer.[54]

The vice of this procedure is aggravated by the fact that the judge is able to act without external restraint. Again in the words of Justice Black:

> . . . the substantive scope of the offense of contempt is inordinately sweeping and vague; it has been defined, for example, as "any conduct that tends to bring the authority and administration of the law into disrespect or disregard." It would be no overstatement therefore to say that the offense with the most ill-defined and elastic contours in our law is now punished by the harshest procedures known to that law. Secondly, a defendant's principal assurance that he will be fairly tried and punished is the largely impotent review of a cold record by an appellate court, another body of judges. Once in a great while a particular appellate tribunal basically hostile to summary proceedings will closely police contempt trials but such supervision is only isolated and fleeting. All too often the reviewing courts stand aside readily with the formal declaration that "the trial judge has not abused his discretion." But even at its rare best appellate review cannot begin to take the place of trial in the first instance by an impartial jury subject to review on the spot by an uncommitted trial judge.[55]

The fears expressed by Justice Black and others have been warranted by empirical evidence. The power to punish summarily tends to lead to severe and arbitrary punishment of defendants and lawyers. As we noted earlier, the defendant in the *Mayberry* case received a sentence of eleven to twenty-two years. No matter how outrageous his words were in court, that sentence imposed by the judge, who was their target, is excessive. As another example, the *New York Times* reported on October 31, 1971, that a civil rights lawyer in Louisville, Kentucky, Daniel T. Taylor III, was sentenced to four and a half years for contempt for his actions in defending the murder case of two black youths in that city. The reason cited for the sentence was that the lawyer argued with the judge, made "flippant" remarks to the prosecution during the trial, and otherwise disobeyed the court's directives. The sentence was later reduced by an appellate court to six months.

In our analysis of the published cases of summary contempt from 1960 to 1972 we found that of a total of seventy-two cases where the trial judge imposed summary punishment, forty (more than sixty

percent) were later reversed by an appeals court. The cases are represented by the following chart:

### REPORTED SUMMARY CONTEMPT CASES
### FROM 1960 to 1972[56]

|  |  | Affirmed | Reversed | | |
| --- | --- | --- | --- | --- | --- |
|  |  |  | MERITS | PROCEDURE | OTHER |
| State (including D.C.) |  |  |  |  |  |
| Parties |  | 9 | 4 | 4 | 0 |
| Attorneys |  | 15 | 12 | 5 | 0 |
| Spectators and |  |  |  |  |  |
| Witnesses |  | 2 | 1 | 2 | 0 |
|  | TOTAL | 26 | 17 | 11 | 0 |
| Federal |  |  |  |  |  |
| Parties |  | 2 | 0 | 3† | 0 |
| Attorneys |  | 2 | 4* | 1 | 0 |
| Spectators and |  |  |  |  |  |
| Witnesses |  | 1 | 2 | 1 | 0 |
| Unspecified |  | 1 | 0 | 0 | 1 |
|  | TOTAL | 6 | 6 | 5 | 1 |
| Federal and Sate Total |  | 32 | 23 | 16 | 1 |

In many of these cases, the arbitrariness of the judge's action is
obvious. In a case involving members of the S.D.S. in Chicago, the
judge held all sixteen defendants in contempt for laughing at one of
his questions ("Who is in charge of the S.D.S.?") and sentenced them
to ten days in jail. The sentences were reversed on appeal.[57]

In reaching our conclusion that the summary contempt power
should be done away with, we have not ignored the justifications that
have been offered for it. The most important of these is that trial
judges require such authority in order to maintain order in the court.
We recognize the importance of a tranquil courtroom to assure the
proper administration of justice, but we do not believe that summary
power is necessary to achieve this end. As Justice Frankfurter said,
dissenting in *Sacher:*

> The administration of justice and courts as its instruments are vindi-
> cated, and lawyers who might be tempted to try similiar tactics are
> amply deterred, by the assurance that punishment will be certain and
> severe regardless of the tribunal that imposes it.[58]

* Including one case, *Tauber* v. *Gordon,* 350 F.2d 843 (3d Cir. 1965) (en
banc), reversed in part on procedural grounds.

† Including one case, *In re Dellinger,* 461 F.2d 389 (7th Cir. 1972), in which
five of the defendants were parties, and two were attorneys.

What Justice Frankfurter says about deterring lawyers is also true about unruly defendants. The availability of the *Allen* remedies provides an answer to the argument that summary contempt is necessary to control defendants with a variety of weapons.

Flexibility is of course desirable, but the use of the summary contempt power is unnecessary for it. As we have shown in chapter 6, a trial judge can act with escalating steps against a defendant—by warning, removal, and then citation for contempt. A defendant who has been cited knows that after trial he will be subject to a hearing and possible conviction and punishment, which should be sufficient to deter him from wayward action, and to enable a judge to control his courtroom. Whatever additional "flexibility" the summary contempt power may provide is outweighed by the significant objections to it.

To the argument that immediate action is necessary to deter others from attempting similar conduct which might abort the trial, our response is that the prompt citation of a defendant or other misbehaving person for contempt is "immediate action." In our judgment the threat of a later criminal trial, with the possibility of a conviction and severe penalties, is a sufficient deterrent to further disobedience within the court.

A related reason offered for the summary contempt power is the need for swift imposition of penalties. If a second contempt hearing before another judge is required, a long period may elapse. In addition, the second hearing may have to be long and complicated, thus adding to the delay in reaching a final decision. This is true, but we do not think it justifies the extraordinary power to punish summarily. All criminal trials involve some delay, and the delay incident to a full contempt hearing is no more dangerous to the administration of justice than the delays incident to the procedural steps required by the Bill of Rights. Procedural safeguards in the legal process always make a criminal trial more complicated and costly than arbitrary arrest and punishment would be. As Justice Black said in the *Green* case:

> It is undoubtedly true that a judge can dispose of charges of criminal contempt faster and cheaper than a jury. But such trifling economies as may result have not generally been thought sufficient reason for abandoning our great constitutional safeguards aimed at protecting freedom and other basic human rights of incalculable value. Cheap, easy convictions were not the primary concern of those who adopted the Constitution and the Bill of Rights. Every procedural safeguard they established purposely made it more difficult for the Government to convict those it accused of crimes. On their scale of values justice occupied at least as high a position as economy.[59]

It is also important to lay to rest the suggestion that a later hearing is unnecessary because the trial judge "has already witnessed directly" the events leading to the contempt citation.[60] This point has been met very well by an analysis in the *Wisconsin Law Review:*

> The existence of eyewitness testimony, even if uncontroverted, has never been considered grounds for abandonment of due process of law. If due process is to mean anything at all, it must mean that guilt may not be presumed, but must be proven. To hold otherwise is to say that when guilt is certain, proof is superfluous. But a legal system which operates according to such tautologies plants the very seeds of despotism, which due process of law seeks to destroy.[61]

Furthermore, since it is clear that a judge can often become personally embroiled or that personal stings may have left their marks, one can no longer assume that the trial judge has dispassionately and clearly viewed what occurred at the trial. Once it is recognized that due process requires an unbiased judge to determine guilt and punishment, the argument that it is "unnecessary" to have a separate hearing loses much force.[62]

A further argument in favor of summary contempt is that appellate review may cure any defect in the summary proceeding. But there are serious shortcomings in appellate review. The appellate court reviewing a summary contempt hearing can decide only on the basis of the original record. If there is a claim of bias or personal embroilment, a defendant should have the right to offer supporting evidence to show that he was not guilty of obstructing the trial. This can be done in a separate due process hearing before another judge but not on appellate review.[63]

Any attempt to abolish the summary contempt power will be met with the claim that it is necessary to maintain respect for and discipline in the courts. The same argument was made when restrictions were placed on the ability of courts to punish printed criticism of court action or to punish conduct outside the courtroom by a term longer than six months.[64] We do not think these claims were justified in the earlier cases, and we do not think they are justified here.

Significantly, some courts and legislatures have concluded that remedies other than summary contempt are adequate to ensure order in the courts. For example, in July 1971 the Alaska Supreme Court held that any contempt (except a fine of less than $100) must be tried before a jury in a full due process hearing.

> . . . a criminal contempt proceeding is criminal prosecution within article I, section 11 of the Alaska Constitution. In the instant case, we believe that considerations of convenience and expediency to the state are convincingly outweighed by the right of an individual to be convicted only by means which are fundamentally fair. . . .
>
> The court has the authority to cite for criminal contempt (i.e. to bind the alleged contemnor over for trial) on its authority alone. The court may order a contumacious defendant to be taken from the court-

room. Unruly spectators, may, in addition to summary fine or citation, be ordered from the courtroom. The court retains the authority to imprison for civil contempt in appropriate instances. Each of these powers involves one degree or another of punishment; in each case the trial court acts summarily. It is thus clear that our trial courts will not be rendered impotent if denied the power summarily to imprison for most direct criminal contempts.[65]

Connecticut enacted a law in 1971 revising its procedure for trying criminal contempts. It specifies:

> Any person who acts in such a manner as to violate the dignity and authority of any court in its presence or so near thereto as to obstruct the administration of justice, or any officer of any court who misbehaves in the conduct of his official duties shall be guilty of contempt and shall be fined not more than five hundred dollars or imprisoned not more than six months or both. No person charged with violating this section should be tried for such violation before the same judge against whom the alleged contempt was perpetrated.[66]

The National Commission on Reform of the Federal Criminal Laws originally recommended in its study draft that the maximum penalty that a judge could summarily impose for improper courtroom conduct should be a five-day jail term.[67] The Commission created a new crime, "hindering proceedings by disorderly conduct," which could be punished by stiffer penalties but would be treated as a separate crime and heard by a different judge in a separate hearing. The Commission stated:

> Even though retention of the criminal contempt power is warranted, it does not follow that Congress should not limit this extraordinary power even more than under existing law. The draft proposal that the imprisonment ceiling be 5 days and the fine ceiling $500 expresses two policies. One is that the kinds of otherwise undefined, petty misbehavior for which the power is reserved does not warrant a greater penalty. The other is that where the conduct also violates a statute, prosecution should proceed in the traditional mode, if a greater penalty is available and appears desirable.[68]

In its final report the Commission increased the maximum penalty that could be imposed to six months but offered the five day limit as an alternative:

> An alternative to the six-month maximum would be to limit the court's summary power to punish for contempt, e.g. to 5 days' imprisonment, relying for greater deterrence on the threat of prosecution as an offense under [other sections of the code]. This might have the advantage of interposing an impartial tribunal between the offending defendant and offended judge prior to the imposition of an extended jail term. Nevertheless, it was thought preferable to recognize a broader need for the court to vindicate its authority. The danger of abuse was acknowledged, but thought not to be, on balance, dispositive.[69]

In our view the need for an impartial tribunal and the danger of abuse far outweigh any demonstrated need for a court to vindicate its authority by this procedure.[70] The *Allen* case, which was not cited by the Commission in its analysis of the contempt power, gives a judge ample power to deal with disorder.

## Conclusion

The contempt power is one of the chief weapons in a judge's arsenal to control courtroom misconduct. It is also one of the most easily abused because existing law permits a judge to punish an individual without the usual safeguards of due process. We believe that a judge has sufficient power to control his courtroom without using the contempt power summarily. By citing for contempt, he sets into motion an effective procedure for protecting the integrity of the proceedings.

It is important that the procedural requirements for the exercise of the contempt power be strictly adhered to. Given the danger of abuse and the purpose of the contempt power, there is no excuse for waiting to apply it summarily when the trial is over. The right to a jury trial should not be evaded by citing separate acts of disorder as separate contempts. A judge contributes to order in the courts by referring the matter to another tribunal for a decision rather than by imposing punishment himself, where his motives can be misconstrued.

# CHAPTER ELEVEN

# The Integrity of
# the Courtroom

One of the most important factors in determining whether judicial proceedings will be conducted in an orderly, rational fashion is the physical surroundings in which a trial is held. The maintenance of security and the management of traffic within the court, including the control of spectators within and immediately outside the courtroom, and the role of the press in reporting on judicial hearings, are related problems which will also be discussed in this chapter.

## The Physical Plant

The physical plant in which the courts operate contributes to the disrespect in which the legal system is often held and to the disorderly way in which justice is frequently dispensed. The courthouses in many of the larger cities are old and dingy, the courtrooms dirty and uncomfortable, the acoustics inadequate, and proper security difficult. *Newsweek* described the Chicago Criminal Court building as

> a melancholy place, flyspecked and grimy, a Hollywood-Egyptian temple squatting heavily and incongruously among the factories, the freight yard and the slum housing projects on Chicago's roiling West Side. . . . Through its cavernous courtrooms have passed generations of Chicago's outlaws and outcasts—a faceless succession of bootleggers, bookies, hit men, drifters, thieves, whores, petty Mafiosi and lately the black young, so thickly involved in the crime of the city streets. In its corridors, in the smell of food and sweat and tears, the People of Illinois through their agents—the police, the prosecutors, the lawyers, the judges—labor imperfectly toward a rough approximation of justice.[1]

In the Boston area many of the courtrooms were built in the nineteenth or even the eighteenth century and are totally inadequate for today's needs. The chief justice of the Massachusetts Superior Court told a *Boston Globe* reporter: "If I had to find room for another judge in the Suffolk County Courthouse, I would have to hang him from a coat hanger in a broom closet."[2]

Robert P. Patterson, Jr., a former president of the Legal Aid Society, describes the Brooklyn Criminal Court building:

> [The courthouse] is about 40 years old. From the outside it looks 60 years old and on the inside it looks 80 years old. The floor is strewn with paper cups and candy wrappers and a large mopping machine is generally stored in the main lobby. At 9:30 in the morning it is a virtual madhouse, clients hunting lawyers, lawyers hunting clients, families trying to find out where their children will be arraigned. How they find out, I don't know. . . .
> It was a warm day and I attended arraignments in the high-ceilinged courtroom on the first floor. There were no seats, so I leaned against the wall where a number of arresting officers waited for their cases to come up. The building is not air-conditioned so the windows were open and the traffic noise was loud. . . .[3]

One of the judges who responded to our questionnaire, a woman judge from the New York Criminal Court, made some trenchant comments about the courtroom in which she presided. She had described two flare-ups in which the defendants tried to hit a court officer and a witness.

> In both of these instances I was holding the hearing in a "back-up" courtroom, about 15 ft. by 20 ft., no bench, but a table on a small dais, dirty and dingy, ill-lit and ill-maintained. . . . I feel strongly, . . . that we cannot separate justice and courtroom conduct from the physical setting of the court. We in my court (as I am honored to term it) are dealing with often violent individuals, some sociopathic, some psychopathic; the courtroom setting as it now exists encourages the volatile and the hostile to violence. Several weeks ago, in a youth part (ages 16–19) I had before me three defendants, concededly members of an alleged militant group, charged with resisting arrest, assault and, as to one of them, possession of a loaded gun. I was hearing the matter, again, in a small back-up room, a former robing room transformed by fiat into a courtroom. Into this room were crammed not only the three defendants, but also their spouses, a set of parents and a few odd siblings and friends.[4]

Although new dignified courthouses are necessary, they are only part of the problem. The lower criminal courts require better administration and management to handle the great traffic that passes through them. Hundreds and thousands of cases are processed every day without the facilities or personnel to handle the overload. The result is assembly-line justice, as the President's Commission on Law Enforcement and the Administration of Justice has described it. The sheer magnitude of the cases in the lower criminal courts creates pressures on judges, clerks, security officers, and other officials that make it difficult for them to do their jobs well. Because of the babble of noise and confusion many participants—defendants, their relatives, witnesses, complainants—can't hear let alone understand what is happening. A reporter for the *Washington Post* described one day in the Recorder's Court in Detroit:

> [A] cluster of perhaps 30 policemen, all in street clothes, . . . [stood] and gossip[ed] idly near the empty jury box on the left side of the courtroom. In the confusion and cacaphony that characterize the criminal courtroom scene, the policemen were balanced by a swirling, changing mass of as many men opposite them. These are the criminal lawyers, most of whom work in Courtroom No. 8 every day. . . .
>
> Lawyers, policemen, clerks and others criss-crossed noisly in front of [the Judge's] bench, streamed back and forth through the swinging gate, and generally kept up an ocean's roar of conversation that crashed around the pronouncements of the judge, occasionally drowning out his words altogether.[5]

Robert P. Patterson, Jr., describes the busyness of a courtroom in the Manhattan Criminal Court:

> Although you could hear the case called, you could not hear much else including the charge, the adjournment date, or the amount of bail. From time to time the words "Legal Aid" would be called out and the defendant led back to the pens. I looked around. There wasn't a comprehending face in the courtroom. How could there be? You couldn't hear what went on. . . .
>
> Because the judge's voice was inaudible, no interest was shown unless someone got mad. Once a lawyer, arguing for lower bail after the judge had set bail, made a lot of loud and ineffective noises at which people up front grimaced. And during a short recess one lawyer yelled at the clerk "who the hell do you think you are, you son of a bitching bastard." Everyone seemed to enjoy this outburst. Anger at the court had had its moment of revenge. It was certainly the most audible event of the day, but to me as a lawyer, it was a distressing event.[6]

A visit to almost any courtroom in the lower criminal courts in a large city will confirm these comments. Witnesses or friends or relatives of the defendants wander in and out, trying to find out what is happening or when they will be needed. Lawyers shout out the names of their clients or of witnesses to locate them before a case is called. In an arraignment part the court clerk or bridgeman cries out the name of every case and the calendar clerk repeats the date of an adjourned hearing to ensure that scheduling is correct. Lawyers argue to the judge about bail while court officers, assistant district attorneys, defendants, Legal Aid lawyers, and policemen wander through the well of the court. Spectators read newspapers or try to puzzle out what is happening. Often a language barrier exists, but no effort is made to translate.

When a defendant appears in the court, he may try to communicate with his family, give them his money or valuables and some last minute instructions. Often in a highly emotional state, he resents the court officers' trying to hurry him along. The abruptness of such last chance meetings often leads to altercations in the courtroom.

Courtroom incidents involving distraught defendants and their families are an almost daily occurrence in the lower courts of the nation and should cause greater concern than the few notorious disruptive trials described in earlier chapters. Since these courts are the first point of contact for most citizens with the criminal law, greater efforts must be made to dignify the setting, make the proceedings more understandable and efficient, and improve the quality of justice that is dispensed.

Many studies have been made on improving the structure, management, and administration of the lower courts.[7] Some of their proposals strike us as having much merit although they raise other problems which have not been fully explored.

New pre-arraignment centers might be established away from the courts to process defendants immediately after their arrest. Bail would be set and some initial screening done to eliminate cases that obviously will not be prosecuted further. A Courthouse Reorganization study in New York City proposes:

> The criminal justice system in New York County beckons for a more effective means of screening and dispersing cases and defendants prior to cases reaching the courts. Based on the Criminal Court's high percentage of dismissed cases, it would seem that police officer, assistant district attorney, probation officer and Legal Aid attorney could work more in unison after an arrest to determine sufficiency of evidence and the best procedure for handling the matter. If it is agreed that there is insufficient evidence to prosecute, then the case should be dismissed and the suspect released without the case ever reaching court. If the matter could best be handled by social agencies, the suspect should be referred to the appropriate agency.[8]

In the criminal courts themselves, some separation should be made between waiting space and judicial working area. Large courtrooms that serve as waiting rooms for hundreds of cases in an arraignment or calendar part are difficult to control. Smaller courtrooms should be established and used for only a few people whose cases are soon to be called. If it is not physically feasible to break up larger courts into smaller ones, a glass barrier between the judicial working area and the waiting space could be installed with microphones and loudspeakers so that spectators can hear.

Separate courts should be established for special types of crimes— housing or administrative code violations could be differentiated from more serious crimes against persons or property. Special narcotics courts might also be established to handle hardcore narcotics felony cases.[9]

In addition, reforms in the system of criminal justice might help reduce the backlog of pending cases and thus reduce congestion and disorder in the courts. Using computers for tracking many aspects of the criminal justice system, centralizing judicial administration, and better management are all necessary. The scope of this study precludes detailed comment on these recommendations.

One proposal for changing the physical make-up of a courtroom that appears to have merit, subject to safeguards, is the introduction of closed circuit television cameras. The use of such cameras in court must be as unobtrusive as possible—no cables or wires must be allowed to snake across a courtroom floor or cameramen to interject themselves into the proceedings. In addition, the transmission should not be used for public dissemination; such use has been forbidden by the Supreme Court.[10] If a trial is broadcast to the public, intense public interest will arise which could distract the jury or create community pressures upon it. Witnesses will also be affected by knowing that their words will be telecast throughout their community: "Some may be demoralized and frightened, some cocky and given to overstatement; memories may falter as with anyone speaking publicly."[11] It may also distract the judge from his important functions. Some of these problems can be minimized with closed circuit television, which might be used with profit in the following instances:

1. To allow defendants removed for disorder to follow what is happening in court. Many judges are reluctant to remove misbehaving defendants if television transmission is not available. While a defendant's actual presence in court would be more desirable, television may reduce the most serious problems of removal and still allow some confrontation between the defendant and the witnesses against him. As new courthouses are built throughout the country, the circuitry necessary for such cameras could be installed at a minimum cost.

2. To supplement or substitute for the written record of a trial an electronic one in the form of sound or television tape. Alaska has used verbal tapes of a trial as the official record on appeal since 1960. Some observers claim they are more accurate than a written record.[12] Films would be especially useful to appellate courts for determining who was responsible for courtroom disorder. Television recording of trials has recently been introduced into courtrooms in Michigan with some success. Five trials were held in a month-long experiment for a local judge, a twenty-four year veteran of the municipal and circuit court bench. He commented:

> So far, it has been moving along smoother than smooth. The cameras are noiseless. I have noticed no interference at all with the traditional procedures.[13]

There are obvious problems involved even with closed circuit television. The cost of technicians and television tape is high. The lighting and microphones may distract witnesses, the jury, or the lawyers. There is still the danger of the psychological reaction noted above, of those who know cameras are trained upon them. Further study is obviously required before such a system is widely installed.

Various commentators have also recommended that a number of protective devices be built in courtrooms to guard against violence. These include the following proposals:

> A concept frequently advanced for multi-courtroom buildings is that of providing in one courtroom an increased number of security measures. This "secure" courtroom, it is argued, would have special provisions for the safety of participants and would limit the capability of spectators to influence proceedings. In this regard, suggestions have been made to provide:
> —A high, bullet-proof, transparent partition at the bar to separate spectators from the trial spaces.
> —A transparent compartment to isolate defendants.
> —Closed circuit television cameras and monitors in the court and detention spaces to transmit proceedings to a defendant being tried in absentia.
> —Weapons-detection devices located in a soundlock at public courtroom entrances to scan all entering persons for concealed weapons.[14]

There are serious legal problems with such proposals because the protective devices could prejudice a defendant. It has long been the law that a defendant may not be brought into court handcuffed or shackled unless there is an immediate possibility of escape or violence. Bullet-proof isolation chambers or mesh fences might be similarly prejudicial. The Courtroom Reorganization program takes a cautious view of this proposal. It concludes that

> it is unlikely that the existence of unusual security measures can be kept from all parties. . . . The temptation might also be great to rely solely on these measures, which would not ensure anyone's safety absolutely, and thereby weaken the use of fundamental security practices, such as good spatial design and adequate, trained staff.[15]

## Security Personnel in the Courtroom

It is obvious that every court must have court officers or marshals to perform a variety of important functions.* They are primarily responsible for courtroom security. They protect the judge, jury, or other

* The terminology regarding security officers in the court is often confusing. Court officers in the federal system are deputy United States marshals. In addition to their courtroom functions, federal marshals serve court papers or subpoenas,

court officials. They guard prisoners when they appear in court, try to defend against escapes, and make sure there are no weapons in court. They must restrain any person seeking to do violence to another. They are the physical arm of the judge, the instrument through which he acts to maintain courtroom decorum. If they are directed to bind or gag a defendant, remove a spectator or defendant, they must act with dispatch but in a manner that will minimize the possibility of disorder.

The marshals are responsible for shepherding and seating spectators in the court. They keep them in line outside the courtroom, direct them to their places, search them if necessary, and make sure that they are orderly when court is in session.

These tasks are often difficult, and it is very important that they be performed in a delicate and dignified way. Ordinary citizens come in closer contact with court officers than with any other court official. How they are treated may shape their view of what the judicial system means to them and how the legal process operates. If they are treated with rudeness and indignities by a marshal, how can they have confidence in the system as a whole?

More generally, courthouses should not become fortresses, with armed guards throughout searching everyone who comes in or out. One federal judge made the following comments concerning security precautions:

> There are current seriously made proposals in this district to place marshals in and outside each courtroom, to provide peepholes on the doors leading to chambers, to lock doors leading to inner corridors so that access to chambers is not possible except through guards and the like. They will, if they are carried out, have a negative impact on the effective administration of justice in this district. It will make it much more difficult for lawyers and litigants to obtain access to the federal courts thereby slowing down litigation and making it even more expensive than it is presently. . . .
>
> Moreover, it will have a deleterious effect on the image of justice to have armed guards in and outside the courtrooms and to use electronic searching devices. Defendants in criminal cases may well complain of the prejudice that such programs may create since juries may be led to believe that our judicial system is in grave danger from physical attacks in the courtrooms or that the extra marshals are necessary to restrain defendants.[16]

There may be situations when some security must be maintained at the entrance of a courthouse. In some places prosecution offices or

---

enforce court orders, guard Congressional hearings, and more recently, screen airline passengers in airports and travel on planes to protect against hijackers. In most state systems the only function of court officers is to maintain courtroom security. In others they may be bailiffs or peace officers under a local sheriff's jurisdiction. In this chapter all will be called "marshals" or "court officers."

those of other government officials are located in the same building as
a courtroom and it may be desirable to provide a check on those coming in or out. But certain safeguards should be taken.

Judges should be careful about establishing security for a particular
case. No one should assume automatically that for the trial of a Black
Panther or other alleged militant all those entering the courtroom
must be searched. Such a practice can easily convey to the jury a
prejudicial attitude about the dangerousness of the defendant and his
friends. In rare cases where a search is desirable, spectators should be
checked at the courthouse entrance or in some other central place so
that the need for security is not associated with a single trial.

Whatever security program is established should be reconciled with
a full acknowledgment of the dignity of the people entering the court.
Court officers must recognize as far as possible the privacy of those
they search. They should be quickly efficient in their search outside
the court and polite in their treatment of defendants and spectators
inside. If court officers do not behave with such restraint, they may
greatly increase the possibility of disorder in the courts. Several of the
disorderly cases mentioned in earlier chapters involved significant
altercations between defendants and court officers.

For example, in the Tacoma Seven trial the defendants claimed that
the marshals kept spectators waiting outside in a December rain and
manhandled many of the defendants' supporters before they came into
the courtroom. On the day that a mistrial was declared, difficulties
arose because spectators were not allowed into the courthouse by the
marshals although it was raining heavily. One of the defendants,
Jeffrey Dowd, knocked loudly on the door of the judge's chambers to
seek his assistance.

> *The Court:*   Mr. Dowd, you a few moments ago were pounding so
> loudly on the door I could hear it clean in here, the door of the entrance
> to my room, I heard it and your counsel heard it, he was standing in the
> corridor. . . . This is contempt of court, I am citing you for contempt,
> and I will issue the citation later this day, and carry on with it. Now,
> what is it you have in mind? . . .
> *Defendant Dowd:*   There's people out in the rain.
> *Mr. [Lee] Holley [attorney for Defendant Kelly]:*   We have been
> waiting outside trying to see your Honor, there are people standing out
> in the rain. . . . There are human beings standing out in the freezing
> rain, and it's just totally unnecessary. . . .
>    Those people are standing out there, and it's just not necessary. There
> is plenty of room inside, and to keep those people that came down here,
> some of them at eight and eight-thirty in the morning, to get into these
> proceedings, at least to let them come in out of the cold and out of the
> rain, you know, that is a very great concern, Judge, because while you
> are concerned with the dignity of the court, they are concerned with
> the dignity of those human beings.[17]

The defendants did not appear in court when the judge was ready to proceed. Another defense attorney explained:

> *Mr. [Jeffrey] Steinborn [attorney for Defendants Abeles and Stern]:* I think it is important that the Judge and the United States Attorney understand what happened. Had it not been for the inhumane and un-civilized conduct of the marshal we would have been ready at 9:00. We felt it important that we speak to you and so did Mr. Dowd and, had it not been for that, if the marshals would begin to act like humans, we would have been ready to start at 9:00.
>
> *The Court:* The Marshal has very serious problems.
>
> *Mr. Steinborn:* He creates his own problems.
>
> *The Court:* Providing security for your clients and, so far as I have personally observed, I have seen him do nothing improper or irregular or not required by the necessities of the occasion. If there have been such, I have not seen or heard them.
>
> *Mr. Steinborn:* Judge, it has been my experience that every incident in which the Marshal has been involved has been provoked by him and encouraged by his functionaries.[18]

The judge then went to the defendants' room and ordered them into the court. After they entered, he declared a mistrial and cited all the defendants present for contempt.

Four days later (December 14, 1970) at the hearing on the contempts, the marshals and the defendants were involved in another dispute. Susan Stern, one of the defendants who had not been present on December 10 and had not been held in contempt, insisted on making a statement. When she refused to stop talking or move from the lectern, the trial judge ordered the marshals to remove her. They started to pull her away from the lectern and were immediately involved in a fracas with defendants and spectators. One of the defense attorneys later stated:

> *Mr. Holley:* I talked to a number of spectators who were physically attacked by the marshals. I have talked to so-called straight people and I have talked to so-called hip people, and I know that the Court was in the same room I was, and I know that the Court's eyes to the extent they were open saw what I saw, and it just points out so totally the different realities under which the Court operates and under which these defendants and, I believe, myself operate, because I saw attacks by the marshals on people.[19]

One of the defendants, Michael Abeles, claimed:

> [T]hey grabbed me, you know, bent my arm back, nearly broke it off, they were bending back my fingers like that (indicating), the marshal had his arm around my neck and I almost passed out and my neck, my throat is still sore from where he grabbed it and where he wouldn't let go and me yelling and saying, "My arm hurts, you are breaking it, I can't breathe, I can't breathe," and that's the thing you support and that's why you're going to lose.[20]

We do not express an opinion on the extent to which the defendants' accusations against the marshals were valid. A written record cannot convey exactly what happens in the court—whether a marshal was unnecessarily severe in trying to restrain a defendant or remove a spectator or who was responsible for the first push or punch. But the incidents show the various functions that marshals perform in court and the crucial role they can play with respect to the problem of courtroom disorder.

These tasks are necessarily difficult since they often involve physical contact with resisting, antagonistic, or confused individuals. There have been many complaints about the attitude and behavior of court officers. Some observers have pointed out that marshals, who generally must have two years of law enforcement background—either in a police force or as a military policeman—tend to identify with the prosecution. Many of them may assume that the prisoners they guard are guilty of the charges against them and that the defendants' friends and relatives need not be treated with respect or sympathy. Sometimes they display racial prejudices. Haywood Burns, the executive director of the National Conference of Black Lawyers, told our committee:

> Someone said that the Government is the greatest teacher for good or for ill. The present treatment of blacks teaches them that the legacy of legally protected and enforced racism is not irrelevant. I would give you a few illustrations. First, we see the attitudes of the court personnel, both the ancillary judicial personnel and judges. You should go sit in Arraignment Part and listen to the insults, racial and other, that are directed to defendants and especially to members of minority groups. These things go beyond mere staffing problems. They reflect an entire attitude.

In many large cities a high percentage of defendants in the lower criminal courts are black or Puerto Rican. Yet few of the court officers are black or speak Spanish. They are given little if any instruction on community relations or basic constitutional law. The main focus of their training, which generally consists of a two-week basic course, is on courtroom security.

Court officers have an extremely difficult job, combining the functions of prison guard, security officer, and courtroom usher. The great majority perform ably and with restraint. But since they bear the actual physical burden of dealing with unruly defendants, emotional relatives, and militant spectators, they should be given adequate instructions and training so that they might learn to deal with potential disorder with words instead of force. Court officers should be involved in pretrial planning for any notorious trial. They should be introduced to the defendants and their counsel as early as possible and get to know the relatives of those on trial so that seating can be arranged for them. The trial judge must impress on them that they should behave as neutral umpires, treating spectators with restraint and understanding.

When performing their security functions, such as searching spectators, they should be careful not to offend and try to avoid incidents. Women spectators should always be searched by women guards in as dignified a manner as possible. Wherever possible mechanical means of searching—such as a magnetometer or a hand-frisker—should be used. One Baltimore judge wrote in the questionnaire:

> Some sort of search for weapons should be made prior to entrance into the courtroom, preferably by way of a mechanical detector rather than a personal frisk. It is most important that security guards or police do not touch or put a hand on any of these demonstrators unless they are going to arrest them, because the touching of them seems to provoke more incidents than anything else.[21]

Judges or court officers should not immediately assume that any breach of decorum by spectators involves an intentional attack on the dignity of the court. Above all, they should never use undue force in restraining an unruly individual in court. We agree with the following comment from the A.B.A. Standards on Trial Disruption:

> In exercising the right to exclude [spectators] the trial judge should not too readily infer contumacious intent on the part of spectators who engage in minor departures from courtroom decorum, as they may be unfamiliar with expected patterns of conduct. A gentle correction quietly delivered by trained court officers should generally be tried first.[22]

The marshals presence in the court should be made as inconspicuous as possible. Federal marshals wear street clothes and only a badge to identify them. During a trial there should not be an inordinate number of court officers in the court; only the minimum necessary to maintain security. As Judge Weinstein pointed out, a courtroom should not be transformed into an armed camp.[23]

It is also important that the judge be firmly in charge of all security arrangements in his courtroom. Court officers should always act on his command unless immediate action is required to prevent violence. A federal court of appeals has emphasized that a judge

> is best equipped to decide the extent to which security measures should be adopted to prevent disruption of the trial, harm to those in the courtroom, escape of the accused, and the prevention of other crimes.[24]

If special security measures are necessary, they should be described carefully for the record.

> Unless the district judge's discretion is to be absolute and beyond review, the reasons for its exercise so as to require special security mea-

sures, must be disclosed in order that a reviewing court may determine
if there was an abuse of discretion. . . . Whenever unusual visible
security measures in jury cases are to be employed, we will require the
district judge to state for the record, out of the presence of the jury, the
reasons therefor and give counsel an opportunity to comment thereon,
as well as to persuade him that such measures are unnecessary.[25]

## Controlling Spectators

Responses to the trial judges questionnaire sent out by the Committee
revealed that a significant proportion of courtroom disorder was perpetrated by spectators. Of the 112 cases of disruption described by trial
judges, three involved relatives of defendants, one involved the complainant, and seventeen involved other spectators. In the prosecutors
questionnaire there were four cases of disruption by spectators of the
twenty-five cases reported. Typical cases involved political activists,
including Black Panther sympathizers, student demonstrators, or anti-
draft protesters. The following reported cases are illustrative:

> Defendant arrested at Black Panther Headquarters and charged with
> possession of illegal weapons, possession of explosives.
>     Audience refused to stand when court was opened, were generally
> loud and disruptive, reacted to various moves of the prosecutor and
> defense counsel. The disturbance was not recorded.
>     General oral reprimand and explanation of the necessity for formality
> and order.[26]

> The defendant and two co-defendants (the latter not yet tried) were
> charged with the ambush-murder of one police officer and assault with
> intent to murder another officer. Only the defendant was charged with
> assault to murder another officer in the third indictment.
>     At the beginning of the trial, the court room was filled with Black
> Panther sympathizers, both black and white. They rose and greeted the
> defendant with outcries of "Right on!", "Power to the People!", "Death
> to the Pigs!", et cetera. When the jury announced the verdicts, a small
> riot ensued, so much so that at first the announcement of the verdicts by
> the jury foreman was inaudible.
>     At the beginning of the trial, after the first demonstration, I informed
> the spectators that anyone engaging in any future demonstrations would
> be summarily ejected from the courtroom for the duration of the trial.
> With a few scattered exceptions, the decorum continued to be accepta-
> ble until the announcement by the jury of the verdicts. Courtroom
> security was excellent at all times.[27]

There were also instances of courtroom disruption by spectators in
trials for ordinary criminal charges. In one case, involving a marijuana
charge, a friend of the defendant made disrespectful gestures toward
the judge:

> During the state's attorney's closing argument spectator-friend of de-
> fendant gave obscene gesture or power salute.
>   The jury was excused and the spectator was warned that another
> incident like that would find him in contempt of court. After the warn-
> ing he gave the same sign to the court. [The spectator was held in con-
> tempt and sentenced to one day in jail.][28]

The cases involving student and anti-draft activists arose in a period
of unusual political unrest when there was widespread violation of
established rules of proper conduct. The courtroom seemed an appropriate place for such activists to demonstrate because the courts are
an arm of the establishment and a protest there is likely to draw public
attention. In addition, the courts were considered responsible for
some of the policies under political attack. One of the defendants in
the Tacoma case told our committee:

> An important perception from the defendants' viewpoints is that the
> court system has never entertained what some weighty, "established"
> legal opinion has clearly determined to be the case, i.e., the unconstitu-
> tionality of the Vietnam war. Thus, the court (the judicial system) sat
> with dirty hands as a result of not only (1) not having ruled against the
> legality of the war, but (2) having sent people to jail for refusing the
> draft or for the exercise of their supposed freedom to demonstrate
> against the war. Therefore, the judges in all cases arising out of the
> anti-war movement (draft refusal, demonstrations, "conspiracy" et al.)
> are in effect partisans, i.e., opposed to such activities and to any persons
> engaging in same.

In nonpolitical cases, disorder by spectators, particularly by relatives
of the defendant, has often occurred at the time of verdict or sentence.
It is understandable that emotions would be at their height at these
moments and judges have generally not been too hard on people in
the audience who act up at that time.

Our conclusions about what a court should do in the face of disorder
by spectators is based in large part upon the responses to the trial
judges questionnaire.

In the first place, a firm effort should be made to persuade spectators to remain quiet. As the A.B.A. Standards indicate, the judge and
court officers should initially assume that spectators are unclear about
what is expected of them and must be told the proper way to act.
They should be warned of possible sanctions if they continue to misbehave.

If disorder continues, the judge should exclude any spectator who
engages in loud, boisterous, or disruptive conduct. The power of a
judge to exclude disorderly spectators is unquestioned and involves
none of the problems of excluding defendants. In particular, it is
established that exclusion of disorderly spectators is not a denial of
a public trial. A federal court of appeals has said that

the right to have the members of the public present is subject to some limitations. There is general agreement that spectators having no immediate concern with the trial need not be admitted in such numbers as to overcrowd the courtroom and take up room needed for those who do have special concern with the trial such as the court officers, jurors and witnesses, and the relatives and friends of the defendant. Moreover those spectators who are admitted must observe proper decorum and if their conduct tends in any way to interfere with the administration of justice in the courtroom they may, of course, be removed.[29]

A spectator, unlike a defendant, may also be excluded for simply not rising at the beginning or closing of court.

> . . . we conclude that the traditional rising in unison of persons present in a court can reasonably be thought to contribute to the functioning of the court. It is a way of marking the beginning and end of the session, and probably serves to remind all that attention must be concentrated upon the business before the court, the judge's control of the court room must be maintained with as little burden on him as possible, and there must be silence, except as the orderly conduct of business calls for speech. We think a court may require such rising, in the interest of facilitating its functions, although the functional virtue of rising at the close of a session is less readily apparent than at the beginning.[30].

Obviously a spectator's interest in being present at a trial is far less than that of a defendant, and sanctions against the former (such as exclusion) usually would be inappropriate for the latter. The Seventh Circuit has permitted exclusion of spectators for not rising in court in the *Malone* case, while denying any sanctions against the defendants for the same conduct in the *Dellinger* case.

In the rare case when a judge feels exclusion is not a sufficient sanction, he may cite a disorderly spectator for contempt. Insults or shouts or manifest acts of disrespect to the court by a spectator are as much substantial interference with the orderly processes of a trial as such acts by a defendant or lawyer. The New York Court of Appeals said in the *Katz* case:

> Petitioner's conduct was a contempt. It is immaterial whether he shouted with the others. It is enough that by rising and raising his arm he joined the others in an unequivocal demonstration of disrespect designed only for that purpose and to interrupt the proceedings. The consciousness and purpose with which he acted, already implicit enough, were made explicit by his response to the court on being arraigned at the bench.[31]

For the reasons outlined in chapter 10, we do not believe that a trial judge should summarily hold a disorderly spectator in contempt. The case should be referred to another judge for a full due process hearing. We recognize that spectator misbehavior may not strike as directly at a judge's sensibilities as misconduct by a lawyer or defendant, but it is a violation of the order in a judge's courtroom and therefore it is desirable that another judge hear the case.

A judge should try not to impose blanket sanctions on a group of spectators. If he singles out one misbehaving spectator, either by removing him or citing him for contempt, this ordinarily will act as a deterrent to others.

Control of spectators in the corridors outside a courtroom and the area immediately surrounding a courthouse may also be necessary to ensure that an orderly trial may take place. We have previously referred in this chapter to the type of orders that a judge may properly issue to meet the problem of possible disorder inside and immediately outside the courthouse.

## Role of the Press

Related to the problem of spectator disorder is the role of the press in reporting on courtroom activities. It is obvious that individuals may engage in courtroom misbehavior because they believe that their actions will be reported in the press. Associate Dean David L. Shapiro of the Harvard Law School, the reporter to the A.B.A.'s Advisory Committee on Fair Trial and Free Press, wrote to one of the authors: "One intuitively suspects that if trials got no publicity, courtroom disruption would be engaged in only by the incompetent and the insane."[32]
A federal judge wrote in his questionnaire:

> It seems to me that publicity of such disturbances in one area has a strong probability of generating like disturbances in other areas which might otherwise not have taken place.[33]

And a colorful Texas judge commented:

> If a brainless, worthless, valueless NOBODY can become an immediate "CELEBRITY" before the eyes and ears of the world by shooting his mouth off in the well of my courtroom screaming and calling me P-I-G and SON-OF-A-BITCH, at the expense of 3 or 30 days in the county jail (during which and wherein he will be INTERVIEWED as to the Whys and Wherefores) for being in contempt, the establishment form of "dealing with" these "THINGS" appears inadequate; yet we must (OR MUST WE?) defend the freedom of the press to report "to the PEOPLE" that Joe Nuts did in fact call me a pig and a son of a bitch while I sat on the Bench clothed in a black robe. For that IS n-e-w-s![34]

The solution is not to bar all press coverage of a trial. The constitutional guarantees of a public trial and the First Amendment's protection of freedom of the press make clear that the press must be admitted to a trial.[35] The fact that their presence may encourage disruption has never been considered an adequate reason for barring them.

In the past ten years three prestigious groups have made detailed recommendations concerning the relation between a fair trial and a free press. In 1965 a Special Committee on Radio and Television of our parent body, the Association of the Bar of the City of New York, under the chairmanship of Judge Harold R. Medina, issued a report.[36] In 1966 the American Bar Association's Project on Minimum Standards for Criminal Justice, with Judge Paul C. Reardon, chairman, issued Standards Relating to Fair Trial and Free Press. In 1968 the Committee on the Operation of the Jury System, with Judge Irving R. Kaufman, chairman, issued a report to the Judicial Conference of the United States on the Fair Trial—Free Press issue.[37]

These reports were concerned with ensuring a fair trial to the defendant and thus focused on the problem of unauthorized disclosure of evidence or other information before trial that would prejudice defendants' rights. They established strict standards on the type of information that might be disclosed by the prosecution and defense before or during a trial. Many media organizations have entered into voluntary agreements with bar organizations to implement these recommendations.

We believe that the suggested restrictions imposed upon the prosecution by the Medina, Reardon, and Kaufman committees, which have been largely followed in the A.B.A. Code of Professional Responsibility (DR 7–107), will also be helpful in reducing trial tension and disorder. Statements by a prosecutor about a defendant's probable guilt or about evidence linking him to a crime not only make an indelible impression on a community and may affect potential jurors, but they also may lead to sharp public counterstatements by the defense. If the defense and prosecution feel free to fight out their case in the press before trial, such publicity can only increase the emotional heat of the trial itself and increase the possibility of disruption.[38]

The press should use restraint in reporting on the events of a trial. That they are free to report whatever occurs does not mean that they should do so. There is no question that some defendants in notorious trials may be inspired to act up because of the wide press coverage of their case. This was obvious in the Nazi sedition trial of 1944. At some point during the trial the *Washington Post* announced in an editorial that it was no longer sending a reporter to cover the trial because it no longer considered the behavior of the defendants newsworthy. The defndants protested against the action of the *Post* because it deprived them of an important outlet for their antics. While the *Post* decision was a reaction to an extreme form of ostentatious misconduct at trial, there may be other cases when a newspaper can responsibly consider taking the same tack.

# CHAPTER TWELVE

## *Synopsis of Report*

### General Observation (Chapters One–Five)

Although the episodes of courtroom disruption are not quantitatively significant, they have an important bearing on public confidence in the judicial system. They underscore the need for each of the participants in the process to perform his defined role to promote a system of orderly judicial procedures that merit public respect and protect the rights of all citizens. These incidents also highlight many injustices— such as overcrowding, court delays, overworked lawyers, plea bargaining, and racism among court personnel—that have occasionally produced anger, frustration, and outrage by those caught up in the process. While it is not surprising that some disruption has occurred, there is no justification for it and it damages the system of justice (pages 10–23).

Historically, both the civil law countries on the European continent and the common law jurisdictions in Great Britain and the United States have experienced recurrent patterns of disorderly court proceedings when one or a combination of the following conditions have occurred:

1. The courts are used to enforce or implement an unpopular policy of the government and thus become the battleground for the contending political forces of the time.

2. Individual opponents of the prevailing regime or members of dissident groups challenging basic government policies are brought before the courts for any reason.

3. The basic criminal procedures under which defendants are tried are thought to be unjust, discriminatory, or improperly invoked by the government (pages 24–32).

In the United States, disorderly trials have occurred in times of political stress, when the courts have tried to enforce unpopular policies of the government. Disorder has also occurred during trials of political dissidents who have tried to explain their political message while also claiming violations of their procedural rights. The frontier tradition in America, in contrast to the English experience, produced a widespread skepticism about the need for decorum and civility by lawyers or defendants (pages 32–42).

There have been a number of widely publicized disorderly trials in American courts since 1940, including the Nazi sedition trial of 1944; the Communist conspiracy case in 1948; the Chicago conspiracy trial of 1969–70; and the New York Black Panther case of 1969–71.

The four cases shared certain significant characteristics: all the defendants represented highly unpopular political currents of the time; a large number of defendants and lawyers were involved in each case; the defendants were charged with conspiracy based in part on their political activities (except in the Black Panther case); all were tried before judges who were accused of bias toward the defendants and their politics; all the trials took many months to finish; and the press reported extensively on what occurred in court (pages 43–76).

The judiciary, the organized bar, and the public reacted very strongly to the Chicago conspiracy case and the New York Black Panther trial. Many meetings were held, speeches made, and new laws passed to deal with the problem of disorderly trials. Nevertheless, our questionnaire results and a close analysis of the reported cases indicate that the numerical incidence of disruption is small (pages 1–9).

Although most courtroom disorder involves defendants in ordinary felony cases, the problem has become associated in the public mind with what are called "political trials." When political activists are brought into court they often express outrage at what they feel is the unfairness of the proceedings, and exhibit undisguised contempt for the political institutions and officials that subjected them to their ordeal. The term "political trial" has been used so long as a vague pejorative expression that it no longer is useful. But political factors in fact have influenced the judicial system in three different ways: the decision to prosecute may be motivated by political factors; the outcome of a case may be affected by political attitudes or considerations; the participants in a case, before or during a trial, may try to maximize the political consequences or impact of their case.

In cases that have political overtones, judges and prosecutors should have a better understanding of the outrage that many representatives of political outgroups feel when the criminal law is invoked against them for what they view as their political opposition to the government. Such defendants are not likely to ignore political considerations during their trial if they feel that politics brought them into the courtroom, and the result often is a disrupted trial that does no credit to the judicial system (pages 77–89).

The following recommendations, reflecting the report as a whole, are designed to assure that the system of justice in the United States will be fair and efficient, and unhampered by courtroom disorder of any kind. Only if these conditions are met will the judiciary and the bar receive from the public the respect that will enable the system to function properly.

# Defendants (Chapter Six)

Most cases of disruption over the years have occurred in criminal proceedings. Some defendants, facing serious charges, have reacted impulsively to the pressure and unfamiliarity of a criminal trial and disrupted the proceedings out of apprehension or fear. Others may consciously and deliberately try to create disorder to bring about a mistrial or gain some other procedural advantage. Still others may do so for ideological reasons. A judge should be attuned to the impulse behind the disruption in order to decide on the appropriate response.

In order to reduce the possibility of a disorderly trial, a judge should initiate certain preventive measures:

1. He should make known the ground rules that all participants will be expected to follow.

2. He should reassure the defendant that all his rights will be respected.

3. He should sever offenses or defendants if he believes that the large number of participants has reached a point unfair to particular defendants or prejudicial to the order of the proceedings.

4. He should issue clear warnings, outside the presence of the jury, promptly after the first instance of disruptive conduct, advising a defendant what the consequences of further disorder will be.

5. He should, in his discretion, call a brief recess to cool off a potentially explosive situation.

In terms of the remedies approved by the Supreme Court in the *Allen* case, a judge has certain powers at his disposal to deal with disorderly defendants which we feel should be limited as follows:

1. After proper warnings, he may remove the defendant from the courtroom without violating the Sixth Amendment right of confrontation. But the power should be exercised only if a fair trial cannot be carried on with the defendant in the courtroom.

2. Although the Supreme Court approved of binding and gagging a defendant "as a last resort," we believe that gagging is so damaging to the orderliness of proceedings that it should never be done. Handcuffing a disorderly defendant to prevent an escape or violence to others is the most physical restraint that should be ordered.

3. Civil contempt may be imposed to imprison a defendant until he

promises to conduct himself properly. But this remedy should be restricted to a maximum of seven full or partial days.

4. Revocation of bail as a substitute for civil contempt is a violation of a constitutional right and should not be used.

5. A judge may cite a defendant for criminal contempt if his behavior obstructs the administration of justice (pages 95–111).

Disorder by a defendant may be divided into the following main categories, which should be dealt with as follows:

1. Passive disrespect. For example, the refusal to address the judge as "Your Honor" or to stand when he enters the courtroom. This conduct should not be punished unless it substantially interferes with the proceedings.

2. The single obscenity or shout. This should generally not be punished by contempt nor should it be ignored by the court. The judge should warn a defendant, outside the presence of the jury, that if such action continues it could lead to punishment or exclusion from the courtroom.

3. Refusal to cooperate with the essential ground rules of the judicial proceeding. For example, a refusal to enter or leave the courtroom voluntarily. A judge should ask a defendant why he refuses to cooperate with the ground rules, and warn him of the sanctions that he faces for repeated refusals: exclusion from the courtroom or contempt. If he persists, sanctions should be imposed.

4. Repeated interruptions of the trial, ranging from insulting remarks to loud shouting, pounding, or cursing. Repeated interruptions may be dealt with by exclusion or contempt after appropriate warnings have been given.

5. Physical violence in the courtroom, with or without weapons. Physical violence cannot be tolerated; a court may deal with it either by exclusion or a contempt citation, or if absolutely necessary, through physical restraint by means of handcuffs (pages 111–18).

Special problems are presented when a defendant wants to act as his own lawyer (appear pro se). Disruption of court proceedings is more likely in these cases since defendants are unfamiliar with legal procedures and rules of evidence and inevitably are emotionally involved. Nevertheless, the right to defend oneself is fundamental and must be permitted unless a defendant is mentally incompetent to handle his own case. A judge in his discretion may refuse a defendant permission to delay proceedings by firing his lawyer at the eve of trial or in its midst. But the mere possibility of disruption is not by itself a justification for denying the right to appear pro se.

For a defendant who does appear pro se, a judge should appoint standby counsel to advise him. If he repeatedly disrupts the trial, the right to appear pro se may be terminated and counsel appointed. In some cases a defendant may act as cocounsel, although the practice has not often been followed and should be used sparingly (pages 118–30).

# Lawyers (Chapter Seven)

The occasions when lawyers have engaged in courtroom disorder are not frequent. Such disorder that does arise is different from that involving defendants. It generally involves forensic misconduct—excessive bickering with the judge, failure to obey court orders or the procedural rules of the judicial process, for example by unnecessarily repeating arguments or questions that have already been rejected by the court or trying to introduce evidence that has been ruled inadmissible. This conduct, particularly in the presence of the jury, is disorderly and disruptive because a lawyer has important responsibilities in conducting a trial and his refusal to perform them in an orderly fashion makes it more difficult for the process to function properly (pages 131–33).

A lawyer has certain specific responsibilities:

1. Responsibility to the client. The lawyer owes the basic duty of vigorous, devoted service to his client. He may be the only person to whom the defendant can turn in total confidence. But this does not mean a lawyer must obey his client's instructions if they conflict with his professional responsibilities.

2. Responsibility to the court. The rules that govern a lawyer's behavior in the courtroom are for the most part undefined. They are loosely couched in terms of high principle and vague generalities, such as the lawyer's duty to act as an "officer of the court." It is often difficult to determine how these general propositions translate into specific rules of conduct.

3. Responsibility to the public interest. The fact that some attorneys feel strongly about public issues does not relieve them of their professional responsibilities to client and court. These obligations themselves embody important public interests—the need for orderly procedures to ensure swift and equal justice (pages 133–42).

Lawyer misconduct in the courtroom that may properly be punished or justify preventive remedies by the court generally falls into the following categories:

1. Disrespectful remarks to the court, the prosecutor, or other parties. A system of orderly justice requires a respectful presentation of a case to ensure that decisions are based upon reasoned principles instead of emotional reaction to insult. Provocative language by a

lawyer thought to be insulting by the judge can be punished only if it obstructs the trial. But there are times when strong language is entirely appropriate, for example, in making a motion for disqualification of a judge.

2. Disobedience of proper court procedures or orders. A lawyer must obey the proper orders of a judge. He may argue points vigorously and preserve a record for appeal, but once the judge decides a point, it must be obeyed unless the court has totally exceeded the bounds of proper procedure.

3. Repetitive or excessive argumentation. The lawyer should be given great latitude in presenting argument, but orderly administration of justice requires that a judge have the power to set a limit (pages 149–57).

If a lawyer acts improperly in any of the above ways, a judge should issue appropriate warnings. If the misbehavior continues, the following sanctions may be appropriate:

1. The judge may hold a lawyer in civil contempt until he promises to conduct himself properly. But he may not commit the lawyer for more than seven full or partial days or impose an excessive monetary fine.

2. The judge may cite the lawyer for criminal contempt.

3. Bar associations may initiate disciplinary proceedings against lawyers who violate their professional responsibilities (pages 157–62).

4. The judge may remove a lawyer from a case only if he believes on careful consideration that the lawyer's behavior is so outrageous that the trial cannot continue with his participation (pages 164–65).

A lawyer does not have an affirmative duty to restrain his client in court, and therefore should not be punished for failing to take such action. Such a requirement would be inconsistent with the duty of devoted service that a lawyer owes to his client, might prejudice the client's case before a court or jury, and is not necessary in view of the ample weapons possessed by a judge to maintain order. But a lawyer is expected to tell his client what the consequences of disorderly conduct in the court would be, and in private he should seek to dissuade the client from improper courtroom behavior. A court should accept a lawyer's representation that he has rendered such advice (pages 142–49).

A judge should not be given the power to suspend a lawyer from practice. This novel sanction, suggested by the American Bar Association and the American College of Trial Lawyers, contains many procedural and possibly constitutional difficulties, such as the appropriate burden of proof and the standards that justify suspension (pages 163–64).

Nor do we believe that special restrictions should be placed on out-of-state lawyers. In many respects the practice of law today is a national profession; a client's desire for an out-of-state lawyer should be respected. Where necessary, a local lawyer should be retained to advise on local law and procedure, and to accept service of papers (pages 166–68).

# Prosecutors (Chapter Eight)

The prosecutor, as the representative of the government in pressing criminal charges, has a crucial role both before and during the trial in determining whether judicial proceedings are orderly.

1. Misuse of the discretion to prosecute. If a prosecutor abuses the wide range of discretion he has in bringing criminal charges, those accused may very likely experience a sense of outrage which could have explosive results during judicial proceedings. To counter this possibility and to ensure that the system of criminal justice is not misused, an accused should have an affirmative defense to a charge if he can carry the heavy burden of showing that the prosecutor's office is engaging in an irrational or discriminatory course of conduct, such as seeking to restrict First Amendment rights.

A claim of prosecutorial abuse should be reviewed by a judge to determine whether a prima facie case has been shown. If sufficient evidence is presented, the ultimate question can then be submitted to the jury (pages 169–78).

2. Mass trials and conspiracy charges. A prosecutor's decision to charge several defendants with conspiracy, and to try them in a single criminal proceeding may increase the potentiality for a disruptive trial. Prosecutors should weigh carefully the gains in judicial economy of a joint trial against the risk of disorder or unfairness to particular defendants. A judge should be prepared to order severance of offenses or defendants if he anticipates unfairness or trial disruption (pages 178–81).

3. Courtroom misconduct by prosecutors. The most frequent form of prosecutorial misconduct in court is the use of arrogant or deliberately provocative language about a defendant or his lawyer. This disrupts proceedings as much as excessive argumentation or disregard of proper procedure. It may also prejudice a jury against a defendant or provoke him to make disorderly counterstatements (pages 180–86).

The most frequent method for dealing with a prosecutor's misbehavior in court is appellate reversal of a conviction tainted by his improper conduct. Prosecutors are concerned with what judges say about their actions and court decisions help to elaborate the standards required of the prosecutor's office. But courts have established a series of obstacles to appellate reversal of cases involving prosecutorial misconduct: some misbehavior by prosecutors is found to be "harmless error," that is, technically incorrect but not serious enough to jeopardize a defendant's right to a fair trial; some courts require proper objection before prosecutorial misconduct will be considered as a basis for reversal; provocation by the defense attorney is sometimes held to be an excuse.

Other remedies—now rarely used—should be given serious consideration. For example, courts should hold prosecutors in contempt for egregrious misconduct and bar associations should overcome their reluctance to initiate disciplinary action in appropriate cases (pages 186–91).

## Judges (Chapter Nine)

Ultimately, the problem of courtroom disorder is one that the trial judge must solve. There are some cases in which a judge was the principal agent in creating disorder or in aggravating potentially disruptive conditions. In most situations, however, the judge's reaction to the conduct of the other participants—defendants, lawyers, prosecutors, and spectators—is critical to whether a proceeding moves along smoothly. A judge not only presides over the trial and decides questions of law, but should be the exemplar of justice, personifying the essential elements of the legal process—the need for fairness, understanding, and evenhanded application of the law (pages 192–94).

When it becomes evident that a potentially disruptive proceeding is about to occur, the judge should hold pretrial conferences to discuss potential problems and endeavor to lay down workable ground rules. When the trial begins, he should tell the defendant that it will be conducted in a fair and impartial way. He may also wish to relax some procedural rules to meet a potentially explosive situation. But he must show that he is firmly in control (pages 194–99).

Judicial misbehavior that causes or contributes to courtroom disorder falls under the following classifications:

1. Arbitrary, biased, or vindictive remarks or rulings. Some judges have acted as if they were an arm of the prosecution, berating the defendant or his counsel or sharply questioning defense witnesses. For a judge to make a prejudicial or humiliating remark about the defendant or his lawyer may lead to counterstatements and misbehavior by the abused party. Even if this does not occur, such remarks are disruptive in that they may distract and improperly influence the jury.

2. Bickering with counsel. For a judge to engage in petty arguments with counsel, in sarcasm and irrelevant colloquy, must interfere with the proceedings and create the wrong kind of atmosphere in court.

3. Interfering with presentation by counsel. Another cause of frequent contention in court which has a disruptive effect is a judge's unnecessary interference with a lawyer's presentation, such as cutting him off before he has had an opportunity to make an argument or present points he thinks important (pages 199–205).

Remedies against judges who engage in improper conduct include the following:

1. Reversal. Appellate courts regularly review charges of judicial misbehavior to determine whether the defendant or litigant received fair treatment. Many cases, including the Chicago conspiracy case, have been reversed because the appeals court thought a judge made a prejudicial remark or improper ruling restricting a defendant's case. But appellate review cannot be wholly effective. In some lower criminal courts there may not be an adequate written record for review. And a written record does not reflect the facial gestures or general demeanor of the trial judge which might indicate hostility to the defendant or litigant. Moreover, even when reversal occurs, it may not sufficiently discipline a judge who has acted egregiously (pages 205–208).

2. Impeachment. This is an ineffectual procedure for curbing courtroom misconduct. It is so heavy a club and involves so cumbersome a procedure that it is rarely invoked for any kind of judicial dereliction and even less often for in-court behavior (pages 208–11).

3. Statutory disciplinary procedures. Within the past fifteen years at least twenty-five states have established new methods for disciplining judges for misconduct, including removal. In most of these states disciplinary boards or courts have been set up, consisting either of judges or a mixed commission of judges, lawyers, and lay persons. Such commissions or courts, which may censure a judge or recommend his removal, have proved an effective method of controlling judges who misbehave. Since they do not rely on the legislature for action and may impose lesser sanctions than removal, they avoid the disadvantages of the impeachment process (pages 211–14).

4. Professional discipline. Bar associations can investigate and recommend disciplinary action against judges who violate the Code of Professional Responsibility or the Canons of Judicial Ethics. Such action has rarely been invoked, but should be considered more often (pages 214–16).

5. Peremptory challenge. California, Illinois, and Wisconsin have permitted litigants to challenge a single judge, disqualifying him from the case, without having to prove that he is biased. This procedure may act as a deterrent to a judge who is particularly offensive. The

bars in the states that have established this system seem to believe it works. It should be evaluated by other states.

In jurisdictions where judges are subject to reappointment or re-election, misbehaving judges should not be returned to the bench (page 216).


# The Contempt Power (Chapter Ten)

The most potent of the remedies for courtroom misconduct is criminal contempt of court. A judge may not only imprison or fine a person for violating the governing rules on courtroom behavior, but he may impose those sanctions "summarily"—on the spot, without complying with the normal procedural requirements for meting out criminal punishment. Recent developments in the law have restricted a judge's power to punish summarily. These restrictions, while desirable, do not go far enough. We believe that the summary contempt power should be eliminated altogether. The essential vice of summary contempt is that it enables a judge to combine in one person the prosecutorial and judicial functions in a criminal case. This power to punish without restraint has led to severe and arbitrary punishment of defendants or lawyers. Other effective remedies to control misbehavior are available.

If a person has been cited and knows that after trial he will be subject to possible conviction and punishment, that should be suffi-cient to deter him for wayward action, and to enable a judge to con-trol the courtroom. The additional "flexibility" gained through the summary contempt power is not needed, and whatever advantages it may have in this respect are plainly outweighed by the significant objections to it (pages 232–38).

Under federal law as presently interpreted (and similarly in most states), a person may be punished for contempt in the following ways:

1. The trial judge can punish the alleged wrongdoer instantly. He cannot wait until the trial is completed.

2. The case can be heard upon notice and hearing. The trial judge can hear the case himself a) during the trial or b) after the trial, or he can c) refer the matter to be heard by another judge at the end of trial.

If the summary contempt power is used, current law permits a judge to punish immediately with no indictment, no notice, no evidentiary hearing, no opportunity for argument. Except where a sentence of more than six months is involved, no jury is necessary. However, the following procedures must be followed:

1. A precise certification of facts by the judge is needed recounting the basis for his decision.

2. It is disputed whether separate acts of disorder at a trial may be punished as separate contempts, with the sentences accumulated beyond the six month maximum without providing for trial by jury. We believe aggregation of sentences is required to satisfy the constitutional principles; if the total sentence is more than six months, a jury is necessary.

3. A trial judge should be disqualified from imposing summary contempt if he is personally embroiled or insulted or if there is any potentiality for bias arising from the contempt. Recent rulings have expanded the situations in which such disqualification is necessary.

4. Recent cases have also indicated that a trial judge cannot wait until the end of the trial to punish summarily for contempt that occured earlier. Since the extraordinary power of summary contempt is justified as a weapon for ensuring an orderly trial, the need disappears when the trial is over. A second judge should then pass on the charges after a full due process hearing (pages 218–30).

If such a hearing is held, the basic evidence is the trial transcript; this may be supplemented by live evidence. In some cases, the second judge may permit the prosecutor and the original trial judge to be called as witnesses (pages 230–32).

# The Integrity of the Courtroom
# (Chapter Eleven)

The physical plant in which many courts function contributes to the disrespect in which the legal system is held. The courthouses in larger cities are often old and dingy, the courtrooms dirty and uncomfortable, the acoustics inadequate, and proper security difficult to achieve. Although new dignified courthouses are necessary, they are only part of the problem. The lower criminal courts require better administration to handle the great traffic that passes through them (pages 239–44).

Courtroom security officers often play a key role in determining whether or not proceedings are orderly. The marshals are responsible for shepherding and seating spectators in the court. They keep them in line outside the courtroom, direct them to their places, search them if necessary, and make sure that they are quiet when court is in session.

Court officers have an extremely difficult job. They often combine the functions of prison guard, security officer, and courtroom usher. The great majority perform ably and with restraint. But since they bear the actual physical burden of dealing with unruly defendants, emotional relatives, and militant spectators, they should be given adequate training so that they can deal with potential disorder with words instead of force. Court officers should be involved in pretrial planning for any notorious trial. They should be introduced to the defendants and their counsel as early as possible and get to know the relatives of those on trial so that seating can be arranged for them. The trial judge, who must be firmly in charge of the marshals, should impress on them that they must behave as neutral umpires, treating spectators with restraint and understanding (pages 244–50).

Courtroom disorder is often caused by spectators who voice their support of the defendants on trial. If a warning is not sufficient to quiet matters, a judge may expel an unruly spectator. In the rare case when a judge feels exclusion is not a sufficient sanction, he may cite a disorderly spectator for contempt. A spectator's insults or shouts or active disrespect of the court interfere with an orderly proceeding as much as similar acts by a defendant or lawyer (pages 250–53).

Related to the problem of spectator disorder is the role of the press in reporting on courtroom activities. It is obvious that individuals may engage in courtroom misbehavior because they believe their actions will receive press attention. The solution is not to bar press coverage. The constitutional guarantees of a public trial and the First Amendment protection of freedom of the press make clear that reporters must be admitted to a trial (pages 253–54).

# APPENDIX A

*Trial Judges Questionnaire*

# LETTERS AND QUESTIONNAIRES TO JUDGES

December 1, 1970

My dear Sir:

The Association of the Bar of the City of New York is engaged in a comprehensive study of courtroom conduct. The purpose of this study is to examine the frequency and form of trial disruption, the causes of the phenomenon, and the danger to the judicial process that such episodes create. It will offer concrete proposals for dealing with the problem to guide the action of lawyers, prosecutors and judges.

The study will deal not only with recent well-publicized cases such as the Chicago "7" trial and the New York Black Panther case, but it will also examine lesser-known instances of disruption. For this reason we have prepared the attached questionnaire which is being sent to trial judges throughout the country. The questionnaire is designed to gather information on the different types of disruption, the effect of such disturbances on trials, and the most effective means for handling them.

We would appreciate your completing the attached questionnaire and returning it to us as soon as possible. No individual judge or court will be identified in the final report without prior written permission.

Thank you for your assistance.

Bernard Botein
President, Association of the Bar

Burke Marshall
Chairman, Special Committee

Name of Judge_____
Court_____
Street_____ City & State_____ (Zip)_____

If you have had experience with a disorderly trial, please answer the following questions for *each* experience. If more than one trial was involved, please use additional copies of this questionnaire as required. (Additional copies will be sent on request.) Please answer questions 17 and 18 *whether or not* you have had any experience with a disorderly trial.

Please use inserted pages if necessary to complete answers.

1. Name of case_____
   _____ Docket No._____
   Citation of case, if reported (please give citation of case on appeal or of any contempt case or disciplinary proceeding relating to this disorder).

   If the media reported the disturbance, please give newspaper or magazine reference.

2. With what crime(s) was defendant(s) charged or what was the nature of the civil case?

3. Briefly, what was the factual background of the case, and what were the main issues before the court?

4. If the case was a criminal action, would you characterize the defendant(s) as
   a) Political activist(s)_____
   b) Ordinary criminal defendant(s)_____
   c) Mentally disturbed defendant(s)_____
   d) Other (please specify)_____

5. a) If the defendant(s) was a political activist or militant, what was his political affiliation or views?
   b) Did he (they) attempt in any way to convey a political message during the trial?
      (i) to whom?
      (ii) how?

6. a) What was the race or nationality of the defendant(s)
      of the lawyers
   b) If there were any racial overtones to the case, please indicate their nature.
   c) How was the racial issue raised, by whom and how was the matter dealt with?

7. Please describe the disruption, including the persons responsible, how it arose, and how long the disturbance lasted?
   If available, please furnish the pages of the minutes of the proceeding relating to the disturbance.

8. How did the court deal with the disturbance?

9. a) Please indicate whether contempt charges were brought and against whom.

    b) By whom were the charges heard?

    c) What sentence was imposed?

    d) Was the sentence actually served?

10. a) What special rules, if any, were established for spectators?

    b) What was the seating capacity for spectators?

    c) Was there enough seating space for all spectators?

11. a) What was the name and address of defendant(s)' counsel?

    b) Was the lawyer(s) local or from outside the jurisdiction?

12. a) Did the defendant's lawyer overtly identify himself with his client's cause?

    b) In what way?

    c) Were charges brought against any lawyer by the local bar association? If so, what was the result of the proceedings? (Please give citation of any reported decision.)

13. a) What was the jury verdict or the court's decision in the action?

    b) If it was a criminal case, what was the maximum sentence possible?

    c) What sentence was imposed by the court?

    d) Was the case appealed?
    What was the appellate decision? (Please give citation of any reported decision.)

14. a) Did the local or national press cover the trial?

    b) Did press or media coverage play any role in the disturbance? If so, in what way?

15. a) Were any pretrial conferences held with a view to minimizing trial disturbances? If so, please describe their nature.

    b) Were pertinent pretrial orders issued?
    If so, please attach copies or quote relevant portions.

    c) Were the orders or agreements followed by the parties? Please be specific.

16. a) Were out-of-court demonstrations held during the trial?

b) Where and by whom?

c) What efforts were made to control them?

d) Were any arrests made?

e) What were the results of the arrests?

## GENERAL QUESTIONS

17. In your view have trial disturbances increased in recent years, or have the media simply been paying more attention to such disorders?

18. Do you have any comments on the way in which trial disturbances should be dealt with?

(DATE)_____     (SIGNED)_____

April 5, 1971

My Dear Sir:

Last December we sent you and every other trial judge in the country the attached questionnaire and explanatory letter. We received over 1,000 returns out of 4,500 inquiries.

About eighty of the returned questionnaires describe specific incidents of trial disruption and indicated how the judges dealt with the problem. Over 900 judges did not experience any court disorders but nevertheless answered the general inquiries in questions 17 and 18. We have found many of these responses at least as important and helpful as the specific episodes described.

We are therefore now sending out a second mailing to those judges who did not respond to the first in the hopes that we may get further thoughts and suggestions about the problem of trial disorder. *A negative response is extremely important so that we may get some idea of the statistical incidence of courtroom disorder.*

We are also attaching a separate sheet containing three additional questions relating to disruption which we would like all judges to answer *whether or not* they have had any experience with a disorderly trial.

Thank you for your cooperation.

Bernard Botein
President, Association of the Bar

Burke Marshall
Chairman, Special Committee

19. How should a judge deal with passive insubordination by a defendant or his counsel, e.g., a refusal to stand at the start of proceedings or to address the court as "your Honor"?

20. How should a judge deal with subtle forms of obstruction, such as a lawyer knowingly asking improper questions, engaging in dilatory tactics beyond the norm, persisting in taking positions overruled by the court, and so on?

21. a) What limits, if any, should be imposed on a defendant's right to appear pro se in court proceedings?

    b) If a defendant is allowed to appear pro se, what precautionary measures, if any, should be taken by the court, e.g., the appointment of standby counsel, etc.?

    c) In your opinion, is a pro se defense more or less likely to result in trial disruption? Why?

## TABULATION AND ANALYSIS OF RESPONSES

JUDGES QUESTIONNAIRE

In December 1970 a total of 4,687 questionnaires were mailed to all trial judges of general jurisdiction throughout the United States and to the criminal court judges in New York City and California. We received the following responses:

|  | TOTAL | STATE | FEDERAL |
|---|---|---|---|
| Mailing | 4,687 | 4,239 | 448 |
| Responses | 1,602 | 1,490 | 112 |
| Alabama | 27 | 25 | 2 |
| Alaska | 4 | 4 | — |
| Arizona | 24 | 21 | 3 |
| Arkansas | 20 | 17 | 3 |
| California | 150 | 144 | 6 |
| Canal Zone | 1 | — | 1 |
| Colorado | 27 | 27 | — |
| Connecticut | 9 | 8 | 1 |
| Delaware | 6 | 4 | 2 |
| District of Columbia | 2 | — | 2 |
| Florida | 50 | 44 | 6 |
| Georgia | 17 | 15 | 2 |
| Guam | 2 | 2 | — |

|  | TOTAL | STATE | FEDERAL |
|---|---|---|---|
| Hawaii | 5 | 4 | 1 |
| Idaho | 13 | 11 | 2 |
| Illinois | 74 | 71 | 3 |
| Indiana | 40 | 38 | 2 |
| Iowa | 45 | 43 | 2 |
| Kansas | 28 | 27 | 1 |
| Kentucky | 25 | 25 | — |
| Louisiana | 25 | 20 | 5 |
| Maine | 10 | 9 | 1 |
| Maryland | 37 | 34 | 3 |
| Massachusetts | 16 | 14 | 2 |
| Michigan | 49 | 45 | 4 |
| Minnesota | 43 | 42 | 1 |
| Mississippi | 17 | 17 | — |
| Missouri | 43 | 38 | 5 |
| Montana | 19 | 17 | 2 |
| Nebraska | 15 | 13 | 2 |
| Nevada | 1 | 1 | — |
| New Hampshire | 3 | 2 | 1 |
| New Jersey | 27 | 24 | 3 |
| New Mexico | 5 | 5 | — |
| New York | 156 | 153 | 3 |
| North Carolina | 19 | 17 | 2 |
| North Dakota | 9 | 9 | — |
| Ohio | 77 | 71 | 6 |
| Oklahoma | 24 | 22 | 2 |
| Oregon | 25 | 24 | 1 |
| Pennsylvania | 82 | 69 | 13 |
| Puerto Rico | 9 | 9 | — |
| Rhode Island | 8 | 8 | — |
| South Carolina | 6 | 5 | 1 |
| South Dakota | 15 | 15 | — |
| Tennessee | 38 | 35 | 3 |
| Texas | 56 | 55 | 1 |
| Utah | 7 | 6 | 1 |
| Vermont | 3 | 2 | 1 |
| Virginia | 46 | 43 | 3 |
| Washington | 42 | 41 | 1 |
| West Virginia | 16 | 14 | 2 |
| Wisconsin | 53 | 51 | 2 |
| Wyoming | 8 | 7 | 1 |
| Unidentified states | 24 | 23 | 1 |

Question 1. *Identifying cases of disruption.*

A total of 107 judges reported on a total of *112* cases of courtroom disruption. (See following chart for complete breakdown of these examples of disorderly trials.)

Question 2. With what crime(s) was defendant(s) charged or what was the nature of the civil case?

17   murder
12   armed robbery
 8   divorce
 7   assault
 7   rape
 7   robbery
 7   burglary
 5   drug law violation
 4   larceny
 3   arson
 3   sale of narcotics
 3   grand theft
 2   violation of Selective Service Act
 2   riot
 2   disorderly conduct
 1   kidnapping and assault
 1   battery, disturbing the peace
 1   extortion
 1   bank robbery
 1   forcible entry and trespass
 1   possession of illegal weapons and explosives
 1   unlawful assembly
 1   civil suit (by Highway Commission to enjoin operation of junkyard)
 1   distribution of obscene literature
 1   illegal voting
 1   child custody case
 1   conspiracy to imprison college dean
 1   escape from Honor Farm
 1   conspiracy to cheat and defraud
 1   aid and abet murder
 1   child molestation
 1   aiding and abetting escape from prison
 1   complaint for mandatory injunction to surrender possession
 1   forgery
 1   obscenity
 1   aggravated battery
 1   attempted escape from prison
 1   (not described)

Question 4. If the case was a criminal action, would you characterize the defendant(s) as:

58   ordinary criminal defendant(s)
21   political activist(s)
20   other
13   mentally disturbed defendant(s)

Question 5. If the defendant(s) was a political activist or militant, what was his political affiliation or views?

| | |
|---|---|
| 7 | Black Panther |
| 5 | against Vietnam war |
| 2 | Students for Democratic Society |
| 2 | radical students |
| 2 | attack on racism |
| 1 | White Panther Organization |
| 1 | Communist Workers Movement |
| 1 | anti-government |

Question 6. Racial overtones to case: 28 cases reported

| | |
|---|---|
| 26 | black defendant(s) |
| 2 | Mexican defendant(s) |

Question 7. Type of disruption

| | |
|---|---|
| 74 | by defendant(s) |
| 17 | by spectator(s) |
| 8 | by party in divorce action |
| 8 | by attorney |
| 3 | by relative of defendant |
| 1 | by complainant |
| 1 | by local sheriff |

Question 8. How did the court deal with the disturbance?

| | |
|---|---|
| 32 | contempt citations |
| 24 | warning |
| 17 | binding and gagging of defendant |
| 13 | removal from courtroom of defendant |
| 2 | removal of spectators from courtroom |
| 1 | mistrial |
| 1 | clearing the courtroom |
| 22 | other |

Question 9. Please indicate whether contempt charges were brought and against whom.

| | |
|---|---|
| 74 | no contempt charges |
| 38 | contempt charges |
| 1 | sheriff |
| 21 | defendant(s) |
| 6 | spectator(s) |
| 3 | party in divorce action |
| 4 | defense attorney |
| 2 | relative of defendant |
| 1 | complainant |

Question 10. What special rules were established for spectators?

| | |
|---|---|
| 11 | court officers to search all spectators upon entering courtroom |
| 3 | no standing allowed in courtroom |

  2     plainclothesmen in audience
  1     any disruption—courtroom to be cleared of spectators

Question 12. Did the defendant's lawyer overtly identify himself with his client's abuse? *10* cases reported

Question 15. Were any pretrial conferences held with a view to minimizing trial disturbances? *21* cases reported

Question 16. Were out-of-court demonstrations held during the trial? *18* cases reported

Represented or Pro se:
  92    represented
  13    pro se
  2     pro se but lawyer stepped in later
  1     represented but attempt to act as own counsel
  1     fired several lawyers and then acted pro se
  3     no answer

Lawyer in any way responsible for disruption?
  89    lawyer not responsible
  8     lawyer responsible
  15    pro se (not applicable)

SUPPLEMENTARY QUESTIONS TO BE ANSWERED BY ALL JUDGES

Mailing: 4,687
Responses: 1,056

Question 19. How should a judge deal with passive insubordination by a defendant or his counsel, e.g., a refusal to stand at the start of proceedings or to address the court as "your Honor"?

*Defendant*
  319   ignore
  162   contempt of court
  120   warning of contempt
  96    explain proper procedure, lecture on bad manners
  59    handled by conference in chambers (reprimand, explain rules of conduct)
  26    treat each situation individually
  23    removal of defendant until he agrees to follow rules
  14    bailiff takes care of situation
  9     no experience in matter
  4     overlook during trial but keep in mind when sentencing

| | |
|---|---|
| 1 | open court without jury so they will not be aware of defendant's insubordination |
| 3 | refuse to start court |
| 2 | publish court rules concerning courtroom etiquette |
| 1 | judge remains standing until everyone in courtroom stands |
| 1 | declare mistrial |
| 1 | warn jury to disregard these actions |
| 1 | open court prior to appearance of those who refuse to stand |
| 214 | no answer |

*Attorney*

| | |
|---|---|
| 216 | ignore |
| 198 | contempt of court |
| 131 | warning of contempt |
| 108 | request conformance to norm |
| 45 | report conduct to bar association |
| 68 | conference in chambers |
| 26 | discipline by bar association |
| 20 | treat each situation individually |
| 11 | disbarment |
| 11 | suspension from practice in trial court |
| 9 | bailiff takes care of situation |
| 9 | no experience |
| 4 | remove attorney from case |
| 3 | refuse to start court |
| 2 | mistrial |
| 2 | revoke lawyer's right to practice in this courtroom in future |
| 2 | publish court rules concerning courtroom etiquette |
| 1 | do not recognize for comments |
| 1 | open court prior to appearance of those who refuse to stand |
| 1 | judge remains standing until everyone in courtroom stands |
| 188 | no answer |

Question 20. How should a judge deal with subtle forms of obstruction, such as a lawyer knowingly asking improper questions, engaging in dilatory tactics beyond the norm, persisting in taking positions overruled by the court, and so on?

| | |
|---|---|
| 329 | warn attorney he will be held in contempt |
| 215 | warn attorney in private |
| 196 | contempt of court |
| 63 | disciplinary action through bar association |
| 50 | use patience and firmness |
| 39 | warn attorney in public |
| 23 | mistrial |
| 21 | recess court and warn lawyer |
| 16 | exclude attorney, appoint substitute counsel |
| 7 | ignore it |
| 6 | no experience |

3      maintain composure
88     no answer

Question 21a. What limits, if any, should be imposed on a defendant's right to appear pro se in court proceedings?
298    none
212    counsel should be present and available to assist (standby counsel)
110    pro se defense should not be permitted in criminal proceedings
78     no limits if court is satisfied defendant understands proceedings and is competent
60     rules of evidence and conduct are to be followed
42     warn defendant of problems of pro se defense
38     no limits if he is not disruptive
33     no general rules—treat each case individually
12     do everything possible to prevent
9      no opinion
8      if defendant's rights are being jeopardized during the proceedings court should appoint counsel
8      no experience
4      pro se only as last resort
1      not permitted if defendant is in custody
143    no answer

b. If a defendant is allowed to appear pro se, what precautionary measures, if any, should be taken by the court, e.g., the appointment of standby counsel, etc.?
694    standby counsel should be appointed
113    none
26     instruct defendant to abide by rules of evidence and conduct in courtroom
25     each case should be treated separately
15     warn the defendant of difficulties of pro se defense on record
12     advise defendant of his rights
12     guidance by the court
4      hearing to determine defendant's legal competency
155    no answer

c. In your opinion, is a pro se defense more or less likely to result in trial disruption? Why?
711    more likely to result in disruption
51     neither
44     depends on individual defendant
40     less likely to result in disruption
3      depends on judge's attitude and leadership
207    no answer

*Pro se defense is more likely to result in trial disruption:*
358    pro se defendant unfamiliar with legal procedure and rules of evidence

| | |
|---|---|
| 45 | defendant is emotionally involved |
| 43 | counsel would be able to quiet unruly defendant |
| 41 | defendant not subject to code of professional responsibility |
| 26 | the purpose of pro se defense is disruption |
| 12 | defendants who appear pro se have mental problems |
| 11 | gives defendant more opportunity to make speeches |
| 10 | same type of individual who would be likely to disrupt any trial |
| 9 | defendant might commit unintentional disruptive acts |
| 7 | cannot appreciate full consequences of his action |
| 5 | difficulty of excluding defendant from courtroom when pro se |
| 144 | no answer |

*Pro se defense is less likely to result in trial disruption:*

| | |
|---|---|
| 7 | defendant may feel he is "doing his thing" |
| 4 | defendant will not be as skilled in the use of disruptive tactics |
| 3 | trial disruption is planned in advance by counsel |
| 3 | so busy he does not have time to disrupt trial |
| 3 | the defendant will usually follow court's advice |
| 2 | pro se defendant usually angry with lawyers not with court |
| 1 | pro se defendant is timid and unsure of himself |
| 1 | court will only have one person to control |
| 16 | no answer |

# TRIAL JUDGES QUESTIONNAIRE

| CASE NUMBER | STATE OR FEDERAL COURT | CRIME TRIED | POLITICAL OR RACIAL OVERTONES | TYPE OF DISRUPTION | WHEN DISRUPTIO OCCURRE |
|---|---|---|---|---|---|
| 1 | state | burglary | no | Sheriff refused to accept judge's authority regarding courtroom decorum or handling a prisoner. He refused to remove his sidearm in court and also refused to remove shackles from the prisoner. | |
| 2 | federal | burglary II and malicious destruction of private property | All defendants opposed to U.S. presence in Vietnam. | Defendants interrupted proceedings by asking questions of court. One unruly spectator was ejected from courtroom. | |
| 3 | state | robbery, grand larceny, assault, sodomy, rape | no | Defendant attempted to frustrate and delay trial. He refused to proceed with competent assigned counsel. | |
| 4 | state | (not described) | Defendants were members of S.D.S. | Defendants were evasive in their answers. They were nonresponsive and they giggled. | during arraignme |
| 5 | federal | possession of illegal weapons, possession of explosives | Defendant was Black Panther who was arrested at Panther Headquarters. | Spectators refused to stand when court was opened. They were loud and disruptive. | |
| 6 | state | armed robbery | no | Spectators used vile language at jurors and bailiffs and blocked hallways at recess. | |

| PRESENTED OR PRO SE | LAWYER IN ANY WAY RESPONSIBLE FOR DISRUPTION | HELD IN CONTEMPT | PENALTY FOR CONTEMPT | FOUND GUILTY OR NOT GUILTY | SENTENCE FOR CRIME | ON APPEAL |
|---|---|---|---|---|---|---|
| presented | no | sheriff held in contempt | $50, suspended | | | |
| presented | Lawyer held in contempt and sentenced to 30 days. | 3 defendants held in contempt | suspended sentence | guilty | varying sentences from 3 months to 1–6 years | on appeal |
| presented | no | no | | guilty | robbery: 10–20 assault: 2–5 rape: 10–20 | affirmed |
| presented | no | 2 defendants held in contempt | 5 days in custody | | | |
| presented | no | no | | trial not complete | | |
| presented | no | no | | guilty | 25 years | on appeal |

| CASE NUMBER | STATE OR FEDERAL COURT | CRIME TRIED | POLITICAL OR RACIAL OVERTONES | TYPE OF DISRUPTION | WHEN DISRUPTION OCCURRED |
|---|---|---|---|---|---|
| 7 | state | armed robbery | no | One of the defendants grabbed a chair and attempted to strike prosecutor and escape through efforts of friends and relatives in court. | when guilt verdict was announced |
| 8 | state | murder, 2nd degree | no | "Unethical" courtroom conduct of defendant's counsel. | throughout trial |
| 9 | federal | violation of Selective Service Act, failure to report and submit to induction | draft resistance movement | 100 spectator sympathizers became outspoken and attempted to argue injustices of draft law. | at time of sentencing |
| 10 | state | assault with intent to kill | no | Defendant insisted on having 12 black jurors hear his case. He refused to accept lawyer assigned by Public Defender's Office. | |
| 11 | state | conspiracy to imprison college dean, false imprisonment with violence and menace | Student members of S.D.S. wanted dean to reinstate discharged black employee. | Student spectators demonstrated in courtroom. | |
| 12 | state | murder | no | Defendants refused to sit down. They later refused to enter courtroom for trial and remained in jail. | during *voir dire* examination of prospective jurors |
| 13 | state | sale of heroin | Defendant claimed persecution because he was a Mexican. | Defendant demanded change of venue because he was not getting a fair trial. He started to walk out of courtroom. | |

| REPRESENTED OR PRO SE | LAWYER IN ANY WAY RESPONSIBLE FOR DISRUPTION | HELD IN CONTEMPT | PENALTY FOR CONTEMPT | FOUND GUILTY OR NOT GUILTY | SENTENCE FOR CRIME | ON APPEAL |
|---|---|---|---|---|---|---|
| represented | no | some of the relatives held in contempt | 30 days | guilty | 21 years | on appeal |
| represented | yes | lawyer held in contempt | $500 and 5 days in jail | not guilty | | |
| represented | no | no | | guilty | 3 years | |
| represented | no | no | | guilty | motion for a new trial pending | |
| pro se | | no | | guilty | sentence suspended, probation —5 years | |
| represented | no | no | | guilty | life imprisonment | on appeal |
| represented | no | no | | guilty | indeterminate | |

| CASE NUMBER | STATE OR FEDERAL COURT | CRIME TRIED | POLITICAL OR RACIAL OVERTONES | TYPE OF DISRUPTION | WHEN DISRUPTION OCCURRED |
|---|---|---|---|---|---|
| 14 | state | murder | no | Defendant did not like the way the trial was going and became difficult. He refused to come to court. | |
| 15 | state | robbery with aggravation | no | Defendant drew knife and threatened officers. He shouted obscenities and curses. | during *voir dire* |
| 16 | state | kidnapping and assault | no | Defendant shouted and pounded the table. | |
| 17 | state | grand larceny, possession of stolen property, possession of heroin | no | Defendant interrupted trial several times and demanded to read a statement to the jury. | |
| 18 | state | extortion, impersonating a police officer | no | Defendant refused to leave cell and enter courtroom. When he was strapped to a movable surgical table and rolled into the courtroom, he yelled and screamed that he would refuse to participate in any trial. | |
| 19 | state | possession of drugs | no | Defendant kept up a series of outbursts: he called witnesses liars, interrupted district attorney during cross-examination. | during jury selection and examination of police witnesses |
| 20 | federal | bank robbery | no | Defendant shouted obscenities directed at the court. | |

| PRESENTED OR PRO SE | LAWYER IN ANY WAY RESPONSIBLE FOR DISRUPTION | HELD IN CONTEMPT | PENALTY FOR CONTEMPT | FOUND GUILTY OR NOT GUILTY | SENTENCE FOR CRIME | ON APPEAL |
|---|---|---|---|---|---|---|
| presented | no | no | | guilty | death | |
| presented | no | no | | guilty | 25 years | no appeal |
| o se | | no | | guilty | 28 years | no appeal |
| presented | no | no | | guilty only of possession of heroin | 6 months | |
| presented | no | no | | guilty | 9–10 years | no appeal |
| presented | no | no | | mistrial | | |
| presented | no | defendant held in contempt | $100 fine | guilty | pending | |

| CASE NUMBER | STATE OR FEDERAL COURT | CRIME TRIED | POLITICAL OR RACIAL OVERTONES | TYPE OF DISRUPTION | WHEN DISRUPTION OCCURRED |
|---|---|---|---|---|---|
| 21 | state | unlawful assembly | Defendants were student activists who held sit-in on main highway alongside university | Student spectators cheered and yelled during proceedings. Obscenities were directed at the court. | during arraignment hearing |
| 22 | state | divorce case | no | Husband shot and killed his wife, his wife's attorney, and wounded the judge. | when the court's decision on the divorce was announced |
| 23 | state | child molestation | no | Defendant attempted to attack judge and other officers of court. | during arraignment |
| 24 | state | distribution of obscene literature | Defendant was a member of White Panther Organization. | Smoke bomb was dropped in doorway leading to courtroom. Smoke and odor permeated courtroom. | |
| 25 | state | forgery | no | Mentally disturbed defendant engaged in 15–20 minute tirade before court. | |
| 26 | state | obscenity | no | Defendant Lenny Bruce, acting pro se, did not follow court directions or procedures. | |
| 27 | federal | destroying and mutilating Selective Service certificate | Defendant was opposed to war in Vietnam. | Disturbance by spectators in courtroom. | when defendant was taken from courtroom |

| REPRESENTED OR PRO SE | LAWYER IN ANY WAY RESPONSIBLE FOR DISRUPTION | HELD IN CONTEMPT | PENALTY FOR CONTEMPT | FOUND GUILTY OR NOT GUILTY | SENTENCE FOR CRIME | ON APPEAL |
|---|---|---|---|---|---|---|
| represented | no | no | | Defendants held for full hearing. | | |
| represented | no | no | | | | |
| | | defendant held in contempt | 5 days and $50 | Case was never tried. Defendant transferred to mental hospital. | | |
| represented | no | no | | Defendant failed to appear for trial. He is now in custody awaiting federal charge on bombing. | | |
| represented | no | no | | Defendant committed to State Hospital for Criminally Insane. | | |
| pro se | | no | | guilty | | reversed |
| represented | no | 19 spectators held in contempt | from reprimand to six months in jail | guilty | 5 years | |

| CASE NUMBER | STATE OR FEDERAL COURT | CRIME TRIED | POLITICAL OR RACIAL OVERTONES | TYPE OF DISRUPTION | WHEN DISRUPTION OCCURRED |
|---|---|---|---|---|---|
| 28 | state | growing marijuana on farm | no | Defendants had to be carried into the courtroom. They refused to stand when judge entered. | |
| 29 | state | disorderly conduct and assault on police officer | Defendants were members of American Communist Workers Movement and had disrupted a "hard hat" parade. | Spectators refused to stand when court opened and screamed about "fascist" court. Defendant grabbed judge's arm. | |
| 30 | state | murder, rape, kidnapping | no | Defendant attempted to escape from courtroom. He used foul language before jury. | |
| 31 | state | burglary | no | Black defendant stated that he refused to continue trial with white jury. | *voir dire* of jury |
| 32 | state | rape | no | Defendant was defiant. He refused to cooperate with his appointed attorneys; he interrupted trial by addressing observers in loud voice. | hearings prior to trial and at beginning of trial itself |
| 33 | state | burglary, 2nd degree & larceny | no | Defendant threatened to escape. He had to be forcibly dragged into court. | |
| 34 | state | murder | no | Defendant made motions and wanted to argue them in open court. | |

| REPRESENTED OR PRO SE | LAWYER IN ANY WAY RESPONSIBLE FOR DISRUPTION | HELD IN CONTEMPT | PENALTY FOR CONTEMPT | FOUND GUILTY OR NOT GUILTY | SENTENCE FOR CRIME | ON APPEAL |
|---|---|---|---|---|---|---|
| presented | no | no | | guilty | 6 months and 2 years probation | |
| ro se | | spectator held in contempt | 10 days and $500 fine | Defendants were minors. They were adjudged delinquent and placed on probation in custody of their father. | | |
| presented | no | no | | guilty | death | reversed |
| presented | no | no | | not guilty | | |
| presented | no | no | | guilty | life imprisonment | |
| presented | no | no | | not guilty | | |
| ro se | | no | | guilty | death | affirmed |

| CASE NUMBER | STATE OR FEDERAL COURT | CRIME TRIED | POLITICAL OR RACIAL OVERTONES | TYPE OF DISRUPTION | WHEN DISRUPTION OCCURRED |
|---|---|---|---|---|---|
| 35 | state | escape from Honor Farm | no | Defendant would not be seated, knocked books and papers off desk, directed obscenities at court. | at beginning of proceedings |
| 36 | state | rape and other related offenses | no | Defendant went into violent tantrum. He was physically and verbally abusive. | when jury announced verdict |
| 37 | state | murder, 1st degree | no | Defendant picked up counsel table and threw it at the bench. | during testimony of witness who testified defendant had admitted the murder |
| 38 | state | divorce case | no | Husband struck wife's attorney. General disturbance in courtroom. | during recess |
| 39 | state | burglary, 2nd degree | no | Defendant interrupted witnesses, called them liars, and shouted he couldn't get a fair trial on perjured testimony. | while witnesses were testifying |
| 40 | state | complaint for mandatory injunction to surrender possession | no | Numerous defendants telling court simultaneously that court had no jurisdiction in matter. Shouting by spectators. | |
| 41 | state | armed robbery | no | Obscene name calling by defendant. He fired lawyer 3 or 4 times. | |

| REPRESENTED OR PRO SE | LAWYER IN ANY WAY RESPONSIBLE FOR DISRUPTION | HELD IN CONTEMPT | PENALTY FOR CONTEMPT | FOUND GUILTY OR NOT GUILTY | SENTENCE FOR CRIME | ON APPEAL |
|---|---|---|---|---|---|---|
| represented | no | no | | guilty | 3½ years | confirmed |
| represented | no | defendant held in contempt | 6 months in prison | guilty | 4–12 years | affirmed |
| represented | no | no | | guilty | death | penalty phase reversed |
| represented | no | no | | mistrial declared | | |
| represented | no | no | | guilty | 3–4 years | |
| pro se | | 13 defendants held in contempt | 3 days | | | |
| represented | no | no | | guilty | 10–25 years | affirmed |

| CASE NUMBER | STATE OR FEDERAL COURT | CRIME TRIED | POLITICAL OR RACIAL OVERTONES | TYPE OF DISRUPTION | WHEN DISRUPTION OCCURRED |
|---|---|---|---|---|---|
| **42** | state | murder, kidnapping | Defendant was Black Panther. | Defendant tried to precipitate altercation with guards, made comments in court about case and conditions of jail. | after trial judge refused bail |
| **43** | state | robbery | no | Defendant became violent, attempted to assault arresting officer, witness. | |
| **44** | state | murder | no | Defendent shouted to disrupt testimony. | |
| **45** | state | murder | Defendant was black militant. | Defendant refused to obey requests. | |
| **46** | state | riot, possession of unlawful weapons | Black defendants opposed to white trustees and rules of college. | Insolence of defendants. | |
| **47** | state | grand theft | no | Defendant interrupted during questioning of witnesses. He pounded table and screamed. | |
| **48** | state | divorce case | no | Husband physically assault wife. | |
| **49** | state | conspiracy to cheat and defraud | no | Defendant interrupted during trial, hired and fired lawyers. | outburst after jury verdict |

| REPRESENTED OR PRO SE | LAWYER IN ANY WAY RESPONSIBLE FOR DISRUPTION | HELD IN CONTEMPT | PENALTY FOR CONTEMPT | FOUND GUILTY OR NOT GUILTY | SENTENCE FOR CRIME | ON APPEAL |
|---|---|---|---|---|---|---|
| represented | no | no | | bail hearing: bail refused | | |
| represented | no | no | | guilty | 5 years to life | affirmed |
| represented | no | no | | not guilty | | |
| represented | no | no | | not guilty | | |
| represented | no | no | | guilty | 18 months or 2 years | pending |
| represented | no | no | | not guilty | | |
| represented | no | husband held in contempt | 10 days in county jail | | | |
| represented but attempted to act as own counsel | no | no | | guilty | 1–5 years | petition for cert. denied in Supreme Court |

| CASE NUMBER | STATE OR FEDERAL COURT | CRIME TRIED | POLITICAL OR RACIAL OVERTONES | TYPE OF DISRUPTION | WHEN DISRUPTION OCCURRED |
|---|---|---|---|---|---|
| 50 | army court | assault, willful disobedience of orders, AWOL | no | Interruptions by defendant, long statements of protest, irrevelant petitions. | |
| 51 | state | armed robbery | no | Defendant refused to be seated or to stop talking or permit his attorney to continue. | when judge refused to allow defendant to fire his third attorney |
| 52 | state | aggravated battery | no | Defendant attacked complaining witness. | as court was beginning |
| 53 | state | armed robbery | no | Defendant stated he would not be tried and attempted to leave the courtroom. | at beginning of trial and when defense rested |
| 54 | state | robbery | no | Convicted defendant, aided by relative, assaulted officer in an effort to escape. | after jury verdict and pronouncement of sentence |
| 55 | state | aiding and abetting an escape from prison | no | Defendant requested armed guards be removed from courtroom. He shouted obscenities at judge when this request was refused. He took off shirt and coat and threw them at judge. | |
| 56 | state | armed robbery | no | Defendant's insistence on representing himself, addressing the court, examining witnesses. | |

| REPRESENTED OR PRO SE | LAWYER IN ANY WAY RESPONSIBLE FOR DISRUPTION | HELD IN CONTEMPT | PENALTY FOR CONTEMPT | FOUND GUILTY OR NOT GUILTY | SENTENCE FOR CRIME | ON APPEAL |
|---|---|---|---|---|---|---|
| represented by several attorneys and pro se | no | defendant held in contempt 3 times | $100 fine and 30 days confinement each time | guilty | dishonorable discharge, forfeitures, 10 years hard labor | conviction set aside, accused found to be insane |
| represented | no | no | | guilty | 5 years | affirmed |
| represented | no | no | | guilty | 3–10 years | affirmed |
| represented | no | no | | guilty | 1–25 years | pending |
| represented | no | defendant and relative held in contempt | $500 fine and 12 months in jail each | guilty | 5 years | |
| represented | no | defendant held in contempt | 3 contempts, 30 days each | mistrial | | |
| pro se | | no | | not guilty | | |

| CASE NUMBER | STATE OR FEDERAL COURT | CRIME TRIED | POLITICAL OR RACIAL OVERTONES | TYPE OF DISRUPTION | WHEN DISRUPTION OCCURRED |
|---|---|---|---|---|---|
| 57 | state | rape | no | Defendants constantly baited judge during trial. | |
| 58 | state | robbery | no | Defendant attempted to walk out of courtroom during trial. When hand-cuffed to his chair he forcibly pulled rungs of chair loose. | |
| 59 | state | auto theft | no | Defendant would berate his counsel, the court, and others by breaking into the dialogue. | |
| 60 | state | breaking and entering and larceny | no | Defendant denounced counsel and refused trial. He refused to answer questions by court. | at beginning of trial |
| 61 | state | rape | no | Defendant disrupted witnesses, accused everyone, ranted about courtroom. | during closing argument by state |
| 62 | state | armed rob-bery, assault with intent to murder | no | Defendant fought with deputies, screamed, cursed, and attempted to lecture the court. | |
| 63 | state | battery, dis-turbing peace, resisting arrest | no | Defendant threatened to approach bench while shouting epithets at judge. | |
| 64A | state | armed robbery | no | Defendant called judge names. | immediately after sentencing |

| REPRESENTED OR PRO SE | LAWYER IN ANY WAY RESPONSIBLE FOR DISRUPTION | HELD IN CONTEMPT | PENALTY FOR CONTEMPT | FOUND GUILTY OR NOT GUILTY | SENTENCE FOR CRIME | ON APPEAL |
|---|---|---|---|---|---|---|
| represented | no | no | | guilty | 2½–6 years | |
| represented | no | no | | | | |
| represented | no | no | | | | |
| represented | no | no | | guilty | 10 years | affirmed |
| represented | no | no | | guilty | | |
| represented | no | no | | guilty | 12 and 12 consecutively | no decision yet |
| represented | no | no | | Defendant removed to hospital. Psychiatrist determined him to be schizophrenic-paranoid. Trial never finished. | | |
| represented | no | defendant held in contempt | 120 days | guilty | | |

| CASE NUMBER | STATE OR FEDERAL COURT | CRIME TRIED | POLITICAL OR RACIAL OVERTONES | TYPE OF DISRUPTION | WHEN DISRUPTION OCCURRED |
|---|---|---|---|---|---|
| **64B** | state | armed robbery | no | Defendant talked in undertones. Told court in loud tones he was being "railroaded." | throughout arraignment |
| **65** | state | armed robbery and breaking and entry | no | Defendant jumped up and ran around in circles and said he didn't want his attorney. | |
| **66** | state | possession of marijuana | no | Defendant blew up in courtroom. He had to be physically subdued. | during disagreement with his lawyer |
| **67** | state | attempted escape from prison | no | Defendant shouted and threw books on table; name calling. | during pre-trial hearing |
| **68** | state | burglary | no | Defendant attempted to attack judge with stapler. | upon sentencing |
| **69** | state | murder, armed robbery, unlawful restraint | no | Defendants interrupted State's Attorney by calling him obscene names. | during closing argument |
| **70** | state | divorce hearing | no | Litigant interrupted attorneys during argument; unruly when testifying. | |
| **71A** | state | assault with deadly weapon | no | Defendant argued with judge and grabbed chair to assault him. | |

| REPRESENTED OR PRO SE | LAWYER IN ANY WAY RESPONSIBLE FOR DISRUPTION | HELD IN CONTEMPT | PENALTY FOR CONTEMPT | FOUND GUILTY OR NOT GUILTY | SENTENCE FOR CRIME | ON APPEAL |
|---|---|---|---|---|---|---|
| pro se | | defendant held in contempt | 150 days | | | |
| represented | no | no | | guilty | | |
| represented | no | no | | guilty | 1½ years | affirmed |
| represented | no | defendant held in contempt | 30 days | guilty | 1–3 years | no decision yet |
| represented | no | no | | guilty | 5 years | |
| represented | no | defendants held in contempt | mail and visitor privileges revoked for 30 days (already in jail) | guilty | 98–100 years | in process |
| represented | no | litigant held in contempt | 4 days in county jail | | | |
| represented | no | no | | guilty | 5 years | |

| CASE NUMBER | STATE OR FEDERAL COURT | CRIME TRIED | POLITICAL OR RACIAL OVERTONES | TYPE OF DISRUPTION | WHEN DISRUPTION OCCURRED |
|---|---|---|---|---|---|
| 71B | state | murder of fellow prisoner | no | Defendant struck guard and attempted to flee before being shot and captured. | when handcuffs were removed |
| 72 | state | illegal voting after loss of status | no | Defendant insulted judge and tried to intimidate jurors by open threats. | |
| 73 | state | civil suit by Highway Com. to enjoin operation of junkyard | no | Defendant assaulted 2 lawyers for Highway Commission. | as attorneys left courtroom |
| 74 | state | murder, attemped armed robbery | no | Defendant created disturbances in courtroom. | |
| 75 | state | rape and assault to kill | no | Defendant badgered witnesses and trial judge by questions and remarks in the presence of jury. | |
| 76 | state | sale of narcotics, assault, 2nd | no | Defendant shouted abusive language to court and jury. | every day during 5 week trial |
| 77 | state | arson, burglary, and theft | Defendants burned draft records, opposed to war in Vietnam. | Defendants cheered, refused to rise, verbal abuse of judge. | when guilty verdicts were read, bedlam broke loose. |

| REPRESENTED OR PRO SE | LAWYER IN ANY WAY RESPONSIBLE FOR DISRUPTION | HELD IN CONTEMPT | PENALTY FOR CONTEMPT | FOUND GUILTY OR NOT GUILTY | SENTENCE FOR CRIME | ON APPEAL |
|---|---|---|---|---|---|---|
| represented | no | no | | guilty | 4 years for man-slaughter, 2nd | |
| pro se, but lawyer stepped in later | lawyer shouted about in-justice in courtroom | defendant held in contempt | one year each for 3 contempts (concur-rent sen-tences) and $2,350 fine | guilty | 1–3 years | verdict re-versed on technicality, contempt upheld |
| represented | no | defendant held in contempt | 1 year in jail, $500 fine | | | |
| represented | no | no | | guilty | 99–175 years— murder; 10–14 years— attempted armed robbery | |
| represented | no | no | | guilty | 20 years | |
| pro se | | defendant held in contempt | 30 days in jail | guilty | 31–41 years | decision pending |
| represented | no | 4 defen-dants held in contempt | fines with alternate jail sen-tences | guilty | 2 years on first count, 4 years con-currently on counts 2 and 3 | |

| CASE NUMBER | STATE OR FEDERAL COURT | CRIME TRIED | POLITICAL OR RACIAL OVERTONES | TYPE OF DISRUPTION | WHEN DISRUPTION OCCURRED |
|---|---|---|---|---|---|
| 78 | state | felony, breaking and entering, and larceny | no | Defendant refused to cooperate with court appointed attorney. He talked out loud and refused to be seated in courtroom. | |
| 79 | state | murder | no | Defendant objected to court rulings, vilified the court, and stated the trial was over. | when defendant (pro se) was examining a police witness |
| 80 | state | arson— burning of law school building | Defendant was Black Panther who raised racial issue throughout trial. | Defendant repeatedly disrupted proceedings. | during *voir dire* of jury, at verdict, and before sentencing |
| 81A | state | robbery, aggravated assault | no | Defendant ripped off his shirt. | when judge decided matters against him |
| 81B | state | murder | no | Defendant shouted and screamed at his lawyer and made obscene gestures to the court. | |
| 82 | state | assault on police officers | antiwar sentiments of defendant | Defendant struck judge on head. | after conviction during proceedings for sentencing |
| 83 | state | larceny and conspiracy | no | Defendant screamed and shouted. | when he was brought into courtroom for trial |

| REPRESENTED OR PRO SE | LAWYER IN ANY WAY RESPONSIBLE FOR DISRUPTION | HELD IN CONTEMPT | PENALTY FOR CONTEMPT | FOUND GUILTY OR NOT GUILTY | SENTENCE FOR CRIME | ON APPEAL |
|---|---|---|---|---|---|---|
| represented | no | no | | | | |
| pro se until disruption; then public defender appointed | no | defendant held in contempt | 3 months | guilty | 30 years | still pending |
| pro se | | defendant held in contempt 6 times | 6 consecutive 30 day sentences | guilty | 10 years | pending |
| represented | no | no | | guilty | 15–30 years 9–10 years | pending |
| represented | no | no | | guilty | death sentence | reversed |
| represented | no | no | | guilty | sent to mental institution | |
| pro se | | defendant held in contempt | 6 months | guilty | | |

| CASE NUMBER | STATE OR FEDERAL COURT | CRIME TRIED | POLITICAL OR RACIAL OVERTONES | TYPE OF DISRUPTION | WHEN DISRUPTION OCCURRED |
|---|---|---|---|---|---|
| 84 | state | armed robbery | no | Shouting in courtroom by defendant. | after verdict of jury |
| 85 | state | divorce case | no | Husband pushed wife's attorney through courtroom door. | |
| 86 | state | sale of marijuana | no | Spectator made an obscene gesture or power salute. | during closing argument of state's attorney |
| 87 | state | drug law violation | no | Grimaces, chuckles, and head nodding by spectators at testimony adverse to defendant. | |
| 88 | state | forcible entry and trespass, University of Maryland | Defendant was student anti-war activist. | The audience laughed and cheered at testimony and rulings. | |
| 89 | state | custody of children | no | Mother, father, and father's sister shouted and voiced disapproval in open court. | |
| 90 | state | assault | no | Complainant called judge names. | when judge dismissed case against defendant |
| 91 | state | assault and battery | no | Spectator beat fist on judge's desk, swore at judge and prosecutor. | after defendant was sentenced |

| REPRESENTED OR PRO SE | LAWYER IN ANY WAY RESPONSIBLE FOR DISRUPTION | HELD IN CONTEMPT | PENALTY FOR CONTEMPT | FOUND GUILTY OR NOT GUILTY | SENTENCE FOR CRIME | ON APPEAL |
|---|---|---|---|---|---|---|
| represented | no | | no | guilty | 50 years | affirmed |
| represented | no | husband held in contempt | 30 days, later reduced to 5 days and $150 fine | | | |
| represented | no | spectator held in contempt | 24 hours in jail | guilty | | |
| represented | no | no | | | | |
| represented | no | no | | guilty | | |
| represented | no | 3 parties held in contempt | one party —3 days in jail, the other 2 were fined | | | |
| | | complainant held in contempt | $100 or 3 days in jail | | | |
| represented | no | spectator held in contempt | 3 days in jail | guilty | $50 fine | |

| CASE NUMBER | STATE OR FEDERAL COURT | CRIME TRIED | POLITICAL OR RACIAL OVERTONES | TYPE OF DISRUPTION | WHEN DISRUPTION OCCURRED |
|---|---|---|---|---|---|
| 92 | state | robbery and aggravated battery | no | Defendant struggled with deputy sheriffs. | when he wa brought into courtroom |
| 93 | state | divorce case | no | Shooting at courtroom door. | |
| 94 | state | murder | | Spectator insulted judge. | after jury was charged and sent out and court re voked defen dant's bail |
| 95 | state | breaking and entering, assault on police officers | Defendant was avowed Communist. | Spectators hissed and stomped. | |
| 96 | state | aid and abet murder, con- spiracy to com- mit murder | Black Panther defendant claimed that police were try- ing to destroy Panther party. | Spectators shouted in courtroom, scuffled with sheriff. | |
| 97 | state | rape and kidnapping | | Attorney refused to be seated. | |
| 98 | state | possession of marijuana | no | Attorney called detective a "liar." He refused to accept ruling of court. | |
| 99 | state | inciting to riot | no | Shouts of "kill the judge" from spectators. A half- hour disturbance by spectators. | upon sentencing |
| 100 | state | armed robbery and sodomy | Defendants were Black Panthers. | Spectators were noisy and threatened to take defendant out by gunfire if verdict was guilty. | throughout trial |

| REPRESENTED OR PRO SE | LAWYER IN ANY WAY RESPONSIBLE FOR DISRUPTION | HELD IN CONTEMPT | PENALTY FOR CONTEMPT | FOUND GUILTY OR NOT GUILTY | SENTENCE FOR CRIME | ON APPEAL |
|---|---|---|---|---|---|---|
| represented | no | no | | guilty | 5–10 years | |
| | | no | | referred to criminal court | | |
| represented | no | no | | guilty | 0–15 years man-slaughter | in process |
| represented | no | no | | guilty | 1 year suspended after 9 months | pending |
| represented | no | 4 spectators held in contempt | 25 days— 4 months | guilty | 15 years | pending |
| represented | yes | no | | hung jury | | |
| represented | yes | no | | guilty | indeterminate | on appeal |
| represented | no | no | | guilty | 1 year in workhouse, $500 fine | affirmed |
| represented | no | no | | guilty | 40 years | affirmed |

| CASE NUMBER | STATE OR FEDERAL COURT | CRIME TRIED | POLITICAL OR RACIAL OVERTONES | TYPE OF DISRUPTION | WHEN DISRUPTION OCCURRED |
|---|---|---|---|---|---|
| **101** | state | disorderly conduct | no | Defendant's wife complained about verdict. | after defen dant was found guilt |
| **102A** | state | grand theft | no | Bickering between attorneys, loud laughing, slamming books on table. | |
| **102B** | state | murder | no | Defense attorney interrupted court's statements. He failed to obey procedural rules. | |
| **103** | state | divorce case | no | Husband threatened wife. | |
| **104** | state | burglary | no | Attorney objected to everything and ignored court rulings. | |
| **105** | state | murder, assault with intent to murder | Defendant was a Black Panther who claimed this was a "political trial." | Spectators rose and greeted defendant with cries of "Power to the People," etc. Riot among spectators when verdict was anounced. | |
| **106A** | state | rape with force and violence | no | Minor interruptions by defendant's relatives throughout trial. | at not guil verdict rel tives bega to cheer a make obscene gestures to family of g involved. |
| **106B** | state | divorce case | no | Present wife of defendant sought to choke former wife who had procured a divorce. | |
| **107** | state | arson | no | Defendant interrupted proceedings and would not be quiet. | during *voi dire* of jur |

| REPRESENTED OR PRO SE | LAWYER IN ANY WAY RESPONSIBLE FOR DISRUPTION | HELD IN CONTEMPT | PENALTY FOR CONTEMPT | FOUND GUILTY OR NOT GUILTY | SENTENCE FOR CRIME | ON APPEAL |
|---|---|---|---|---|---|---|
| pro se | | wife held in contempt | 10 days in jail | guilty | fine | |
| represented | yes | district attorney and defense counsel held in contempt | none imposed at end of trial | guilty | indeterminate | pending |
| represented | yes | no | | guilty | | |
| represented | no | no | | | | |
| represented | yes | attorney held in contempt | $100 fine | mistrial | | |
| represented | no | no | | guilty | life imprisonment | on appeal |
| represented | no | brother of girl held in contempt for attempting physical violence | $10 fine | not guilty | | |
| represented | no | present wife held in contempt | 10 days in jail | | | |
| pro se | — | no | | guilty | 5–7 years | affirmed |

# APPENDIX B

*Attorneys General Questionnaire*

# LETTER AND QUESTIONNAIRE TO ATTORNEYS GENERAL

July 26, 1971

My dear Sir:

The Association of the Bar of the City of New York is engaged in a comprehensive study of courtroom conduct. The purpose of this study is to examine the frequency and form of trial disruption, the causes of the phenomenon, and the danger to the judicial process that such episodes create. It will offer concrete proposals for dealing with the problem to guide the action of lawyers, prosecutors and judges.

As part of the study, we have sent a questionnaire to every trial judge of general jurisdiction in the nation. We received an excellent response from judges concerning their experiences and views on disorderly trials.

As part of the study, we would like to know what new laws the states have passed or proposed to deal with the phenomenon. We would also like to know what other recommendations for action have been advanced within each jurisdiction. Accordingly, we have prepared the attached questionnaire for each of the State Attorneys General focusing on these problems.

We would appreciate your completing the attached questionnaire and returning it to us as soon as possible.

Thank you for your assistance.

Sincerely yours,

Leon Friedman
Associate Director

QUESTIONNAIRE FOR ATTORNEYS GENERAL

1. Have any new laws been passed in your jurisdiction since January 1, 1970 relating in any way to the problem of trial disruption?
   a. If so, please give citation or attach a copy of such law.

   b. Were such laws passed in response to a specific incident of trial disruption within your jurisdiction, or because of the highly publicized trials in Chicago or New York or for some other reasons? Please explain.

2. Have any bills been introduced in your jurisdiction since January 1, 1970 which were not enacted relating in any way to the problem of trial disruption?

   a. If so, please describe the proposals or attach a copy of the bill.

   b. Are the proposals still pending?

   c. If they were rejected by the legislature, please indicate why.

   d. Were such bills introduced in response to a specific incident of trial disruption within your jurisdiction, or because of the highly publicized trials in Chicago or New York or for some other reasons? Please explain.

3. To your knowledge, have trial disruptions increased in your jurisdiction in recent years?

4. Please describe any cases of trial disruption in your jurisdiction in recent years that have come to the attention of your office.

   a. What was the result of the disruption (contempt citation, disciplinary proceeding initiated, etc.)?

   b. If the incident is now a matter of public record, please give citation of case, including the citation of any contempt action that grew out of the episode.

   c. Please give name of judge who heard the action or passed on contempt citation.

5. Please describe form of disciplinary procedures against lawyers in force in your jurisdiction (integrated bar, non-integrated bar, etc.). Describe the various agencies or committees responsible for initiating and hearing a complaint against an attorney and generally how the procedure operates. (Please give exact names and addresses of disciplinary agencies.) Please cite the relevant statutes or regulations dealing with disciplinary procedures.

   a. If a lawyer from your jurisdiction is disruptive, who may initiate a complaint aagainst him?

   b. If a lawyer from a foreign jurisdiction is disruptive, what sanctions can be imposed within your jurisdiction?

   c. What procedures are available to send a complaint to his home jurisdiction?

6. Have any proposals been made in recent years to change these disciplinary procedures?
   What changes have been suggested and what is their current status?

7. Are statistics available in your jurisdiction on the number of disciplinary actions taken in recent years against disorderly attorneys?

   If so, please indicate how many complaints were initiated and what the final outcome was. (If your office does not maintain such statistics, please indicate where such information may be found.)
8. How do you think the problem of disorderly trials should be dealt with?

Name_____
Title_____
Address_____
_____
Date_____

## TABULATION AND ANALYSIS OF RESPONSES

On July 26, 1971, 50 questionnaires were mailed to the Attorneys General in all states.

Responses received: 42

Question 3. To your knowledge, have trial disruptions increased in your jurisdiction in recent years?

39    No
3    Yes

Question 4. Please describe any cases of trial disruption in your jurisdiction in recent years that have come to the attention of your office.

34    no cases of trial disruption
5    *cases of trial disruption*
      South Carolina—1 case
      Illinois—*Allen* v. *Illinois;* Chicago conspiracy trial
      Delaware—cases involving members of black militant groups
      Connecticut—Black Panther trials in New Haven
      California—Manson trial
3    no answer

Question 8. How do you think the problem of disorderly trials should be dealt with?

7    contempt of court
4    *Illinois* v. *Allen*
2    firmly by judge
1    removal of defendant to room where he can view proceedings, etc.
1    binding and gagging
27    no answer

# APPENDIX C

*Bar Association Presidents Questionnaire*

# LETTER AND QUESTIONNAIRE TO BAR ASSOCIATION PRESIDENTS

July 26, 1971

My dear Sir:

The Association of the Bar of the City of New York is engaged in a comprehensive study of courtroom conduct. The purpose of this study is to examine the frequency and form of trial disruption, the causes of the phenomenon, and the danger to the judicial process that such episodes create. It will offer concrete proposals for dealing with the problem to guide the action of lawyers, prosecutors and judges.

As part of the study, we have sent a questionnaire to every trial judge of general jurisdiction in the nation. We received an excellent response from judges concerning their experiences and views on disorderly trials.

We think it extremely important to obtain the views of the bar associations on proposals for action, particularly with respect to disciplinary proceedings against allegedly disruptive attorneys. Accordingly, we have prepared the attached questionnaire for the Presidents of each bar association focusing on these problems.

We would appreciate your completing the attached questionnaire and returning it to us as soon as possible.

Thank you for your assistance.

*Bernard Botein*

Bernard Botein
President, Association of the Bar

## QUESTIONNAIRE FOR BAR ASSOCIATION PRESIDENTS

1. To your knowledge, have trial disruptions increased in your jurisdiction in recent years?

2. Please describe any cases of trial disruption in your jurisdiction that have come to the attention of your organization. (If disciplinary proceedings have been initiated as a result of the incident and secrecy must be maintained, please describe the general nature of the incident without using the names of the principals.)

    a. What was the result of the disruption (contempt citation, disciplinary proceeding initiated, etc.)?

    b. If the incident is now a matter of public record, please give citation of case, including any contempt citation that grew out of the episode.

    c. Please give name of judge who heard the action or passed on contempt citation.

3. Please describe form of disciplinary procedures against lawyers in force in your jurisdiction (integrated bar, non-integrated bar, etc.). Describe the various agencies or committees responsible for initiating and hearing a complaint against an attorney and generally how the procedure operates. (Please give exact names and addresses of disciplinary agencies.) Please cite the relevant statutes or regulations dealing with disciplinary procedures.

    a. If a lawyer from your jurisdiction is disruptive, who may initiate a complaint against him?

    b. If a lawyer from a foreign jurisdiction is disruptive, what sanctions are possible within your jurisdiction?

    c. What procedures are available to send a complaint to his home jurisdiction?

4. Have any proposals been made in recent years to change these disciplinary procedures? What changes have been suggested and what is their current status?

5. Are statistics available in your jurisdiction on the number of disciplinary actions taken in recent years against disorderly attorneys? If your office does not maintain such statistics, please indicate where such information may be found.

6. Is a grievance committee of your organization responsible for initiating disciplinary proceedings? If so, please indicate how many complaints were initiated in recent years against disorderly attorneys and what the final outcome was. (It is not necessary to give the names of the principals involved.)

7. How do you think the problem of disorderly trials should be dealt with?

8. What actions has your organization taken in recent years to deal with the problem of trial disruption?

9. Have any new court rules been established in recent years dealing with the courtroom behavior of attorneys? If so, please attach a copy of such new rules or indicate where they might be obtained.

10. Who was responsible for the drafting and promulgating of such rules?

# TABULATION AND ANALYSIS OF RESPONSES

On July 26, 1971, 89 questionnaires were mailed to the state bar association and local bar association presidents of organizations represented in the American Bar Association House of Delegates.

Responses received: 37

Question 1. To your knowledge, have trial disruptions increased in your jurisdiction in recent years?

| | |
|---|---|
| 26 | No |
| 3 | Yes |
| 8 | no answer |

Question 3. Please describe form of disciplinary procedures against lawyers in your jurisdiction (integrated bar, non-integrated bar, etc.).

| | |
|---|---|
| 12 | integrated bar |
| 10 | bar association grievance committee |
| 3 | non-integrated bar |
| 1 | Supreme Court appointed grievance committee consisting of lawyers |
| 11 | no answer |

Question 4. Have any proposals been made in recent years to change these disciplinary procedures?

| | |
|---|---|
| 10 | No |
| 8 | Yes |
| 19 | no answer |

Question 6. Is a grievance committee of your organization responsible for initiating disciplinary proceedings?

| | |
|---|---|
| 12 | No |
| 12 | Yes |
| 13 | no answer |

Question 7. How do you think the problem of disorderly trials should be dealt with?

| | |
|---|---|
| 9 | contempt of court |
| 5 | by presiding judge |
| 5 | no experience with disorderly trials |
| 1 | mistrial |
| 1 | bar association should discipline lawyers |
| 16 | no answer |

Question 8. What actions has your organization taken in recent years to deal with the problem of trial disruption?

| | |
|---|---|
| 21 | none |
| 1 | educational programs at state conventions |
| 1 | bar association resolution condemning trial disruption by lawyers |
| 1 | strengthening rules governing practice of law |
| 13 | no answer |

# APPENDIX D

*Prosecutors Questionnaire*

# LETTER AND QUESTIONNAIRE TO U.S. ATTORNEYS AND DISTRICT ATTORNEYS

February 14, 1972

My dear Sir:

The Association of the Bar of the City of New York is engaged in a comprehensive study of courtroom conduct. The purpose of this study is to examine the frequency and form of trial disruption, the causes of the phenomenon, and the danger to the judicial process that such episodes create. It will offer concrete proposals for dealing with the problem to guide the action of lawyers, prosecutors and judges.

As part of the study, we have sent a questionnaire to every trial judge of general jurisdiction in the nation. We received an excellent response from judges concerning their experiences and views on disorderly trials.

We would like to learn about the experience and point of view of prosecutors with respect to this problem. We also want to know what recommendations for action they would like to see advanced. Accordingly, we have prepared the attached questionnaire for each of the United States Attorneys and District Attorneys in the larger cities focusing on these problems.

We would appreciate your completing the attached questionnaire and returning it to us as soon as possible.

Thank you for your assistance.

Sincerely yours,

*Leon Friedman*

Leon Friedman
Associate Director

QUESTIONNAIRE FOR UNITED STATES ATTORNEYS AND
DISTRICT ATTORNEYS

1. Have any new rules been issued in your jurisdiction since January 1, 1970 relating in any way to the problem of trial disruption?

   a. If so, please give citation or attach a copy of such rules.

   b. Were such laws passed in response to a specific incident of trial disruption within your jurisdiction, or because of the highly publicized trials in Chicago or New York or for some other reasons? Please explain.

2. To your knowledge, have trial disruptions increased in your jurisdiction in recent years?

3. Please describe any cases of trial disruption in your jurisdiction in recent years that have come to the attention of your office.

a. Name of case_____ Docket No._____
Citation of case, if reported (please give citation of case on appeal or of any contempt case or disciplinary proceeding relating to this disorder).
If the media reported the disturbance, please give newspaper or magazine reference.

b. With what crime(s) was defendant(s) charged or what was the nature of the civil case?

c. Briefly, what was the factual background of the case, and what were the main issues before the court?

d. If the case was a criminal action, would you characterize the defendant(s) as
Political activist(s)
Ordinary criminal defendant(s)
Mentally disturbed defendant(s)
Other (please specify)

e. If the defendant(s) was a political activist or militant, what was his political affiliation or views?

f. Did he (they) attempt in any way to convey a political message during the trial?
To whom?
How?

g. Please describe the disruption, including the persons responsible, how it arose, and how long the disturbance lasted?
If available, please furnish the pages of the minutes of the proceeding relating to the disturbance.

h. How did the court deal with the disturbance?

i. Please indicate whether contempt charges were brought and against whom.
By whom were the charges heard?
What sentence was imposed?
Was the sentence actually served?

j. What special rules, if any, were established for spectators?

k. Did the defendant's lawyer overtly identify himself with his client's cause?
In what way?
Were charges brought or complaints filed against any lawyer? If so, what was the result of the proceedings? (Please give citation of any reported decision).

l.  Did the local or national press cover the trial?

m.  Did press or media coverage play any role in the disturbance? If so, in what way?

n.  Were any pretrial conferences held with a view to minimizing trial disturbances? If so, please describe their nature.

o.  Were pertinent pretrial orders issued?
    If so, please attach copies or quote relevant portions.

p.  Were the orders or agreements followed by the parties? Please be specific.

q.  Were out-of-court demonstrations held during the trial?
    Where and by whom?
    What efforts were made to control them?
    Were any arrests made?
    What were the results of the arrests?

4.  Do you have any comments on the way in which trial disturbances should be dealt with?

DATE_____
NAME_____
ADDRESS_____
_____

## TABULATION AND ANALYSIS OF RESPONSES TO U.S. ATTORNEYS QUESTIONNAIRE

On February 14, 1972, 93 questionnaires were mailed to all United States Attorneys in the United States. A second mailing was sent on April 13, 1972, to those who had not responded.

Responses received: 53

Question 2. To your knowledge, have trial disruptions increased in your jurisdiction in recent years?

41    No
3     Yes
9     no answer

Question 3. Please describe any cases of trial disruption in your jurisdiction in recent years that have come to the attention of your office.

10 cases of disruption (see following chart for complete breakdown)

Question 3.

b) Crimes defendants charged with:
   2     murder
   2     robbery
   1     blowing up CIA office
   1     theft of government property
   1     burglary
   1     blocking driveway at Federal Center
   1     demonstration at military base
   1     draft evasion

d) Defendant characterized as:
   5     political activist
   3     ordinary criminal defendant
   1     mentally disturbed
   1     no answer

i) Contempt charges brought:
   9     No
   1     Yes

j) Special rules for spectators:
   10    No

k) Did defendant's lawyer overtly identify himself with client's cause?
   2     Yes
   8     No

n) Were any pretrial conferences held?
   3     Yes
   7     No

q) Were out-of-court demonstrations held during trial?
   3     Yes
   7     No

Who was responsible for disruption?
   9     defendant(s)
   1     spectators

Lawyer in any way responsible for disruption?
   10    No

Represented or Pro se:
   10    represented

Question 4. Do you have any comments on the way in which trial disturbances should be dealt with?

   8     removal from courtroom
   7     contempt of court
   1     strong and firm judge
   1     disbarment for attorneys
   36    no answer

U. S. ATTORNEYS QUESTIONNAIRE: TABLE

| CASE NUMBER | CRIME TRIED | POLITICAL OR RACIAL OVERTONES | TYPE OF DISRUPTION | REPRESENTED OR PRO SE | LAWYER IN ANY WAY RESPONSIBLE FOR DISRUPTION | HELD IN CONTEMPT | PENALTY FOR CONTEMPT |
|---|---|---|---|---|---|---|---|
| A-1 | conspiracy to and actual blowing up of CIA office | yes | Clenched-fist salutes, muttered comments, laughter, applause, and booing by defendants and spectators. | represented | no | no | |
| A-2 | murder | no | Defendant made loud outbursts. He struck his appointed counsel. | represented | no | no | |
| A-3 | robbery | yes | Two black defendants protest trial by all white jury and attempted to leave courtroom. | represented | no | 1 defendant held in contempt for refusing to answer questions | 1 year |
| A-4 | theft of gov't. property | yes | Defendant assaulted prosecutor and shouted obscenities at judge. | represented | no | no | |

| CASE NUMBER | CRIME TRIED | POLITICAL OR RACIAL OVERTONES | TYPE OF DISRUPTION | REPRESENTED OR PRO SE | LAWYER IN ANY WAY RESPONSIBLE FOR DISRUPTION | HELD IN CONTEMPT | CONTEMPT FOR PENALTY |
|---|---|---|---|---|---|---|---|
| A-5 | bank burglary conspiracy | no | Defendants talked out loud, cursed prosecutor and judge, fought among themselves. | represented | no | no | |
| A-6 | murder | no | Defendant used profanities against court. | represented | no | no | |
| A-7 | armed bank robbery | no | Defendant verbally interrupted trial 3 times, protesting competency of his appointed attorney. | represented | no | no | |
| A-8 | blocking driveway at Federal Center | yes—war protest demonstrations | Defendant was insolent and insulting to judge. Spectator called judge a "tyrant." | represented | no | no | |
| A-9 | unlawful demonstration on military base | yes—war protest demonstration | Defendants sang songs in courtroom and had to be dragged in and out of courtroom. | represented | no | no | |
| A-10 | draft evasion | yes | Disruption by spectators consisted of chanting slogans. | represented | no | no | |

# TABULATION AND ANALYSIS OF RESPONSES TO DISTRICT ATTORNEYS QUESTIONNAIRE

On February 14, 1972, 69 questionnaires were sent to the 69 district attorneys who have jurisdictions of 500,000 and over. A second mailing was sent on April 13, 1972, to those who had not responded.

Responses received: 25

Question 2. To your knowledge, have trial disruptions increased in your jurisdiction in recent years?

| | |
|---|---|
| 14 | No |
| 7 | Yes |
| 4 | no answer |

Question 3. Cases of trial disruption (see chart which follows)

15 cases of disruption

b) Crimes defendants charged with:

| | |
|---|---|
| 3 | murder |
| 2 | criminal trespass |
| 1 | burglary |
| 1 | kidnapping |
| 1 | attempted murder |
| 1 | possession of explosives and bombs |
| 1 | perjury |
| 1 | robbery |
| 1 | doctor prescribed drugs to addicts |
| 1 | conspiracy to destroy private property |
| 1 | burning Selective Service records |
| 1 | unknown crime |

d) Defendant characterized as:

| | |
|---|---|
| 8 | ordinary criminal defendant(s) |
| 7 | political activist(s) |

i) Contempt charges brought:

| | |
|---|---|
| 9 | No |
| 6 | Yes |

j) Special rules for spectators:

| | |
|---|---|
| 10 | Yes |
| 4 | No |
| 1 | no answer |

k) Did defendant's lawyer overtly identify himself with client's cause?
- 7     Yes
- 2     No
- 1     pro se (not applicable)
- 5     no answer

n) Were any pretrial conferences held?
- 8     Yes
- 2     No
- 5     no answer

q) Were out-of-court demonstrations held during trial?
- 9     Yes
- 3     No
- 3     no answer

Who was responsible for disruption?
- 8     defendant(s)
- 4     attorney
- 3     spectators

Represented or pro se:
- 14     represented
- 1     pro se

Question 4. Do you have any comments on the way in which trial disturbances should be dealt with?
- 6     strong judges
- 2     contempt of court
- 1     limit spectators
- 1     removal of defendant from courtroom
- 15     no answer

# DISTRICT ATTORNEYS QUESTIONNAIRE: TABLE

| CASE NUMBER | CRIME TRIED | POLITICAL OR RACIAL OVERTONES | TYPE OF DISRUPTION | REPRESENTED OR PRO SE | LAWYER IN ANY WAY RESPONSIBLE FOR DISRUPTION | HELD IN CONTEMPT | PENALTY FOR CONTEMPT |
|---|---|---|---|---|---|---|---|
| B-1 | criminal trespass | yes | Defendants yelled at prosecutor and threw paper at him. | represented | no | 1 defendant | $25 fine and 10 day sentence, suspended |
| B-2 | criminal trespass | yes—defendants antiwar activists | Defendants interrupted trial with extraneous objections and dialogues with witnesses during cross-examination. | represented | no | no | |
| B-3 | murder and attempted robbery | no | Spectators behaved wildly in courtroom. | represented | yes | no | |
| B-4 | burglary | no | Defendant fought violently with court officers on three occasions. | represented | no | no | |
| B-5 | kidnapping, coercion, possession of weapon | case arose out of riots in Manhattan House of Detention | Defendant used profane language to judge and his own attorney. | represented | no | defendant held in contempt | |

| CASE NUMBER | CRIME TRIED | POLITICAL OR RACIAL OVERTONES | TYPE OF DISRUPTION | REPRESENTED OR PRO SE | LAWYER IN ANY WAY RESPONSIBLE FOR DISRUPTION | HELD IN CONTEMPT | CONTEMPT FOR PENALTY |
|---|---|---|---|---|---|---|---|
| B-6 | conspiracy, possession of weapons, attempted murder and robbery | no | Defendants made profane comments to judge, court personnel, district attorney, and witnesses. | represented | no | no | |
| B-7 | possession of explosives and bombs | yes | Spectators laughed, stamped their feet, cheered, made power salutes. | represented | no | no | |
| B-8 | perjury | no | Hundreds of spectators brought placards and decals and pasted them on court corridors. Use of sound trucks and organized demonstrations outside courtroom. | represented | no | no | |
| B-9 | robbery | no | Defendants refused to listen to judge's instructions. They spoke to jury while witnesses were testifying. | represented | no | no | |
| B-10 | murder and armed robbery | no | Attorneys for defendants precipitated disturbances by courtroom antics and statements to media. | represented | yes | no | |

| CASE NUMBER | CRIME TRIED | POLITICAL OR RACIAL OVERTONES | TYPE OF DISRUPTION | REPRESENTED OR PRO SE | LAWYER IN ANY WAY RESPONSIBLE FOR DISRUPTION | HELD IN CONTEMPT | PENALTY FOR CONTEMPT |
|---|---|---|---|---|---|---|---|
| B-11 | doctor prescribed drugs to addicts | no | Attorney for defendant precipitated disturbances by courtroom antics and statements. | represented | yes | no | |
| B-12 | conspiracy to destroy private property | yes | Attorney for defendant precipitated disturbance by courtroom antics and statements. | represented | yes | no | |
| B-13 | murder of 2 police officers | no | Attorney responsible for disruption. | represented | yes | attorney held in contempt for 8 specific incidents | total of 5 years |
| B-14 | burning Selective Service records | yes | Disturbances in court by defendants and spectators. | pro se | | 2 defendants | 30 days |
| B-15 | | no | Defendant addressed court in profane and obscene terms. | represented | no | defendant | |

# APPENDIX E

*Lists of Witnesses Appearing Before Committee,
Papers Prepared by Consultants, Legal Consultants and
Assistants, and Other Persons Interviewed*

# EXPERT GUESTS OF COMMITTEE

In the course of its deliberations the Committee met with a number of people who were in a position to help it in forming its conclusions. The following persons were interviewed:

*November 20, 1970*
Louis Nizer, trial lawyer, New York City
Melvin Wulf, Legal Director, American Civil Liberties Union
Richard Uviller, Professor, Columbia Law School

*January 15, 1971*
William Kunstler, defense counsel in Chicago conspiracy case
Sanford Katz, counsel for Black Panther defendants in New York

*February 19, 1971*
Thomas Foran, prosecutor in Chicago conspiracy case
Joseph Phillips, prosecutor of Black Panther defendants in New York

*February 20, 1972*
Judge Jon O. Newman, United States District Judge, District of Connecticut
   (former U.S. Attorney for Connecticut)

*March 25, 1971*
Sheila Rush Okpaku, Associate Director, Community Law Offices, currently
   Associate Professor, Hofstra Law School
Haywood Burns, National Director, National Conference of Black Lawyers
Ray Brown, New Jersey attorney who has represented the Black Panthers

*May 10, 1971*
Justice Arthur Markewich, Appellate Division, First Department
Judge Jack B. Weinstein, United States District Judge, Eastern District of
   New York

*September 27, 1971*
Judge George H. Boldt, Chief United States District Judge, Western District
   of Washington (trial judge in Tacoma conspiracy case)

*October 7, 1971*
George Vradenburg, defense counsel for Tacoma conspiracy case defendants
Michael Lerner, defendant in Tacoma conspiracy case

PAPERS PREPARED BY CONSULTANTS

"The Morality of Disruption," by Graham Hughes, Professor of Law, New York University School of Law

"Racism in American Courts: Cause for Black Disruption or Despair?" by Derrick A. Bell, Jr., Professor of Law, Harvard Law School

"The Politics of Courtroom Conduct," by Jerome H. Skolnick, Professor of Criminology, University of California (Berkeley)

"Courtroom Misconduct by Prosecutors and Trial Judges," by Albert W. Alschuler, Professor of Law, Texas Law School

OTHER LEGAL CONSULTANTS

Monroe H. Freedman, Dean, Hofstra Law School; formerly Professor of Law, George Washington University Law School

Daniel Rezneck, Arnold and Porter; former Assistant U.S. Attorney

LEGAL RESEARCH ASSISTANTS

Margaret Bancroft
William Birtles
Anthony S. Kaufman
Ralph K. Nickerson
Henry Rossbacher
Patricia S. Skigen

STUDENT RESEARCH ASSISTANTS

Peter Bienstock
Sharyn Campbell
Constance Cardin
Sandra Mitchell Caron
Jane Fankhanel
Nancy Jacoby
Randolph Jonakait
Eric Lieberman
Joan Lowy
Jack Novick
Nicholas Waranoff

STUDENT TECHNICAL ASSISTANTS

Howard Goldstein
Shelly Korman
Charles Newman
Leroy Richie
Terry Rose
Elizabeth Schneider

OTHER PERSONS INTERVIEWED

| | |
|---|---|
| Kenneth Conboy | Assistant District Attorney, N.Y. County |
| Professor Alan Dershowitz | Harvard Law School |
| Professor Thomas I. Emerson | Yale Law School |
| Chief Louis A. Hulnick | New York Criminal Court |
| John Jennings | Rand Corporation |
| Frank Juliano | Deputy U.S. Marshal |
| Professor Delmar Karlen | Institute for Judicial Administration, New York University Law School |
| Reise S. Kash | Marshals Service, Department of Justice |
| Professor Arthur Kinoy | Rutgers Law School |
| James A. McCafferty | Administrative Office, U.S. Courts |
| Bernard Newman | Administrator, New York Criminal Court |
| Richard T. Penn, Jr. | National Bureau of Standards |
| O. John Rogge | Former Federal Prosecutor |
| Dean Albert M. Sacks | Harvard Law School |
| Professor Herman Schwartz | State University of N.Y. at Buffalo Law School |
| Whitney North Seymour, Sr. | Former President, American Bar Association |
| Associate Dean David L. Shapiro | Harvard Law School |
| Lawrence Siegel | Courthouse Reorganization Project |
| Anson Smith | Boston *Globe* |
| Jeffrey Tand | Court Specialist, Law Enforcement Assistance Administration |
| Michael Wong | Courthouse Reorganization Project, Appellate Division, 1st Department |
| Professor Peter Zimroth | New York University Law School |

# APPENDIX F

*American College of Trial Lawyers Report and*
*Recommendations on Disruption of the Judicial Process*

# PRINCIPLES AS TO DISRUPTION OF THE JUDICIAL PROCESS OF THE AMERICAN COLLEGE OF TRIAL LAWYERS

## I. EQUAL JUSTICE FOR ALL

Courts exist to administer equal justice to the rich and the poor, the good and the bad, the strong and the weak, the native born and the foreign born of every race, color, nationality and religion, to men and women of every shade of political belief, to those who enjoy popular favor and to those who are popularly despised, feared, or hated.

All persons who come before the courts are entitled to vigorous and zealous representation within the law by qualified counsel—representation which is sanctioned, encouraged and protected by the judiciary and the organized bar.

## II. COURTROOM ATMOSPHERE AND THE
### RIGHT TO A FAIR TRIAL

In administering justice, courts are required to perform two difficult tasks: discovering where the truth lies between conflicting versions of the facts, and applying to the facts so found the relevant legal principles. These tasks are as demanding and delicate as a surgical operation, and, like such an operation, they cannot be performed in an atmosphere of bedlam.

Unless order is maintained in the courtroom and disruption prevented, reason cannot prevail and constitutional rights to liberty, freedom and equality under law cannot be protected. The dignity, decorum and courtesy which have traditionally characterized the courts of civilized nations are not empty formalities. They are essential to an atmosphere in which justice can be done.

The right to a fair trial is the most basic of all constitutional guarantees, underlying and conditioning all other legal rights, constitutional or otherwise.

## III. THE LAWYER'S OBLIGATIONS

A lawyer has these professional obligations:
   (a) to represent every client courageously, vigorously, diligently and with all the skill and knowledge he possesses;

(b) to do so according to law and the standards of professional conduct as defined in codes and canons of the legal profession;

(c) to conduct himself in such a way as to avoid disorder or disruption in the courtroom;

(d) to advise any client appearing in a courtroom of the kind of behavior expected and required of him there, and to prevent him, so far as lies within the lawyer's power, from creating disorder or disruption in the courtroom.

A lawyer is not relieved of these obligations by any shortcomings on the part of the judge, nor is he relieved of them by the legal, moral, political, social or ideological merits of the cause of any client.

## IV. THE JUDGE'S OBLIGATIONS

A judge has these professional obligations:

(a) to consider objectively any challenge of his right to preside; to deny it courageously if the challenge is unfounded; to allow it if it is well founded; and to disqualify himself without challenge if he is biased or plausibly may be suspected of bias;

(b) to recognize the obligation of every lawyer to represent his clients courageously and vigorously, and to treat every lawyer with the courtesy and respect due one performing an essential role in the trial process;

(c) to avoid becoming personally involved in any case before him, to preside firmly and impartially, and to conduct himself and the trial in such a way as to prevent, if possible, disorder or disruption in the courtroom.

He is not relieved of these obligations by any shortcomings on the part of any lawyer, or by the legal, moral, political, social or ideological deficiencies of the cause of any litigant.

## V. CONTEMPT POWER

The power of a judge to punish contempt committed in his presence is not designed to protect his own dignity or person, but to protect the rights of litigants and the public by ensuring that the administration of justice shall not be thwarted or obstructed.

A trial judge has power to punish summarily for contempt any lawyer who in his presence willfully contributes to disorder or disruption in the courtroom. The judge may exercise this power without a jury, without making a new record and without referring the matter to another judge. He may do so at any stage of the proceedings without waiting for their conclusion, and he may do so as many times as appears necessary to ensure fair and orderly proceedings.

## VI. SANCTIONS

In lieu of imposing a traditional fine or imprisonment (for not more than six months), a judge, if permitted by law, may impose any of the following lesser sanctions, which are necessarily implicit in the power to impose imprisonment:

    (a) Termination of the lawyer's right to continue as counsel in the case in which the contempt was committed;

    (b) Suspension for 6 months or less of his right to appear in any case in the particular court where the contempt was committed; or

    (c) Suspension for 6 months or less of his right to appear in any court of the jurisdiction where the contempt was committed.

The judge may stay the execution of any contempt sentence pending appeal.

## VII. CONTINUANCE OR MISTRIAL

In the event any contempt sentence prevents a lawyer from continuing to represent his clients in the case, the judge may grant such continuance as may be necessary to secure new counsel, or, if that is not practicable, may declare a mistrial.

## VIII. WARNING

In any case where there is reason to anticipate disorder or disruption, the judge should make known in open court the type of behavior required in his courtroom and the nature and extent of his contempt powers. He should do so at the outset of the proceeding if possible, and should repeat the warning as often as he deems necessary.

## IX. APPELLATE REVIEW

The rules of appellate procedure should provide that an appeal from any contempt sentence imposed on a lawyer for courtroom disorder or disruption shall receive a preference over all other pending appeals; that the reviewing court may dispense with written briefs at its discretion, may specify the record it requires, and may order the trial court and the court reporter to expedite its preparation; that it shall possess all powers it has in other cases, including the power to consider the judge's conduct of the case in relation to the lawyer's behavior, to modify any sentence imposed, to suspend its execution pending final determination of the appeal and to remand the proceeding for a new trial of the contempt on some or all issues before the original or another judge.

## X. ADMISSION PRO HAC VICE

A judge to whom an application is made on behalf of a lawyer not licensed to practice in his court for permission to appear in a particular case may deny such application if it is established that the lawyer has willfully engaged in disorderly or disruptive tactics in any other court. He may grant permission conditioned on proper behavior, and in any event:

(a)  shall advise the lawyer of the kind of behavior expected of him;
(b)  may require him to promise proper conduct;
(c)  may require him to disclose all courts in which he is authorized to practice; and
(d)  may require local counsel to be appointed as well, with responsibility to be prepared to step in and assume control of the client's case if primary counsel is removed.

## XI. DISCIPLINARY PROCEEDINGS

Court rules should provide that the trial judge and the appellate court, respectively, shall without delay certify the record and result of any contempt proceeding for courtroom disorder or disruption involving any lawyer to the body having authority to disbar, suspend or impose other disciplinary sanctions on him in any state where he has been admitted to the bar.

Disciplinary proceedings involving disruptive tactics should receive a preference over all other disciplinary proceedings, and should be commenced and concluded as expeditiously as possible.

Rules of appellate procedure should provide that if any appellate court reviewing a contempt sentence imposed on a lawyer for disruptive conduct believes that the trial judge was himself guilty of serious courtroom misconduct beyond the appellate court's own power to correct, it shall certify that fact, along with its own opinion and the trial record, to any official body having authority to impose disciplinary sanctions against the judge or to express censure or admonition with respect to his conduct.

Disciplinary proceedings against judges for courtroom misconduct should receive a preference over all other disciplinary proceedings against judges, and should be commenced and concluded as expeditiously as possible.

## XII. LITIGANTS AND SPECTATORS—OTHER
### TYPES OF CONTEMPT

Nothing in the foregoing is intended to curtail a judge's power and duty to deal with disorderly litigants in one of the manners specified in *Illinois* v.

*Allen,* 90 S. Ct. 1057 (1970); or with disorderly spectators by traditional contempt powers; or with other contempts (including those committed by lawyers) which do not involve courtroom disruption or disorder.

COMMITTEE ON DISRUPTION
OF THE JUDICIAL PROCESS
Hicks Epton
Lewis, F. Powell, Jr., *ex officio*
C. Brewster Rhoads
Simon H. Rifkind
Whitney North Seymour, *chairman*
Edward Bennett Williams
Delmar Karlen, *Reporter*

*July 1970*

# APPENDIX G

*American Bar Association Project on Standards
for Criminal Justice, Standards Relating to
the Judge's Role in Dealing with Trial Disruptions*

## PART A. GENERAL PRINCIPLES

A.1 General responsibility of the trial judge.

In the administration of criminal justice, the trial judge has the responsibility for safeguarding both the rights of the accused and the interests of the public. The adversary nature of the proceedings does not relieve the trial judge of the obligation of raising on his own initiative, at all appropriate times and in an appropriate manner, matters which may significantly affect a just determination of the trial.

A.2 The judge's responsibility to maintain order.

The purpose of a criminal trial is to determine whether or not the defendant is guilty of the offense charged. No one has the right to disrupt or prevent the orderly course and completion of the trial. The trial judge has the obligation to use his judicial power to prevent distractions from and disruptions of the trial.

A.3 Judge's use of his powers to maintain order.

If the judge determines to impose sanctions for misconduct affecting the trial, he should ordinarily impose the least severe sanction appropriate to correct the abuse and to deter repetition. In weighing the severity of a possible sanction for disruptive courtroom conduct to be applied during the trial, the judge should consider the risk of further disruption, delay or prejudice that might result from the character of the sanction or the time of its imposition.

A.4 Special rules for order in the courtroom.

The trial judge, either before a criminal trial or at its beginning, should prescribe and make known the ground rules relating to conduct which the parties, the prosecutor, the defense counsel, the witnesses, and others will be expected to follow in the courtroom, and which are not set forth in the code of criminal procedure or in the published rules of court.

## PART B. CONDUCT OF THE JUDGE

B.1 Judge's responsibility for self-restraint.

The trial judge should be the exemplar of dignity and impartiality. He should exercise restraint over his conduct and utterances. He should suppress his personal predilections, and control his temper and emotions. He should not permit any person in the courtroom to embroil him in conflict, and he should otherwise avoid conduct on his part which tends to demean the proceedings or to undermine his authority in the courtroom. When it becomes necessary during the trial for him to comment upon the conduct of witnesses, spectators, counsel, or others, or upon the testimony, he should do so in a firm, dignified and restrained manner, avoiding repartee, limiting his comments and rulings to what is reasonably required for the orderly progress of the trial, and refraining from unnecessary disparagement of persons or issues.

## PART C. CONDUCT OF THE DEFENDANT

C.1 The disruptive defendant.
A defendant may be removed from the courtroom during his trial when his conduct is so disruptive that the trial cannot proceed in an orderly manner. Removal is preferable to gagging or shackling the disruptive defendant. If removed, the defendant should be required to be present in the court building while the trial is in progress, be given the opportunity of learning of the trial proceedings through his counsel at reasonable intervals, and be given a continuing opportunity to return to the courtroom during the trial upon his assurance of good behavior. The removed defendant should be summoned to the courtroom at appropriate intervals, with the offer to permit him to remain repeated in open court each time.

C.2 The defendant's election to represent himself at trial.
A defendant should be permitted at his election to proceed in the trial of his case without the assistance of counsel only after the court makes thorough inquiry and is satisfied that he
(a) possesses the intelligence and capacity to appreciate the consequences of his decision; and
(b) comprehends the nature of the charges and proceedings, the range of permissible punishments, and any additional facts essential to a broad understanding of the case.

C.3 Standby counsel for defendant representing himself.
When a defendant has been permitted to proceed pro se, the court should consider the appointment of standby counsel to assist the defendant when called upon and to call the court's attention to matters favorable to the accused upon which the court should rule on its own motion. Standby counsel should always be appointed in cases expected to be long or complicated or in which there are multiple defendants.

C.4 Misconduct of defendant representing himself.
If a defendant appearing pro se engages in conduct which is so disruptive that the trial cannot proceed in an orderly manner, the court should, after appropriate warnings, revoke permission for the defendant to proceed pro se and require representation by counsel. If standby counsel has pre-

viously been appointed, he should be asked to represent the defendant. In any event, the trial should be recessed only long enough for counsel to prepare himself to go forward.

## PART D. CONDUCT OF ATTORNEYS

D.1  Deterring and correcting misconduct of attorneys.

The trial judge should require attorneys to respect their obligations as officers of the court. When an attorney causes a significant disruption in a criminal proceeding, the trial judge, having particular regard to the provisions of section A.3, should correct the abuse and, if necessary, discipline the attorney, using such powers as are available to him, including one or more of the following:

(a)  censure or reprimand;

(b)  citation or punishment for contempt;

(c)  removal from the courtroom;

(d)  suspension for a limited time of the right to practice in the court where the misconduct occurred;

(e)  informing the appropriate disciplinary bodies in every jurisdiction where the attorney is admitted to practice of the nature of the attorney's misconduct and of any sanction imposed.

D.2  Attorneys from other jurisdictions.

If any attorney who is not admitted to practice in the jurisdiction of the court petitions for permission to represent a defendant, the trial judge may

(a)  deny such permission if the attorney has been held in contempt of court or otherwise formally disciplined for courtroom misconduct, or if it appears by reliable information that he has engaged in courtroom misconduct sufficient to warrant disciplinary action;

(b)  grant such permission on condition that

(i)  the petitioning attorney associate with him as co-counsel a local attorney admitted to practice in the jurisdiction,

(ii)  the local attorney will assume full responsibility for the defense if the petitioning attorney becomes unable or unwilling to perform his duties, and

(iii)  the defendant consents to the foregoing conditions.

## PART E. CONDUCT OF SPECTATORS AND OTHERS

E.1  Misconduct by spectators and others.

The right of the defendant to a public trial does not give particular members of the general public or of the news media a right to enter the courtroom or to remain there. Any person who engages in conduct which disturbs the orderly process of the trial may be admonished or excluded, and, if his conduct is intentional, may be punished for contempt. Any person whose conduct tends to menace a defendant, an attorney, a witness, a juror, a court officer, or the judge in a criminal proceeding may be removed from the courtroom.

E.2  Arrangements for the news media.
Although the news media may observe the trial of a criminal case in order that information be obtained for circulation to the general public, the trial judge should, nevertheless, require that the conduct of their representatives not jeopardize the order and decorum of the courtroom. He should make reasonable arrangements to accommodate them consistent with the opportunity of other members of the public to attend the trial.

## PART F.  USE OF THE CONTEMPT POWER

F.1  Inherent power of the court.
The court has inherent power to punish any contempt in order to protect the rights of the defendant and the interests of the public by assuring that the administration of criminal justice shall not be thwarted. The trial judge has the power to cite and, if necessary, punish summarily anyone who, in his presence in open court, willfully obstructs the course of criminal proceedings.

F.2  Admonition and warning.
No sanction other than censure should be imposed by the trial judge unless
(a)  it is clear from the identity of the offender and the character of his acts that disruptive conduct was willfully contemptuous, or
(b)  the conduct warranting the sanction was preceded by a clear warning that the conduct is impermissible and that specified sanctions may be imposed for its repetition.

F.3  Notice of intent to use contempt power; postponement of adjudication.
(a)  The trial judge should, as soon as practicable after he is satisfied that courtroom misconduct requires contempt proceedings, inform the alleged offender of his intention to institute such proceedings.
(b)  The trial judge should consider the advisability of deferring adjudication of contempt for courtroom misconduct of a defendant, an attorney or a witness until after the trial, and should defer such a proceeding unless prompt punishment is imperative.

F.4  Notice of charges and opportunity to be heard.
Before imposing any punishment for criminal contempt, the judge should give the offender notice of the charges and at least a summary opportunity to adduce evidence or argument relevant to guilt or punishment.

F.5  Referral to another judge.

The judge before whom courtroom misconduct occurs may impose appropriate sanctions, including punishment for contempt, but should refer the matter to another judge if his conduct was so integrated with the contempt that he contributed to it or was otherwise involved, or his objectivity can reasonably be questioned.

ADVISORY COMMITTEE ON
THE JUDGE'S FUNCTION
Frank J. Murray, *Chairman*
Thomas J. O'Toole, *Reporter*
Steven Duke, *Associate Reporter*

*May 1971*

# APPENDIX H

*New York State Appellate Division,*
*First and Second Departments,*
*Special Rules Concerning Court Decorum*

On March 24, 1971, the Appellate Division, First and Second Departments, adopted special rules setting forth standards of courtroom behavior for lawyers and judges; guidelines for judicial exercise of contempt and other powers; and provisions for discipline of attorneys who participate in disruptive trial conduct. These rules, which were drafted by a committee chaired by Herbert Brownell, former Attorney General of the United States, are set forth below:

# SPECIAL RULES CONCERNING COURT DECORUM

SEC. 609.1 OBLIGATION OF ATTORNEYS AND JUDGES

(a) *Application of Rules*

These Rules shall apply to all actions and proceedings, civil and criminal, in courts subject to the jurisdiction of the Appellate Division of the Supreme Court in the First Judicial Department. They are intended to supplement, but not to supersede, the Code of Professional Responsibility and the Canons of Judicial Ethics, as adopted by the New York State Bar Association. In the event of any conflict between the provisions of these Rules and that Code or those Canons, the Code and the Canons shall prevail.

(b) *Importance of Decorum in Court*

The courtroom, as the place where justice is dispensed, must at all times satisfy the appearance as well as the reality of fairness and equal treatment. Dignity, order and decorum are indispensable to the proper administration of justice. Disruptive conduct by any person while the court is in session is forbidden.

(c) *Disruptive Conduct Defined*

Disruptive conduct is any intentional conduct by any person in the courtroom that substantially interferes with the dignity, order and decorum of judicial proceedings.

(d) *Obligations of the Attorney*

(1) The attorney is both an officer of the court and an advocate. It is his professional obligation to conduct his case courageously, vigorously, and with all the skill and knowledge he possesses. It is also his obligation to uphold the honor and maintain the dignity of the profession. He must avoid disorder or disruption in the courtroom, and he must maintain a respectful attitude to-

ward the court. In all respects the attorney is bound, in court and out, by the provisions of the Code of Professional Responsibility.

(2) The attorney shall use his best efforts to dissuade his client and witnesses from causing disorder or disruption in the courtroom.

(3) The attorney shall treat each witness with courtesy and respect.

(4) No attorney shall argue in support of or against an objection without permission from the court; nor shall any attorney argue with respect to a ruling of the court on an objection without such permission.

(5) The attorney has neither the right nor duty to execute any directive of a client which is not consistent with professional standards of conduct. Nor may he advise another to do any act or to engage in any conduct which is in any manner contrary to these Rules.

(6) Once a client has employed an attorney who has entered an appearance, the attorney shall not withdraw or abandon the case without (i) justifiable cause, (ii) reasonable notice to the client, and (iii) permission of the court.

(7) The attorney is not relieved of these obligations by what he may regard as a deficiency in the conduct or ruling of a judge or in the system of justice; nor is he relieved of these obligations by what he believes to be the moral, political, social, or ideological merits of the cause of any client.

(e) *Obligations of the Judge*

(1) In the administration of justice, the judge shall safeguard the rights of the parties and the interests of the public. The judge at all times shall be dignified, courteous, and considerate of the parties, attorneys, jurors, and witnesses. In the performance of his duties and in the maintenance of proper court decorum the judge is in all respects bound by the Canons of Judicial Ethics.

(2) The judge shall use his judicial power to prevent disruptions of the trial.

(3) A judge before whom a case is moved for trial shall preside at such trial unless he is satisfied, upon challenge, or sua sponte, that he is unable to serve with complete impartiality, in fact or appearance, with regard to the matter, or parties in question.

(4) Where the judge deems it appropriate in order to preserve or enhance the dignity, order and decorum of the proceedings, he shall prescribe and make known the rules relating to conduct which the parties, attorneys, witnesses and others will be expected to follow in the courtroom.

(5) The judge should be the exemplar of dignity and impartiality. He shall suppress his personal predilections, control his temper and emotions, and otherwise avoid conduct on his part which tends to demean the proceedings or to undermine his authority in the courtroom. When it becomes necessary during trial for him to comment upon the conduct of witnesses, spectators, counsel, or others, or upon the testimony, he shall do so in a firm and polite manner, limiting his comments and rulings to what is reasonably required for the orderly progress of the trial, and refraining from unnecessary disparagement of persons or issues.

(6) The judge is not relieved of these obligations by what he may regard

as a deficiency in the conduct of any attorney who appears before him; nor is he relieved of these obligations by what he believes to be the moral, political, social, or ideological deficiencies of the cause of any party.

## SEC. 609.2 JUDICIAL EXERCISE OF CONTEMPT POWER

(a) *Exercise of the Summary Contempt Power*

(1) The power of the court to punish summarily contempt committed in its immediate view and presence shall be exercised only in exceptional and necessitous circumstances, as follows:

(i) Where the offending conduct either

(A) disrupts or threatens to disrupt proceedings actually in progress; or

(B) destroys or undermines or tends seriously to destroy or undermine the dignity and authority of the court in a manner and to the extent that it appears unlikely that the court will be able to continue to conduct its normal business in an appropriate way; and

(ii) The court reasonably believes that a prompt summary adjudication of contempt may aid in maintaining or restoring and maintaining proper order and decorum.

(2) Wherever practical punishment should be determined and imposed at the time of the adjudication of contempt. However, where the court deems it advisable the determination and imposition of punishment may be deferred following a prompt summary adjudication of contempt which satisfies the necessity for immediate judicial corrective or disciplinary action.

(3) Before summary adjudication of contempt the accused shall be given a reasonable opportunity to make a statement in his defense or in extenuation of his conduct.

(b) *Exercise of the Contempt Power After Hearing*

In all other cases, notwithstanding the occurrence of the contumacious conduct in the view and presence of the sitting court, the contempt shall be adjudicated at a plenary hearing with due process of law including notice, written charges, assistance of counsel, compulsory process for production of evidence and an opportunity of the accused to confront witnesses against him.

(c) *Judicial Warning of Possible Contempts*

Except in the case of the most flagrant and offensive misbehavior which in the court's discretion requires an immediate adjudication of contempt to preserve order and decorum, the court should warn and admonish the person engaged in alleged contumacious conduct that his conduct is deemed contumacious and give the person an opportunity to desist before adjudicating him in contempt. Where a person so warned desists from further offensive conduct, there is ordinarily no occasion for an adjudication of contempt. Where a person is summarily adjudicated in contempt and punishment deferred and such person desists from further offensive conduct, the court should consider carefully whether there is any need for punishment for the adjudicated contempt.

(d) *Disqualification of Judge*

The judge before whom the alleged contumacious conduct occurred is disqualified from presiding at the plenary hearing or trial (as distinguished from summary action) except with the defendant's consent:

(1) If the allegedly contumacious conduct consists primarily of personal disrespect to or vituperative criticism of the judge; or

(2) If the judge's recollection of, or testimony concerning the conduct allegedly constituting contempt is necessary for an adjudication; or

(3) If the judge concludes that in view of his recollection of the events he would be unable to make his decision solely on the basis of the evidence at the hearing.

## SEC. 609.3 CONDUCT OF CRIMINAL TRIAL THREATENED BY DISRUPTIVE CONDUCT

(a) *Removal of Disruptive Defendant*

(1) If a defendant engages in disruptive conduct by word or action in the courtroom in the course of his trial, the trial judge may order the defendant to be removed from the courtroom and placed in custody, and the trial judge may proceed with the trial in the absence of the defendant.

(2) The trial judge may not exclude the defendant except after warning that further disruptive conduct will lead to removal of the defendant from the courtroom.

(3) The defendant shall be returned to the courtroom immediately upon a determination by the court that the defendant is not likely to engage in further disruptive conduct.

(b) *Communication between Defendant and Courtroom*

If the defendant is removed from the courtroom under the provisions of Rule 609.3(a)(1), the trial judge shall make reasonable efforts to establish methods of communication linking the defendant with the courtroom while his trial is in progress. For such defendant the judge may provide methods of communication in any way suitable to the physical facilities of the courthouse and consonant with the goal of providing adequate communication to the courtroom and to defense counsel.

(c) *Restraint of Defendant*

(1) If a defendant engages in disruptive conduct in the course of the trial, and the trial judge determines not to take action under subdivision (a) of this section, the trial judge may order the defendant to be physically restrained in the courtroom while his trial continues.

(2) The trial judge shall not apply the restraints authorized in the preceding subdivision unless he has warned the defendant, following disruptive conduct by the defendant, that further misconduct will lead to the physical restraint of the defendant in the courtroom.

(3) The physical restraint of the defendant shall be terminated immediately upon a determination by the court that the defendant is not likely to engage in further disruptive conduct.

## SEC. 609.4 DISCIPLINE OF ATTORNEYS

(a) *Disciplinary Jurisdiction Over Attorneys, Admitted pro hac vice*

An attorney from another state, territory, district, or foreign country admitted pro hac vice to participate in the trial or argument of a particular cause in any court in this Judicial Department shall be subject to the disciplinary jurisdiction of this court.

Where an attorney admitted pro hac vice is guilty of misconduct in the argument or trial of a particular cause in any court in this Judicial Department, this court may discipline the attorney under Section 90 (2) of the Judiciary Law.

(b) *Discipline of Attorneys for Disruptive Conduct in Courts*
*of Foreign Jurisdiction*

(1) This Court may discipline in accordance with this Rule, an attorney who is admitted to practice or who has an office in this Judicial Department and who has been disciplined in another state, territory, or district because of disruptive conduct.

(2) Upon receipt from the foreign jurisdiction of a certified or exemplified copy of the order imposing such discipline and of the record of the proceedings upon which such order was based, this court, directly or by the Committee on Grievances of the Association of the Bar of the City of New York, shall give written notice to such attorney pursuant to Section 90(6) of the Judiciary Law, according him the opportunity within twenty days of the giving of such notice, to file a verified statement setting forth any defense to discipline enumerated under paragraph (3), below, and a written demand for a hearing at which consideration shall be given to any and all defenses enumerated in said paragraph (3) below. Such notice shall further advise the attorney that in default of such filing by him, this court will impose such discipline or take such disciplinary action as it deems appropriate.

(3) This court, in default of the attorney's filing a verified statement and demand as provided for in paragraph (b) (2) of this section, may discipline such attorney unless an examination of the entire record before this court, including the record of the foreign jurisdiction and such other evidence as this court in its discretion may receive, discloses (i) that the procedure in the foreign jurisdiction was so lacking in notice or opportunity to be heard as to constitute a deprivation of due process; or (ii) that there was such an infirmity of proof establishing the disruptive conduct as to give rise to the clear conviction that this court could not, consistent with its duties, accept as final the finding of the court in the foreign jurisdiction as to the attorney's disruptive conduct; or (iii) that the imposition of discipline by this court would be unjust.

(c) *Discipline of Attorneys Convicted of Misdemeanor of Criminal Contempt in any Court in any Jurisdiction*

(1) Where an attorney, who is admitted to practice or has an office in this Judicial Department, has been convicted of the misdemeanor of criminal contempt in a court of record of any state, territory, or district, including this State, this court may discipline such attorney so convicted, upon notice in accordance with this Rule.

(2) Upon receipt of a certified or exemplified copy of the judgment of conviction of the misdemeanor of criminal contempt and of the record of the proceedings upon which such conviction was based, this court, directly or by the Committee on Grievances of the Association of the Bar of the City of New York, shall give written notice to such attorney pursuant to Section 90(6) of the Judiciary Law according him the opportunity within twenty days of the giving of such notice to file with this court a verified statement setting forth any defense to discipline enumerated under paragraph (3), below, and to file a written demand for a hearing. At that hearing consideration shall be given to any and all defenses enumerated in paragraph (3) below. Such notice shall further advise the attorney that in default of such filing by him, the court will take such disciplinary action as it deems appropriate.

(3) This court, in default of the attorney's filing a verified statement and demand as provided for in paragraph (b)(2) of this section, may suspend such attorney for such period as it sees fit unless an examination of the entire record before it, and such other evidence as this court in its discretion may receive, discloses (i) that the procedure leading to the conviction of the misdemeanor of criminal contempt was so lacking in notice or opportunity to be heard as to constitute a deprivation of due process; or (ii) that there was such an infirmity of proof establishing the conviction that this court could not, consistent with its duties, accept as final the conclusion on that subject; or (iii) that the imposition of suspension by this court would be unjust.

(d) *Opportunity for Hearing*

Where an attorney shall have duly filed both his verified statement setting forth any defense (as described in the preceding Rules) to the imposition of discipline by this court and his written demand for a hearing with respect to such defense, no discipline, by way of suspension or otherwise, shall be imposed without affording the attorney an opportunity to have a hearing.

(e) *Preference for Appeals from Criminal Contempt Convictions*

Any appeal by an attorney of his conviction for the misdemeanor of criminal contempt which is pending in any court in this Judicial Department, shall be granted a preference by the court.

(f) *Other Sanctions*

The imposition of a suspension or other discipline pursuant to these rules shall not preclude the imposition of any further or additional sanctions prescribed or authorized by law.

# APPENDIX I

*State Laws and Court Rules Dealing with*
*Discipline of Lawyers for Courtroom Misbehavior*

## ALABAMA
**Ala. Code title 46, §§21 *et seq.* (1958)**
The Board of Commissioners of the state bar has the power, subject to the approval of the Supreme Court, to establish rules governing the procedure in cases of alleged misconduct and administer discipline deemed warranted.

## ALASKA
**Alaska Stat. title 8, §§08.08.010 *et seq.* (1968)**
The Board of Governors of the state bar has the power to establish and enforce rules of professional conduct for bar members which shall conform to but need not be limited to "the standards of the ABA Code of Professional Responsibility subject to review by the Supreme Court" (§08.08.110, Supp. 1971).

## ARIZONA
**Arizona Rev. Stat. Ann. §§32–201 *et seq.* (1956)**
The Board of Governors of the state bar may formulate and enforce rules of professional conduct, subject always to the approval of the Supreme Court (§32–237 (2) Supp. 1970).

## ARKANSAS
**Arkansas Stat. Ann. §§25–101 *et seq.* (1962)**
The grounds for disbarment are stated in the statute and includes "any ungentlemanly conduct in the practice of his profession" (§25–401). Trial of offenses is held and decided by the county court with a jury unless waived. The accused may prosecute an appeal to the Supreme Court (§25–414).

## CALIFORNIA
**California Bus. & Prof. Code §§6000 *et seq.* (West 1962)**
The Board of Governors of the state bar may formulate and enforce rules of professional conduct subject to the approval of the Supreme Court (§6076). The Board may reprimand or recommend suspension to the Supreme Court (three year maximum) for any attorney who violates those rules (§6077). In addition, an attorney may be disbarred or suspended for any cause listed in the statutes (§6100).

## COLORADO
**Colorado Rev. Stat. Ann. §§12–1–1 *et seq.* (1963)**
The Supreme Court, in open court, may strike from the rolls the name of any attorney for "malconduct in his office" (§12–1–8).

## CONNECTICUT
**Connecticut General Statute Ann. §§51–80 *et seq.* (1958)**
Attorneys admitted by the Superior Court are subject to all rules and orders of the courts before which they practice, and those courts may fine attorneys for violation of the rules and may suspend or discipline for just cause (§51–84).

## DELAWARE
**Del. Code Ann. title 10, §1950 (1953)**
Attorneys admitted to practice shall behave "justly and faithfully" and for misconduct are subject to "such disciplinary measures as the Supreme Court, in its discretion may determine" (§1905).

## DISTRICT OF COLUMBIA
**D.C. Code Ann. §§2101 *et seq.* (Supp. IV, 1965)**
The U.S. District Court for D.C. may censure, suspend, or expel a member of the bar for crime, fraud, deceit, malpractice, professional misconduct, or "conduct prejudicial to the administration of justice" (§11–2102).

**D.C. Code Ann. §§2501 *et seq.* (Supp. IV, 1971)**
Effective April 1, 1972, the Court of Appeals of D.C. may censure, suspend, or expel a member of the bar for causes stated, which include "professional misconduct or conduct prejudicial to the administration of justice" (§11–2505).

## FLORIDA
**Florida Statute Ann. §§454.01 *et seq.* (1965)**
"All attorneys are deemed officers of the court for the administration of justice and are amenable to the rules and discipline of the court in all matters of order or procedure not in conflict with the constitution or laws of this state" (§454.11).

## GEORGIA
**Ga. Code Ann. §§9–101 *et seq.* (Supp. 1970)**
The Supreme Court is given the power, upon recommendation of the Georgia Bar Association, to adopt rules regarding the regulation of attorneys within the state (§§9–702). Disbarment is governed by statute (§9–501). The proceedings are conducted by a county Superior Court (§9–501) and may be begun by the court on its own motion or upon the motion of an individual (§§9–505). The proceedings are prosecuted by the state's attorney in Superior Court before a jury (§§9–507 *et seq.*).

## HAWAII
**Hawaii Rev. Stat. §§605–1 *et seq.* (1968)**
The Supreme Court has the sole power to revoke or suspend an attorney's license for "malpractice, fraud, deceit or other gross misconduct" (§605–1). The practitioners are summarily amenable to courts of record and may be

fined or imprisoned for "satisfactory cause upon the complaint of any party aggrieved by their malpractice . . . or for any fraud, deceit or other gross misconduct" (§605–9).

## IDAHO
**Idaho Code Ann. §§3–101 et seq. (1947)**
The duties of an attorney include among others, the maintenance of "respect due to the courts of justice and judicial officers" (§3–201 (2)). The Supreme Court and District Court may remove, suspend, or reprimand an attorney on complaint of the state Board of Governors on grounds specified by statute, which includes "willful disobedience or violation of an order of the court . . . and any violation of the oath taken by him or his duties as such attorney . . ." (§§3–301).

## ILLINOIS
**Ill. Ann. Stat. Ch. 13, §§1 et seq. (Smith-Hard Supp. 1963)**
The Supreme Court is given the power to strike the name of any attorney for malconduct in office (§6) and any circuit or Superior Court may suspend for like cause subject to the right of appeal to the supreme court (§6).

## INDIANA
**Ind. Ann. Stat. §§4–7401 et seq. (1968)**
The Supreme Court has exclusive jurisdiction to prescribe rules for admission and conduct (§4–7405).

## IOWA
**Iowa Code Ann. §§610.1 et seq. (150)**
The duties of an attorney include: "To maintain the respect due to the courts of justice and judicial officers" (§610.14). The Supreme Court will appoint three district court judges to hear and decide complaints against an attorney (§610.30) and appeal lies to the Supreme Court if removal or suspension is ordered (§610.37).

## KANSAS
**Kansas Statute Ann. §§7–101 et seq. (Supp. 1970)**
The Supreme Court has authority to make rules concerning disbarment and discipline (§7–103). The grounds for disciplinary action include: "(1) For willful disobedience of an order of court . . . ; (2) For a willful violation of his oath; or any duty imposed upon an attorney at law . . ." (§7–111).

## KENTUCKY
**Ky. Rev. Stat. §§30.010 et seq. (1971)**
The Court of Appeals is required to adopt and promulgate rules which among other things prescribe a code of ethics and establish practice and procedure for disciplining, suspending, and disbarring attorneys (§30.170).

## LOUISIANA
**La. Rev. Stat. Ann. title 37, §§211 et seq. (1964)**
The Louisiana Constitution gives the Supreme Court "exclusive original juris-

diction of disbarment cases involving misconduct of members of the bar with the power to suspend or disbar under such rules as the court may adopt . . ." (La. Const. Art. 7, §10).

## MARYLAND
**Md. Ann. Code art. 10 §§11 *et seq.* (1968)**
When a judge has reason to believe an attorney is guilty of "professional misconduct . . . conduct prejudicial to the administration of justice, or is a subversive person . . ." he may order the bar association and/or states attorney to prosecute the charge (§12).

## MASSACHUSETTS
**Mass. Gen. Laws Ann. Ch. 221, §§37 *et seq.* (1958)**
An attorney may be removed by the supreme judicial or superior court for "deceit, malpractice or other gross misconduct." The court will appoint an attorney to prosecute the case for removal of the charged attorney (§40).

## MICHIGAN
**Mich. Comp. Laws Ann. §§600.091 *et seq.* (1968)**
The supreme court has the power to adopt rules and regulations regarding the conduct and activities of the members of the bar and the "discipline, suspension and disbarment of its members for misconduct . . ." (§600.904). The state bar has investigatory powers for "aiding in cases of discipline, suspension and disbarment . . ." (§600.907). The Supreme Court and each circuit court has jurisdiction to disbar or suspend an attorney for misconduct (§600.910).

## MINNESOTA
**Minn. Stat. Ann. §§481.01 *et seq.* (1971)**
The supreme court may remove or suspend an attorney for certain cases which include "(3) For willful disobedience of an order of court . . . (4) For a willful violation of his oath, or any duty imposed upon an attorney" (§481.15). The proceedings may be begun by the Supreme Court upon its own motion or upon accusation. The accusation will be "investigated, prosecuted, heard and determined in accordance with rules which may be made . . . by the Supreme Court" (§481.15).

## MISSISSIPPI
**Miss. Code Ann. §§8647 *et seq.* (1957)**
The duties of an attorney includes the obligation "(2) to maintain the respect due to courts of justice and judicial officers" and "(5) to abstain from all offensive personality . . ." (§8665). An attorney who is found guilty of misbehavior or willful violation of his duties shall be disbarred by any court in which he may practice (§8675). The Board of Commissioners of the state bar shall investigate and pass upon all complaints regarding the professional conduct of attorneys and may institute disciplinary proceedings in all circuit or chancery court (§8708–8711).

## MISSOURI
**Mo. Ann. Stat. §484.010 (1952)**
Charges against lawyers may be preferred by any member of the bar or a judge and proceedings shall be held in the Supreme Court, Court of Appeals, or Circuit Court (§484.200). The trial shall be by the court and if guilt is determined the court shall pronounce sentence of removal or suspension (§484.250).

## MONTANA
**Mont. Rev. Codes Ann. §§93–2001 *et seq.* (1964)**
When a complaint is filed with the Supreme Court or attorney general charging an attorney with violation of his oath or other conduct authorizing or justifying his suspension or disbarment the attorney general will investigate, and if brought to trial, will prosecute the case (§93–2016 or 2017).

## NEBRASKA
**Neb. Rev. Stat. §§7–101 *et seq.* (1970)**
The duties of an attorney includes the obligation to "(1) maintain the respect due to the courts of justice and to judicial officers (§7–105).

## NEVADA
**Nev. Rev. Stat. §§6.939 *et seq.* (1969)**
The state bar association is under the executive jurisdiction and control of the Supreme Court (§7.275). The Supreme Court may make rules for the government of the bar (§2.120).

## NEW HAMPSHIRE
**N.H. Rev. Stat. Ann. §§311.1 *et seq.* (1966)**
"The Court shall inquire in a summary manner into any charges of fraud, malpractice or contempt of court against an attorney, and upon satisfactory evidence of his guilt, shall suspend him from practice, or may remove him from office" (§311.8).

## NEW JERSEY
**N.J. Stat. Ann. §§2A:13–1 *et seq.* (1954)**
The state constitution provides that "the Supreme Court shall have jurisdiction over the admission to the practice of law and the discipline of persons admitted."

**N.J. Const. article 6, §2**
The statutory provisions regulating the practice of law contains no provisions for the discipline of attorneys.

## NEW MEXICO
**N.M. Stat. Ann. §§18–1–1 *et seq.* (1970)**
The duties of an attorney include the obligation "(2) To maintain the respect due to courts of justice and judicial officers" (§18–1–9). An attorney may be disbarred or suspended by the Supreme Court for, among other things,

"(2) Willful disobedience or violation of an order of the court . . . and any violation of the oath taken by him or his duty as such attorney" (§18–1–17).

## NEW YORK
**N.Y. Judiciary Law §90 (1968)**
The appellate division of the Supreme Court in each department is authorized to censure, suspend, or remove from office an attorney guilty of "professional misconduct" or "any conduct prejudicial to the administration of justice" (§90(2)). Prior to disciplinary action charges must be served on the attorney accused and an opportunity to defend against the charges must be afforded (§90(6)).

## NORTH CAROLINA
**N.C. Gen. Stat. §84–1 *et seq.* (1965)**
The council of the state bar has "control of the discipline, disbarment and restoration of attorneys . . . and from any order disbarring an attorney, an appeal shall be . . . to the Superior Court of the county . . ." (§84–23). Further the council shall have the power to "formulate and adopt rules of professional ethics and conduct" (§84–23).

## NORTH DAKOTA
**N.D. Cent. Code Ann. §§27–; 3–01 *et seq.* (1960)**
The duties of an attorney are specified and include the obligation to "(1) maintain the respect due to the courts of justice and judicial officers" (§27–13–01). The power to revoke or suspend certification of attorneys is vested in the supreme court (§27–14–01).

## OHIO
**Ohio Rev. Code Ann. §§4705.01 *et seq.* (Page 1953)**
The Supreme Court, Court of Appeals, or Court of Common Pleas may suspend or remove any attorney or reprimand him for "misconduct or unprofessional conduct in office involving moral turpitude" (§4705.02).

## OKLAHOMA
**Okla. Stat. Ann. title 5 *et seq.* (1966)**
The duties of an attorney includes, among others, "first to maintain, while in the presence of the courts of justice, or . . . judicial officers . . . the respect due to the said courts and judicial officers, and . . . to obey all lawful orders . . . of the court; . . . Fifth to abstain from all offensive personalities . . ." (§3). The supreme court "shall have exclusive power and authority to discipline attorneys . . . and the rules of conduct of attorneys . . . shall be as . . . prescribed by the statutes of Oklahoma and the rules of the Supreme Court" (§13).

## OREGON
**Ore. Rev. Stat. §§9.010 *et seq.* (1969)**
The duties of an attorney are specified and include the obligation to "(2) maintain the respect due the courts and judicial officers . . . (6) abstain from

all offensive personality . . ." (§9.460). The Supreme Court may disbar attorneys when, upon proceedings, it appears the attorney has committed certain specified acts which include "an act of such a nature that if applying for the bar the application would be denied" and willfully disobeying an order of the court (§9.480). The Board of Governors of the state bar may recommend disciplinary action to the Supreme Court after having investigated the charges (§9.540).

### PENNSYLVANIA
**Pa. Stat. Ann. title 17, §§1601 *et seq.* (1962)**
An attorney who "shall misbehave himself in his office" is liable to suspension, removal, or other penalties (§1661). In all cases of any proceedings, in any court, for unprofessional conduct, the attorney charged is entitled to appeal to the Supreme Court (§1663).

### RHODE ISLAND
Rhode Island does not statutorily regulate the discipline of attorneys.

### SOUTH CAROLINA
**S.C. Code Ann. §§56–96 *et seq.* (1962)**
The Supreme Court may appoint committees to investigate suspected violation of the rules, hear all cases involving disciplinary matters, and make recommendations to the Court (§56–98).

### SOUTH DAKOTA
**S.D. Comp. Laws Ann. §§16–19–1 *et seq.* (1969)**
The Supreme Court has the sole power to disbar or suspend an attorney (§16–19–1). Disciplinary proceedings may be instituted by the court, attorney general, grievance committee of the state bar, or an individual (§16–19–5).

### TENNESSEE
**Tenn. Code Ann. §§29–101 *et seq.* (1955)**
An attorney may be disbarred or suspended if he is "guilty of any unprofessional conduct" (§29–308). Proceedings may be instituted in any circuit, chancery, or criminal court by the court, bar association, or individual aggrieved (§29–309).

### TEXAS
**Tex. Rev. Civ. Stat. Ann. article 304 *et seq.* (1959)**
An attorney may be fined or imprisoned by any court for "misbehavior or for contempt of such court," but no attorney shall be stricken from the roles or suspended for contempt unless it involves fraudulent or dishonorable misconduct or malpractice (art. 312). Proceedings may be instituted by a judge, attorney, county commissioner, or justice of the peace, by filing a sworn complaint (art. 314). The attorney charged will then be ordered to show cause why his license should not be revoked (art. 315).

UTAH
**Utah Code Ann. §§78–51–1 *et seq.* (1953)**
The Board of Commissioners of the state bar shall establish rules governing
the conduct of all persons admitted to the bar and they shall "investigate and
pass upon all unethical questions or improper conduct" of any attorney and
shall establish rules governing the procedure in cases involving alleged misconduct (§78–51–12). The Board shall make findings and report to the
Supreme Court on all investigations with recommendations for disciplinary
action if that be deemed necessary (§78–51–18).

VERMONT
**Vt. Stat. Ann. title 4 *et seq.* (1958)**
A complaint for disbarment may be filed in the Supreme Court and the court
will order the accused to answer (§843). The court may appoint a committee
to investigate and report on the charges (§843).

VIRGINIA
**Va. Code Ann. §54–42 (1967)**
The Supreme Court of Appeals may adopt rules prescribing a code of ethics
and establishing procedure for the disciplining of attorneys (§54–48). Any
court, if it observes or if a complaint is made as to "unprofessional conduct,"
may issue an order for the attorney to show cause why his license should not
be revoked or suspended (§54–74).

WASHINGTON
**Wash. Rev. Code Ann. §§2.48.010 *et seq.* (1961)**
The Board of Governors of the state bar shall have power subject to the approval of the Supreme Court, to adopt rules of professional conduct, to
investigate, prosecute, and hear all causes involving disciplinary matters and
make recommendations to the Court (§2.48.060). An attorney may be disbarred for, among other things, willful disobedience of a court order, violation of his oath of office, or violation of the ethics of the profession
(§2.48.220).

WEST VIRGINIA
**W. Va. Code Ann. §§30–2–1 *et seq.* (1966)**
Any court which observes malpractice, or if a complaint is filed so charging,
shall order the attorney to show cause why his license should not be revoked
(§30–2–7). The court will try the case without jury, and if he is found guilty
the court may suspend or disbar him (§30–2–7).

WISCONSIN
**Wis. Stat. Ann. §256.283 (Supp. 1971)**
When the Board of State Bar Commissioners receives reliable information that
an attorney is guilty of misconduct which would, if true, warrant disciplinary
action, the Board shall investigate and if warranted file a complaint with the
Supreme Court (§256.283 (2)). The court may order the defendant to an-

swer the charges (§256.284(4)). The court shall appoint a referee to hear the case, report findings, and if requested give recommendations (§256.283(6)).

## WYOMING
**Wyo. Stat. Ann. §§33–39 *et seq.* (1957)**
The Supreme Court and district courts may revoke or suspend the license of an attorney for, among other things, "(2) Willful disobedience or violation of the order of the court . . . (3) Willful violations of any of the duties of an attorney" (§33–54). The state Board of Law Examiners shall enforce the laws regarding attorneys and shall have general charge of suspension and disbarment proceedings (§33–56). The proceedings shall be held before a three judge court without jury (§33–56).

# APPENDIX J

*State Laws and Constitutional Provisions*
*Governing Misconduct of Judges*

## ALABAMA
**Ala. Const. Amend. 317**
Judicial Commission (5 judges, 2 attys., 2 laymen) to investigate and may recommend censure, suspension, removal, or retirement of all state judges to state Supreme Court for decision (adopted 1972).

## ALASKA
**Alas. Stats. tit. 22, §§22.05.120 (supreme court justices), 22.10.170 (superior court judges) (1971)**
Impeachment originated by ⅔ vote of Senate; judgment by ⅔ vote of the House of Representatives.

**Alas. Stats. tit. 22, §§22.30.010, 22.30.070 (1971); Alas. Const. art IV, §10**
Commission on Judicial Qualifications (5 judges, 2 attys., 2 laymen) may recommend censure or removal of all state judges to Supreme Court for decision.

## ARIZONA
**Ariz. Const. Art. 6.1, §§1, 4**
Commission on Judicial Qualifications (5 judges, 2 attys., 2 laymen) may recommend censure or removal of state judges to Supreme Court for decision.

**Ariz. Rev. Stat. §38–311 et seq. (1956); Ariz. Const. Art. 8, Pt. 2**
Impeachment originated by House of Representatives; judgment by ⅔ vote of Senate.

## ARKANSAS
**Ark. Const. Art. 15, §1; Ark. Stats. §12–2201 (1968)**
Judges of supreme and circuit courts may be impeached; originated by House of Representatives, judgment by ⅔ vote of Senate.

**Ark. Const. Art. 15, §3**
Address—for cause, governor may remove judges of the supreme and circuit courts upon joint address of ⅔ of each house.

## CALIFORNIA
**Cal. Const. Art. VI, §§8, 18**
Commission on Judicial Qualifications (5 judges, 2 attys., 2 laymen) may recommend censure or removal of judges to Supreme Court for decision (adopted 1966).

**Cal. Const. Art. IV, §18, West's Ann. Gov. Code §§3020–3040 (1966)**
Impeachment of judges originated in assembly; judgment by ⅔ vote of Senate.

COLORADO
**Colo. Const. Art. VI, §23 (3)**
Commission on Judicial Qualifications (5 judges, 2 attys., 2 laymen) may recommend removal of judges to Supreme Court for decision (adopted 1967).

**Colo. Const. Art. XIII**
Impeachment (except county judges and justices of the peace) originated by House of Representatives, judgment by ⅔ vote of Senate.

**Colo. Const. Art. XXI**
Recall—originated by at least 25% of those who voted for the office in last election; judgment by "Yes"/"No" election (affects every elected public officer—includes Supreme Court justices, district and county judges (**Colo. Rev. Stats. 49–2–2 [1963]**).

CONNECTICUT
**Conn. Const. Art. IX, §§1–3**
Impeachment originated by House of Representatives, judgment by ⅔ vote of Senate.

**Conn. Gen. Stat. Ann. §51a–c (Supp. 1972)**
Judicial Review Council hears and investigates complaints and may recommend impeachment (to the House) or no reappointment (to the governor).

DELAWARE
**Del. Const. Art. 4, §37**
Court on the Judiciary (5 highest state judges) may, after notice and hearing, remove or censure any state judge by ⅔ vote (adopted 1969). Proposed Del. Const. (effective July 1, 1973) retains the substance of this provision (**Art. 4 §4.14**). (Impeachment extends only to criminal acts [**Del. Const. Art 6§2, Proposed Del. Const. Art. 2, §2.18**]).

DISTRICT OF COLUMBIA
**D.C.C.E. §§11–1521, 1526 (Supp. 1972)**
Commission on Judicial Disabilities and Tenure (5 members—1 federal judge, at least 1 atty., and 1 layman) may suspend or remove D.C. judges by vote of four members. Appeal lies in special 3-judge federal court convened by chief justice of U.S. Supreme Court (**D.C.C.E. §11–1529**).

FLORIDA
**Fla. Const. Art. 5§12**
Judicial Qualifications Commission (6 judges, 2 attys., 5 laymen) may, by ⅔ vote, recommend discipline or removal of state judges to the Supreme Court for decision (adopted 1972).

**Fla. Const. Art. 4, §7**
a) Governor may suspend any county officer by executive order and make temporary reappointment; b) Senate may remove or reinstate the suspended officer. (Impeachment extends only to misdemeanor in office [**Fla. Const. Art. 5, §17 (3)**].)

GEORGIA

**Ga. Const. Art. III, §§ V,VI**

Impeachment originated in the House of Representatives; judgment by ⅔ of Senate. (Grounds for impeachment of judges enumerated in statutes seem to be exclusive: Supreme Court justice or court of appeals judge receiving favors from public utilities [**Ga. Stat. Ann. 24–103 (1971)**]; any judge repeatedly refusing to reach a decision [**Ga. Stat. Ann. 24–2621 (1971)**]; any judge refusing to disqualify himself when appropriate [**Ga. Stat. Ann. 24–2624 (1971)**].)

HAWAII

**Hawaii Rev. Stats. tit. 32, §610–1–16 (Supp. 1971)**

Commission for Judicial Qualifications (5 members appointed by governor) conducts private investigation into complaints of judicial misconduct. Certifies any findings of misconduct to governor who appoints 3-member board of judicial removal (including chief justice or associate justice) which, after notice and hearings may, by majority vote, remove judge.

IDAHO

None. (Impeachment limited to state officers for any misdemeanor in office [**Idaho Code 19–4001 (1948)**]. Provisions for discipline and removal of judges shall be as provided by law (**Idaho Const. Art. 5, §28**) (adopted 1968).)

ILLINOIS

**Ill. Const. Art. 6, §15**

Judicial Inquiry Board (2 judges, 3 attys., 4 laymen) initiate or receive complaints of judicial misconduct. If 5 members of board find misconduct, certify to Courts Commission (5 state judges), which, after notice and hearing, may by majority vote remove judge.

**Ill. Const. Art. 4, §14**

Impeachment originated in House of Representatives; judgment by ⅔ vote of Senate.

INDIANA

**Ind. Const. Art. 7, §§9,11**

Commission on Judicial Qualifications (same as Judicial Nominating Commission)—chief justice, 3 attys., 3 laymen—may recommend censure or removal of state judges to supreme court for decision (adopted 1970).

(Impeachment limited to misdemeanors (**Burns Ind. Stats. §49–801 [1964]**) or corruption or other high crimes [**§49–819, 820 (1964)**].)

IOWA

**Iowa Code Ann. §§605.26–605.32 (Supp. 1972)**

Petition for removal of judge of the supreme or district court for cause initiated by chief justice, atty. genl., or 25 members of state bar. Hearing before 3 judges appointed by chief justice. Removal by 3 judges may be reviewed by Supreme Court (adopted 1963).

**Iowa Const. Art. 3, §§19,20 Iowa Code Ann., §§68.1–68.14 (1950)**
Impeachment (all state officers for malfeasance) originates in House of Representatives; judgment by ⅔ vote of the Senate.

KANSAS
**Kans. Const. Art. 3, §15**
Removal of Supreme Court justices and district court judges by ⅔ vote of each house of legislature.

(Impeachment of state officers limited to misdemeanors [**Kans. Const. Art. 2, §§27,28; Kans. Stats. Ann. §§37–101** *et seq.*)

**Kans. Const. Art. 5, §§3–5**
Recall of all public officers (elected or appointed) by majority of electors of state or county. Initiated by petition signed by percentage of those voting for officer or appointing officer (percentage depends on whether county-, district-, or state-wide).

KENTUCKY
**Ky. Const. §§112, 129**
Address—court of appeals and circuit court judges shall be removed by the governor for reasonable cause upon joint resolution passed by ⅔ vote of each house of the General Assembly.

(Impeachment limited to misdemeanors in office [**Ky. Const. §68**].)

LOUISIANA
**La. Const. Art. IX, §§1–2**
Impeachment of all state and district officers for *inter alia* "incompetency, corruption . . . or oppression in office, or for gross misconduct" originated by House of Representatives; judgment by ⅔ vote of Senate.

**La. Const. Art. IX, §3**
Address—removal of any state officer for any reasonable cause by ⅔ vote of each house.

**La. Const. Art. IX, §§4**
Removal of judge of Supreme Court for causes enumerated in §1 by judgment of not less than 7 judges, including Supreme Court judges not involved, and sufficient number of court of appeals judges. Suit originated by atty. gen'l., 100 citizens, 25 practicing attorneys, or 2 Supreme Court justices.

**La. Const. Art. 5, La. Stat. Ann.—Rev. Stat. 13: 5001–5006 (1968)**
Removal of any judge for causes enumerated in §1 heard before Supreme Court. Suits originated by atty. gen'l. or district atty. or at request of governor, 25 citizens, or ½ of practicing attorneys in district.

MAINE
**Me. Const. Art. VI §4, Art. IX §5**
Any civil officer, including all judicial officers, may be removed for stated cause by governor (on advice of Council Cabinet) after hearing and address (apparently majority) by both houses of legislature.

(Impeachment limited to misdemeanors—same const. provision.)

## MARYLAND
**Md. Const. Art. IV, §§4A, 4B**
Commission on Judicial Disabilities (4 judges, 2 attys., 1 layman) investigates complaints against judges and may recommend removal of judge for misconduct. Decision by Court of Appeals (highest court) after hearing (adopted 1970).

**Md. Const. Art. IV, §4**
Address—removal of any judge on ⅔ vote of each house of the General Assembly.

**Md. Const. Art. IV, §4, Art. III, §26**
Impeachment originated by House of Delegates; judgment by ⅔ vote of Senate.

## MASSACHUSETTS
**Mass. Const. Pt. 2, C. 3, Art. I**
Address—governor (with consent of Council) may remove all judicial officers upon address of both houses of the legislature (apparently a majority of each).
   (Judicial officers explicitly excluded from initiative and referendum [Amend. Art. 48, Pt. 2, §2, Pt. 3, §2].)
**Mass. Const. Pt. 2, C.1, §2, Art. VIII, §3, Art. VI**
Impeachment of any state officer for misconduct or maladministration initiated by the House of Representatives; judgment, after hearing, by Senate.

## MICHIGAN
**Mich. Const. Art. 6, §30**
Judicial Tenure Commission (4 judges, 3 attys., 2 laymen) to investigate and may recommend censure, suspension, or removal of judge for misconduct to supreme court for decision (adopted 1968).

**Mich. Const. Art. 6, §25**
Address—governor shall remove any judge for cause (insufficient for impeachment) on ⅔ vote of each house of legislature.

**Mich. Const. Art. 11, §7**
Impeachment (including for corrupt conduct in office) initiated by House of Representatives; judgment after trial by ⅔ vote of Senate.

## MINNESOTA
**Minn. Stats. Ann. §§490.15–16 (Supp. 1972)**
Commission on Judicial Standards (3 judges, 2 attys., 4 laymen) to investigate and may recommend censure or removal of any judge for misconduct to Supreme Court for decision (effective upon amendment to constitution authorizing such removal (See **Proposed Amendments Minn. Const. Art. VI, §10 [Supp. 1972]**).

**Minn. Stats. Ann. §351.03 (1972)**
Governor may remove lower court judges (municipal court, justice of the peace) for misconduct after notice and hearing.

**Minn. Const. Art. 4, §14, Art. XIII, §§k, 3–5**
Impeachment of Supreme Court and district court judges by House of Representatives; judgment by ⅔ vote of Senate.

## MISSISSIPPI
**Miss. Const. Art. 4, §53**
Address—governor shall remove any state court judge for reasonable cause (insufficient for impeachment) on ⅔ vote of each branch of the legislature.
 (Impeachment limited to crimes. [**Const. Art. 4, §50**].)

## MISSOURI
**Mo. Const. Art. 5, §27**
Commission on retirement, removal, and discipline (2 judges, 2 attys., 2 laymen) by 4-member vote may recommend, after notice and hearing, removal of any judge for misconduct to Supreme Court (en banc) for decision (adopted 1970).

**Mo. Const. Art. 7, §§1–4 Vernon's Ann. Mo. Stat. §106.020 *et seq.* (1966)**
Impeachment (including for misconduct) initiated by House of Representatives; judgment by at least ⅝ of state Supreme Court.
 (Elaborate procedures for recall of *city* elective officers [**Vernon's Ann. Mo. Stat. 73.550–73.640, 74.200, 75.350–75.380 (1952)**].)

## MONTANA
**Mont. Const. Art. V, §17; Rev. Code Mont. 94–5401 *et seq.* (1969)**
Impeachment of judicial officers (except justices of the peace) for malfeasance in office initiated by House of Representatives; judgment by ⅔ vote of Senate.

**Rev. Code Mont. 94–5516 (1969)**
Removal of public officers for willful refusal or neglect to perform official duties may be heard in a summary hearing before district court, which may order removal. Appeal allowed (probably applies only to those not subject to impeachment).

## NEBRASKA
**Neb. Const. Art. V, §§28–31; Rev. Stat. Neb. §24–721–728 (1972 supp.)**
Commission on Judicial Qualifications (6 judges, 2 attys., 2 laymen) investigate and may recommend removal of any state judge for misconduct to Supreme Court for decision (adopted 1966).
 (Impeachment limited to misdemeanors in office [**Neb. Const. Art. IV, §5, Art. III, §17**].)

## NEVADA
**Nev. Const. Art. VII, §1–2**
Impeachment of judicial officers (for malfeasance in office) initiated by Assembly; judgment by ⅔ vote of Senate.

**Nev. Const. Art. VII, §3**
Address—Supreme Court justices and district judges may be removed for

reasonable cause by ⅔ vote of each branch of the leigslature, after notice and hearing.

**Nev. Const. Art. II, §9**
Recall—of all public officers—initiated by petition of 25% of those voting in last election. New election held.

## NEW HAMPSHIRE
**N.H. Const. Pt. 2, Art. 73**
Address—governor may remove any judge upon address of both houses of the legislature after notice of reasonable cause and opportunity to be heard.

**N.H. Const. Pt. 2, Arts. 17, 19, 38**
Impeachment of all state officers for malpractice or maladministration in office initiated by House of Representatives; judgment by Senate.

## NEW JERSEY
**N.J. Const. Art. 6, §6, ¶4, N.J. Stat. Ann. 2A: 1B–1–11 (Supp. 1972)**
Any state judge may be removed for misconduct, after hearing, by Supreme Court. Complaint initiated by either house of legislature, governor, Supreme Court, or filing of complaint with Supreme Court.
    (Impeachment limited to misdemeanors [**Const. Art. 7, §3, ¶1**].)

## NEW MEXICO
**N.M. Const. Art. VI, §32**
Judicial standards commission (2 judges, 2 attys., 5 laymen) to investigate and recommend discipline or removal of any judge for misconduct to Supreme Court for decision (adopted 1967).

**N.M. Const. Art. IV, §§35, 36**
Impeachment of state judges for malfeasance initiated in House of Representatives; judgment by ⅔ vote of Senate.

## NEW YORK
**N.Y. Const. Art. 6, §22**
Court on the Judiciary (6 senior judges) may remove or retire most state judges for cause after notice and hearing initiated by court *sua sponte,* by governor, by presiding justice of the appellate division, or by majority of exec. comm. of State Bar Association. City court judges may be so removed by appellate division after notice and hearing (adopted 1962).

**N.Y. Const. Art. 6, §23**
Address—court of appeals or Supreme Court judges may be removed for cause by joint resolution passed by ⅔ vote of each house of legislature after notice and hearing. Lower court judges may be removed for cause by ⅔ vote of Senate after notice and hearing.

**N.Y. Const. Art. 6, §24**
Impeachment initiated by Assembly; judgment by ⅔ vote of Senate (plus judges of court of appeals).

NORTH CAROLINA
**Gen. Stat. N.C. §§7A–375–377 (Supp. 1971)**
Judicial Standards Commission (3 judges, 2 attys., 2 laymen) may, after investigation, recommend censure or removal of any judge for misconduct to Supreme Court for decision (after notice and opportunity for argument) (adopted 1971).

**N.C. Const. Art. IV, §4; Gen. Stat. N.C. §123 (1964)**
Impeachment of all state officers for misconduct may be originated by House of Representatives; judgment by ⅔ vote of Senate.

NORTH DAKOTA
**N.D. Const. Art. XIV, §§194–204; N.D. Century Code**
**§§44–09–01 *et seq.* (1960)**
Impeachment of all judicial officers (except county justices and judges and police magistrates) for malfeasance initiated by House of Representatives; judgment by ⅔ vote of Senate.

**N.D. Const. Art. XIV, §197; N.D. Century Code §§44–10–01 *et seq.***
Judges not liable for impeachment may be removed for malfeasance through judicial proceedings, including jury trial.

**N.D. Const. Amend. 33**
Recall of all elected judicial officers upon petition signed by 30% of voters in jurisdiction's last election. New election held.

OHIO
**Ohio Const. Art. II, §38; Page's Ohio Rev. Code Ann. §§2701.11–12 (Supp. 1971)**
Commission of 5 appointed state judges may remove or suspend for misconduct any judge upon receipt of a recommendation (agreed upon by ⅔ vote) of the commission's Board on Grievances and Discipline. Appeal to state Supreme Court (adopted 1964).

**Ohio Const. Art. IV, §17**
Address—judges may be removed by joint resolution passed by ⅔ vote of each house of assembly.
    (Impeachment limited to misdemeanor Const. Art. II, §24.)

OKLAHOMA
**Okla. Const. Art. 7–A §§1–7**
Court on the Judiciary (trial and appellate divisions—each with 8 judges and 1 atty.) may remove any judge for misconduct. No review past app. div. of this court. Proceeding initiated by Supreme Court, attorney general, governor, resolution of either house of legislature, or majority of executive committee of state bar association (adopted 1966).

**Okla. Const. Art. 8; Okla. Stat. Ann. tit. 51, §51 *et seq.***
Impeachment of state Supreme Court justices for misconduct initiated by House of Representatives; judgment by ⅔ vote of Senate. (Lower court judges, not subject to impeachment, may be removed for misconduct by

civil action initiated by complaint of five citizens. Supreme Court has concurrent original jurisdiction over such actions. [**Okla. Stat. Ann. tit. 51, §§91–105 (1962)**].)

## OREGON
**Ore. Rev. Stat. §§1.410–1.480 (1971)**
Commission on Judicial Fitness (3 judges, 3 attys., 3 laymen) may, after hearing, recommend removal, suspension, or censure of any state judge to Supreme Court for decision (adopted 1967).

**Ore. Const. Art. VII (orig.), §20**
Address—governor may remove judges of the Supreme Court for misconduct after joint resolution passed by ⅔ vote of each house.

**Ore. Const. Art. VII, §19**
For incompetence, corruption, malfeasance, or delinquency in office any public officer may be removed from office after criminal-style proceeding.

**Ore. Const. Art. II, §18**
All public officers subject to recall on petition of 25% of those voting for Supreme Court justice in district: "Yes"/"No" election.

## PENNSYLVANIA
**Pa. Const. Art. 5, §18**
Judicial Inquiry and Review Board (5 judges, 2 attys., 2 laymen) may recommend, after hearing, suspension, removal, or discipline for misconduct to Supreme Court for decision (adopted 1968).

**Pa. Const. Art. 6, §§1–3**
Impeachment of all civil officers for misconduct initiated by House of Representatives; judgment by ⅔ of Senate.

(Address provision Art. 6, §7 explicitly excludes judges of courts of record.)

## RHODE ISLAND
**R.I. Const. Art. 10, §4**
Address—any judge may be removed by joint resolution passed by each house of legislature.

(Impeachment limited to "official misdemeanor.")

## SOUTH CAROLINA
**S.C. Const. Art. 15, §§1–2**
Impeachment of any state judges for "serious misconduct" initiated by ⅔ vote of House of Representatives; judgment by ⅔ vote of Senate.

**S.C. Const. Art. 15, §3**
Any judicial officer shall be removed for cause (insufficient for impeachment) by the governor upon joint resolution passed by ⅔ vote of each house of the legislature.

## SOUTH DAKOTA
**S.D. Const. Art. XVI, §§1–3**
Impeachment of any judicial officer (except county judges, justices of the peace, and police magistrates) for misconduct initiated by the House of Representatives; judgment by ⅔ vote of the Senate. (County judges, etc., may be removed for misconduct by the governor, after notice and hearing [**S.D. Compiled Laws §3–17 (1967)**].)

## TENNESSEE
**Tenn. Const. Art. 6, §6; Tenn. Code Ann. §17–801–816 (1972)**
Judicial Standards Comm. (3 judges, 3 attys., 3 laymen or attys.) may recommend removal of any judge for misconduct, after hearing and investigation. Recommendations acted on by joint resolution passed by ⅔ vote of each house of the legislature. (Address procedure merged with commission system.) (adopted 1971).

(Impeachment limited to any crime [**Tenn. Code Ann. 8–2601 (1956); Tenn. Const. Art. 5, §4**].)

## TEXAS
**Texas Const. Art. V, §1–a**
Judicial Qualifications Commission (4 judges, 3 attys., 2 laymen) may, after hearing, recommend censure or removal of any state judge for misconduct to Supreme Court for decision (adopted 1965).

**Texas Const. Art. XV, §§1–6; Vernon's Ann. Civ. Stat. Art. 5961–5963**
Impeachment of state judges initiated by House of Representatives; judgment by ⅔ vote of Senate.

**Texas Const. Art. XV, §8; Vernon's Ann. Civ. Stat. Art. 5964**
Address—any state judge shall be removed by governor for misconduct upon joint resolution passed by ⅔ vote of each house of the legislature.

## UTAH
**Utah Code Ann. §49–7a–38 (Supp. 1971)**
Commission on Judicial Qualifications (2 state legislators, 3 members of board of commissioners of state bar) may recommend suspension censure or removal of any state judge for misconduct to Supreme Court for decision.

**Utah Const. Art. VIII, §11**
Address—judges may be removed for cause by joint resolution passed by each house of the legislature.

**Utah Const. Art. VI, §§17–20; Utah Code Ann. §77–6–(1–19) (1953)**
Impeachment of state judges (except justices of the peace) for malfeasance initiated by ⅔ vote of House of Representatives; judgment by ⅔ vote of Senate.

## VERMONT
**Vt. Const. Ch. II, §§53–54**
Impeachment of all state judicial officers initiated by ⅔ vote of House of Representatives; judgment by ⅔ vote of Senate.

**Vt. Stat. Ann., tit. 4, §3 (1972)**
Supreme Court has general supervisory power over all judicial officers and
may suspend such officers for balance of term where appropriate.

## VIRGINIA
**Va. Const. Art. VI, §10; Code of Va. §2.1–37.1–37.16 (Supp. 1972)**
Judicial Inquiry and Review Commission (2 judges, 2 attys., 1 layman) may
recommend, after hearing, removal of any judge for misconduct to Supreme
Court for decision.
   (Address—general assembly may remove for misconduct judges of courts
not of record [some constitutional provision].)

**Va. Const. Art. IV, §17**
Impeachment of all state judges for malfeasance initiated by the House of
Delegates; judgment by ⅔ vote of Senate.

## WASHINGTON
**Wash. Const. Art. IV, §9**
Address—removal of any judge of court of record by joint resolution passed
by ¾ vote of each house of legislature.

**Wash. Const. Art. V**
Impeachment of all judges of courts of record for malfeasance initiated by
House of Representatives; judgment by ⅔ vote of Senate.
   (Recall limited to judges of courts not of record [**Wash. Const. Art. I,
§33 (Amend. 8)**].)

## WEST VIRGINIA
**W.Va. Const. Art. 4, §9; W.Va. Code §6–6–3 (Supp. 1971)**
Impeachment of any judge for misconduct initiated by House of Delegates;
judgment by ⅔ vote of Senate.
   (Address limited to aged or physical or mental disability [Const. Art. 8,
§17].)

## WISCONSIN
**Wisc. Const. Art. 7, §13; Wisc. Stat. Ann. §17.06 (1972)**
Address—any state judge may be removed for misconduct by joint resolution
passed by ⅔ of each house of the legislature.

**Wisc. Const. Art. 7, §1; Wisc. Stat. Ann. §17.06 (1972)**
Impeachment—for corrupt conduct in office or crimes and misdemeanors, of
all civil officers—initiated by Assembly; judgment by ⅔ vote of Senate.

**Wisc. Const. Art. 13, §12**
Recall of all elective officers one year after last election; by petition signed by
25% of number voting for governor in last election. New election held.

## WYOMING
**Wyo. Const. Art. 3, §§17, 18**
Impeachment of judicial officers for misconduct initiated by House of Repre-
sentatives; judgment by ⅔ vote of Senate.

# APPENDIX K

*Analysis of Total Number of Criminal Trials
in United States (Jury and Non-Jury)*

In order to ascertain the ratio of disorderly trials to the total number of criminal trials held in the United States, it is important to discover how many criminal trials are held in both state and federal courts each year. While precise figures are available for the federal courts, only a few states maintain accurate totals on their criminal trials. Many states account for the total defendants disposed of, but since the large majority of criminal defendants plead guilty to the charges, it is difficult to determine the actual number of trials held, that is, where proof was completed and submitted to the trier of fact.

An earlier study prepared by the American Jury Project undertaken at the University of Chicago Law School determined that in 1955 there were 55,670 jury trials. Figures on non-jury trials were not available.

Using the Chicago figures as a base, we have determined that there were approximately 130,000 jury trials held in 1971 in the United States. We derived this figure by projecting the increase in criminal jury trials in those states where precise figures are available onto the national average. Thus, comparative figures are available for the following jurisdictions:

|  | CRIMINAL JURY TRIALS | | PERCENTAGE OF INCREASE |
|---|---|---|---|
|  | 1955 | 1971 |  |
| Federal | 2,290 | 4,533 | 198% |
| California | 4,940 | 9,174 | 185% |
| Maryland | 440 | 1,278 | 290% |
| Connecticut | 70 | 234 | 334% |
| New Jersey | 850 | 3,767 | 443% |
| Michigan | 1,010 | 3,480 | 344% |
| Wisconsin | 210 | 583 | 282% |
| Totals | 9,810 | 23,049 |  |
| Average increase in seven jurisdictions |  |  | 235% |

If the 235 percent increase held for the entire country, the total number of criminal jury trials would be 235 percent of 55,670, or 130,268.

Determining the number of non-jury trials held was far more difficult. Large numbers of traffic offenses and disorderly conduct or drunkenness charges are handled informally in justice of the peace courts or their equivalent in many states. Accurate figures for such dispositions are not kept.

Working from the figures that are available, we estimate that there are approximately 500,000 non-jury criminal trials in the United States each year.

We found that the F.B.I. reported that 2,251,647 individuals from 2,990 cities with a total population of 63,269,000 were held for prosecution for all crimes other than minor traffic offenses in 1971. Projecting these figures to a national total would mean approximately 7,000,000 persons were formally charged with a crime other than minor traffic offenses. If we assume that only 10 percent of those charged actually went to trial, which is a figure often cited in this regard, it would mean that 700,000 total criminal trials were held in 1971. Eliminating the 130,000 jury cases leaves 570,00 non-jury cases, a figure close to that determined above.

# APPENDIX L

*Selected Bibliography*
*on Courtroom Disorder*

# BOOKS

Becker, Theodore, ed. *Political Trials*. New York: Bobbs-Merrill Co., 1971.

Bishop, George. *Witness to Evil*. New York: Nash Publishing Corp., 1971.

Chevigny, Paul. *Cops and Rebels*. New York: Pantheon Books, 1972.

Epstein, Jason. *The Great Conspiracy Trial*. New York: Random House, 1970.

Kirchheimer, Otto. *Political Justice*. Princeton: Princeton University Press, 1961.

Lefcourt, Robert, ed. *Law Against the People*. New York: Random House, 1971.

Lieberman, Jethro K. *How the Government Breaks the Law*. New York: Stein and Day, 1972.

Marks, F. Raymond, with Kirk Leswing and Barbara A. Fartinsky. *The Lawyer, The Public and Professional Responsibility*. Chicago: American Bar Foundation, 1972.

# ARTICLES

Alschuler, Albert W. "Courtroom Misconduct by Prosecutors and Trial Judges." 50 *Texas Law Review* 629 (1971).

Berger, Raoul. "Impeachment of Judges and 'Good Behaviour' Tenure." 79 *Yale Law Journal* 1475 (1970).

Brennan, William J. "The Responsibilities of the Legal Profession." 54 *American Bar Association Journal* 121 (1968).

Burger, Warren E. "The Necessity for Civility." 52 Federal Rules Decisions 211 (1971).

Comment. "Controlling Lawyers by Bar Associations and Courts." 6 *Harvard Civil Rights-Civil Liberties Law Review* 301 (1970).

Comment. "Defense Pro Se." 23 *University of Miami Law Review* 551 (1969).

Comment. "Invoking Summary Criminal Contempt Procedures—Use or Abuse? *United States* v. *Dellinger*—The 'Chicago Seven' Contempts." 69 *Michigan Law Review* 1549 (1971).

Comment. "Violent Misconduct in the Courtroom—Physical Restraint and Eviction of the Criminal Defendant." 28 *University of Pittsburgh Law Review* 443 (1967).

Comment. "Prosecutorial Discretion on the Initiation of Criminal Complaints." 42 *Southern California Law Review* 519 (1969).

Conner, Leslie L. "The Trial Judge, His Facial Expressions, Gestures and General Demeanor—Their Effect Upon the Administration of Justice." *American Criminal Law Quarterly* 175 (1968).

Dorsen, Norman. "The Role of the Lawyer in America's Ghetto Society." 49 *Texas Law Review* 50 (1970).

Ferrick, John D. "Impeaching Federal Judges: A Study of the Constitutional Provisions." 39 *Fordham Law Review* 1 (1970).

Flaum, Joel M. and James R. Thompson. "The Case of the Disruptive Defendant: *Allen v Illinois.*" 61 *Journal of Criminal Law* 327 (1970).

Freedman, Monroe H. "Professional Responsibility of the Criminal Defense Lawyer; The Three Hardest Questions." 64 *Michigan Law Review* 1469 (1966).

Freedman, Monroe H. "The Professional Responsibility of the Prosecuting Attorney." 55 *Georgetown Law Review* 1030 (1967).

Friedman, Leon. "Political Power and Legal Legitimacy, A Short History of Political Trials." 30 *Antioch Review* 157 (1970).

Freund, Paul. "Contempt of Court." 1 *Human Rights* 4 (1970).

Fuld, Stanley H. "The Right to Dissent: Protest in the Courtroom." 44 *St. John's Law Review* 581 (1970).

Garry, Charles R. "Who's an Officer of the Court." *Trial Magazine*, Jan./Feb. 1971.

Harper, Fowler, and David Haber. "Lawyer Troubles in Political Trials." 60 *Yale Law Journal* 1 (1951).

Hazard, Geoffrey C., Jr. "Securing Courtroom Decorum." 80 *Yale Law Journal* 433 (1971).

Hobbs, Don. "Prosecutors Bias: An Occupational Disease." 2 *Alabama Law Review* 40 (1949).

Karlen, Delmar. "Disorder in the Courtroom." 44 *Southern California Law Review* 996 (1971).

Katz, Harvey. "Some Call it Justice." *Washingtonian Magazine*, March 1971.

Koskoff, Theodore I. "Quest for a Fair Trial." *Trial Magazine*, Jan./Feb. 1971.

Laub, Burton. "The Problem of the Unrepresented, Misrepresented and Rebellious Defendant in Criminal Court." 2 *Duquesne University Law Review* 245 (1964).

Lewis, Anthony. "Lawyers and Civilization." 120 *University of Pennsylvania Law Review* 860 (1972).

Murray, Daniel E. "The Power to Expel a Criminal Defendant from his Own Trial: A Comparative View." 36 *University of Colorado Law Review* 171 (1964).

Newman, Jon O. "Is the Problem Simple?" *Trial Magazine*, Jan./Feb. 1971.

Nizer, Louis. "What to Do When the Judge is Put Up Against The Wall." *New York Times Magazine*, April 5, 1970, p. 30.

Note. "The Contemptuous Attorney and Problems Concerning His Summary Punishment Under Rule 47(a) of the Federal Rules of Criminal Procedure." 4 *John Marshall Journal of Practice and Procedure* 74 (1970).

Note. "Criminal Law—Contempt—Conduct of Attorney During Course of Trial." 1971 *Wisconsin Law Review* 320.

Note. "Dealing with Unruly Persons in the Courtroom." 48 *North Carolina Law Review* 878 (1970).

Note. "Disbarment; A Case for Reform." 17 *New York Law Forum* 792 (1971).

Note. "*Illinois v. Allen:* The Unruly Defendant's Right to a Fair Trial." 46 *New York University Law Review* 120 (1970).

Note. "Misconduct of Judges and Attorneys During Trial." 49 *Iowa Law Review* 531 (1964).

Note. "The Nature and Consequences of Forensic Misconduct in the Prosecution of a Criminal Case." 54 *Columbia Law Review* 946 (1954).

Note. "Right to Defend Pro Se." 48 *North Carolina Law Review* 678 (1970).

Note. "The Power of the Judge to Command Order in the Courtroom; The Options of *Illinois v. Allen.*" 65 *Northwestern University Law Review* 671 (1970).

Note. "Prosecutorial Forensic Misconduct—Harmless Error?" 6 *Utah Law Review* 108 (1958).

Note. "The Sedition Trial: A Study in Delay and Obstruction." 15 *University of Chicago Law Review* 691 (1948).

Note. Special Project; "Judicial Response to the Disruptive Defendant." 60 *Georgetown Law Journal* 281 (1971).

Note. "Summary Punishment for Contempt." 39 *Southern California Law Review* 483 (1966).

Schwartz, Herman. "Judges as Tyrants." 7 *Criminal Law Bulletin* 129 (1971)·

Singer, Richard G. "Forensic Misconduct by Federal Prosecutors—and How it Grew." 20 *Alabama Law Review* 227 (1968).

Thompson, Frank, Jr. and Daniel H. Pollett. "Impeachment of Federal Judges: An Historical Overview." 49 *North Carolina Law Review* 87 (1970).

Wright, Eugene A. "Courtroom Decorum and the Trial Process." 51 *Judicature* 378 (1968).

# NOTES

## Notes to Chapter One

1. Circuit Judge Arlin M. Adams, concurring and dissenting in United States v. Dougherty, __F.2d __ (D.C. Cir. June 30, 1972).
2. Chief Justice Warren E. Burger, "The Necessity for Civility," 52 F.R.D. 211, 212, 213–14 (1971).
3. See *New York Times,* September 13, 1970, at 21; *New York Law Journal,* April 28, 1971, p. 1; 57 *American Bar Association Journal* 48 (1971); *New York Times,* August 9, 1971, at 1; *Trial Magazine,* January/February 1971.
4. Cal. Penal Code §169 (West 1972).
5. N.Y. Crim. Pro. Law §§260.20, 340.50 (McKinney 1972) (Ch. 789, 1971, Laws of New York).
6. Nev. Rev. Stat. §§175, 387 (1972) (Ch. 425, 1971 Statutes of Nevada); Minn. Stat. Ann. §631.015 (1972).
7. Ch. 524 of Massachusetts Laws of 1971.
8. A full list of state laws and court rules on discipline of lawyers for courtroom misbehavior is found in Appendix I.
9. See Appendix H, pp. 349–55 above.
10. General Rule 5.
11. Rules Creating and Controlling the Oklahoma Bar Association, August 7, 1971.
12. S.2039, 92d Cong., 1st Sess. §1364:
    "Censure, suspension and disbarment of attorneys:
    (a) Any United States district court shall have jurisdiction to make an order in a disciplinary proceeding disbarring, suspending, or censuring, or taking such other action as justice may require, with respect to any attorney who is a member of the bar of such court and has:
    (1) been convicted of a crime involving moral turpitude in any State, territory, Commonwealth, possession or the District of Columbia; or (2) is guilty of conduct unbecoming a member of the bar of such court. Without limiting the generality of the foregoing, conduct unbecoming a member of the bar of a United States district court shall be deemed to include fraud, deceit, malpractice, conduct prejudicial to the administration of justice, incitement to arson, riot, espionage, or sabotage or violation of the Code of Professional Responsibilities of the American Bar Association or of the bar association of the State in which such United States district court has jurisdiction."
13. 117 *Cong. Rec.* S8810 (daily ed. June 10, 1971).
14. See *New York Times,* June 10, 1971, at 13.
15. Illinois v. Allen, 397 U.S. 337, 343 (1970).
16. A complete description and analysis of the trial judges questionnaire results appear in appendix A.
17. We also received one report of disruption from an army court-martial.
18. See chapter 10, note 56 for a breakdown of the cases.
19. Ibid.
20. Kentucky State Bar Association v. Taylor, __ Ky. __, 482 S.W.2d 574 (June 30, 1972).
21. *New York Times,* August 9, 1971, at 1.
22. The totals taken from the annual reports of the past five years are as follows:

| FISCAL YEAR | TOTAL TRIALS IN FEDERAL SYSTEM | TOTAL CRIMINAL TRIALS IN FEDERAL SYSTEM | CRIMINAL CONTEMPT CONVICTIONS |
|---|---|---|---|
| 1967 | 12,500 | 4,405 | 32 |
| 1968 | 14,221 | 5,533 | 49 |
| 1969 | 14,397 | 5,563 | 68 |
| 1970 | 16,032 | 6,583 | 54 |
| 1971 | 17,549 | 7,456 | 56 |

The fifty-six cases noted in fiscal year 1971 are not all instances of court-room disruption. A contempt citation can arise out of the violation of a court order or injunction as well as from in-court misbehavior. In 1971, 43 of the 56 convictions resulted from a nolo contendere plea. And in only 12 cases was the contemnor convicted by the court (one person was convicted by a jury). This indicates that a high percentage of the federal convictions related to out-of-court violations since it would be unusual for a federal judge to accept a nolo plea from a person who disrupted court proceedings.

In summary, in 1971 the incidence of courtroom disorder in federal courts was at most in the order of 12/7,456 or .16% of criminal trials. If civil cases are included, the ratio is 12/17,549 or .068%.

23. *See* appendix K for discussion of the statistics.
24. *See* Note, Special Project: "Judicial Response to the Disruptive Defendant," 60 *Georgetown Law Journal* 281, 487 n.1195 (1971).

## Notes to Chapter Two

1. People v. Julio Roldan and Robert Lemus, Docket # A–20005, A–20006, 110/150 P.L. Arraignment, October 14, 1970, Transcript of Proceedings, at 2–3.
2. Ibid. at 3–5.
3. "A Report by the New York City Board of Correction on the Investigation into the Death of Julio Roldan," November 17, 1970, at 11.
4. Letter, William vanden Heuvel, Chairman, Board of Corrections, to Honorable John V. Lindsay, November 17, 1970.
5. Illinois v. Allen, 397 U.S. 337, 347–48 (1970) (Brennan, J., concurring).
6. Charge to Grand Jury—Civil Rights Act, 30 F. Cas. 1005, 1006–07 (Case No. 18,260) (C.C.W.D. Tenn. 1875).
7. Moore v. Dempsey, 261 U.S. 86, 89–90 (1923). The many trials of the Scottsboro boys in the 1930s saw similar events. *See* Powell v. State, 224 Ala. 540, 555, 141 So. 201, 214–15 (1932) (Anderson, C. J., dissenting), *reversed*, Powell v. Alabama, 287 U.S. 45 (1932). For a full account of the *Scottsboro* case, *see* Dan T. Carter, *Scottsboro: A Tragedy of the American South* (Baton Rouge, 1969).
8. Frank v. Magnum, 237 U.S. 309, 346 (1915) (Holmes, J., dissenting).
9. Anthony Lewis, "Lawyers and Civilization," 120 *University of Pennsylvania Law Review* 860 (1972).
10. "The Necessity for Civility," 52 F.R.D. 211, 214–215 (1971). *See also* remarks of Chief Judge Stanley H. Fuld, "The Right to Dissent: Protest in the Courtroom," 44 *St. John's Law Review*, 581, 593 (1970).
11. Thurman W. Arnold, *The Symbols of Government* 129 (New Haven, 1935).
12. *See* John C. Flugel, *Man, Morals and Society* 169–70 (New York, 1945). *See also* Jean-Paul Sartre, *Saint Genet* 29 (New York, 1963).
13. *See* Hannah Arendt, "Civil Disobedience" in *Is Law Dead?* ed., Eugene Rostow 212 (New York, 1971).

14. *See* "Report on the State of the Federal Judiciary," 117 *Cong. Rec.* S15013 (daily ed. September 24, 1971).
15. United States v. Dougherty, ___F.2d ___ (D.C. Cir. June 30, 1972) (Adams, J., concurring and dissenting).
16. *The Challenge of Crime in a Free Society,* Report of President's Commission on Law Enforcement and Administration of Justice 128 (Washington, 1967).
17. *Report of the National Advisory Commission on Civil Disorders* 337 (New York, Bantam ed. 1968).
18. *See* reference in note 28.
19. Criminal Justice Coordinating Council, "City of New York Criminal Justice Plan for 1971," at 1.
20. *See* Statement of District Attorney of New York County, "Proposal for Reducing Delays in Criminal Justice in New York City," 1970, at 3. *See also* Paul Chevigny, *Police Power* (New York, 1969). A recent study has suggested that in 10 percent of police-citizen contacts, the police have acted in a belittling or authoritarian manner. *See* Albert J. Reiss, Jr., *The Police and the Public* 141–50 (New Haven, 1971).
21. *See* 117 Cong. Rec. S4242 (daily ed. April 1, 1971).
22. A graphic case is described in James Mills's article, "I Have Nothing to do with Justice," *Life,* March 12, 1971, pp. 61–62. *See also* Peter L. Zimroth, "101,000 Defendants Were Convicted of Misdemeanors Last Year: 98,000 of Them Had Pleaded Guilty—To Get Reduced Sentences," *New York Times,* May 28, 1972, §6 (Magazine), at 14ff.
23. Stephen R. Bing and S. Stephen Rosenfeld, *The Quality of Justice in the Lower Criminal Courts of Metropolitan Boston,* A Report by the Lawyers Committee for Civil Rights Under Law 31 (Boston, 1970).
24. Ibid., at 87.
25. Harvey Katz, "Some Call It Justice," *Washingtonian Magazine,* March 1971, at 46. *See* discussion at pp. 200–204 below.
26. *See New York Times,* December 21, 1970, at 52.
27. *See Report of the National Advisory Commission on Civil Disorders;* A. Downs, *Racism in America and How to Combat It* (U.S. Commission on Civil Rights, 1970); Haywood Burns, "Can a Black Man Get a Fair Trial in This Country?" *New York Times,* July 12, 1970, §6 (Magazine), at 5.
28. Since published in somewhat revised form, 61 *California Law Review* 165 (1973).
29. Donald J. Warren, "Justice in the Recorder's Court in Detroit: An Analysis of Misdemeanor Cases During the Months of September to December, 1969," A Preliminary Report of the Court Watching Project for the Equal Justice Council, February 16, 1970.
30. Henry A. Bullock, "Significance of the Racial Factor in the Length of Prison Sentences," 52 *Journal of Criminal Law, Criminology and Political Science* 411 (1961).
31. Haywood Burns had written in the *New York Times:* "Blacks usually receive longer prison sentences than whites for most criminal offenses. A study of persons convicted of burglary and auto theft in Los Angeles County, most of them first offenders and unskilled laborers, revealed that on the average whites were treated much less severely than blacks. Forty-five per cent of the whites and 27 per cent of the blacks were given sentences for these crimes of four months' imprisonment or less, or probation; 42 per cent of the whites and 47 per cent of the blacks received four to nine months; and 13 per cent of the whites and 27 per cent of the blacks got 10 to 20 months." ("Can a Black Man Get a Fair Trial in This Country?" note 27 above, p. 38.)

## Notes to Chapter Three

1. *See New York Times,* December 10, 1970, at 1.
2. *See New York Times,* February 8, 1970, at 10.

3. *The Times* (London), October 12, 1971, at 2, November 13, 1971, at 2, December 19, 1971, at 2.
4. *New York Times,* February 7, 1971, §1, at 10, February 9, 1971, at 2.
5. Ibid., August 26, 1971, at 3.
6. *See Time,* October 23, 1972, at 49.
7. *See* Barbara Tuchman, *The Proud Tower,* ch. 2 (New York, 1966).
8. Nicholas Halasz, *Captain Dreyfus: The Story of a Mass Hysteria* 139–40 (New York, 1955).
9. Ibid., at 232.
10. Bertram D. Wolfe, *Three Who Made a Revolution* 333 (New York, 1948).
11. *See* Ronald Florence, *Fritz: The Story of a Political Assassin,* ch. 17 (New York, 1971).
12. The 1922 case of Matthias Erzberger, one of the first Weimer ministers, is discussed in Richard N. Watt, *The Kings Depart* 522–23 (New York, 1968). The libel cases of Friedrich Ebert, president of the Weimer Republic, are analyzed by Otto Kirchheimer in *Political Justice* 76–84 (Princeton, 1961).
13. *See* Jason Epstein, *The Great Conspiracy Trial* 128–29 (New York, 1970); Gerald Dickler, *Man on Trial* 219–20 (Garden City, 1962).
14. *See* Kirchheimer, *Political Justice,* at 252.
15. Ibid.
16. *See* Kirchheimer, *Political Justice,* at 253; John Steward Ambler, *Soldiers Against the State* 117 (New York, Anchor ed. 1968).
17. John Toland, *The Rising Sun* 10–11 (New York, 1970).
18. In some cases—as in the Adler case discussed above—the very purpose of the criminal act bringing on the trial may have been to provide a forum for the political complaints of the accused.
19. *See* 2 *Howell's State Trials* 1, 8 ff. (1603).
20. 3 *Howell's State Trials* 1320 (1637).
21. For an excellent account of Lilburne's trial and its effect on English law, *see* Leonard Levy, *Origins of the Fifth Amendment* 271–82 (New York, 1968).

    In addition to the Lilburne case, another action occurred in 1637 which has often been cited as a disorderly trial in English law. Under the instigation of William Laud, Archbishop of Canterbury, Puritan, Presbyterian, and nonconformist sects were suppressed by the royal High Commission and the infamous Star Chamber. Anyone who preached or wrote anti-Anglican tracts was subject to interrogation and punishment. Those who refused to answer the judges questions fully and truthfully were subject to judgment *pro confesso*— were taken to have confessed the charges against them. Three Puritan pamphleteers, Dr. John Bastwick, Henry Burton, and William Prynn were charged with sedition in the Star Chamber in 1637 and ordered to answer the charges against them, signed by their counsel. Their answers contained long attacks on the Anglican Church hierarchy and their lawyers refused to sign them. The defendants sought to submit the answers under their own signature but the Star Chamber judges refused to accept them. Frequent arguments arose with the judges on this point. In addition, the defendants claimed that the bishops who sat in the Star Chamber were prejudiced against them, and tried to have them removed. *See* 3 *Howell's State Trials* 717–25.
22. 6 Howell's State Trials 955–56.
23. Bushell's Case, 6 *Howell's State Trials* 999, 1021 (1670).
24. Disruption marked other state trials in England in the seventeenth and eighteenth centuries. Charles I constantly objected to the jurisdiction of the High Court of Justice which tried him for high treason in 1649. 4 *Howell's State Trials* 993, 1000 (1649). There were altercations in court during the many trials of John Wilkes, the Parliamentary champion of free speech, in the late 18th century. *See* 19 *Howell's State Trials* 1075, 1381, 1407–08 (1770). The famous impeachment trial of Warren Hastings also had disorderly moments. *See The History of the Trial of Warren Hastings* (1796), part V, p. 107. And the sedition trial of Thomas Paine in 1792 witnessed exchanges between his

lawyer, Sir Thomas Erskine, and members of the jury. *See* 22 *Howell's State Trials* 357, 445 (1792).

25. Lord Campbell, 4 *Lives of the Lord Chancellors of England* 343–44 (1834).
26. In 1871 an Australian butcher who called himself Thomas Castro brought suit to regain possession of the Tichborne baronetcy and estate, claiming to be Roger Tichborne (the eldest son of the tenth baronet) who had been lost at sea in 1854 and believed drowned. The claimant's suit was supported by Lady Tichborne (Roger's mother) and many family servants and friends who insisted he was the missing son. Other members of the family fought the claim and the suit (which went on for many months) became the subject of intense public interest. The claimant elected to non-suit his case in the middle of the trial when it became clear that the jury did not believe his evidence. He was then prosecuted for perjury, found guilty, and sentenced to seven years in jail. *See* Douglas Woodruff, *The Tichborne Claimant* (New York, 1957).
27. *New York Weekly Tribune,* February 22, 1851, at 4.
28. 2 *Journal of Richard Henry Dana* 412 (Cambridge, Robert Lucid, ed. 1968).
29. Ibid. at 629–30.
30. 5 *American State Trials* 645, 651–53 (1854).
31. *Reminiscences of Levi Coffin* 550–51 (Cincinnati, 1876).
32. For other Ohio cases, *see* William C. Cochran, *The Western Reserve and the Fugitive Slave Law* 154–55 (Cleveland, 1920).
33. *New York Times,* April 28, 1933, at 1, col. 4.
34. 6 *American State Trials* 687, 692 (1798).
35. 3 *American State Trials* 1, 49–50 (1873).
36. Ibid. at 50–53.
37. *See* Wayne G. Broehl, *The Molly Maguires* 270–340 (Cambridge, 1964). In a similar case, a group of radical labor leaders and anarchist theoreticians were indicted and tried for murder in the 1886 Haymarket affair. (12 *American State Trials* 1 [1886]).
38. William D. Haywood, *Bill Haywood's Book: The Autobiography of William D. Haywood* 212 (New York, 1929).
39. Irving Stone, *Clarence Darrow for the Defense* 235 (Garden City, 1941).
40. Richard H. Frost, *The Mooney Case* 256–57 (Stanford, 1968).
41. Ibid.
42. Lowell S. Hawley and Ralph Bushnell Potts, *Counsel for the Damned: A Biography of George Francis Vanderveer* 240 (Philadelphia, 1953).
43. Haywood, *Bill Haywood's Book,* at 311.
44. Ray Ginger, *Eugene V. Debs* 384 (New York, Collier ed., 1962).
45. 15 *American State Trials* 465, 491–92 (1885).
46. Ibid. at 483–85.
47. 15 *American State Trials* at 568–69.
48. The contempt finding was upheld by the United States Supreme Court, *Ex parte Terry,* 128 U.S. 289 (1888) (Mr. Justice Field did not participate). The Terry case became one of the leading cases on the scope of a judge's contempt power. *See* Sacher v. United States, 343 U.S. 1, 35 n.2 (1952) (Frankfurter, J., dissenting).
49. The case eventually came to the United States Supreme Court which decided in Neagle's favor, *In re Neagle,* 135 U.S. 1 (1890). While the case is not political in the same sense as earlier cases and while it led to no important procedural reforms, it is the leading case on the scope of the protected activities of federal officers vis-a-vis the state criminal law.

## Notes to Chapter Four

1. Hartzel v. United States, 322 U.S. 680 (1944) and Keegan v. United States, 325 U.S. 478 (1945). In addition, charges were brought against George Viereck for failure to supply material information when he registered as a

foreign agent for Germany. That case was also reversed, Viereck v. United States, 318 U.S. 236 (1943).

2. Francis Biddle, *In Brief Authority* 238 (New York, 1962).
3. Indictment, United States v. McWilliams, Criminal No. 73083 (D.D.C. 1943).
4. *New York Times,* April 18, 1944, at 9.
5. Ibid., April 20, 1944, at 12.
6. The court of appeals concluded that such motions were not made in good faith but only to publicize the case. It noted that at the time the motions were made, Laughlin

> knew that motions to subpoena defense witnesses at Government expense would not be taken up for disposition until after the jury had been impaneled. In spite of this, every few days he filed motions to subpoena as alleged defense witnesses men conspicious in public and private life, and he accompanied these motions with written statements of what he expected to prove by these persons. We have considered the statements and find in them nothing which appears to us in any respect relevant to the subject matter of the case on trial and hence we think, as Judge Bailey thought, that their only purpose was to disrupt and interfere with the orderly conduct of the trial and their wholesale publication in newspapers a further effort to this end. [Laughlin v. United States, 151 F.2d 281, 284 (D.C. Cir. 1945)]

7. Laughlin v. United States, 151 F.2d 281 (D.C. Cir. 1945).
8. *New York Times,* May 18, 1944, at 17. According to the *Chicago Tribune,* the day's proceedings "approached the proportions of a riot." After almost every sentence the defendants shouted "mistrial," "does this court believe in the Constitution," "this is Moscow," and so on. Even after additional marshals were called in, the defendants booed and hissed and shouted "that's not true," and "that's a lie" in reference to Rogge's statement. *See Chicago Tribune,* August 8, 1944, at 5.
9. Jones was eventually held in contempt for refusing to stop arguing after the judge ordered him to stop. Jones v. United States, 151 F.2d 289 (D.C. Cir. 1945).
10. Laughlin v. Eicher, 145 F.2d 700, 702 (D.C. Cir. 1944).
11. Ibid.
12. That holding was reversed by the court of appeals on the ground that the misbehavior did not take place in the presence of the court and therefore summary contempt proceedings were unavailable. *See* Klein v. United States, 151 F.2d 286 (D.C. Cir. 1945).
13. *See* United States v. McWilliams, 69 F. Supp. 812 (D.D.C. 1946), *affirmed,* 163 F.2d 695 (D.C. Cir. 1947).
14. A law review note on the trial agreed:

> Any sort of organized procedure was made impossible by what seemed at times a complete lack of respect for the court. Thus attempts to procure smooth handling of the trial were frustrated, and in many situations collateral questions were raised which had to be handled while the main proceedings were temporarily halted. Further, persistent attempts were made to becloud the issue involved by picturing the trial as a political or ethnological fight. . . .
> It can reasonably be asked why the Government, at least when defense strategy became clear, did not seek to sever the various cases and move against the defendants individually. Possibly the Government's case against some of the defendants rested on its ability to prove the conspiracy, but it is doubtful whether a result in which some of the defendants might have been convicted and others not prosecuted would have been of less value than the fiasco which actually occurred. [Note, "The Sedition Trial: A Study in Delay and Obstruction," 15 *University of Chicago Law Review* 691, 701, 702 (1948)]

15. United States v. Sacher, 182 F.2d 416, 430 (2d Cir. 1950).

16. Ibid. at 431.

17. United States v. Sacher, 182 F.2d 416 (2d Cir. 1950).

18. Sacher v. United States, 343 U.S. 1 (1952).

19. Ibid. at 346.

20. 182 F.2d at 447; Trial Tr. 11,369–11, 371.

21. 182 F.2d at 446; Trial Tr. 11,031.

22. 182 F.2d at 433; Challenge Tr. 2494.

23. 182 F.2d at 436; Challenge Tr. 4416–17.

24. 182 F.2d at 446; Trial Tr. 11,031.

25. 182 F.2d at 453. Trial Tr. 13893–94.

26. 182 F.2d at 444–45.

27. 182 F.2d at 442.

28. Sacher v. Ass'n of the Bar of the City of New York, 347 U.S. 388 (1954).

29. In re Isserman, 9 N.J. 269, 87 A.2d 903 (1952).

30. In re Isserman, 345 U.S. 286 (1953), *reversed,* 348 U.S. 1 (1954).

31. In re Isserman, 35 N.J. 198, 172 A.2d 425 (1961).

32. Association of the Bar of the City of New York v. Isserman, 271 F.2d 784 (2d Cir. 1959).

33. Note, "The Nature and Consequences of Forensic Misconduct in the Prosecution of a Criminal Case," 54 *Columbia Law Review* 946, 980 (1954).

34. 36 *American Bar Association Journal* 948, 972 (1950). *See* Comment, "Controlling Lawyers by Bar Associations and Courts," 6 *Harvard Civil Rights-Civil Liberties Law Review* 301, 330 (1970).

35. 76 *American Bar Association Reports* 53 (1951).

36. 80 *American Bar Association Reports* 461–62 (1955).

37. Fowler Harper, "Loyalty and Lawyers," 11 *Lawyers Guild Review* 205 (1951).

38. Bobby Seale, the eighth defendant, had no connection with the planning of the demonstrations but was asked only at the last minute to appear and speak at one of the rallies. He came to Chicago on August 27 and did speak at Lincoln Park that evening. He was reported to have made certain remarks to the effect that "now is the time to act, to go buy a . . . carbine . . . and kill the pigs."

39. Daniel Walker, *Rights in Conflict* 5 (New York, Bantam ed. 1968).

40. United States v. Seale, 461 F.2d 345, 374 (7th Cir. 1972); Tr. 3.

41. The "captured cake" episode led to five separate contempt citations, three against Seale and one against Davis and Dellinger. The transcript of the episode reads as follows:

*The Court:* Oh, the defendants are not here? Will you please get the defendants, Mr. Marshal?

*Mr. Davis:* They arrested your cake, Bobby. They arrested it. . . .

*The Court:* One more outburst like that, ladies and gentlemen on the spectator seats, and the courtroom will be cleared of spectators. Just one more. That is the second time that has occurred.

*Mr. Seale:* Don't say nothing no more, brothers. Just sit in the court and observe the proceedings. OK? All right. . . .

*Mr. Seale:* They don't take orders from racist judges, but I can convey the orders for them and they will follow them.

*The Court:* If you continue with that sort of thing, you may expect to be punished for it. I warned you right through this trial and I warn you again, sir. Bring in the jury. [461 F.2d at 377, Tr. 3640–42]

42. 461 F.2d at 375; Tr. 2206.

43. *See* 461 F.2d at 358.

44. 461 F.2d at 381; Tr. 4607 *et seq.*

45. 461 F.2d at 382; Tr. 4632.

46. Tr. 4765.
47. *In re* Dellinger, 461 F.2d 389, 437–38 (7th Cir. 1972); Tr. 4815.
48. *See New York Times,* September 28, 1972, at 28.
49. 461 F.2d at 448; Tr. 19,108–109.
50. 461 F.2d at 450; Tr. 19,154–55.
51. Tr. 19,093–94.
52. 461 F.2d at 415; Tr. 19,669–70.
53. Tr. 19,671.
54. In the Matter of David T. Dellinger, No. 18294, Brief and Appendix for Appellee in the United States Court of Appeals for the Seventh Circuit, 5.
55. The breakdown for each participant was as follows:

| NAME | NO. OF CITATIONS | TOTAL PUNISHMENT |
|---|---|---|
| William M. Kunstler | 24 | 4 years, 13 days |
| Leonard I. Weinglass | 14 | 1 year, 8 months, 5 days |
| Rennard C. Davis | 23 | 2 years, 1 month, 19 days |
| David T. Dellinger | 32 | 2 years, 2 months, 9 days |
| John R. Froines | 10 | 6 months, 15 days |
| Thomas E. Hayden | 11 | 1 year, 2 months, 14 days |
| Abbott H. Hoffman | 23 | 8 months |
| Jerry C. Rubin | 15 | 2 years, 1 month, 23 days |
| Lee Weiner | 7 | 2 months, 18 days |
| Bobby Seale | 16 | 4 years |

See 461 F.2d at 402–403.
56. *In re* Dellinger, 461 F.2d 389 (7th Cir. 1972).
57. Ibid. at 395.
58. United States v. Seale, 461 F.2d 345 (7th Cir. 1972).
59. The contempt trial was assigned to Judge Edward T. Gignoux of the District Court of Maine who was specially designated to hear the case. At the time of this writing (summer 1973), no hearing had been held on the contempt charges.
60. United States v. Dellinger, 472 F.2d 340 (7th Cir. 1972).
61. Of the twenty-one indicted, three were never apprehended and two others were already incarcerated on other charges. Two of the younger defendants were granted youthful offender treatment and one other defendant who was seriously ill was severed. Thirteen stood trial.
62. Arr. Tr. 15.
63. People v. Lumumba Abdul Shakur, Indictment No. 1848–1969. Transcript of Proceedings, November 17, 1969, at 43–44.
64. Ibid. at 46.
65. Transcript of Proceedings, February 2, 1970, Pretrial Tr. 32–33.
66. Pretrial Tr. 34.
67. Ibid. at 96.
68. Ibid. at 107–108.
69. Ibid. at 108–109.
70. Ibid. at 1716.
71. Ibid. at 4310.
72. Ibid. at 5284.
73. Ibid. at 5283.
74. Trial Tr. 3828.
75. Ibid. at 3858.
76. Ibid. at 4351.
77. Ibid. at 4732-3.
78. Ibid. at 5019–20.

79. Ibid. at 3269.
80. Ibid. at 6132.
81. Ibid. at 6132.
82. Ibid. at 6133.
83. Ibid. at 6133.
84. Ibid. at 6251.
85. Ibid. at 6258.
86. Ibid. at 6259–60.
87. Ibid. at 7215.
88. *See* George Bishop, *Witness to Evil* 99 (New York, Dell ed. 1971).
89. Ibid. at 100.
90. Ibid. at 136.
91. People v. Manson, et al, Indictment No. ___. Trial Tr. 12,764.
92. Ibid. at 12,765–66.
93. All the convictions were later reversed by the Court of Appeals. United States v. Dougherty, ___F.2d ___ (D.C. Cir. June 30, 1972).
94. *See* chapter 11 for a more detailed account of the Tacoma trial.
95. *See New York Times,* August 13, 1970, at 19.
96. *See New York Times,* August 19, 1971, at 28.
97. Ibid., December 24, 1971, at 14. The defendants were acquitted of the charges.
98. Ibid., March 19, 1972, at 21; March 28, 1972, at 1.
99. The New York case involved the murder of a Marine sergeant in Greenwich Village. *See New York Times,* November 19, 1970, at 52.
100. The Cleveland case involved a murder at sea, *Cleveland Press,* November 30, 1970, at 2.

## Notes to Chapter Five

1. See Delmar Karlen, "Disorder in the Courtroom," 44 *Southern California Law Review* 996, 1007 (1971); remarks of Judge John M. Murtagh reported in the *New York Times,* October 21, 1970, at 53.
2. Illinois v. Allen, 397 U.S. 337, 352 (1970) (Justice Douglas, concurring).
3. *See* p. 4 above.
4. "What Is a Political Trial?" 28 *The Guild Practitioner* 33 (Spring 1969).
5. Theodore Becker, ed., *Political Trials* xi (New York, 1971).
6. Otto Kirchheimer, *Political Justice* 47 (Princeton, 1961).
7. *See, e.g.,* Karlen, "Disorder in the Courtroom," note 1 above.
8. *See* Lon Fuller, *Legal Fictions* 125 (Stanford, 1967).
9. *See* pp. 35–36 above for a discussion of a trial under those laws.
10. *See* Lewis L. Lorwin, "Criminal Syndicalism," 2 *Encyclopedia of the Social Sciences* 583 (New York, 1937). The same two witnesses—renegade members of the organization—appeared in almost every case to testify against their former comrades. The state would arrest any defense witnesses who admitted to membership in the I.W.W. It also secured an injunction against the very acts classed as crimes under the law so that a judge could try violations without a jury. *See also* Roberta S. Feuerlicht, *America's Reign of Terror* (New York, 1971).
11. *See* Debs v. United States, 249 U.S. 211 (1919). See p. 39 above.
12. Geoffrey C. Hazard, Jr., "Securing Courtroom Decorum," 80 *Yale Law Journal* 433, 449 (1971).
13. For a full account of the Bridges case, *see* C. P. Larrowe, "Did the Old Left Get Due Process: The Case of Harry Bridges," 60 *California Law Review* 39 (1972).
14. 86 *Cong. Rec.* 9031 (1940). *See* Bridges v. Wixon, 326 U.S. 135, 158 (1945).
15. Bridges v. Wixon, 326 U.S. 135 (1945). Justice Frank Murphy began his con-

curring opinion by saying: "The record of this case will stand forever as a monument of man's intolerance of man. Seldom, if ever, in the history of this nation has there been such a concentrated and relentless crusade to deport an individual because he dared to exercise the freedom that belongs to him as a human being and that is guaranteed to him by the Constitution" (326 U.S. at 157).

16. United States v. Bridges, 199 F.2d 845 (9th Cir. 1951).
17. Bridges v. United States, 346 U.S. 209 (1953).
18. United States v. Bridges, 133 F. Supp. 638 (N.D. Cal. 1955).
19. *See* Hallinan v. United States, 182 F.2d 880, 884 (9th Cir. 1951), and MacInnis v. United States, 191 F.2d 157, 159 (9th Cir. 1951).
20. J. Woodford Howard, Jr., *Mr. Justice Murphy: A Political Biography* 212–13 (Princeton, 1968).
21. Biddle later wrote about the prosecution:

> I have since come to regret that I authorized the prosecution. I should not have tried to test the criminal provisions of the statute in this particular case. The two Dunne brothers and their twenty-seven associates were the leaders of the Trotskyist Socialist Workers' Party, a little splinter group, which claimed 3000 members, and by no conceivable stretch of a liberal imagination could have been said to constitute any "clear and present danger" to the government, which, it was alleged, they were conspiring to overthrow. There had been no substantial overt act outside of talk and threats, openly expressed in the time-honored Marxist lingo. [*In Brief Authority* 152 (New York, 1962).]

22. "Political Offenders," 6 *Encyclopedia of the Social Sciences* 202 (New York, 1937).
23. There are many instances of police spies instigating the commission of crimes they were supposed to detect. Company spies or army agents regularly joined the I.W.W. in the 1910s and led the Wobblies, as the members were called, to extravagant actions later put down by the authorities. During World War I, secret army agents spurred a call for a general strike in the Butte, Montana, copper mines and prepared leaflets that were clearly in violation of the Espionage Act (Melvyn Dubofsky, *We Shall Be All* 45 [Chicago, 1969]. After the war, Bureau of Investigation agents from the Justice Department joined the Communists and helped to draft propaganda planks that brought the party within the terms of the Deportation Act. A distinguished panel of lawyers, including Zechariah Chafee, Felix Frankfurter, and Roscoe Pound issued a pamphlet in 1920 which stated that "agents of the Department of Justice have been introduced into radical activities for the purpose of informing on their members or inciting them to activities; these agents have even been instructed from Washington to arrange meetings upon certain dates for the express object of facilitating wholesale raids and arrests" (National Popular Government League, *Report Upon the Illegal Practices of the United States Department of Justice* 5 [1920]). More recently, the police have placed agents among the Black Panthers to encourage them to step beyond the limits of the law. In one recent case in New York, a police agent lured three Panthers into a hotel robbery, supplied maps and an escape car, and then helped to arrest them. A jury could not agree on a verdict, ten members believing that the defendants had been entrapped into committing the crime. They were later acquitted of all charges except for carrying weapons. (*See* Paul Chevigny, *Cops and Rebels* [New York, 1972].)
24. *See* Leon Friedman, ed., *Southern Justice* (New York, 1965).
25. *See* Max Lerner, "Political Offenders," note 22 above.
26. The Pennsylvania Supreme Court reversed the trial judge's ruling and ordered the lawyer reinstated, Schlesinger v. Musmanno, 367 Pa. 476, 478, 81 A.2d 316, 317 (1951).
27. United States v. Daniels, 446 F.2d 967, 969 (6th Cir. 1971). The sentence was reversed by the court of appeals.

28. Jerome Frank, *Law and the Modern Mind* 111, 105 (New York, 1931).
29. Herbert B. Ehrmann, *The Case That Will Not Die* 140 (Boston, 1969).
30. Jessica Mitford, *The Trial of Dr. Spock* 228 (New York, 1969).
31. United States v. Dellinger, 472 F.2d 340 (7th Cir. 1972).
32. Ibid.
33. Charles Garry, "Who's an Officer of the Court," *Trial Magazine,* January/February 1971, at 19.
34. B-1. (The trial judges' questionnaires discussed in chapter 1 and analyzed in appendix A have been numbered consecutively and will be cited by number, J-1, J-2, J-3, etc. Supplementary questionnaires to the trial judges will be cited as SJ-1, SJ-2, SJ-3, etc. The United States attorneys' questionnaires will be cited as A-1, A-2, A-3, etc. The district attorneys' questionnaires are numbered B-1, B-2, B-3, etc. The questionnaires are available in the files of the Association of the Bar of the City of New York.)
35. J-77.
36. *See* Peter Nabokov, *Tijerina and the Courthouse Raid* (Berkeley, 1969).
37. Arthur Kinoy, "The Role of the Radical Lawyer and Teacher of Law" in *Law Against the People,* ed. Robert Lefcourt (New York, 1971).

## Notes to Chapter Six

1. 397 U.S. 337 (1970).
2. Rule 609.1 (c).
3. *See* 18 U.S.C. §401. The issue is somewhat more complex when a *lawyer* refuses to obey a judge's direct order; that issue is treated in the next chapter.
4. 397 U.S. at 343.
5. Ibid. at 346.
6. A judicial survey conducted by the *Georgetown Law Journal* after the *Allen* decision revealed that more than one-quarter of the trial judges believed that the Supreme Court has not provided adequate guidelines (Note, Special Project; "Judicial Response to the Disruptive Defendant," 60 *Georgetown Law Journal* 281, 487 n.1197 [1971]).
7. J-12.
8. *In re* Michael, 326 U.S. 224, 227 (1945), quoting Anderson v. Dunn, 6 Wheat. 204, 231 (1821). *See also* Shillitani v. United States, 384 U.S. 364, 371 (1966).
9. *See* discussion in chapter 10 below.
10. A.B.A. Project on Standards for Criminal Justice, Standards Relating to the Judge's Role in Dealing with Trial Disruptions (Approved Draft, 1971) (hereafter "A.B.A. Trial Disruption Standards"), Standard A.4.
11. J-46.
12. *See* discussion in chapter 8 below.
13. In case J-12, there was a clear indication that one of the three defendants would disrupt the proceedings. The trial judge dealt with this by severing that defendant; "There was no further difficulty."
    Another aspect of pretrial precautions concerns the physical security of the courtroom. This subject will be dealt with in chapter 11.
14. 397 U.S. at 346.
15. Ibid. at 350.
16. Joel M. Flaum and James R. Thompson, "The Case of the Disruptive Defendant: *Allen* v. *Illinois,*" 61 *Journal of Criminal Law* 327, 333 (1970). The warnings in our view should relate not only to the removal sanction, but also to the other *Allen* remedies.
17. *See* J-47. A judge first warned a disorderly defendant in the presence of the jury, and then more forcefully after excusing the jury.
18. J-25.
19. J-77. J-69 involves a similar situation.

20. United States v. Samuel, 431 F.2d 610, 615–16 (4th Cir. 1970).
21. *See* McCloskey v. Boslow, 349 F.2d 119, 121 (4th Cir. 1965); Dennis v. Dees, 278 F. Supp. 354, 357–58 (E.D. La. 1968). *But see* Odell v. Hudspeth, 189 F.2d 300, 301 (10th Cir. 1951).
22. Note, 60 *Georgetown Law Journal* at 493.
23. *See* discussion in chapter 11 below.
24. *Compare* Lanza v. New York, 370 U.S. 139 (1962).
25. *See, e.g.*, United States v. Bollenbach, 125 F.2d 458 (2d Cir. 1942).
26. *See* United States v. Galante, 298 F.2d 72, 75 (2d Cir. 1962).
27. For a discussion of how other countries deal with this problem, *see* Daniel E. Murray, "The Power to Expel a Criminal Defendant from his Own Trial: A Comparative View," 36 *University of Colorado Law Review* 171 (1964).
28. Note, *"Illinois v. Allen:* The Unruly Defendant's Right to a Fair Trial," 46 *New York University Law Review* 120, 126–28 (1971).
29. 223 U.S. 442 (1912).
30. Ibid. at 458.
31. Snyder v. Massachusetts, 291 U.S. 97 (1934).
32. Ibid. at 105–106.
33. 397 U.S. at 343.
34. Contempt was also employed against the one defendant representing himself. There was no contempt citation in the case where the defendant was warned about possible removal.
35. J-15.
36. 397 U.S. at 351. *See also* Note, 60 *Georgetown Law Journal* at 497: "Whenever removal is utilized . . . its adverse effects must be minimized to the greatest extent possible."
37. A.B.A. Trial Disruption Standards, Standard C.2.
38. J-53 and J-74.
39. *See* State v. Roberts, 86 N.J. Super. 159, 296 A.2d 200 (Super. Ct. 1965).
40. Williams v. Florida, 399 U.S. 78 (1970); Thompson v. Utah, 170 U.S. 343 (1898).
41. See the Tacoma conspiracy trial and J-55.
42. 397 U.S. at 344.
43. Frank v. Mangum, 237 U.S. 309, 349 (1915) (Holmes, J., dissenting).
44. It has been argued that if the defendant and his lawyer conclude that binding and gagging is preferable to exclusion of the defendant from the courtroom—that is, if they would rather absorb any prejudice to the defendant because of his trussed up condition than lose the benefits of confrontation of witnesses—a trial judge in his discretion could permit the trial to go forward with the defendant bound and gagged. This was the choice of an Alabama judge during a burglary trial (J-39):

    Defendant, from time to time, interrupted witnesses, calling them liars and shouting that he couldn't get a fair trial on perjured testimony. 3 or 4 interruptions of 1 to 2 minutes each.

    Recessed trial; sequestered jury; informed Defendant that further interruptions could not be permitted and that Court had only two courses of action: gag Defendant and tie him to chair, or remove him from Court Room and try him in absentia. Defendant was informed that Court had no preference and he could select whichever solution he found most agreeable. Defendant was given a few minutes to confer in private with his Attorney, after which he requested one more chance to comply with court rules governing decorum of the parties.

45. *E.g.*, Odell v. Hudspeth, 189 F.2d 300 (10th Cir. 1951).
46. *E.g.*, DeWolf v. State, 245 P.2d 107 (Okla. Crim. 1952).
47. *E.g.*, State v. Temple, 194 Mo. 237, 92 S.W. 869 (1906).
48. J-31. A federal court has held that if handcuffs are used, the district judge must state reasons on the record for imposing the sanction so that an appeals court may review his decision. *See* United States v. Samuel, 431 F.2d 610 (4th Cir. 1970).

49. J-37.
50. J-35.
51. The *New York University Law Review* likewise was able to discover no evidence that civil contempt has been used for this purpose. *See* Note, 46 *New York University Law Review* at 146–47, 151. A case that approaches the civil contempt remedy is People *ex rel* Shakur v. McGrath, 62 Misc. 2d 484, 309 N.Y.S.2d 483 (Sup. Ct. 1970), decided the day before the Supreme Court decided Allen v. Illinois. In *Shakur*, involving the trial of Black Panthers in New York County, the judge indefinitely postponed a preliminary hearing until the defendants promised to behave. The defendants being held in lieu of bail were in effect held in civil contempt. The appellate court indicated, however, that even had the defendants been free on bail, the judge had power to terminate the bail and remand the defendants to jail, a point discussed more fully in the text below.
52. Civil contempt is often used, for example, to jail witnesses until they agree to testify, or parties to a case until they cease violating an order of the court. The remedy is not ordinarily invoked by a judge on his own motion, but rather is moved by one of the parties.
53. McCrone v. United States, 307 U.S. 61, 64 (1939). *See also* Gompers v. Buck Stove & Range Co., 221 U.S. 418, 443 (1911).
54. Shillitani v. United States, 384 U.S. 364, 368–72 (1966).
55. 397 U.S. at 345.
56. Bitter v. United States, 389 U.S. 15 (1967); Fernandez v. United States, 81 S. Ct. 642 (1961) (Harlan J., In chambers).
57. J-47. In addition, the remedy was successfully used as a threat in J-57.
58. 397 U.S. at 345.
59. J-3, where the trial judge believed that the defendants were intentionally courting a mistrial by acting in a disorderly manner.
60. *E.g.*, J-57.
61. *E.g.*, *Shakur* case, *see* note 51.
62. N.Y. Judiciary Law §774 (McKinney 1968).
63. 62 Misc. 2d at 491, 309 N.Y.S.2d at 491.
64. *See* discussion in Note, 46 *New York University Law Review* at 153.
65. Bitter v. United States, 389 U.S. 15, 16 (1967).
66. An expert consultant to the National Commission on Reform of Federal Criminal Laws suggested:

> It is recommended, therefore, that as a matter of policy, no custody summarily imposed as a civil contempt sanction exceed one week. . . . When custody exceeds one week, it is fair to say that it has become punishment, not inducement; if it warrants longer punishment, it should only be imposed pursuant to prosecution and conviction for a specific offense. [Appendix, "Consultant's Report on Contempt," 1 Working Papers of the National Commission on Reform of Federal Criminal Laws 656 (1970).]

67. *Compare* Stack v. Boyle, 342 U.S. 1 (1951). The courts have drawn a distinction between the right to bail before trial and during trial. In the latter case, it is maintained, bail can be aborted because the "public interest in efficient criminal prosecution becomes more pressing once a defendant goes to trial" (United States v. Bentvena, 288 F.2d 442, 444 [2d Cir. 1961]).
68. 18 U.S.C. §401.
69. *Ex parte* Terry, 128 U.S. 289, 303 (1888), quoting Anderson v. Dunn, 6 Wheat. 204, 227 (1821).
70. Harris v. United States, 382 U.S. 162, 164 (1965).
71. 397 U.S. at 345.
72. Note, 46 *New York University Law Review* at 146–47.
73. *In re* Michael, 326 U.S. 224, 227 (1945), quoting Anderson v. Dunn, 6 Wheat 204, 231 (1821).
74. The federal statute, 18 U.S.C. §401 reads as follows:

> A court of the United States shall have power to punish by fine or imprison-

ment, as its discretion, such contempt of its authority, and other, as—(1) Misbehavior of any person in its presence or so near thereto as to obstruct the administration of justice.

Most state statutes follow this wording. *See* Dan B. Dobbs, "Contempt of Court: A Survey," 56 *Cornell University Law Review* 183, 222, n.152 (1971).

75. *See* United States v. Seale, 461 F.2d 345 (7th Cir. 1972); *compare* Katz v. Murtagh, 28 N.Y.2d 234, 238, 269 N.E.2d 815, 820 (1971).
76. 397 U.S. 337, 343 (1970).
77. United States v. Seale, 461 F.2d at 367.
78. United States v. Marshall, 451 F.2d 372, 375 n.6 (9th Cir. 1971).
79. *See* Harlan, J., dissenting, in *In re* McConnell, 370 U.S. 230, 237 (1962).
80. *See* cases cited at pp. 114–15.
81. *In re* Michael, 326 U.S. 224, 227 (1946). *See also Ex parte* Hudgings, 249 U.S. 378, 383 (1919).
82. Brown v. United States, 356 U.S. 148 (1958).
83. *In re* McConnell, 370 U.S. at 236.
84. *In re* Michael, 326 U.S. at 227.
85. Brown v. United States, 356 U.S. at 161 (dissenting opinion).
86. Ibid. at 153.
87. Craig v. Harney, 331 U.S. 367, 376 (1947).
88. *See e.g.*, Walker v. City of Birmingham, 388 U.S. 307 (1967); United States v. United Mine Workers, 330 U.S. 258 (1947). *See* pp. 152–54 below where a lawyer's refusal to obey a court order is discussed.
89. 397 U.S. at 347.
90. *E.g.*, Morissette v. United States, 342 U.S. 246, 250 (1952). ("The contention that an injury can amount to a crime only when inflicted by intention is no provincial or transient notion.") *Compare* Blackstone's sweeping statement that to constitute any crime there must first be a "vicious will" (4 W. Blackstone, *Commentaries* \*21).
91. 190 U.S. 1 (1903).
92. Ibid. at 32 (emphasis added).
93. Ibid. at 35.
94. Kelly v. United States, 250 Fed. 947, 950 (9th Cir. 1918); *also* United States v. Sanders, 290 Fed. 428 (W.D. Tenn. 1923).
95. Offutt v. United States, 232 F.2d 69, 72 (D.C. Cir.), *cert. denied,* 351 U.S. 988 (1956).
96. *In re Brown*, 454 F.2d 999, 1007 (D.C. Cir. 1971).
97. 119. Some of the most perplexing problems have arisen in connection with enforcement of federal civil rights laws. *Compare* Screws v. United States, 325 U.S. 91 (1945) and Collins v. Hardyman, 341 U.S. 651 (1951) *with* Griffin v. Breckenridge, 403 U.S. 88 (1971) (overruling *Collins*).
98. United States v. Seale, 461 F.2d at 368, quoting from United States v. Polizzi, 323 F. Supp. 222, 226 (C.D. Calif. 1971).
99. United States v. Seale, 461 F.2d at 368. Great reliance was put on United States v. Sopher, 347 F.2d 415, 418 (7th Cir. 1965), in which the court noted the absence of "positive evidence of a deliberate intent to pursue a course of improper argument or prohibited conduct."
100. United States v. Seale, 461 F.2d at 368 (emphasis added).
101. *Compare* United States v. Cullea, 454 F.2d 386, 392 (7th Cir. 1971).
102. United States v. Seale, 461 F.2d at 368–69. The court of appeals relied on the *Morissette* and *Brown* cases. *See* notes 82 and 90.
103. *See* New York Times Co. v. Sullivan, 376 U.S. 254 (1964). *See also* St. Amant v. Thompson, 390 U.S. 727 (1968).
104. United States v. Seale, 461 F.2d at 363.
105. *See* Cooke v. United States, 267 U.S. 517, 538 (1925).
106. Two student writers have concluded that *Allen* does not authorize "serious sanctions" for mere disrespect unaccompanied by more serious forms of mis-

behavior. *See* Note, 46 *New York University Law Review* at 135–36; Note, 60 *Georgetown Law Journal* at 490.
107. 461 F.2d 389, 401 (7th Cir. 1972).
108. U.S. *ex rel.* Robson v. Malone, 412 F.2d 848, 850 (5th Cir. 1969). *See* the discussion of this case as it applies to spectators in chapter 11. In a more recent case in the Seventh Circuit, *In re* Chase, 468 F.2d 128 (7th Cir. 1972), a defendant was held in contempt for disobeying ninety-nine direct instructions by a judge to rise. The court of appeals affirmed the contempt but reduced the sentence from 297 to 30 days. One judge dissented, claiming that since a defendant was not voluntarily in the courtroom, he should not be subject to the normal ceremonial rules. *See also* Comstock v. United States, 419 F.2d 1128, 1131 (9th Cir. 1969).
109. *In re* Little, 404 U.S. 553, 554 (1972).
110. Ibid. at 556.
111. United States v. Bollenbach, 125 F.2d 458 (2d Cir. 1942); State v. Watson, 182 Neb. 692, 157 N.W.2d 156 (1968); Banks v. Markowitz, 4 App. Div. 2d 1022, 1168 N.Y.S.2d 852 (1st Dept. 1957).
112. State v. Jones, 105 N.J. Super 493, 253 A.2d 193 (1969).
113. 253 A.2d at 195.
114. Ibid. at 199. The court did uphold a second count of contempt against Jones for his conduct in attempting to speak directly to the court after being directed to do so only through his attorney, calling the court a kangaroo court, and attempting to leave the courtroom while the trial was in progress. We will deal with these issues below. *See also* Adams v. State, 89 Ga. App. 882, 81 S.E.2d 507 (1959).
115. J-12.
116. *See e.g.,* Commonwealth v. Snyder, 275 A.2d 312 (1971).
117. J-60.
118. J-3.
119. 397 U.S. at 345.
120. J-76.
121. J-70.
122. J-50.
123. J-36.
124. J-83.
125. *See also* J-20.
126. J-69.
127. J-36.
128. J-64.
129. *But see* the Supreme Court decision in *In re* Little, 404 U.S. 553 (1972), which casts doubt on this ruling.
130. J-41.
131. J-80.
132. United States v. Bentvena, 319 F.2d 916, 929–30 (2d Cir. 1963).
133. J-23.
134. J-73.
135. J-7.
136. J-52.
137. *See* Donald H. Zergler and Michele G. Hermann, "The Invisible Litigant: An Inside View of Pro Se Actions in the Federal Courts," 47 *New York University Law Review* 157 (1972).
138. A defendant will sometimes be better off representing himself when there are no local lawyers available who are sympathetic to his cause, as in some civil rights cases in the 1960s. The choice for a defendant faced with an unsympathetic bar is to represent himself or engage an out-of-state lawyer.
139. *See* A.B.A. Trial Disruption Standards at 11.
140. J-83.
141. J-41.

142. In addition, 51 felt that *pro se* representation had no effect on disorder, 44 stated that it depended on the individual defendant, and 3 said it depended on the judge's attitude. The remaining 207 judges expressed no opinion.
143. Burton Laub, "The Problem of The Unrepresented, Misrepresented and Rebellious Defendant in Criminal Court," 2 *Duquesne Law Review* 245, 245–46 (1964).
144. SJ-1.
145. SJ-2.
146. United States v. Dougherty, ___F.2d ___ (D.C. Cir. June 30, 1972). *See* Note, "Right to Defend Pro Se," 48 *North Carolina Law Review* 678 (1970). In June 1972, the California constitution was amended to remove the right of a defendant to appear pro se and place this determination in the trial judge's discretion. The California Supreme Court in People v. Sharp, 103 Cal. Rptr. 233, 499 P.2d 489 (1972), narrowed the right as it previously existed in a decision handed down a week after the constitutional change was made.
147. United States v. Denno, 348 F.2d 12, 15 (2d Cir. 1965), quoting from Adams v. United States ex rel McCann, 317 U.S. 269, 279 (1942) and United States v. Mitchell, 137 F.2d 1006, 1011 (2d Cir. 1943).
148. Carter v. Illinois, 329 U.S. 173, 175 (1946).
149. United States v. Plattner, 330 F.2d 271, 273–74 (2d Cir. 1964). *See also* United States v. Dougherty, ___F.2d ___ (D.C. Cir. June 30, 1972); Bayless v. United States, 381 F.2d 67 (9th Cir. 1967); Juelich v. United States, 342 F.2d 29, 32 (5th Cir. 1965); United States v. Denno, 239 F. Supp. 851 (S.D.N.Y. 1965), *affirmed*, 348 F.2d 12 (2nd Cir. 1965), *cert. denied*, 384 1007 (1966). Some courts have found the right only statutory in nature, Johnson v. United States, 318 F.2d 855 (D.C. Cir. 1959).
150. United States v. Dougherty, ___F.2d ___ (D.C. Cir. June 30, 1972).
151. Johnson v. Zerbst, 304 U.S. 458 (1938).
152. United States v. Plattner, 330 F.2d 271, 276 (2d Cir. 1964).
153. People v. Carter, 66 Cal. 2d 666, 673, 427 P.2d 214, 220 (1967).
154. *See, e.g.,* United States v. Birrell, 286 F. Supp. 885, 894–98 (S.D.N.Y. 1968); United States v. Davis, 260 F. Supp. 1009 (E.D. Tenn. 1966) *affirmed* 365 F.2d 251 (6th Cir. 1966). *See also* Westbrook v. Arizona, 384 U.S. 150 (1966).
155. *See* State v. Kolocotronis, 73 Wash. 2d 92, 99, 436 P.2d 774, 781 (1968); United States v. Odom, 423 F.2d 875, 877 (9th Cir. 1970) (concurring opinion); United States v. Dougherty, ___F.2d___ (D.C. Cir. 1972).
156. United States v. Dougherty, ___F.2d ___ (D.C. Cir. 1972).
157. *See, e.g.,* United States v. Bentvena, 319 F.2d 916 (2d Cir. 1963).
158. *See* Reynolds v. United States, 267 F.2d 235 (9th Cir. 1959); United States v. Plattner, 330 F.2d 271, 273 (2d Cir. 1964).
159. State v. Bullock, 431 P.2d 195, 199 (Wash. 1967).
160. United States v. Dougherty, ___F.2d ___, ___. *See also* United States *ex rel.* Maldonando v. Denno, 348 F.2d 12, 15 (2d Cir. 1965).
161. United States v. Bentvena, 319 F.2d 916, 936 (2d Cir. 1963).
162. United States v. Llanes, 374 F.2d 712, 717 (2d Cir. 1967).
163. United States v. Seale, 461 F.2d 345, 359–60 (7th Cir. 1972).
164. Ibid.
165. *See* United States v. Bentvena, 319 F.2d 916, 934–38 (2d Cir. 1963).
166. Mayberry v. Pennsylvania, 400 U.S. 455, 462 (1971); *see also* Illinois v. Allen, 397 U.S. 337, 353–55 (1970) (Douglas, J., concurring).
167. United States v. Dougherty ___F.2d ___.
168. Ibid. at ___.
169. Ibid. at ___.
170. A.B.A. Trial Disruption Standards, p. 13.
171. Note, 60 *Georgetown Law Journal* at 401, n.1240.
172. *In re* McConnell, 370 U.S. 230, 236 (1962).

173. *See* the analysis in Note, 46 *New York University Law Review* at 155–56.
174. Commonwealth v. Fletcher, 441 Pa. 28, 269 A.2d 727 (1970).
175. 441 Pa. at 30, 269 A.2d at 728–29.
176. 441 Pa. at 32, 269 A.2d at 730.
177. People v. Cole, 113 Cal. App. 2d 253, 260, 248 P.2d 141, 146 (Ct. App. 1952).
178. Ibid.
179. Note, 60 *Georgetown Law Journal* at 500 n.1238.
180. A.B.A. Trial Disruption Standards, p. 12.
181. The D.C. Circuit field in *Dougherty:*

> The Supreme Court has recently emphasized that even constitutional litigation prerogatives of a defendant are available for the purpose of choice in conduct of a trial, and do not extend so far as to permit subversion of the core concept of a trial. *Illinois* v. *Allen,* 397 U.S. 337 (1970). The same principle means that obstreperous behavior may constitute waiver of the pro se right.

182. *E.g.,* Brown v. United States, 264 F.2d 363, 367, 369 (D.C. Cir. 1959).
183. *E.g.,* Shelten v. United States, 205 F.2d 806, 813 (5th Cir. 1953).
184. A.B.A. Trial Disruption Standards, at 12.
185. Mayberry v. Pennsylvania, 400 U.S. 455, 468 (1971) (concurring opinion).
186. *See* A.B.A. Trial Disruption Standards, Standard C.3.
187. *See* Wilson v. State, 76 Ga. App. 257, 45 S.E.2d 709 (1947); Patterson v. State, 21 Ala. App. 108 So. 265 (1926).
188. *E.g.,* Duke v. United States, 255 F.2d 721 (9th Cir. 1958); People v. Hill, 70 Cal. 2d 678 (1969); Foster v. State, 148 Tex. Crim. 372, 187 S.W.2d 575 (1945).
189. Strosnider v. Warden of Maryland Penit. 245 Md. 692 226 A.2d 545 (1967); Thompson v. State, 194 So. 2d 649 (Fla. App. 1967).
190. United States v. Foster, 9 F.R.D. 367, 372 (S.D.N.Y. 1949).
191. United States v. Dennis, 183 F.2d 201 (2d Cir. 1950).
192. People v. Mattson, 51 Cal. 2d 777, 797, 336 P.2d 937, 952 (1959).
193. Juelich v. United States, 342 F.2d 29, 33 (5th Cir. 1965).
194. Bayless v. United States, 381 F.2d 67, 71 (9th Cir. 1967).
195. United States v. Davis, 260 F. Supp. 1009, 1018 (E. D. Tenn. 1966).
196. United States v. Mesarosh, 116 F. Supp. 345, 352 (W.D. Penn. 1953).
197. *See* United States v. Warner, 428 F.2d 730 (8th Cir. 1970).
198. Overholser v. De Marcos, 149 F.2d 23, 26 (D.C. Cir. 1945). *See also* Brasier v. Jeary, 256 F.2d 474 (8th Cir. 1958).

## Notes to Chapter Seven

1. Joseph W. Bishop, Jr., "Will Mr. Kunstler Please Step Down?" *Esquire Magazine,* April 1971, at 115.
2. Seven of the trial judges who answered our questionnaire thought that pro se defendants would be less likely to cause disruption because they felt that disruption was "planned in advance by the lawyer" or that the defendant would not be as "skilled in the use of disruptive tactics" as the defense counsel.
3. A recent law review note has pointed out:

> If past cases are any guide, American lawyers have had demonstrably greater respect for the legal system than is implied by the continuing existence of the summary contempt power. Research of cases from 1900 to the present reveals no case in the federal courts in which the contumacious conduct of an attorney succeeded in forcing the trial judge to declare a mistrial, nor does that research provide any case in which an attorney has committed an

assault and battery or other act of violence in the courtroom. [Note, "Criminal Law-Contempt-Conduct of Attorney During Course of Trial," 1971 *Wisconsin Law Review* 329, 351–52]

4. J-98.
5. J-102A.
6. J-102B.
7. A.B.A. Project on Standards for Criminal Justice, Standards Relating to the Prosecution Function and the Defense Function (Approved Draft, 1971) (hereafter "A.B.A. Defense Function Standards") state:

> Human experience with deliberative and judicial processes demonstrates that certain rules or standards of conduct are needed to ensure that, notwithstanding differences in their objectives, contending advocates will work in harmony for what is their common cause, the administration of justice. They must not allow themselves to be diverted by irrelevant, extraneous or disrupting factors. Basic to an efficient and fair functioning of our adversary system of justice is that at all times there be an atmosphere manifesting mutual respect by all participants. This can be achieved only by strict adherence to firm standards of what may be called, for want of better terms, professional etiquette and deportment. There is no place and no occasion for rudeness or overbearing, oppressive conduct. The control of courtroom decorum lies in the advocates' acceptance of standards of elementary courtesy and politeness in human relations. [457–58]

8. A.B.A. Defense Function Standards, at 153.
9. Ibid. at 148.
10. Ibid. at 146.
11. For a general discussion of this phenomenon see Daniel H. Pollitt, "Counsel for the Unpopular Cause: The 'Hazard of Being Undone,'" 43 *North Carolina Law Review* 9 (1964).
12. A.B.A. Defense Function Standards, at 147.
13. *See* discussion on pp. 176–78 below.
14. F. Raymond Marks with Kirk Leswing and Barbara A. Fortinsky, *The Lawyer, the Public and Professional Responsibility* 242–43 (American Bar Foundation, 1972). *See also* Norman Dorsen, The Role of the Lawyer in America's Ghetto Society, 49 *Texas Law Review* 50 (1970).
15. 22 *Howell's State Trials,* 414 (1792).
16. American Bar Association Special Committee on Evaluation of Ethical Standards, Code of Professional Responsibility (Final Draft, July 1, 1969) (hereafter "A.B.A. Code of Professional Responsibility").
17. *See, e.g.,* periodic reports of Committee on Professional and Judicial Ethics, Association of the Bar of the City of New York.
18. People v. Kurz, 35 Mich. App. 643, 192 N.W.2d 594 (1971).
19. *In re* Ruffalo, 390 U.S. 544, 555 (1968) (White, J., concurring).
20. Kentucky State Bar Association v. Taylor, __ Ky. __, 482 S.W.2d 574, 582–83 (1972).
21. Personal interview, Professor Monroe H. Freedman, September 20, 1972.
22. Anthony Lewis, "Lawyers and Civilization," 120 *University of Pennsylvania Law Review* 860, 862 (1972).
23. Ibid. at 863.
24. In 1970 there were only fourteen complaints against English barristers, four of whom were overseas. In five cases, formal charges were presented. None of the charges involved in-court misbehavior. (Annual Statement, The Senate of the Four Inns of Court, 1969–1970; Letter, Nancy Gow to William Birtles, September 29, 1971).
25. Lewis, "Lawyers and Civilization," at 862–63.
26. William J. Brennan, "The Responsibilities of the Legal Profession," 54 *American Bar Association Journal* 121, 122 (1968).
27. Rule 609.1(d)(2), First Department; Rule 700.4(b), Second Department.

28. American College of Trial Lawyers, Report and Recommendations on Disruption of the Judicial Process (hereafter "Trial Lawyers Report"), p. 6.
29. Canon 16 of the American Bar Association's Canons of Professional Ethics included similar language but the rule was not formally interpreted to require an attorney to act as a disciplining agent of his client in court: See A.B.A. Committee on Professional Ethics, Opinions no. 44 (1931), no. 75 (1932).
30. *Contempt: Transcript of the Contempt Citations, Sentences and Responses of the Chicago Conspiracy 10* 209 (Chicago, 1970).
31. *In re* Lord, 255 Minn. 370, 375, 97 N.W.2d 287, 291 (1959).
32. A.B.A. Code of Professional Responsibility, EC 9-6.
33. "Is the Problem Simple," *Trial Magazine,* January/February 1971, p. 27.
34. Cammer v. United States, 350 U.S. 399, 405 n.3 (1956).
35. *In re* Bergeron, 220 Mass. 472, 467, 107 N.E. 1007, 1008-9 (1915).
36. Noone v. Fisher, 45 F. Supp. 653 (E.D. Tenn. 1942).
37. Powell v. Alabama, 287 U.S. 45, 73 (1932).
38. Cammer v. United States, 350 U.S. 399, 405 (1956).
39. Johns v. Smyth, 176 F. Supp. 949, 952 (E.D. Va. 1959).
40. *In re* Dellinger, 461 F.2d 389, 399 (7th Cir. 1972).
41. Hal H. Rowland, "The Crucial Code," *Trial Magazine,* January/February 1971, at 17.
42. Melvin Kodas and Robert Joost, "The American Trial Lawyers Association: Its Argument," *Trial Magazine,* January/February 1971, at 33.
43. EC 7-8.
44. United States v. Marshall, No. 51942 (W.D. Wash. 1970) Transcript of Proceedings, Voir Dire, 3, 5–6. *See also* Monroe H. Freedman, "The Three Hardest Questions," 64 *Michigan Law Review* 1469, 1471–72 (1966).
45. Under DR 7-102(a) (7) of the A.B.A. Code of Professional Responsibility, a lawyer may not "counsel or assist his client in conduct that the lawyer knows to be illegal or fraudulent." DR 7-101(b) (2) states that a lawyer may "refuse to aid or participate in conduct that he believes to be unlawful."
46. Newman, "Is the Problem Simple?" at 27.
47. A.B.A. Code of Professional Responsibility, EC 7-36.
48. Warren E. Burger, "The Necessity for Civility," 52 F.R.D. 211, 212 (1971).
49. United States v. Schiffer, 351 F.2d 91, 93 (6th Cir. 1965).
50. MacInnis v. United States, 191 F.2d 157, 159 (9th Cir. 1951).
51. United States v. Seale 461 F.2d 345, 369–70 (7th Cir. 1972), quoting from *In re* Little, 404 U.S. 553 (1972).
52. *See* United States v. Seale, 461 F.2d at 370:

> . . . the manner in which insulting remarks, not obstructive of themselves, are leveled may accomplish an obstruction. For example, shouting the remarks or accompanying their utterance with physical demonstration may provide the necessary element. Moreover, the very delay of the proceedings occasioned by a disrespectful outburst or other misbehavior may be sufficient to constitute a material obstruction. Thus, if a not insubstantial delay is entirely unnecessary and the misconduct serves, for instance, solely to vent the speaker's spleen, the requisite obstruction would be present.

53. *In re* Philip Hirschkop, 346 F. Supp. 972, 982–83 (D.D.C. 1972).
54. Ibid. at 978.
55. O'Brien v. State, 261 Wisc. 470, 572–73, 53 N.W.2d 534, 535 (1952).
56. J-232.
57. Va. Code Ann. §18.1–292.
58. Holt v. Virginia, 381 U.S. 131 (1965).
59. *In re* Dellinger, 461 F.2d at 398–99.
60. Hallinan v. United States, 182 F.2d 880, 877 (9th Cir. 1950).
61. *In re* McConnell, 370 U.S. 230, 236 (1962).
62. Cooper v. Superior Court, 359 P.2d 274, 276–77 (1961).

63. Ibid. at 280.

64. Walker v. City of Birmingham, 388 U.S. 307 (1967).

65. Ibid. at 320.

66. Interlocutory appeals (i.e., appeals to a high court before a final judgment is issued) are available in only a limited number of situations and hardly ever for in-court procedural rulings of a judge.

67. United States v. Sopher, 347 F.2d 415 (7th Cir. 1965).

68. *In re* Osborne, 344 F.2d 611, 613 (9th Cir. 1965).

69. Phelan v. People Territory of Guam, 394 F.2d 293, 394–95 (9th Cir. 1968).

70. People v. Harrington, 301 Ill. App. 185, 21 N.E.2d 903 (1939).

71. *In re* Abse, 251 A.2d 655 (D.C.C. of A., 1969).

72. State v. Yates, 302 P.2d 719 (Oreg. 1956).

73. *In re* Dellinger, 461 F.2d 389, 398–99 (7th Cir. 1972).

74. *See In re* Hallinan, 81 Cal. Rptr. 1, 459 P.2d 255 (1969).

75. *See* People v. Sears, 49 Ill. 2d 14, 273 N.E.2d 380 (1971) where a fine of fifty dollars per hour was imposed on a special prosecutor until he called certain witnesses before a grand jury. The order was reversed by the Illinois Supreme Court.

76. The New York State Committee on Disciplinary Enforcement has explained in a report to the Administrative Board of the New York State Judicial Conference:

> There are cogent reasons for that practice. For one, there is the desire to avoid a situation where two tribunals, simultaneously considering the same matter, may arrive at inconsistent results. This is not a remote possibility where different burdens of proof are involved and the result turns on the resolution of questions of fact and credibility. . . .
>
> Another reason [for] justifying the present practice is that simultaneous prosecution of the disciplinary proceeding may improperly affect the outcome of either the proceeding or the related litigation. If the accused attorney is required to invoke his privilege against self-incrimination in the disciplinary proceeding to avoid the use of his testimony in the criminal proceeding, he will be deprived of his right to defend himself fully in the disciplinary proceeding. If, on the other hand, he testifies fully in the disciplinary proceeding and produces all witnesses and evidence available to him, his adversaries in the pending litigation obtain an unfair advantage in having the strengths and weaknesses of his defense prematurely disclosed.

77. Schofield Discipline Case, 362 Pa. 201, 215 (1949).

78. *In re* Ruffalo, 390 U.S. 544, 551 (1968). *See also* Spevack v. Klein, 385 U.S. 511 (1967).

79. In one case in the Canal Zone, a lawyer was suspended by the court for two years for using offensive and insulting language to the judge in open court and in chambers. He refused to apologize. The court of appeals suggested that upon proper apology, the order of suspension could be modified (*In re* Collins, 210 F.2d 373 [5th Cir. 1954]). In a New York case, one lawyer physically attacked another in an examination before trial and was suspended for six months (*In re* Simon, 302 N.Y.S.2d 159 [1st Dept. 1969]). These actions go far beyond the kind of forensic misconduct discussed in the text.

80. *Legal Ethics* 46–47 (New York, 1953).

81. *In re* Isserman, 345 U.S. 286 (1953).

82. *In re* Isserman, 348 U.S. 1 (1954).

83. *In re* Isserman, 345 U.S. 286, 292 (1953).

84. *In re* Isserman, 345 U.S. 286, 294 (1953).

85. Kentucky State Bar Association v. Taylor, ___ Ky. ___, 482 S.W.2d 574, 584 (1972).

86. *See* note 53.

87. Personal interview, M-K, March 1, 1972.

88. Trial Lawyers Report, at 14.

89. A.B.A. Trial Disruption Standards, at 14.
90. Trial Lawyers Report, at 15.
91. *See* Phelan v. People of Territory of Guam, 394 F.2d 293 (9th Cir. 1968).
92. *Ex parte* Garland, 4 Wall. 333, 379 (1867).
93. A.B.A. Trial Disruption Standards, at 14.
94. Trial Lawyers Report, at 15.
95. Laughlin v. Eicher, 145 F.2d 700, 702 (D.C. Cir. 1944).
96. Ibid. at 705.
97. The power to remove an attorney from a civil case has also been exercised. In a case in New York City, the attorney for one of the parties in a long and complicated condemnation case made repeated insulting and personal remarks about opposing counsel, a distinguished former judge, and accused the court of favoring his opponent in every ruling that he made. He was warned to stop his remarks but he continued. Finally the judge stopped the proceedings and told the condemnor to replace its trial counsel (*In re* Port Authority Trans-Hudson Corporation, Docket No. ___). As a practical matter, any client in a civil case who is told by a judge that he thinks counsel should be replaced is likely to obey the direction. As far as a judge's power to do so over the client's objections, we believe that a judge's authority to control the courtroom and to ensure that proceedings are properly conducted encompasses the power to remove an attorney from a civil case as well as a criminal action under proper circumstances.
98. Trial Disruption Standards, Standard D.2. The Trial Lawyers suggest a similar sanction. *See* Recommendation X.
99. 353 U.S. 232, 238–39 (1956). The *Schware* doctrine was reiterated in 1971: Baird v. Arizona, 401 U.S. 1, 8 (1971).
100. *See* New York State Judiciary Law, §478.
101. *See* Spivak v. Sachs, 16 N.Y.2d 163, 263 N.Y.S.2d 953 (1965).
102. Spanos v. Skouras Theaters Corp. 364 F.2d 161, 170 (2d Cir. 1966). *See also* Banks v. Halder, TH72, Cr.47, no. 73–1332 (7th Cir. May 17, 1973), where the Seventh Circuit granted a petition for mandamus ordering a federal district judge in Indiana to permit William M. Kunstler to appear as counsel for a federal prisoner charged with assaulting a guard.
103. Lefton v. City of Hattiesburg, 333 F.2d 280 (5th Cir. 1965).
104. United States v. Bergamo, 154 F.2d 31, 35 (3rd Cir. 1946) (relying on the Sixth Amendment right to counsel).
105. Cooper v. Hutchinson, 184 F.2d 119 (3rd Cir. 1950).

## Notes to Chapter Eight

1. A.B.A. Code of Professional Responsibility, EC 7-13.
2. A.B.A. Project on Standards for Criminal Justice, Standards Relating to The Prosecution Function and the Defense Function (Approved Draft, 1971), at 44 (hereafter "A.B.A. Prosecution Function Standards").
3. A.B.A. Prosecution Function Standards, at 45.
4. Trial Lawyers Report, at 9.
5. Robert H. Jackson, "The Federal Prosecutor," 24 *Journal of American Judicature Society* 18, 19 (1940).
6. *See* Note, "An Examination of the Grand Jury in New York," 1 *Columbia Journal of Law and Social Problems* 88 (1965); Patricia Mar, "The California Grand Jury: Vestige of Aristocracy," 1 *Pacific Law Journal* 36 (1970). *See also* Wayne L. Morse, "A Survey of the Grand Jury System," 10 *Oregon Law Review* 102 (1931).
7. *See* New York Criminal Procedure Law §§100, 170, and 190.
8. *See* Coates v. City of Cincinnati, 402 U.S. 611 (1971) and Papachristou v. City of Jacksonville, 405 U.S. 56 (1972).

9. Comment, "Prosecutorial Discretion in the Initiation of Criminal Complaints," 42 *Southern California Law Review* 519, 333 (1969).
10. *See* Otto Kirchheimer, *Political Justice* 193 (Princeton, 1961).
11. *See* Patrick Lord Devlin, *The Criminal Prosecution in England* 25–26 (New Haven, 1958), for an interesting account of the situation.
12. *See* Kirchheimer, *Political Justice,* at 188 ff.
13. Yick Wo v. Hopkins, 118 U.S. 356, 373–74 (1886).
14. *E.g.,* Buxbom v. City of Riverside, 29 F. Supp. 3 (S.D. Cal. 1939) (handbill distribution): Society of Good Neighbors v. Mayor of Detroit, 324 Mich. 22, 36 N.W.2d 308 (1949) (lottery laws). And *see* cases cited in Note, "The Right to Nondiscriminatory Enforcement of State Penal Laws, 61 *Columbia Law Review* 1102, 1106 n.12 (1961).
15. Wade v. City and County of San Francisco, 82 Cal. App. 2d 337, 186 P.2d 181 (1st Dist. Ct. App. 1957) (court upheld complaint charging discriminatory enforcement of anti-solicitation ordinance); City of New Orleans v. Levy, 233 La. 844, 98 So. 2d 210 (1957) (injunction sought under zoning ordinance held to be discriminatory since many other unprosecuted violations shown to exist). And *see* cases cited in Note, 61 *Columbia Law Review* at 1106 n.12.
16. Edelman v. California, 344 U.S. 357 (1953); Ah Sin v. Wittman, 198 U.S. 500, 506 (1905); Edelman v. California, 344 U.S. 357 (1953); Snowden v. Hughes, 321 U.S. 1 (1944).
17. 342 P.2d 538 (Super. Ct. 1959).
18. Ibid. at 540.
19. Ibid.
20. People v. Utica Daw's Drug Co. 225 N.Y.S.2d 128, 133 (4th Dept. 1962) (emphasis added).
21. Discriminatory arrests by the police may properly be subject to a federal court injunctive relief. *See* Lewis v. Kugler, 446 F.2d 1343 (3d Cir. 1971).
22. Coates v. City of Cincinnati, 402 U.S. 611 (1971).
23. Ibid. at 616 (1971); *see also* Papachristou v. City of Jacksonville, 405 U.S. 156, 1970 (1972) ("Where, as here, there are no standards governing the exercise of discretion . . . the scheme permits and encourages an arbitrary and discriminatory enforcement of the law"); L.I. Vietnam Moratorium Comm. v. Cahn, 437 F.2d 344, 350 (1970). *See also* United States v. Crowthers, 456 F.2d 1074 (4th Cir. 1971).
24. Lenske v. United States, 383 F.2d 20, 27 (9th Cir. 1967).
25. Ibid. at 26.
26. Ibid. at 27. It has recently become known that, beginning in August 1969, the Internal Revenue Service had a special division that investigated liberal and radical organizations and their sponsors for possible violations of tax law. It was abolished in August 1973. *See New York Times,* August 10, 1973, at 29.
27. United States v. Steele, 461 F.2d 1149, 1151–52 (9th Cir. 1972). In a more recent case in the Seventh Circuit, a young man was indicted for failure to have his draft card in his possession. He claimed that he was being prosecuted because he was a draft counselor and was active in opposing the draft and the Vietnam war. He offered evidence to show that it was the policy of the Selective Service not to prosecute charges of non-possession, that the U.S. Attorney's office knew of his draft counseling activities, and that the government waited three years to indict him. The court of appeals held in an en banc opinion that there was a prima facie showing of purposeful discrimination in enforcement of the law and that the government had the burden of proving non-discrimination. United States v. Falk, 6 SSLR 3200 (7th Cir. April 19, 1973).
28. 225 N.Y.S.2d at 135.
29. District of Columbia v. Thompson Co., 346 U.S. 100, 117 (1953).
30. Arthur E. Bonfield, "The Abrogation of Penal Statutes by Non-Enforcement," 49 *Iowa Law Review* 389, 414–15 (1964).
31. Ibid. at 412.

32. One case has been found in which the non-enforcement of a law against government officials who violated the statute was held to be a defense for a private individual who did the same. In a federal case in Missouri, a private detective was indicted for engaging in illegal wiretapping. The judge dismissed the indictment on the ground that many government agencies tapped telephone wires illegally but were not prosecuted for doing so. (*See* United States v. Robinson, 331 F. Supp. 1003 [W. D. Mo. 1969].) It is not clear whether the defense would have been available if a number of other private individuals had violated the law and not been prosecuted.
33. 225 N.Y.S.2d at 135.
34. City of Covington v. Gausepohl, 250 Ky. 323, 62 S.W.2d 1040 (1933).
35. City of New Orleans v. Levy, 233 La. 844, 98 So. 2d 210 (1957).
36. *E.g.,* People v. Utica Daw's Drug Co., 225 N.Y.S.2d at 134.
37. *See* Bloom v. Illinois, 391 U.S. 194, 202 (1968); Osborn v. United States, 385 U.S. 323, 331 (1966).
38. *See* Jackson v. Denno, 378 U.S. 368 (1964).
39. Hearings Before the Subcommittee of the Committee on Appropriations, Department of Justice, 84th Cong., 1st Sess., at 85–96 (1955).
40. *Discretionary Justice* 211–12 (Baton Rouge, 1965).
41. Bruton v. United States, 391 U.S. 123 (1968).
42. Ibid. at 134.
43. Ibid. at 135.
44. Krulewitch v. United States, 336 U.S. 440, 446–48, 450, 453 (1949).
45. Personal interview, Leon Friedman, November 1, 1971.
46. *See* discussion in Model Penal Code, §5.03 (Criminal Conspiracy Comments) (Tent. Draft, Nov. 10, 1960), at 136.
47. *See* Bruton v. United States, 391 U.S. 123 (1968) and cases cited at 129 n.4.
48. *See generally* Note, "Joint and Single Trials under Rules 8 and 14 of the Federal Rules of Criminal Procedure," 74 *Yale Law Journal* 553 (1965).
49. Opper v. United States, 348 U.S. 84, 95 (1954).
50. William F. Walsh, "Fair Trials and the Federal Rules of Criminal Procedure," 49 *American Bar Association Journal* 853 (1963).
51. *See* Note, "The Threat of Unfairness in Conspiracy Prosecutions: A Proposal for Procedural Reform," 2 *New York University Review of Law & Social Change* 1, 12–17 (Summer 1972).
52. Harrison v. United States, 7 F.2d 259, 263 (2d Cir. 1925).
53. Prosecutors have been known to criticize the behavior of judges outside of court. *See New York Times,* June 17, 1971, at 45.
54. *See Dallas Morning News,* February 26, 1971, §D, at 1.
55. *See* Albert W. Alschuler, "Courtroom Misconduct by Prosecutors and Trial Judges" (hereafter "Alschuler"), 50 *Texas Law Review* 629, 631 n.9; *see also* Roscoe Pound, *Criminal Justice in America* 187 (1930); Richard G. Singer, "Forensic Misconduct by Federal Prosecutors—And How It Grew," 20 *Alabama Law Review* 227 (1968); Don Hobbs, "Prosecutor's Bias: An Occupational Disease," 2 *Alabama Law Review* 40 (1949); Note, "Prosecutor Forensic Misconduct—'Harmless Error'? 6 *Utah Law Review* 108 (1958).
56. *See* Alschuler at 633–34 and cases cited.
57. State v. Brice, 163 La. 392, 111 So. 798 (1927).
58. Blocker v. State, 112 Tex. Crim. 275, 16 S.W.2d 253 (1929).
59. State v. Moore, 212 La. 943, 33 So. 2d 691 (1947).
60. Yett v. State, 110 Tex. Crim. 23, 24, 7 S.W.2d 94, 94 (1928).
61. King v. State, 141 Tex. Crim. 257, 148 S.W.2d 199 (1941).
62. United States v. Hughes, 389 F.2d 535, 536 (2d Cir. 1968).
63. Volkmor v. United States, 13 F.2d 594, 595 (6th Cir. 1926). The prosecutor also said, "A skunk is always a skunk; you can decorate him any way you want to. . . . I also presume you cannot make a rose out of an onion, no matter what you do. . . . Take a weak-faced weasel, such as the defendant—." At this point, the defense counsel interjected an objection, but the prosecutor continued with the remark quoted in the text.
64. State v. Owen, 73 Idaho, 394, 408, 253 P.2d 203, 211 (1953).

65. Horner v. Florida, 312 F. Supp. 1292, 1295 (M.D. Fla. 1967), *affirmed,* 398 F.2d 880 (5th Cir. 1968). This statement was not the only ground for reversal. The prosecutor failed to correct a material false statement made by a prosecution witness; he characterized the defense attorney as "an expert in the rackets"; he asserted facts not in evidence; and he said, "It isn't viciousness that you see from the prosecutor here. What it is, is venom, for this reason: I represent the law."

66. People v. Hickman, 34 App. Div. 2d 831, 312 N.Y.S.2d 644 (1951).

67. United States v. Dellinger, 472 F.2d 340, 388 (7th Cir. 1972).

68. People v. Elder, 25 Ill. 2d 612, 614, 186 N.E.2d 27, 29 (1962), *cert. denied,* 374 U.S. 814 (1963).

69. Williams v. State, 93 Okla. Crim. 260, 275, 226 P.2d 989, 997 (1951).

70. Commonwealth v. Capps, 382 Pa. 72, 79, 114 A.2d 338, 342 (1955).

71. Commonwealth v. Narr, 173 Pa. Super. 148, 153, 96 A.2d 155 (1950).

72. United States v. Markham, 191 F.2d 936, 939 (7th Cir. 1951).

73. Stephan v. United States, 133 F.2d 87, 98 (6th Cir.), *cert. denied,* 318 U.S. 781 (1943).

74. Johnston v. United States, 154 F. 445, 449 (9th Cir. 1907).

75. State v. Goodwin, 189 La. 443, 446, 179 So. 591, 599 (1938).

76. United States v. Walker, 190 F.2d 481, 484 (2d Cir. 1951).

77. Miller v. State, 226 Ga. 730, 731, 177 S.E.2d 253, 254 (1970).

78. United States v. Dellinger, 472 F.2d 340, 388 (7th Cir. 1972).

79. Ibid.

80. People v. Alpine, 81 Cal. App. 456, 468, 254 P. 281, 286 (1927).

81. People v. Weller, 123 Ill. App. 2d 421, 258 N.E.2d 806, 809 (1970); *see also* People v. Garippo, 321 Ill. 157, 151 N.E. 584 (1926).

82. People v. Gilyard, 124 Ill. App. 2d 95, 108, 260 N.E.2d 364, 370 (1970). Courts have also found the error harmless when a prosecutor referred to unscrupulous, shyster lawyers who got criminals free (People v. Cummings, 388 Ill. 636,170 N.E. 750 [1930]); to the deplorable conduct of an attorney who would represent a murderer (Adams v. State, 176 Ark. 916, 5 S.W.2d 946 [1928]); to the dollars jingling in the defense attorney's pocket (Gatlin v. State, 113 Tex. Crim. 247, 20 S.W.2d 431 [1929]); and to the asserted fact that the defense attorney was a "poor, humble, simple little fellow" who talked "out of two sides of his mouth, or as the Indian might say a forked tongue" (State v. Gonzales, 105 Ariz. 434, 436, 466 P.2d 388, 390 [1970]).

83. Berger v. United States, 295 U.S. 78, 88 (1935). *See also* Viereck v. United States, 318 U.S. 236, 247–48 (1943).

84. Dunlop v. United States, 165 U.S. 486, 498 (1897).

85. *See* Ballard v. United States, 152 F.2d 941, 943 (9th Cir. 1945), *reversed on other grounds,* 329 U.S. 187 (1946). *See also* United States v. Wexler, 79 F.2d 526, 530 (2d Cir. 1935) (L. Hand, J.), *cert. denied,* 297 U.S. 703 (1936). Judge Hand had written the decision that, seven months earlier, had been reversed in *Berger.* This statement can be viewed as his response. *See also* Gray v. State, 90 Miss. 235, 241, 43 So. 289, 290 (1907).

86. Di Carlo v. United States, 6 F.2d 364, 368 (2d Cir.), *cert. denied,* 268 U.S. 706 (1925); Fitter v. United States, 258 F. 567, 572 (2d Cir. 1919); Bynum v. State, 35 Ala. App. 297, 298, 47 So. 245, 247, *cert. denied,* 245 Ala. 22, 47 So. 2d 247 (1950).

87. United States v. Cook, 432 F.2d 1093, 1106–07 (7th Cir. 1970), *cert. denied,* 401 U.S. 996 (1971); State v. Brown, 214 La. 18, 24, 36 So. 2d 624, 626 (1948); State v. Dallao, 187 La. 392, 434, 175 So. 4, 18 *cert. denied,* 302 U.S. 635 (1937); State v. Graziani, 168 La. 397, 302, 121 So. 872, 874 (1929).

88. Trial Lawyers Report, at 9.

89. People v. Kirkes, 243 P.2d 816, 831 *affirmed,* 39 Cal. 2d 719, 249 P.2d 1 (1952). *See* Berger v. United States, 295 U.S. 78, 88 (1935).

90. Alschuler at 632.

91. *National Commission of Law Observance and Enforcement Report on Law-lessness in Law Enforcement* 268 (1931).
92. Ibid.
93. Commonwealth v. Nicely, 130 Pa. 261, 270, 18 A. 737, 738 (1889).
94. Pierce v. United States, 86 F.2d 949, 953 (6th Cir. 1936).
95. Alschuler at 674; Singer, "Forensic Mis-Conduct by Federal Prosecutors—And How It Grew" at 276.
96. *In re* Sanborn, 208 Kan. 4, 490 P.2d 598 (1971); Brutkiewicz v. State, 280 Ala. 218, 191 So. 2d 222 (1966).
97. Castle v. Commonwealth, 269 Ky. 168, 170, 106 S.W.2d 626, 627 (1937). *Cf.* Rogers v. State, 8 Okla. Crim. 226, 243, 127 P. 365, 372 (1912).
98. *In re* Maestretti, 30 Nev. 187, 191, 93 P. 1004, 1005 (1908).
99. See the full discussion in Alschuler at 671–72, of the Illinois disciplinary proceedings following Miller v. Pate, 386 U.S. 1 (1967), in which the Supreme Court freed a prisoner on the ground that the prosecutor had "deliberately misrepresented the truth" in securing the conviction. The Grievance Committee, in a strained interpretation, converted the issue from one of misrepresentation to one of innocent non-disclosure, and declined to recommend disciplinary action.
100. Commonwealth *ex rel.* Buckingham v. Ward, 267 Ky. 627, 103 S.W.2d 117 (1937).
101. *E.g.*, Melville v. Wettengel, 98 Colo. 529, 57 P.2d 699 (1936); *In re* Maestretti, 30 Nev. 187, 93 P. 1004 (1908); Snyder's Case, 301 Pa. 276, 152 A. 33 (1930).
102. United States v. Lotsch, 102 F.2d 35, 37 (2d Cir.), *cert. denied*, 307 U.S. 622 (1939).
103. Goddard v. State, 143 Fla. 28, 38, 196 So. 596, 601 (1940); Commonwealth v. Nelson, 172 Pa. Super. 125, 148, 92 A.2d 431, 444 (1952), *reversed on other grounds*, 377 Pa. 58, 104 A.2d 133 (1954), *affirmed*, 350 U.S. 497 (1956).
104. People v. Podwys, 6 Cal. App. 2d 71, 44 P.2d 377, 379 (1935); People v. Esposito, 244 N.Y. 370, 372, 121 N.E. 344, 345 (1918).
105. Stunz v. United States, 27 F.2d 575, 577 (8th Cir. 1928).
106. United States v. Antonelli Fireworks Co., 155 F.2d 631, 637–38 (2d Cir.), *cert. denied*, 329 U.S. 742 (1946); Commonwealth v. Wilcox, 316 Pa. 129, 146, 173 A. 653, 660 (1934).
107. People v. Milewski, 316 Ill. 288, 291, 147 N.E. 246, 247 (1925).
108. United States v. Antonelli Fireworks Co., 155 F.2d 631, 661 (2d Cir.) (Frank, J., dissenting), *cert. denied*, 329 U.S. 742 (1946).
109. Chapman v. California, 386 U.S. 18, 24 (1967).
110. United States v. Socony-Vacuum Oil Co., 310 U.S. 150, 239 (1940).
111. *See, e.g.*, Malone v. United States, 94 F.2d 281, 288 (7th Cir. 1938).
112. Alschuler at 658.
113. *Nat'l. Comm'n. of Law Observance and Enforcement Report on Lawlessness in Law Enforcement*, at 15.

## Notes to Chapter Nine

1. Sacher v. United States, 343 U.S. 1, 37–38 (1952) (dissent).

   The A.B.A. Standards on the Judge's Role in Dealing with Trial Disruptions recognize the central role of the judge in all courtroom proceedings:

   > It is ultimately the authority and responsibility of the trial judge which must be exercised to maintain the atmosphere appropriate for a fair, rational and civilized determination of the issues and the governance of the conduct of all persons in the courtroom, including the attorneys. [Commentary to A.2]

2. J-113.
3. J-77. *See also* J-114.

4. A.B.A. Prosecution Function Standards, at 1.
5. J-242.
6. J-18.
7. J-244.
8. *See* State v. Pierce, 208 Kan. 19, 490 P.2d 584 (1971).
9. Comments of Judge Robert T. Stephan at National Conference of Trial Judges meeting, St. Louis, Missouri, August 7, 1970, Transcript of Proceedings, at 57–59.
10. Ibid. at 58.
11. *See In re* Stevens, 20 N.J. 177, 119 A.2d 9, 10 (1955).
12. If many defendants are involved in a case, it may also be desirable to allow one counsel to object on behalf of all defendants.
13. *See* note 3 above, p. 59.
14. J-1.
15. Trial Disruption Standards, at 3.
16. J-218. *See also* the Detroit case described by Judge James L. Ryan at National Conference of Trial Judges meeting, St. Louis, Missouri, August 7, 1970, Transcript of Proceedings, at 68–69.
17. Trial Disruption Standards, at 5–6.
18. Herman Schwartz, "Judges as Tyrants," 7 *Criminal Law Bulletin* 129–30 (1971).
19. *Los Angeles Times,* December 4, 1972, Part II, at 1.
20. United States v. Marzano, 149 F.2d 923, 926 (2d Cir. 1945).
21. United States v. Dellinger, 472 F.2d 340, 387 (7th Cir. 1972).
22. Ibid. at 388. n.84.
23. People v. Russell, Docket YO-125/69, Criminal Court of City of New York, Queens County, Record of Proceedings, June 22, 1970, at 32–33.
24. *New York Times,* December 21, 1970, at 52.
25. Stephen R. Bing and S. Stephen Rosenfeld, "The Quality of Justice in the Lower Criminal Courts of Metropolitan Boston, A Report by the Lawyers Committee for Civil Rights Under Law" 80 (Boston, 1970). *See also Time Magazine,* June 5, 1972.
26. The reporter wrote about one judge:

> In one case, two defendants were to be tried together on narcotics charges. One fell asleep in court, and Judge Beard sentenced both to thirty days in jail for contempt. "But I'm all right," the other said. "Why me?" "You are guilty by association," Beard shouted. "Get them out of here."

He described another case involving a Virginia judge:

> "Judge [L. Jackson] Embrey is strongly prejudiced against blacks and makes no attempt to hide it. During a recent visit, I watched him take over the cross-examination of a young, black defendant charged with trespassing:
>
> EMBREY: How old was this boy you were with?
>
> DEFENDANT: I don't know, maybe eighteen or nineteen.
>
> EMBREY: You say this boy is a friend of yours?
>
> DEFENDANT: Yes, sir. He's a friend.
>
> EMBREY: And you don't know how old he is?
>
> DEFENDANT: Not exactly. No, sir.
>
> EMBREY: Have you ever had your head examined?
>
> DEFENDANT: No, sir.
>
> EMBREY: I think that would be a good idea, don't you?"

Harvey Katz, "Some Call It Justice," *Washingtonian Magazine,* September 1970, at 48, 74–75.
27. Eager v. State, 205 Tenn. 156, 166, 325 S.W.2d 815, 820 (1959).
28. Moore v. State, 147 Neb. 390, 397, 23 N.W.2d 552, 556 (1946).

29. United States v. Chikata, 427 F.2d 385, 388 (9th Cir. 1970).
30. Alschuler at 684.
31. *See* Leon Friedman, ed., *Southern Justice* (New York, 1965).
32. B-16.
33. Sacher v. United States, 343 U.S. at 38.
34. Ibid. at 63. Trial Tr. 2276–77.
35. Kent v. State, 53 Okla. Crim. 276, 10 p.2d 733, 734 (1932).
36. People v. Pearson, 240 N.E.2d 337, 341–42 (Ill. App. Ct. 1968).
37. *In re* Dellinger, 461 F.2d 389, 446 (7th Cir. 1972); Trial Tr. 17, 371.
38. United States v. Sacher, 182 F.2d 416, 430 (2d Cir. 1950).
39. State v. Zwillman, 112 N.J. Super. 6, 20, 270 A.2d 284, 291 (1970).
40. Alschuler at 687.
41. Leslie L. Conner, "The Trial Judge, His Facial Expressions, Gestures and General Demeanor—Their Effect on the Administration of Justice," 6 *American Criminal Law Quarterly* 175, 178 (1968).
42. Schwartz, "Judges as Tyrants," at 133.
43. Alschuler at 692.
44. Albert Beveridge, 3 *Life of John Marshall* (1916) 170–210.
45. "Impeaching Federal Judges: A Study of the Constitutional Provisions," 39 *Fordham Law Review* 1, 43 (1970).
46. Frank Thompson, Jr., and Daniel H. Pollitt, "Impeachment of Federal Judges: An Historical Overview," 49 *North Carolina Law Review* 87, 116 (1970).
47. Alschuler at 697.
48. *In re* Sobel and Leibowitz, 8 N.Y.2d a (following p. 1158) (Ct. on the Jud. 1950).
49. Another judicial supervisory commission was established in New York in 1968. The Appellate Division of the First Department set up a Judiciary Relations Committee to "process and take action . . . [with respect to] the qualifications, conduct or fitness to perform" of judicial officers in that department (Rules of Practice of the Appellate Division, First Department, 22 N.Y. Codes, Rules & Regs. §607.1—.11 [1970]). The Committee consists of five judges, two attorneys, and one lay person, all appointed by the presiding justice of the First Department. The judicial members include two justices of the supreme court, one judge of the civil court, one judge of the family court, and one judge of the criminal court. (For a discussion of the procedures in force *see* Edwin L. Gasperini, Arnold S. Anderson, and Patrick W. McGinley, "Judicial Removal in New York: A New Look," 40 *Fordham Law Review* 1, 20 (1971).) The Committee has the use of the Appellate Division staff which investigates charges by interviewing the complainant and others with relevant knowledge. It may "make suggestions and recommendations to the judicial officer under investigation if the complaint deals with his deportment as a judge" (Ibid. at 21). A full hearing is held by the Committee if the charges warrant plenary proceedings. The Committee itself has no power of removal but may refer action to the Court on the Judiciary or the Appellate Divisions themselves.
50. Alschuler at 703–704.
51. Alschuler at 707.
52. Alschuler at 706. *See also* William T. Braithwaite, "Judicial Misconduct and How Four States Deal With It," 35 *Law and Contemporary Problems*, 151, 152–53 (1970).
53. S.1506, Judicial Reform Act, 91st Cong., 1st Sess. (1969).
54. The Supreme Court upheld the action of the Judicial Council of the Tenth Circuit to reassign all cases away from one judge charged with serious misconduct (Chandler v. Judicial Council, 398 U.S. 74 [1970]). However that case did not involve actual removal from office.
55. *See* Frank J. Battisti, "The Independence of the Federal Judiciary," 13 *Boston College Industrial and Commercial Law Review* 421 (February 1972), reprinted 118 *Cong. Rec.* E4561 (daily ed. May 2, 1972).
56. Missouri Const. Art. V, 927; Wisconsin St. Bar R. 10, §5.
57. *In re* Mattera, 34, N.J. 259, 168 A.2d 38, 41, 42 (1961).

58. The Massachusetts Supreme Judicial Court has recently held:

> We now rule that this court has jurisdiction to impose appropriate discipline upon a member of the bar, who is also a judge, for misconduct or acts of impropriety, whether such acts involve his judicial conduct or other conduct. This, we hold, even though, because he is a judge, he is not permitted to engage in the practice of law. [*In re* De Saulnier, 274 N.E.2d 454, 456 (1971).]

*See also* Gordon v. Clinkscales, 215 Ga. 843, 114 S.E.2d 15, 19 (1960); *In re* Copland, 66 Ohio App. 304, 33 N.E.2d 857 (Ct. App. (1940); and cases cited 53 A.L.R. 2d 305 (1957).

59. *In re* Watson, 286 P.2d 254, 256 (Nev. 1955). There are other cases to the same effect. *See* Chambers v. Central Committee Bar Assoc., 203 Okla. 583, 224 P.2d 583 (1950) and cases cited at 53 A.L.R. 2d 307–308.

60. *In re* Breen, 30 Nev. 164, 93 Pac. 997 (1908); Chambers v. Central Committee Bar Association, 203 Oka. 583, 224 P.2d 583 (1950).

61. Jenkins v. Oregon State Bar, 405 P.2d 525, 527 (1965).

62. Ibid.

63. *See* remarks of Charles Garry, before A.B.A., Young Lawyers Section, "A New Challenge to our Court System: the Spirited Lawyer Representing Political Defendants" 20 (1970).

64. A.B.A. Trial Disruption Standards, at 67.

## Notes to Chapter Ten

1. 1 Stat. 73, 83.

2. Act of March 2, 1831, 4 Stat. 487.

3. 18 U.S.C. §401, 62 Stat. 701 (1948).

4. Rule 42 provides:
   "(a) Summary Disposition. A criminal contempt may be punished summarily if the judge certifies that he saw or heard the conduct constituting the contempt and that it was committed in the actual presence of the court. The order of contempt shall recite the facts and shall be signed by the judge and entered of record.
   "(b) Disposition Upon Notice and Hearing. A criminal contempt except as provided in subdivision (a) of this rule shall be prosecuted on notice. The notice shall state the time and place of hearing, allowing a reasonable time for the preparation of the defense, and shall state the essential facts constituting the criminal contempt charged and describe it as such. The notice shall be given orally by the judge in open court in the presence of the defendant or, on application of the United States attorney or of an attorney appointed by the court for that purpose, by an order to show cause or an order of arrest. The defendant is entitled to a trial by jury in any case in which an act of Congress so provides. He is entitled to admission to bail as provided in these rules. If the contempt charged involves disrespect to or criticism of a judge, that judge is disqualified from presiding at the trial or hearing except with the defendant's consent. Upon a verdict or finding of guilt the court shall enter an order fixing the punishment."

5. Pietsch v. President of the United States, 434 F.2d 861 (2d Cir. 1970). *See also* Nye v. United States, 313 U.S. 33 (1941).

6. The Supreme Court in 1958, following a line of precedent, held that criminal contempt is not an "infamous crime" within the meaning of the Fifth Amendment (Green v. United States, 356 U.S. 165 [1958]). Therefore, a grand jury indictment is unnecessary even when an individual is punished for contempt in excess of one year, the usual standard for requiring a grand jury in criminal cases. (*See* Mackin v. United States, 117 U.S. 348 [1886], 18 U.S.C. §4083.) Despite the later decision in Bloom v. Illinois, 391 U.S. 194 (1968), discussed

later in this chapter, holding that serious criminal contempts must be tried to a jury, the Supreme Court has never overruled the *Green* case, and some lower courts have refused to assume that it no longer governs. (*See, e.g.,* United States v. Bukowski, 435 F.2d 1094, 1099–1102 [7th Cir. 1970].) Because criminal contempt "is a crime in every fundamental respect" and its penalties are indistinguishable from those obtained under ordinary criminal laws" (Bloom v. Illinois, 391 U.S. at 201, 207–208), the usual standard for invoking the grand jury should be applicable. A degree of uncertainty as to the grand jury requirement will exist, as in the case of the petit jury, because the contempt statute does not express a maximum penalty. But this problem can be mitigated if the prosecutor states in advance whether or not a sentence of more than one year will be sought. Because the Supreme Court has not yet held that the grand jury requirement of the Fifth Amendment is applicable to state criminal trials, the indictment problem cannot arise in connection with criminal contempts in state courts.

7. Tauber v. Gordon, 350 F.2d 843, 845 (3d Cir. 1965).
8. United States v. Marshall, 451 F.2d 372, 383–84 (9th Cir. 1971).
9. Ibid. at 386.
10. Ibid. at 377.
11. *See* Green v. United States, 356 U.S. 165, 187 (1958). Earlier cases rejecting a claim of jury include Savin, Petitioner, 131 U.S. 267, 278 (1889); *In re* Debs, 158 U.S. 564, 594–96 (1895); Gompers v. United States, 233 U.S. 604, 610–11 (1914). United States v. Barnett, 376 U.S. 681 (1964), signaled a possible change of view, which culminated in the decision in the *Bloom* case, discussed below. *See* note 6, supra.
12. 391 U.S. 194, 202 (1968).
13. Duncan v. Louisiana, 391 U.S. 145 (1968).
14. Baldwin v. New York, 399 U.S. 66, 72–74 (1969).
15. Frank v. United States, 395 U.S. 147, 148–50 (1969); Cheff v. Schnackenberg, 384 U.S. 373 (1966).
16. United States v. Seale, 461 F.2d 345 (7th Cir. 1972).
17. Ibid. at 353.
18. Ibid. at 354. But *see In re* Chase, 468 F.2d 128 (7th Cir. 1972).
19. *See* "Contempt of Court," 1 *Human Rights* 4, 6 (A.B.A. Section of Individual Rights and Responsibilities, 1970).
20. United States v. Seale, 461 F.2d at 354.
21. *See* Yates v. United States, 355 U.S. 66, 72–74 (1957).
22. Bloom v. United States, 391 U.S. at 209.
23. *See* United States v. Seale, 461 F.2d at 356.
24. *In re* Murchison, 349 U.S. 133, 137 (1955).
25. Ibid. *See also* the application of this doctrine in Ward v. Village of Monroeville, 409 U.S. 57 (November 13, 1972).
26. 267 U.S. 517, 539 (1925).
27. Offutt v. United States, 348 U.S. 11, 14 (1954).
28. 400 U.S. 455 (1971).
29. Ibid. at 466.
30. *See* Note, "The Supreme Court, 1970 Term," 85 *Harvard Law Review*, 3, 296 (1971).
31. Sacher v. United States, 343 U.S. 1, 12 (1952). *Compare* the venerable comment by Edward Livingston: "But what jesuit will teach me how I may tell a court that it has decided against the plainest principles of law, without showing that I think they had been careless, prejudiced or worse?" *The Complete Works of Edward Livingston on Criminal Jurisprudence* 260 (1873).
32. 343 U.S. 1 (1952).
33. 348 U.S. 11 (1954).
34. United States v. Meyer, 462 F.2d 827, 838 (D.C. Cir. 1972).
35. 400 U.S. 455, 465 (1971).
36. United States v. Meyer, 462 F.2d 827 (D.C. Cir. 1972).

37. *In re* Dellinger, 461 F.2d 389, 394–95 (7th Cir. 1972).
38. 343 U.S. at 10–11.
39. Ibid. at 11.
40. Ibid. at 36–37.
41. Note, 85 *Harvard Law Review* at 299.
42. *See* Note, 85 *Harvard Law Review* at 296.
43. *See* United States v. Meyer, 462 F.2d 827 (D.C. Cir. 1972).
44. Cooke v. United States, 267 U.S. at 537.
45. Offutt v. United States, 232 F.2d 69 (D.C. Cir. 1956), *cert. denied,* 351 U.S. 988 (1956). *See* p. 225 above.
46. *See* Offutt v. United States, 348 U.S. 11 (1954).
47. 232 F.2d at 71.
48. Ibid. at 72.
49. Ibid.
50. United States v. Seale, 461 F.2d at 373.
51. *See* Note, 85 *Harvard Law Review* at 299.
52. *Ex parte* Terry, 128 U.S. 289, 313 (1888).
53. Green v. United States, 356 U.S. 165, 193–94 (1958) (Black, J., dissenting).
54. Ibid. at 199.
55. Ibid. at 199–200.
56. REVERSALS:
*Federal:*
*In re* McConnell, 370 U.S. 230 (1962), appealed from 294 F.2d 310 (7th Cir.); United States v. Meyer, 462 F.2d 827 (D.C. Cir. 1972); *In re* Dellinger, 461 F.2d 389 (7th Cir. 1972); United States v. Seale, 461 F.2d 345 (7th Cir. 1972); Phillips v. United States, 457 F.2d 1313 (8th Cir. 1972); United States v. Peterson, 456 F.2d 1125 (10th Cir. 1972); United States v. Marshall, 451 F.2d 372 (9th Cir. 1971); *In re* McClure—Appeal of Swicegood, 442 F.2d 836 (D.C. Cir. 1971); Pietsch v. President of United States, 434 F.2d 861 (2d Cir. 1970); Tauber v. Gordon, 350 F.2d 843 (3d Cir. 1965) (en banc); United States v. Sopher, 347 F.2d 415 (7th Cir. 1965); Parmelee Transportation Co. v. Keeshin, 292 F.2d 806 (7th Cir. 1961)

*State (including D.C.):*
United States: *In re* Little, 404 U.S. 553 (1972); Johnson v. Mississippi, 403 U.S. 212, 91 S. Ct. 1778 (1971); Mayberry v. Pennsylvania, 400 U.S. 455 (1971); Holt v. Virginia, 381 U.S. 131 (1965); Johnson v. Virginia, 373 U.S. 61 (1963)
*Alaska:* State v. Browder, 486 P.2d 925 (Alaska, 1971)
*California:* *In re* Hallinan, 81 Cal. Rptr. 1, 459 P.2d 255 (1969); Thorne v. Municipal Court, City and County of San Francisco, 46 Cal. Rptr. 749 (Cal. App. 1965); *In re* Hagan, 36 Cal. Rptr. 828 (Cal. App. 1964); Cooper v. Superior Court in and for Los Angeles, 10 Cal. Rptr. 842, 359 P.2d 274 (1961)
*D.C.:* *In re* Abse, 251 A.2d 655 (D.C. App. 1969)
*Georgia:* White v. State, 218 Ga. 290, 127 S.E.2d 668 (1962)
*Illinois:* People v. Thor, 286 N.E.2d 769 (Ill. App. 1972); George v. Tool, 286 N.E.2d 41 (Ill. App. 1972); People v. Tecza, 4 Ill. App. 3d 1058, 283 N.E.2d 111 (Ill. App. 1972); People v. Javaras, 51 Ill. 2d 296, 281 N.E.2d 670 (1972); Katowski v. Katowski, 3 Ill. App. 3d 231, 278 N.E.2d 856 (Ill. App. 1971); People v. Tomashevsky—Appeal of Boudin, 48 Ill. 2d 559, 273 N.E.2d 398 (Ill. 1971); People v. Pearson, 240 N.E.2d 337 (Ill. App. 1968)
*Kansas:* *In re* Sanborn, 208 Kan. 4, 490 P.2d 598 (1971)
*Michigan:* People v. Ravitz, 26 Mich. App. 263, 182 N.W.2d 75 (1970); *In re* Henry, 369 Mich. 347, 119 N.W.2d 671 (1963)
*New Jersey:* *In re* Logan, 52 N.J. 475, 246 A.2d 441 (1968); State v. Zoppi, 72 N.J. Super. 432, 178 A.2d 632 (A.D. 1962)
*Oklahoma:* Fulreader v. State, 408 P.2d 775 (Okla. 1965)
*Pennsylvania:* Commonwealth v. Fletcher, 269 A.2d 727 (Pa. 1970)
*Virginia:* Harvey v. Commonwealth, 164 S.E.2d 636 (Va. 1968)

*Washington:* Dike v. Dike, 448 P.2d 490 (Wash. 1968)
AFFIRMANCES:
*Federal:*
Comstock v. United States, 419 F.2d 1128 (9th Cir. 1969); United States
*ex rel.* Robson v. Malone, 412 F.2d 848 (7th Cir. 1969); United States v.
Schiffer, 351 F.2d 91 (6th Cir. 1965), *cert. den.,* 384 U.S. 1003, *reh. den.,* 385
U.S. 890; *In re* Osborne, 344 F.2d 611 (9th Cir. 1965); United States v.
Galante, 298 F.2d 72 (2d Cir. 1962); Robles v. United States, 279 F.2d 401
(9th Cir. 1960), *cert. den.,* 365 U.S. 836, *reh. den.,* 365 U.S. 890 (1961)

*State (including D.C.):*
*Arizona:* Weiss v. Superior Ct. Pima Cty., 106 Ariz. 577, 480 P.2d 3 (1971)
*California: In re* Grossman 24 Cal. App. 3d 624, 101 Cal. Reptr. 176 (1972)
*(aff'd.* in part, *rev'd.* in part); Vaugh v. Municipal Court of Los Angeles
Judicial District, 60 Cal. Rptr. 575 (Cal. App. 1967)
*D.C.: In re* Ellis, 264 A.2d 300 (D.C. App. 1970); *In re* Gates, 248 A.2d 671
D.C. App. 1968)
*Georgia:* Hodges v. Thibadeau, 122 Ga. App. 334, 177 S.E.2d 127 (1970);
Jackson v. State, 225 Ga. 553, 170 S.E.2d 281 (1969); Cohran v. Sosebee,
120 Ga. App. 115, 169 S.E.2d 624 (1969); Crudup v. State, 106 Ga. App.
833, 129 S.E.2d 183 (1962); Salem v. State, 101 Ga. App. 905, 115 S.E.2d
447 (1960); Garland v. State, 101 Ga. App. 395, 114 S.E.2d 176 (1970)
*Illinois:* People v. Clark, 4 Ill. App. 3d 301, 280 N.E.2d 723 (Ill. App. 1972);
People v. Carr, 3 Ill. App.3d 227, 278 N.E.2d 839 (Ill. App. 1971); People
v. Miller, 265 N.E.2d 175 (Ill. App. 1970)
*Iowa:* Knox v. Harrison, 185 N.W.2d 718 (Iowa 1971)
*Michigan: In re* Burns, 173 N.W.2d 1 (Mich. App. 1969)
*New Jersey:* State v. Jones, 105 N.J. Super 493, 253 A.2d 193 (1969)
*New York: In re* Katz, 62 Misc. 2d 342, 309 N.Y.S.2d 76 (Sup. Ct. 1970),
*aff'd* 28 N.Y.2d 234, 321 N.Y.S.2d 104, 269 N.E.2d 816 (1971); Hayden v.
Helfand, 28 A.D.2d 567, 280 N.Y.S.2d 420 (2d dept, 1967)
*Ohio:* State v. Wilson, 30 Ohio St. 2d 312, 285 N.E.2d 38 (Ohio S.Ct. 1972),
*cert. den.,* 41 LW3306 (1972)
*Oklahoma:* Champion v. State, 456 P.2d 571 (Okl. Cr. 1969)
*Oregon:* Taylor v. Gladden, 377 P.2d 14 (Ore. 1962)
*Pennsylvania:* Commonwealth v. Snyder, 275 A.2d 312 (Pa. 1971); Common-
wealth v. Mayberry, 255 A.2d 548 (Pa. 1969)
*Texas: Ex parte* Clayton, 350 S.W.2d 926 (Tex. Cr. App. 1961)
*Washington:* State v. Caffrey, 422 P.2d 307 (Wash. 1966)
57. People v. Tomashevsky—Appeal of Boudin, 48 Ill. 2d 559, 273 N.E.2d 398
(Ill. 1971). *See also* People v. Tecza, 4 Ill. App. 2d 1058, 283 N.E.2d Ill. 113
(1972)
58. 343 U.S. at 37.
59. 356 U.S. at 216.
60. *See* Trial Lawyers Report, at 13.
61. Note, "Criminal Law—Contempt—Conduct of Attorney During Course of
Trial," 1971 *Wisconsin Law Review* 329, 347.
62. One other contention of the Trial Lawyers deserves brief comment. It is that
"if the original trial was disrupted, it is by no means inconceivable that a
second trial may be disrupted in much the same way." But experience does
not support the hypothesis. Indeed, it seems far more likely that defendants or
lawyers held in contempt will be more likely to disrupt a contempt hearing
held before the same judge who cited them initially. The personal embroilment
may not have disappeared when the trial is over, thereby increasing the chances
for another uproar, as in the Tacoma Seven trial in December 1970. A new
proceeding before a new judge some time after the original action terminated
may have cooled the passions heated in the earlier case.
63. *See* Note, "Summary Punishment for Contempt," 39 *Southern California Law
Review* 463, 466 (1966). A final justification for summary contempt is that it

obviates the unseemly or undignified spectacle of a judge appearing as a witness in the later contempt proceedings. We have explained above at pp. 231–32 why it would ordinarily be unnecessary for a judge to appear as a witness in the second proceeding, and if he did appear, why there would be no loss of dignity involved.

64. *See* Bridges v. California, 314 U.S. 352 (1941); Nye v. United States, 313 U.S. 33 (1941); Bloom v. Illinois, 391 U.S. 194 (1968).

65. State v. Browder, 486 P.2d 925, 937–39 (Alaska 1971).

66. Public Act No. 779.

67. *See* Study Draft of a New Federal Criminal Code, §1341 (2), at 113.

68. Working Papers of the National Commission on Reform of the Federal Criminal Laws 604.

69. Final Report, Comment to §1341.

70. In some civil law countries, a judge may have the power both to expel disorderly participants and to impose summary fines or a brief jail sentence, generally not exceeding three days. This corresponds to our suggestion that civil contempt may be imposed summarily to ensure continued order in a trial, but the maximum penalty should be seven days. *See* discussion at pp. 104–105. Representative foreign laws include the following:

    *France:* expulsion and/or a twenty-four hour term for disturbing proceedings (Code of Civil Procedure art. 89). For forcibly resisting an order to leave the court, a person may be summarily sentenced to a longer term (Code of Criminal Procedure, art. 404).

    *Germany:* fine or three days imprisonment (Judiciary Code 6V6 §§178 ss).

    *Italy:* expulsion (Code of Criminal Procedure, art. 433 and 434).

    *Spain:* expulsion; fine or imprisonment for resisting order of expulsion (Civil Procedure Law, art. 439 and 440).

    *Sweden:* expulsion and/or a sixty dollar fine and three day maximum sentence (RB 5:9(1), 9:5).

## Notes to Chapter Eleven

1. Peter Goldman and Don Holt, "How Justice Works: The People vs. Donald Payne," *Newsweek,* March 8, 1971, at 20.

2. *See* Stephen R. Bing and S. Stephen Rosenfeld, *The Quality of Justice in the Lower Criminal Courts of Metropolitan Boston* (1970); Anson Smith, "Disorder in the Courts," *Boston Globe,* March 11, 1971, at 1.

3. Robert P. Patterson, Jr., "Our Lower Courts Are Disgraceful," 67 *Legal Aid Review* 5, 8–9 (1970).

4. J-235.

5. Leonard Downie, Jr., "Crime in the Courts: Assembly Line Justice," *Washington Monthly,* September 1970, at 27.

6. Patterson, *op. cit.* at 8–9.

7. Courthouse Reorganization and Renovation Program, First and Second Appellate Divisions, New York, Foley Square Court Complex (1972). EDC Supreme Court Task Force, *Phase One Organization Report* (1972).

8. Ibid., Final Report, at 13.

9. Such courts have been established in New York City, and five parts were operational in September 1972.

10. Estes v. Texas, 381 U.S. 532 (1965).

11. Ibid. at 547.

12. *See* Robert H. Reynolds, "Alaska's Ten Years of Electronic Reporting," 56 *American Bar Association Journal* 1080 (1970). *But see* Edgar Paul Boyko, "The Case Against Electronic Courtroom Reporting," 57 *American Bar Association Journal* 1008 (1971).

13. *New York Times,* November 26, 1971, at 24.

14. Courthouse Reorganization and Renovation Program, Appendix E *Courtroom Security,* at 16–17.
15. Ibid. at 18.
16. Letter, December 7, 1970, Judge Jack B. Weinstein to Senator Harry F. Byrd, Jr.
17. Trial Transcript, 1942–1945.
18. Ibid. at 1951–52.
19. Ibid. at 2136.
20. Ibid. at 2143. The Chicago conspiracy trial also involved problems about the conduct of marshals. *See In re* Dellinger, 461 F.2d 389, 437–38 (7th Cir. 1972); Trial Tr. 4618; Trial Tr. 4815–17.
21. J-42.
22. A.B.A. Trial Disruption Standards, at 17.
23. During the trial of the Soledad Brothers in San Francisco in late 1971 their lawyers objected to the strict security measures in force including a protective shield between the court well and the spectator section and the large number of guards in court. *See New York Times,* August 10, 1971.
24. United States v. Samuel, 431 F.2d 610, 615 (D.C. Cir. 1970).
25. Ibid.
26. J-5.
27. J-105. *See also* J-95 (action against college students); J-77 (draft case).
28. J-63. There are also a number of other reported cases involving spectator disorder. In the New York Black Panther case one of the spectators was held in contempt for shouting "all power to the people" and was given a thirty day jail sentence (Katz v. Murtagh, 28 N.Y.2d 234, 236, 321 N.Y.S.2d 104, 106 [1971]; *see also* Patten v. Harrison, 185 N.W.2d 720, 721 [Iowa Sup. Ct. 1971]).
29. United States v. Kobli, 172 F.2d 919, 921–22 (2d Cir. 1949).
30. United States *ex rel* Robinson v. Malone, 412 F.2d 848, 850–51 (7th Cir. 1969).
31. 321 N.Y.S.2d at 107.
32. Letter, January 11, 1971 to Leon Friedman.
33. J-249.
34. J-216.
35. *See* United Press Assn. v. Valente, 308 N.Y. 71 (1954); Oliver v. Postel, 30 N.Y.2d 171 (1972). The only conceivable exception would be when secret government information is involved, and even here the right to close the courtroom doors to spectators or the press is disrupted.
36. *Radio, Television and the Administration of Justice* (1964). More recently, the Civil Rights Committee of the City Bar Association has issued a new report on the subject endorsing the earlier Medina report.
37. *See* 45 F.R.D. 391, 51 F.R.D. 135.
38. It may be that different rules should apply in this area to the prosecution and the defense. The mere fact that criminal charges are brought against a person makes a strong impression on the public, generally according great credibility to the prosecution. Instead of a presumption of innocence, a presumption of guilt may exist after an indictment is returned. Perhaps some leeway ought to be afforded the defense to counter the impression made by the filing of charges.

# INDEX